THE KOSOVO CRISIS

The last American war in Europe?

EDITED BY

ANTHONY WEYMOUTH AND STANLEY HENIG

REUTERS

Publishd by **Pearson Education**

London / New York / San Francisco / Toronto / Sydney
Tokyo / Singapore / Hong Kong / Cape Town / Madrid / Amsterdam / Munich / Paris / Milan

PEARSON EDUCATION LIMITED

Head Office:
Edinburgh Gate
Harlow CM20 2JE
Tel: +44 (0)1279 623623
Fax: +44 (0)1279 431059

London Office:
128 Long Acre, London WC2E 9AN
Tel: +44 (0)207 447 2000
Fax: +44 (0)207 240 5771
Website: www.business-minds.com

First published in Great Britain in 2001

ISBN 0 273 65158 7

British Library Cataloguing in Publication Data
A CIP catalogue record for this book can be obtained from the British Library

10 9 8 7 6 5 4 3 2 1

Typeset by Pantek Arts Ltd, Maidstone, Kent
Printed and bound in Great Britain by Biddles Ltd, Guildford and King's Lynn

The Publishers' policy is to use paper manufactured from sustainable forests.

CONTENTS

CHRONOLOGY OF EVENTS
KOSOVO 1946–99, COUNTDOWN TO CRISIS

1946   Formation of the Federal Republic of Yugoslavia headed by former communist partisan, Marshall Tito.

1948   Yugoslavia enjoys special position between East and West under Tito's 'independent' stance. In consequence Stalin expels Yugoslavia from Eastern Bloc.

1968   Kosovo Albanians involved in first significant post-war demonstration for self-determination.

1974   Tito allows the establishment of Kosovo as an autonomous province of Serbia.

1980   Death of Tito and the resulting weakening of Belgrade's hold on the Federation previously sustained by Tito's personality and political skills.

1981   Kosovo Albanians demonstrate in favour of an independent Kosovo.

1987   Emergence of Slobodan Milosevic as leader of Serbian Socialist Party with the major objective of reclaiming Kosovo.

1989   Serbian National Assembly votes for constitutional changes which return control of Kosovo police and judiciary to Belgrade.

        May: Milosevic appointed president.

1990   Serbian National Assembly dissolves Kosovo Assembly. Kosovo Albanian legislators declare Kosovo's independence.

1991   Slovenia, Croatia and Muslim-dominated government of Bosnia-Herzegovina declare independence.

        Bosnian Serbs vow to oppose the break-up of the Yugosalav Federation.

In a secret referendum, Kosovo Albanians announce the establishment of the Independent Republic of Kosovo.

1992   Civil War breaks out in Croatia and Bosnia. Bosnian Serbs declare their Republic inside Serbia.

Ibrahim Rugova is elected president of the Republic of Kosovo and a provincial assembly is established. Serbia rejects the legality of both.

1995   UN 'Safe Areas' in Bosnia are overrun by Bosnian Serbs, initiating a Nato bombardment of Bosnian Serb forces.

US-brokered Dayton Accord signed creating the Muslim–Croat Federation and the Bosnian Serb Republic.

1996   Emergence of the Kosovo Liberation Army claiming responsibility for attacks on Serbian police targets.

1997   KLA attacks continue while Serb forces put down Albanian student demonstrations.

1998   Year marked by rapid acceleration of events

February: KLA kills two Serb policemen resulting in severe reprisals against Kosovo Albanians, many deaths and mass displacement of refugees from the violence.

April: Contact Group imposes additional sanctions on Yugoslavia.

June: US envoy Richard Holbrooke meets separately with Milosevic and Kosovo Albanian leaders.

UN Secretary-General, Kofi Annan warns Nato to seek UN approval before engaging in any military action against Serbia.

July: France and Britain draft a UN Security Council resolution aimed at bringing about a cease-fire in Kosovo.

Kosovo Albanians inaugurate parliament and elect speaker. Serbian police order delegates to disperse.

Serbs launch offensive to recapture areas of Kosovo controlled by the KLA.

August: KLA stronghold of Junik taken by Serb military.

October: News and pictures of Kosovo Albanians allegedly massacred by the Serbs appear in the Western media.

US Defence Secretary, William Cohen warns of air attacks within two weeks.

Russia threatens to veto any UN move to authorize air strikes.

President Clinton says Nato is ready to take action.

US envoy Richard Holbrooke outlines deal to avoid air strikes and Nato gives Milosevic four days to end the Serb offensive.

Serbian security forces comply at the end of the month by partially withdrawing from Kosovo and Nato halts immediate threat of air strikes.

1999   January: Violence erupts once again: KLA capture eight Yugoslav soldiers; Serbs use artillery against KLA strongholds in full view of world media.

Bodies of 45 Kosovo Albanians discovered at Racak, South Kosovo. William Walker, US head of international monitoring group, the Organization for Security and Cooperation in Europe (OSCE), calls it a Serb police 'massacre'.

Contact Group orders the Serbs and the Kosovo Albanians to attend peace talks at Rambouillet, Paris.

February: US mediator Chris Hill tells Milosevic to make concessions or face air strikes.

Milosevic opposes deployment of Nato peacekeepers and the KLA rejects calls to disarm.

Milosevic declares: 'We will not give up Kosovo, even if we are bombed.' Western diplomats and aid workers start leaving Serbia.

At Rambouillet, both sides conditionally agree to greater autonomy for Kosovo.

The Kosovo Albanians agree in principle to sign a political accord but the Serbs find the conditions unacceptable. Both sides agree to meet again in Paris in mid-March.

March: Milosevic flatly rejects international peacekeepers for Kosovo.

US House of Representatives backs deployment of US troops in Kosovo as part of any Nato peacekeeping force.

Peace talks resume in Paris.

Forensic report on the deaths of Kosovo Albanians in Racak refers to 'crime against humanity' but refuses to term it a massacre or blame the Serbs.

Kosovo Albanians sign the international peace deal in Paris but the Serbs boycott the event and Russia refuses to sign as witness. Peace talks are adjourned.

All 1,380 international monitors withdraw from Kosovo as the Yugoslav army sends in reinforcements.

On 22 March, Holbrooke arrives in Belgrade for last ditch attempt to persuade Milosevic to accept the accord.

On 23 March, the Serb parliament rejects Nato demands to send peace-keeping troops into Kosovo. Holbrooke ends his mission saying that Milosevic has refused to agree to a plan for autonomy for Kosovo. This failure of the mission opens the way for air strikes against Serbia.

Sources: Stratfor and New York Times (www).

PREFACE

THERE IS A WIDESPREAD BELIEF THAT THE REMOVAL of the Iron Curtain heralded an era in which war would, hopefully, never again be considered as an instrument of national policy within the continent of Europe. The conflict in Kosovo may seem a quintessential '*fin-de-siècle*' event: perhaps, the very last armed conflict to pitch nation against nation in the 'old' continent; or, alternatively, the very first of a new kind of 'just' war. When the Western powers took military action in 1999, they claimed as their sole justification the need to avert the forceful subjugation of a people by the internationally recognized government of an independent, sovereign state. Whatever view one takes of the honesty or legitimacy of such a claim, it makes the war over Kosovo a unique event in history.

Modern technology has shrunk our world; instant reporting provokes a near universal response to every crisis that 'something must be done'. As this book demonstrates it is never easy to agree on what that 'something' should be. Whether or not the end ever justifies the means, it certainly does not automatically beget the means.

Yugoslavia and its successor states are very much a part of Europe; for most of the contributors to this book it is 'our' continent. The implosion within the former Yugoslavia has involved a series of humanitarian catastrophes of which Kosovo will, hopefully, turn out to be the last. Perhaps it will also be the final occasion on which a rapidly uniting Europe will be unable to resolve its own 'domestic' problems without the involvement of the USA.

This book is not about Kosovo itself or even about Yugoslavia. It is about external reactions to an internal crisis. It places the events of the late 1990s in a series of contexts viewed from a variety of perspectives. It focuses particularly on the motivations that led the West into war in 1999. It is also about the implications of the West's action for the post-Cold War international system in the new century.

Time, it is said, waits for no man, and its impatience with human projects is perfectly illustrated in the production of this book. All the chapters, with the exception of the introduction and conclusion, were finished before Milosevic's eviction from power in early October 2000. Milosevic's departure, however, makes little difference to the essential thrust of argument contained in these pages. Whatever the reasons for his rejection by the Serbian people (it would be naïve in the extreme to identify these objections with those of Nato), it can be safely assumed that the bombing and the sanctions were instrumental in bringing about Milosevic's downfall. Whilst the architect of Serbian ambitions in the Balkans is gone, Yugoslavia is now entering a new and highly problematic phase of post-war development. As far as Kosovo is concerned, it is most unlikely that Kostunica's election to the presidency will resolve very much in the short and medium terms. Thus, while Nato has achieved an important part of its strategic objective, namely the removal of Milosevic as Head of State, the other part – its commitment to resolving the Kosovo entanglement, and the ramifications that this has for the international community – remains. Our book examines the costs and benefits for the West of Nato's intervention in Yugoslavia in the long term. We have revised our conclusion to include Milosevic's fall from power as an undoubted benefit from the West's point of view, but have left the substance of the other chapters unchanged.

The editors would like to offer warm thanks to Peter Anderson and Christopher Williams for many helpful comments on the entire work; to Saleel Nurbhai for his invaluable assistance in preparing the final manuscript; to Joe Stretch for his cartographic skills and to the Languages Development Centre of St. Martin's College, Lancaster, for much technical assistance in preparing the text.

Lancaster, November 2000

LIST OF CONTRIBUTORS BY CHAPTER

Tony Weymouth has taught in universities in the United States and continental Europe. Until recently he was Principal Lecturer in French and European Studies at the University of Central Lancashire, England. He is now a freelance writer specializing in the European media and Politics.

Christopher Williams is Reader in Russian Studies at the University of Central Lancashire, England. He is widely published on social and polictical trends in Russia, the Baltic States, East-Central Europe and the Balkans. In 2000 he was elected member of the Russian Academy of Political Science.

Stanley Henig, formerly a Member of Parliament, and Lecturer at the Civil Service College, was Professor in European Studies at the University of Central Lancashire, England, until 1997. He is the author of several books on European Politics.

Umberto Morelli is Professor of the History of International Relations at the University of Turin, and of the History of European Integration at the School of Applied Military Studies, Turin, Italy, where he has published widely in both fields.

Sabrina Ramet is Professor of International Studies at the University of Washington, Seattle, USA. She is an internationally recognised specialist on the Balkans and the author of several books on the region.

Phil Lyon is a post graduate student at the School of Advanced International Studies at The John Hopkins University, Washington DC, USA, having previously studied at the University of Washington, specializing in Czech and Yugoslav history.

Bernard Lamizet is Professor of Politics and Communication Science at the Institut d'Etudes Politiques at the University of Lyon, France. He is the author of several books on the media and communication theory.

Sylvie Debras is a research student who recently completed her doctorate in information and communication science at the University of Paris II, France.

Juan Diego Ramirez is Senior Lecturer in politics at the College of Europe in Bruges, Belgium, specializing in European common foreign and security policy, the Council of Ministers, and the Internal Market.

Manuel Szapiro is Assistant Lecturer at the College of Europe, Bruges, Belgium, specializing in European common foreign and security policy, the political economy of European integration and issues of constitutional reform.

Peter J. Anderson is Senior Lecturer in Political Science at the University of Central Lancashire and has published several works in the fields of international relations, security and the environment, and the media.

Zinaida T. Golenkova is Professor and Deputy Director of the Institute of Sociology, Moscow and a member of the Russian Academy of Social Sciences. She is a specialist sociologist for the Balkans and Russia.

John Simons is Professor and Head of the School of Humanities at the Edge Hill College of Higher Education, Ormskirk, England. He has extensive experience of working in and visiting universities in the Balkans.

David Travers is Director of MA Studies and Lecturer in the Department of Politics and International Relations at Lancaster University, England, specializing in foreign policy analysis, international institutions and diplomacy. He was a specialist advisor to the House of Commons Foreign Affairs Committee on the UN.

WIDELY USED ABBREVIATIONS

EC European Community

ESDP European Security and Defence Policy

EU European Union

FRY Federal Republic of Yugoslavia

FYROM Former Yugoslav Republic of Macedonia

ICTY International Criminal Tribunal for the former Yugoslavia

KFOR Kosovo Force

KLA Kosovo Liberation Army

KVM Kosovo Verification Mission

Nato/NATO North Atlantic Treaty Organization

OSCE Organization for Security and Cooperation in Europe

UN United Nations

UNHCHR United Nations High Commissioner for Human Rights

UNHCR United Nations High Commissioner for Refugees

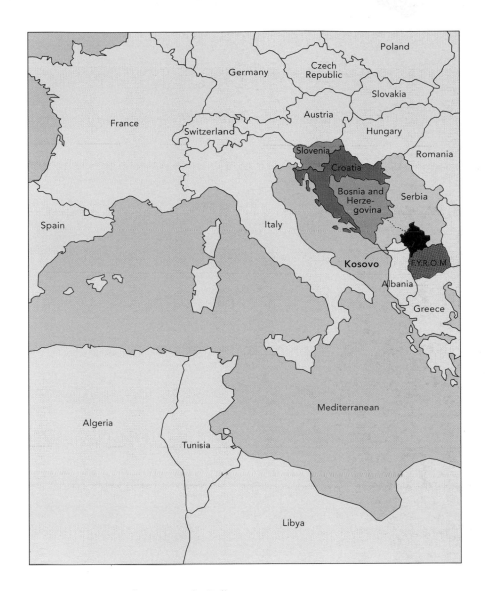

Map 1 The location of Kosovo in the Balkans.

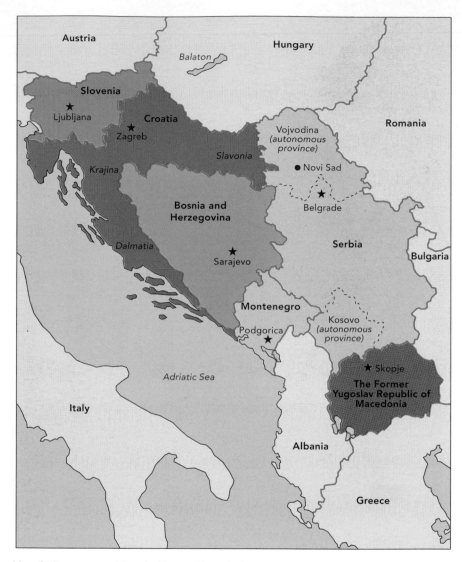

Map 2 States comprising the Former Yugoslavia.

Map 3 The Central Balkans Region.

Map 4 Kosovo: main towns, roads and railways.

1

WHY WAR, WHY NATO?

ANTHONY WEYMOUTH

VOICES IN SEARCH OF ANSWERS

Conflicts involving the Western allies in the 1945–91 period were characterized by ideological, strategic and economic interests of singular clarity. In the Korean and Vietnam wars there were clear, ideological collisions between East and West in which the Great Powers and their allies attempted to establish regional spheres of influence in the name of either communism or capitalism. In the Gulf War it was oil, and the perceived destabilization of the Middle East by Iraq's annexation of Kuwait, which drew the West into conflict. However, in Kosovo, in the apparent aftermath of the Cold War, a clear Western motive was more difficult to perceive. The Balkans, historically turbulent, geographically inaccessible and of little directly strategic or economic interest to the West, seemed a most unlikely region for Nato to intervene militarily, and yet that is precisely what happened.

The *prima facie* reasons for military intervention were humanitarian. The West, in Nato guise, intervened in order to save a whole ethnic group of people from the repression of the Serbs, bent on mass deportation and the indiscriminate killing of civilians. However, beyond this 'popular' dimension it was alleged that there were indeed others of a more complex, strategic nature. It has been argued both here and elsewhere that

Nato's military intervention was dictated predominantly by the need to establish a new role for itself in the post-Cold War conflict. Events in Kosovo, it is alleged, provided the ideal opportunity to do so. Supporters of this view point to a perceived implacable stance adopted by Nato with regard to Milosevic in March 1999 and its refusal to pursue a diplomatic solution, preferring instead to impose terms it knew were too humiliating for the Serbs to accept. This perception was honed by the left to depict Nato as the instrument of dominant capitalist states, intervening in an illegal and aggressive way to the long-term benefit of the forces of global capitalism. A final more pragmatic and less conspiratorial interpretation depicted Nato in a firefighting role: Kosovo was not a crisis engineered by the United States of America or the alliance; on the contrary, it was a conflagration sparked off by the post-Cold War implosion of Yugoslavia. Nato, it could be argued, in the absence of decisive UN action, moved pre-emptively in order to fill a dangerous vacuum and prevent the spread of further destabilizing events of a potentially more serious and global nature.

Why, in 1999, in the aftermath of the collapse of world communism, and in a region of little direct economic interest to the West, did the remaining superpower, the USA and its Western allies, intervene with such awesome and costly displays of military force?

This book is an attempt to address this overriding question to which, as the reader will see, there is not one, but several possible answers, depending on the perspective from which it is viewed. As is often the case, a question of this magnitude, involving a number of world players, gives rise to a series of further questions concerning the motivation and response of each to the crisis. From a Western viewpoint some of the answers may be more plausible than others.

Despite the momentous impact events in the Balkans had on Europe in the twentieth century, the understanding of the reasons for the current political turbulence of that region, or why the outcomes of this instability have such ramifications for European security, varied considerably among the peoples of the member states of Nato and among those of the former Eastern Bloc. How many British or Americans, before the crisis started making the headlines, had even heard of a semi-autonomous province of Serbia called Kosovo, let alone knew of its geographical location?

What are the social, cultural and political factors that combined in the past and at the end of the twentieth century to make the Balkans a threat to European stability and even world peace?

There is an irony in the fact that the peoples of the two most hawkish nations of the Nato alliance knew so little about the place where Nato would go to war for the first time since 1945. In Britain, despite its historic 'off-shore' attitude towards continental Europe and its apparent diffidence towards deepening relations with the European Union, there is a folk memory of the consequences of appeasement in Europe that was almost certainly reactivated by events in Kosovo in 1998–9 and which may have been sufficient to justify cross-party support for Prime Minister Tony Blair's assertive anti-Milosevic stance. In the USA, there were constitutional objections to President Clinton's military commitment of troops to Nato fuelled by what one observer called 'an appalling level of ignorance' on the part of some politicians about the Kosovo situation, an ignorance moreover that was almost certainly shared by most of the population. But, in the most enlightened US government circles at least, it was understood that the political unrest and resulting ethnic cleansing policies in Kosovo might have serious consequences for other Nato states which, by reason of its commitment to the Atlantic alliance, the USA could not afford to ignore.

However, beyond these generalities, what were the reasons that persuaded the British and American governments to lead Nato into a war of intervention between Serbs and ethnic Albanians within the recognized boundaries of a sovereign state?

Such possible motives for military intervention as those of the USA and Britain were not shared by all Nato members, nor indeed by non-Nato countries such as Russia, nor countries of the former Eastern Bloc. Each brought to the crisis its own particular agenda and each viewed the events through its own particular optic.

In Italy, for example, opinions were divided. Historically, the geopolitical and geo-economic proximity of the Balkans have ensured close attention from all Italian governments in modern times. In the past, political turbulence in the Balkans has led to economic loss (Italy has always had important investment links and strong trading relations with the region) and social tensions resulting from the arrival on its shores of thousands of refugees fleeing the consequences of endemic political and social upheaval. In addition, there was the question of committing Italian troops, ports and other military installations (as the Nato country best placed for aerial operations) to an American-led alliance, while at the same time remaining on speaking terms with Serbia.

What were the motives of the prime minister D'Alema, a former communist, and the Italian government for supporting Nato in the Kosovo operation?

For Germany with its 'special history' in the twentieth century, the engagement of its troops in military combat in, of all places, the Balkans, where just over fifty years ago Hitler's army had committed its own acts of barbarism, participation in the Nato operation constituted a massive step away from the post-war pacifism that previously characterized its foreign policy.

What factors account for Germany's first military operation outside its national frontiers since 1944?

For France, a former staunch ally of the Serbs since 1913, the crisis provoked serious contradictions related to its historical associations with Serbia and to its own special position *vis-à-vis* the European Union, the USA and Nato themselves.

In what circumstances could the neo-Gaullist president, Jacques Chirac, be seen to accept the views and leadership of the American-dominated alliance against its former ally and friend, Serbia?

If the Kosovo crisis provoked some searching questions for the individual member states of Nato, it also raised important issues for the present and future roles of the European Union (EU) as a political player on the world stage. In the same way as it had acted during the United Nations (UN) intervention in Bosnia, in Kosovo, the EU cooperated with many of the principal actors to bring about and sustain an end to hostilities. Its actions ranged from long-term economic pacts and agreements with the countries of south-eastern Europe, to the organizing of emergency meetings such as those in Rambouillet and Paris, and the provision of negotiators who, along with those of Russia, were finally crucial to bringing the hostilities to an end. In the aftermath of the war, the EU was and continues to be the biggest contributor of humanitarian aid to the region. But beyond these not-inconsiderable strategies for extending to the rest of Europe the principles of respect for human rights, international law, democratic freedoms, and the inviolability of frontiers, the EU lacks further means for their imposition. While the collective European Security and Defence Policy (ESDP) is firmly on the EU table as an agenda item for discussion and development, there is a long way to go before any initiative towards its implementation gets underway. In the meantime, the dilemma for the EU is one of having to rely on the UN and Nato for peace-making roles, backed up by force, or to experience collective impotence in the face of flagrant violations of human rights, not only outside Europe, but in its own backyard.

Was the EU's involvement in the Kosovo crisis inconsequential and to what extent is the concept of a collective European Defence Community a realizable objective in the light of internal differences of emphasis, and of external opposition?

So far we have touched on the perceptions of the Kosovo crisis from viewpoints grounded firmly in the West, that is to say, Nato and its European partners. But what about Russia, and Serbia itself? In retrospect, it is clear that Russia played a crucial role in bringing Milosevic to the negotiating table and in securing an end to the immediate crisis in Kosovo. However, this subsequently undisputed peace-making role developed within tumultuous and complex circumstances not least of which were Russia's own internal crisis in Chechnya; its own political instability; and its increasing economic reliance on the West. During the crisis, the media and public opinion were predominantly pro-Serb and anti-Nato and in some political circles, including those of President Yeltsin himself, the bombing was perceived as being tantamount to an attack on Russia. But, despite the public utterances of political outrage, it was indeed Russia that played the crucial mediating role that brought about the end to the hostilities. Many claim, however, that the price to pay on the part of the West will be a significant drop in the temperature of the 'Cool Peace' that succeeded the Cold War at the end of the twentieth century.

How was Nato's intervention in Kosovo perceived by the Russians? What prompted the Russians finally to cooperate with Nato and what is the likely effect of the crisis on Russia's future relations with the West?

With regard to Serbia itself, defenders of its position *vis-à-vis* the Western alliance point to the widespread incredulity among Serbs concerning the manner in which they were treated by Nato. They saw themselves as being singled out by Nato for special treatment with regard to policies in Kosovo while the violations of human rights by others, notably China and Turkey, remained unpunished. Furthermore, against a background of anti-Serb propaganda in the West, verging on demonization, there was widespread resentment at the apparent ease with which the world appeared to have forgotten the heroic stand of the Serbs against Germany during World War II. The Serbs saw their attachment to their cultural past in Kosovo and the provocation offered to them by the increasingly violent attacks by the Kosovo Liberation Army (KLA) to have been largely ignored by a Western alliance determined for its own ends to see the crisis from the point of view of the Kosovo Albanians.

To what extent did the West understand the complexities and significance of the Serbian presence in Kosovo and the likely political consequences for Nato's intervention in terms of further regional disturbances?

For the UN, the Kosovo crisis was and continues to be the source of many testing questions. In the early stages of the conflict the perceived need to retain the good will of Milosevic in order to maintain the peace in Bosnia meant that the Security Council's hands were tied in its attempts to initiate preventative diplomacy. When the Council did become involved in 1998 the momentum of events and their nature – the spiralling violence and their complexity – were both too strong and complicated to be brought under control. In any case, the Security Council was divided. Two of the permanent members, Russia and China, and other non-permanent members had deep misgivings about the legitimacy of Nato's intervention in Kosovo and the resolutions passed by the Council reflected the delicate path it had to tread in order achieve consensus. But despite these obstacles, the UN, from the Secretary-General himself to the many practical services and missions launched by its agencies, was extremely active both in the theatre of war and on the international stage in promoting peace and a return to law and order in Kosovo.

What was the role of the United Nations, as the world's principal guarantor of peace, security and respect for human rights, in the Kosovo crisis? Was this role subverted by the intervention of Nato? Is there now a precedent for a concept of human rights of a higher order which could override the rights of national sovereignty and, if so, what are the consequences for international law?

In addition to the topics and questions raised above, there is an important issue of a different kind concerning the manner in which information relating to the Kosovo crisis was conveyed to the people in whose name governments were, or were becoming, involved. For more than fifty years, East and West had stared at each other through an ideological lens that represented the world on either side in starkly different ways. Despite the perceived ending of the Cold War, it was interesting to see how quickly both West and East European media used their former ideological perceptions, supported by historical analogy, as a frame of reference for reporting the crisis and hostilities.

To what extent were the media, and particularly the Western media, justified in representing the events leading up to the war, and the war itself, in the manner in which they did? Were there distortions and, if so, what was their nature and why did they occur?

THE STRUCTURE OF THE BOOK

Many of the issues, and the questions they raised, both at the time and in the longer term for Europe and the wider world, figure in the chapters that follow. In retrospect, if we had wished for greater coherence in their treatment, we would have been disappointed. In reality, our aspirations were more modest. Our task in this project was to hold the topic – Kosovo – constant and allow the crisis to be portrayed through the eyes of fourteen contributors representing the principal, national and institutional players involved in the war. Thus, given the wide spectrum of perspectives covered, overt coherence in approach and attitude would have been neither possible nor desirable. However, this is not to say that the overall perception for the reader will be one of a mere re-statement on behalf of the major players of their positions, of the intractable nature of Balkans politics and the pious expression of a hope that resolution of some kind will ultimately be found this century. We hope that this book amounts to more than the sum total of its fourteen chapters, that is to say, more than a mere collection of diverse and often contradictory opinions (although both epithets apply in some measure). Whether we have succeeded will be inevitably a judgement to be made by our readers.

The book divides essentially into four sections. The first contains two foundation chapters of which this introduction is the first and where, in Chapter Two, Christopher Williams sets out the significance of Kosovo for both Serbia and for the Balkans region as a whole. Williams's analysis shows that Kosovo has been an area of widespread ethnic tension for most of the twentieth century, thus making the current crisis one of many between Kosovo and Serbia. A detailed analysis is offered of the roots of this ethnic conflict and the consequences in terms of Albanian and Serbian nationalism. Williams challenges the widely held perception in government and among the general public that the Kosovo crisis is primarily ethnic in origin. In addition, he undertakes what may be considered a controversial analysis of Nato's motives for military intervention in Kosovo and the possible long-term consequences for the region as a whole.

The second section comprises six chapters and is dedicated first to the responses of the four main European participants in the Nato campaign: Britain, Italy, Germany and France. We place Britain (Chapter 3) first as the most hawkish of the four and the country having the fewest internal tensions, followed by the two least bellicose and more problematic participants, Italy and Germany (Chapters 4 and 5) and finally France, which also experienced its own particular problems in coming to terms with the crisis (Chapter 6). Having presented the respective positions of these countries in their capacity as Nato members, we then revisit them in their 'civilian' European context via an analysis in Chapter 7 of the position of the EU itself. The section is brought to a close in Chapter 8 by an examination of the manner in which the events in Kosovo were represented to the West by its media.

The four chapters on Britain, Italy, Germany and France are fascinating as much for the things they have in common – respect for human rights, democracy and the rule of law – as for those that keep them apart – their past history, geopolitical factors and attitudes towards the United States. The EU chapter is equally fascinating for its sub-text of 'common-denominator realism' with regard to European unity and influence, mixed with more idealistic concepts such as real cooperation in matters of foreign policy and collective security.

In Chapter 3 Henig paints a picture of Britain broadly united behind the Labour government in its approach to the crisis in Kosovo. At the time the internal position of the British government was stronger than that of any of the other major allies. Tony Blair emerged as the Western leader most obviously outraged by the treatment of the Albanians. Henig points out that throughout the crisis and the bombing campaign the government received support from the bulk of the media as well as from general public opinion. Government rhetoric claimed that the war was being fought solely for humanitarian purposes. The rhetoric of government ministers also laid much stress on the dangers of appeasement and the lessons of history. There was little discernible difference in the attitudes of the major political parties; the opposition was mainly from those parts of the left traditionally suspicious of Nato and Western imperialism.

Italy, as Morelli points out in Chapter 4, was probably the least enthusiastic of the Nato allies to embark upon a military campaign against Yugoslavia. According to Morelli, the fact that it did so, notwithstanding the reservations, the demands for suspension of the bombings to allow negotiations to take place, and its generally conciliatory stance with regard to Belgrade, is due largely to the skills of prime minister D'Alema. The latter, treading a delicate path between public opinion, the Communists and the Greens and, heading the first government of the left for some years, gambled shrewdly on the reluctance of other parties to bring him down. The outcome, Morelli points out, is that Italy saw the crisis through to the end, having participated significantly and, by so doing, maintained its status on the world stage and avoided a national crisis. In Chapter 5, Lyon and Ramet provide a perceptive analysis of what they claim to be a new phase in Germany's post-war history. Despite the deep political cleavages provoked by the crisis, which they examine in detail, they point to the SPD/Green coalition government's qualified endorsement of Germany's participation in Nato's intervention as an important milestone on the road to its 'normalization' within the context of its recent past. In France too, events in Kosovo caused widespread political realignments and reassessment of positions in the face of the conflict. In Chapter 6, Lamizet and Debras point to the fact that for the French, the issue of national identity, which lay at the heart of the Serb–Kosovo Albanian struggle, had special resonances in the light of French identity also being called into question in modern times. They examine the nature of the political turbulence among the parties and offer a tentative view on the common agreement between the right and left as represented by president Chirac and the prime minister, Lionel Jospin, as well as on the relationship of Chirac's RPR party and the extreme right. The acceptance of France of the American-led Nato campaign in the light of France's past attitudes towards the United States is also examined.

Having examined the positions adopted by the four most active of the European member states of Nato *vis-à-vis* the crisis in Kosovo, we add, by way of contrast in Chapter 7, an examination of the position of the 'civilian' home of these states, the EU. Here Ramirez and Szapiro set out the distinctly 'civilian approach' to this and other crises that characterizes the EU's foreign policy, comprising a judicious mixture of dialogue, diplomacy and economic pressure, used in both 'stick' and 'carrot' modes, which in the Kosovo context resulted in the Stability Pact for South-Eastern Europe. Notwithstanding its considerable economic clout, Ramirez and Szapiro point out that the EU may be deemed to have been sidelined once hostilities broke out and that this incapacity to back up diplomacy by force, and its dependence on the USA/Nato for this purpose, have injected the debate within the EU on the establishing of a common European Security and Defence Policy with additional urgency.

Finally in this section, Weymouth, in Chapter 8, examines the performance of the Western media and the manner in which they presented the conflict to the people. He proposes that, in many ways, and frequently because of the ideological straitjackets they put on in order to engage with the crisis, the mass media misrepresented the facts and exaggerated the widespread comparison of the Serbian violence with Nazi barbarism earlier in the century. He concludes, however, that such distortions are more likely to have been generated by ill-judged opinion which, in the absence of hard information, passed for fact, than they were by deliberate attempts to mislead. Weymouth's conclusions, perhaps understandably, are not shared by Williams (Chapter 11), Simons (Chapter 12) or Ramet (Chapter 9).

In the third section, we present the Kosovo crisis from the perspectives of the principal actors: first, the USA and Nato (Chapters 9 and 10), thus completing the Western position; second, two eastern viewpoints, Russia and the initiator/victim, Serbia itself, depending on the lens through which the latter is viewed (Chapters 11 and 12); finally, in Chapter 13, we offer the UN perspective, the organization that had to encompass all views relating to the crisis.

In Chapter 9, Ramet examines both the immediate context and the longer-term implications of US involvement in Kosovo. She identifies the obstacles in the way of presidential action, ranging from the interpretation of the constitution itself to specific cases of ignorance about the Balkans, poor judgement and partisan politics engaged more with the intent of frustrating Clinton's objectives than of thwarting those of Milosevic. Ramet confirms the view, reported by Weymouth in Chapter 8, that it was the media and other reports of the massacre at Racak that finally concentrated the minds of Congress to endorse Nato/US action. In addition, Ramet briefly questions the reluctance on the part of some commentators to use the term 'genocide' when discussing the nature of Serbian oppression of the Kosovo Albanians.

In a key chapter, Chapter 10, Anderson offers a wide-ranging and balanced analysis of Nato's motivation and ethical/legal position *vis-à-vis* its military intervention in Kosovo. If Ramet's analysis in the previous chapter provides an in-depth picture of the internal workings of the US political process involved in ultimately backing Nato, Anderson's provides an excellent, external, European point of view of the same events and their relevance to Nato and to the development of European defence initiatives. Anderson examines the range of motives attributed to Nato's intervention to be found in several of the other chapters and counsels restraint in the acceptance of any on the grounds that it would be unwise to rush to judgement particularly when all the facts are not yet fully accessible. Even so, and with this proviso concerning the facts, he offers some support to the 'humanitarian' dimension of Nato's claims and advances arguments for the limited legal/ethical justification for its actions. Importantly, too, the issue raised by Ramirez and Szapiro in Chapter 7, relating to the significance of the Kosovo conflict for the development of a European defence capability, is addressed from the Nato standpoint.

In a chapter that frequently challenges and contrasts with many of the other commentaries in this book, Williams sets out, in Chapter 11, the Russian perspective and explains how Nato's intervention was seen by most Russians as the aggressive pursuit of the West's strategic interests in central and south-eastern Europe. Williams, while emphasizing the 'tightrope walking' nature of Russia's predicament – its weakening influence in Europe on one hand and reliance on Western finance on the other – highlights its successful crossing of the divide and crucial participation in the political end-game of the conflict. He also points out, significantly, the downside for the alliance: that there are already adverse consequences in the shape of new Russian thinking on foreign policy concerning its post-Cold War relations with the West.

Chapter 12, by Simons, provides the second pro-Serbian text of the book. In a personal account of his perceptions of the Serbian point of view, he emphasizes what he considers major mitigating factors in the Yugoslav action against the Kosovo Albanians. He argues that the West failed to understand the cultural/historical importance of Kosovo to the Serbs, and failed also to comprehend that the violence had been orchestrated by the KLA and reported to the West by a credulous media. He suggests that Nato singled out Serbia as a pariah state in the same way as it had demonized Iraq – for its own purposes: to reassert itself in the post-Cold War era as the principal global enforcer. Simons ascribes part of Nato's motives to a particularly pejorative concept of the region east of the Danube which he calls 'Orientalism'.

The position of the UN was problematic in many ways, some familiar to political analysts and others specific to the nature of Nato's intervention in the case of Kosovo. In Chapter 13, Travers examines and distinguishes between the diverse elements of the crisis from the UN's point of view, and the measures adopted in its attempts to engage with them. He also discusses attempts by the international community to deal with Kosovo that go back to the London talks of 1992, and analyzes the UN's complicated response to the use of force by Nato against Yugoslavia which had to accommodate the wrath of two permanent members of the Security Council as well as that of some of the non-permanent members. Travers's chapter ends with what may be seen as a positive assessment of the achievements of the UN in the post-crisis period.

In the final section (Chapter 14), Henig brings together multifarious strands drawn from substantive chapters in the book. He focuses particularly on the longer-term implications of the war in Kosovo for the sub-region, the participants, international institutions and for international law at the beginning of a new millennium. Based on the views expressed he concludes that the outlook for Kosovo is highly uncertain, even taking into account Milosevic's fall from power.

None of the suggestions for future status – a multi-ethnic community, re-integration with Serbia, absorption into Albania, partition – seem likely to win general support within the sub-region and there is no obvious solution in sight. Henig visualizes the war in Kosovo pushing the EU towards acquiring a defence and security capacity of its own. As far as the international system is concerned, he argues that the role of Russia in bringing about a cease-fire was sufficient to ensure the continuation of the shaky international system which has emerged from the ending of the Cold War. In the last analysis it is the impact of Kosovo on international law that may prove to be most significant. Henig accepts that, according to the classic, somewhat static approach to international law, Nato's actions could be considered illegal, but he suggests that in a more dynamic interpretation the war itself has helped in the evolution of an alternative concept of international law that pays more regard to human rights and which recognizes that people as well as states can be its legitimate subjects.

As we have noted in the Preface, Milosevic was ousted from the presidency in October 2000 by a combination of electoral defeat and public demonstrations at the time when this book was going to press. In Chapter 14, Henig has added an analysis and commentary on the latest developments in Belgrade in which he identifies the reasons for Milosevic's political undoing and discusses its possible consequences for the West.

Whilst all our questions relating to the response of the international community to Serbian repression in Kosovo remain valid, others are beginning to be formulated surrounding the emergence of a new Yugoslav president. The tasks of rebuilding Serbia, reconstructing its shattered economy, negotiating its relationships with Bosnia, Montenegro and Kosovo, and avoiding civil war in the process, are indeed awesome. None of the foregoing tasks can be achieved unless Kostunica holds all the reins of government in his hands. Given the well-known fractiousness of the parties opposed to the Milosevic regime, on the one hand, and the continuing entrenched powerbase of the Socialist Party, on the other, the means by which Kostunica asserts his authority (with political caution, or with radical authority drawn from his popular rise to power) may be a critical factor in the unfolding of events in Yugoslavia and beyond. All this is speculation, but for the moment at least our text, if not the last word, stands among the latest commentaries on the international response to the Kosovo crisis and to Yugoslavia after Milosevic.

EDITORIAL NOTE

Both in the formulation of the questions and in the account in this chapter of how the contributors have set about their responses, we have placed some particular priority upon the accessibility of our text, trying to present the issues as clearly as possible without, we hope, falling into the trap of oversimplification. We have asked the questions in order that the detailed issues and themes of the book may be more easily identified in the individual chapters. In the concluding chapter, the major issues and themes are collected and discussed. There is one final point on the issue of accessibility and style: our original manuscript was bristling with a wide range of acronyms which, although making perfect sense to the specialist in politics or international relations, in our view are off-putting and exclusive to a less-specialized reader. We have therefore considerably reduced in the text original references to the Federal Republic of Yugoslavia (FRY) and to the Former Yugoslav Republic of Macedonia (FYROM) in favour of Yugoslavia and Macedonia respectively; this should be borne in mind in the reading of the text. For our purposes too, references to Belgrade and Serbia are synonymous with the use of the term Yugoslavia as just defined. If reference is made to the *former* Republic of Yugoslavia (i.e. pre-1992) or to that part of Greece which is also called Macedonia, but which is not the Former Yugoslav Republic of Macedonia, then this is made clear locally in the text.

This marks the end of this chapter and the rapid tour of the sites of debate and argument that make up this book. The reader, we hope, is now better equipped to re-visit them at leisure, not necessarily in the order they are placed in the text, in order to better understand and evaluate the causes, nature and possible outcome for the West of its last war of the twentieth century in Europe.

2

KOSOVO: A FUSE FOR THE LIGHTING

CHRISTOPHER WILLIAMS

Whether Kosovo is brought in the end to a peaceful solution or plunged into a conflict ... will depend to a large extent on the ability of ordinary Serbs to challenge the fixed pattern of thought that has held them in its grip for so long ... When ordinary Serbs learn to think more rationally and humanely about Kosovo, and more critically about some of their national myths, all the people of Kosovo and Serbia will benefit, not least the Serbs themselves.

(Malcolm, Kosovo)

Everything started with Kosovo and everything will finish with Kosovo.

(Miranda Vickers, Between Serb and Albanian)

To the Western media, the cause of the Kosovo crisis in 1998–9 was simple: Serb atrocities against Kosovo Albanians. However, as with any war, and especially one conducted through the media, things are never quite as simple as they first appear.

DEFINING THE BALKANS

One of the most controversial issues is the manner in which the Balkans are perceived both internally and externally. In her book, *Imagining the Balkans* (1997), Maria Tomova stresses the importance of the perceptions of the people of the region as well as those of outsiders to the 'Balkans'. This is a highly significant point because from the mid-nineteenth century onwards when Western, in particular, British, travellers, went to the region, two views were formed: first, Westerners sided with the Ottoman Turks (against the Serbs); and second, Westerners also tended to view those who inhabited the region as 'backward'. By the early twentieth century, a third view was added to the previous two. Prompted by the origins of World War I, Westerners now saw the Balkans as a source of violence and unrest. These views prevail to this day. The international community, especially the Western powers, for ethnocentric and other reasons, still hold anti-Serbian views, and retain the inaccurate stereotype that the region is backward (but in different ways and for different reasons by the late twentieth century). Finally, the former Yugoslavia throughout the 1980s and 1990s is viewed as being constantly plagued by violence, rising nationalism and widespread political violence. Mark Mazower has warned scholars against falling into the trap of viewing recent events in the Balkans as largely of ethnic origin.[1] Thus one journalist recently commented:

> 66 The international community still hold anti-Serbian views and retain the inaccurate stereotype that the region is backward 99

What has consumed the Balkans over the course of generations is the hatred of Serbs for Croats; Croats for Slovenes; Slovenes for Montenegrins; Montenegrins for Muslims; Muslims for Macedonians; Macedonians for Albanians ...

(Fields 1999)

We must be careful not to draw the same conclusion about Serbs and Kosovo Albanians. Mazower goes on to conclude that the causes of war in this region lie 'in the relationship of ethnicity *not* to history and society, but to politics and power' and he adds that 'It is in the struggle for power following Tito's death that *ethnicity assumes a central role*' (Mazower 1997). Although these remarks relate to Bosnia in 1995, they apply equally to Kosovo in 1998–9. These variables and the so-called 'Wars of Secession' in the last two decades have put the Balkan Question firmly back on the agenda.

CONTESTED PAST: THE ORIGINS OF THE CONFLICT

Although it may appear that the ongoing conflict between Serbs and Albanians has its origins in rising nationalism or human rights abuses in the 1980s and 1990s, and Vickers implies that the conflict is of fairly recent origin,[2] most scholars would disagree, suggesting instead that the tendency by both groups to contest their rights to Kosovo is clear evidence of the long-term origins of the Kosovo crisis. Thus it is not simple hatred of one group for another; instead the meaning of 'ethnicity', 'nation', 'national identity' and so forth all need to be taken into account in order for those living in the twenty-first century to be able to appreciate the origins and consequences of the war in Kosovo.

> 66 Although it may appear that the ongoing conflict between Serbs and Albanians has its origins in the 1980s and 1990s, the tendency by both groups to contest their rights to Kosovo is clear evidence of the long-term origins of the Kosovo crisis 99

Both Serbs and Albanians have constructed their own 'myths' around the historical importance of Kosovo for the origins of their nations and their national identity. However, as the opening quote from Noel Malcolm shows, until both sides challenge these 'fixed patterns of thought' nothing much will change. The Battle of Kosovo in 1389 is a case in point. So much myth, symbolism and legend is associated with this battle it is difficult even to this day to separate fact from fiction. The Serbs argue that they have been in Kosovo since the seventh century, that their medieval kings were crowned there and but for a defeat by the Ottoman Turks at the Battle of Kosovo Polje in 1389 Serbs would have retained control in Kosovo; while the Albanians suggest that they arrived in Kosovo prior to the Serbs and that they are the direct descendants of the region's earliest inhabitants.

Both sides challenge their opponents' claim that Kosovo was, first, the cradle of Serb/Albanian civilization and, second, that their (Serb or Albanian) nationality was the largest group in Kosovo. For Malcolm most of the evidence does not support Serb claims over Kosovo; whereas Miranda Vicker's 1998 work, *Between Serb and Albanian: A History of Kosovo*, suggests instead that neither group has an irrefutable case.

Besides contested historical claims to Kosovo, there are other major differences between Serbs and Albanians. They speak different languages and have different religions. Most Albanians are Muslim, with a small proportion being orthodox or Catholic. Even here, there is no consensus among scholars. For instance, Vickers believes that many Kosovo Albanians are really Serbs who during the period of Ottoman domination were forced to give up their national identity by the Turks.[3] As with the historical importance of Kosovo, it is difficult to reach any firm conclusions.

A HISTORY OF TURMOIL AND SUPPRESSION: KOSOVO BEFORE AND DURING THE COMMUNIST ERA

As Table 2.1 shows, relations between the Serbs, Kosovo Albanian and other parties have been strained for many centuries. During the rise of the Ottoman Empire, each side accused the other of supporting the Turkish enemy. It is clear that most states, such as Serbia and Albania, did not gain their independence until relatively late, in the 1870s and early twentieth century respectively. By the start of World War I, most Balkan states contained numerous ethnic groups. In what was to become Yugoslavia, for example, Slovenes, Croats, Bosnians, Macedonians, Serbs and Albanians co-existed. But the marriage of convenience did not last for long. Soon the Serbs suppressed the Albanians, closing their schools in the 1920s and 1930s and seizing their land. This had an impact on Yugoslavia's as well as Kosovo's ethnic composition (see Table 2.2). Although some Albanians left, this repressive stance did not entirely remove the Albanian presence in Kosovo. Thus according to Ramet, there were 800,000 Albanians in the area in 1931 and, even by 1940, their number had only declined to 700,000.[4]

During World War II, Kosovo was occupied by Mussolini's forces. Although Kosovo was divided into three zones, things were much better than under the Serbs because:

[Kosovo Albanians found] Italian occupation *less harsh* [in terms of culture, education and language] *than [under] rule by Belgrade.*   (Ramet 1999: 303)

TITO'S RESPONSE TO THE KOSOVO QUESTION, 1945–80

When Tito and the communists took power in Yugoslavia from the mid–late 1940s, they inherited various types of ethnic or nationality conflicts, such as those between the dominant nationality and the minorities as typified by the history of the Serbs and Albanians. Yugoslavia, like the USSR and east-central Europe, was a melting pot. Tito expected his comrades and citizens to remain loyal, so he sup-

Year	Event
1389	Battle of Kosovo
1815	Serbia gains autonomous status
1878	Bulgaria, Serbia, Romania and Montenegro declared independent
1912	Albania gains independence
1913	Kosovo handed over to Serbia not Albania
1918	Kingdom of Serbs, Croats and Slovenes proclaimed
1918–20	Suppression and Serbianization of Albanians Closure of all Albanian-language schools
1920	Albanian state created
1939–44	Italian fascists occupy Albania and Kosovo
1945	Tito establishes government in Yugoslavia
1948	Yugoslavia breaks with USSR and is expelled from *Cominform*; Albania funds Kosovo terrorism
1960s	Albanians' demands for republican status for Kosovo fail but University of Pristina (Albanian language) established
1963	Kosovo made 'autonomous province' (*automnia prokrajina*) of Yugoslavia
1974	Kosovo made 'constituent province' of Yugoslavia
1980	Tito's death
1980s	Gradual Serbianization of Kosovo
1988–97	Milosevic's rise to power, clamp-down and reduction in Kosovo Albanian autonomy
1990	Kosovo Albanians demand secession from Serbia but not Yugoslavia
1990s	Albanians' loyalty to Yugoslavia wanes Gradual break-up of Yugoslavia Serb clamp-down on Kosovo Albanians Increased tension in Kosovo Emergence of KLA
Mid-1990s	Increasing Western concern about Milosevic
1995–date	Wars of Secession, Rambouillet agreement, Nato strikes and Western occupation of Kosovo

TABLE 2.1 The major events in Balkan and Kosovo history

pressed national identity, contained nationalism and above all kept a tight grip on ethnic tension among so-called disruptive ethnic minorities, like the Kosovo Albanians. As Lee notes:

The party now stressed Yugoslav unity: the right to self-determination was *put to one side* and advocating *the secession of disaffected regions condemned once again as nationalism.*   (Lee 1983: 77; my emphasis)

Country	Ethnic groups	Number	Percentage
Yugoslavia	Serbo-Croat	10.7 million	77.01
	Slovene	1.1 million	8.15
	Czech	52,909	0.38
	Slovak	76,411	0.11
	Magyar	468,185	3.36
	Romanian/Vlach	137,879	0.98
	Albanian	505,259	3.63
	Turkish	132,924	0.95
	Gypsy	70,424	0.51

Source: Joseph Rothschild, *East Central Europe between the Two World Wars* (University of Washington Press, Seattle 1983), pp. 36, 89, 192, 203, 284, 328

TABLE 2.2 Ethnic composition of Yugoslavia, 1931

Tito's 'iron glove approach' on Kosovo in the 1940s and 1950s gradually gave way to a more flexible cultural policy which tolerated Kosovo Albanians. Although the Albanians wanted much more – autonomy – Tito only made, what Ramet terms 'minor cosmetic concessions' which included, among other things, granting Kosovo autonomous status within the Republic of Serbia in 1963, allowing the Albanians to control the Yugoslav Communist Party apparatus in Kosovo and establishing the University of Pristina.[5] By the late 1960s, Tito even allowed Albanians to display their flag in Kosovo. The Yugoslav Constitution was finally amended in 1974 to upgrade Kosovo's status to that of a 'constituent republic', equal, in theory, to all the others. Ramet implies that these changes were minor and, in the sense that they did not fundamentally alter the *status quo*, she is correct. When seen in a broader comparative communist framework, Kosovo's higher status can be seen as a marked improvement to the Soviet response to the Prague Spring of 1968. Nevertheless, Kosovo Albanians were dissatisfied with these changes. As Lee points out:

disappointment at the failure to make Kosovo Yugoslavia's seventh republic spilled into the streets in 1968 and there were demonstrations again in 1974–5.   (Lee 1983: 88)

Despite different reactions to the National Question, all the communist regimes shared one thing in common: a concern that ethnicity and rising nationalism were major issues capable of re-shaping their states and societies. Seen in this light, Tito's policy on Kosovo can be viewed as an attempt to curb Albanian separatism and prevent the possible disintegration of Yugoslavia. The outcome was a mass Serb exodus – 45,000 Serbs left Kosovo between 1968 and 1981.[6] Moreover, the 1974 Constitutional amendments were resented by many Serbs who thought that Tito had given too much power to Kosovo Albanians. In the long-term, Tito's so-called 'softly softly approach' would contribute to the deterioration of Serb–Albanian relations in Kosovo, especially after Milosevic came to power.

> 66All the communist regimes shared one thing in common: a concern that ethnicity and rising nationalism were major issues capable of re-shaping their states and societies 99

THE POST-TITO PERIOD AND THE KOSOVO QUESTION

The above analysis shows that although Kosovo Albanians struggled to preserve their national identity and ethnic status throughout the communist era, many had nevertheless more or less assimilated and become accustomed to the benefits and disadvantages that communism had brought. However, Tito's death in 1980 opened up a new, more uncertain, phase in Yugoslavia's history.

In early 1981, the first signs that there were flaws in Yugoslavia's communist experiment occurred when riots took place in Kosovo. The number of Albanians living in Kosovo had been steadily rising throughout the 1960s and 1970s, so that they constituted over three quarters of the population of Kosovo by 1981.[7] Kosovo Albanians rioted against poverty, economic neglect, high unemployment (three times the national average) and deteriorating socio-economic conditions.[8] For decades the socio-economic indicators had been lower in Kosovo than in other republics.[9] Calls were made for Kosovo to be granted republican status in order to help it overcome these difficulties, but this did not happen. The difficulty now, as Lee notes, was how to transform Kosovo's status while not siding with the enemy. This necessitated taking a middle road between acknowledging the importance of Albanian concerns over Kosovo while at the same time not threatening Serb identity.[10]

> 66 The difficulty was how to transform Kosovo's status while not siding with the enemy 99

Throughout the 1980s, against the backdrop of a series of power struggles between various Yugoslav elites, there was a gradual shift in perceptions of Kosovo. Thus according to Ramet, between 1981 and 1987 the Yugoslav Federal authorities increasingly viewed Albanian nationalism, especially in Kosovo, as 'dangerous' and 'irredentist' (Ramet 1999: 307). Yugoslavia remained a melting pot and it was still very ethnically diverse (see Table 2.3).

Country	Population	Ethnic groups	Percentage of population
Yugoslavia	23.41 million	Serbian	35.0
		Croatian	18.8
		Turks, Gypsies, Slovaks and Romanians	12.8
		Slav Moslem	8.5
		Slovenes	7.7
		Albanian	7.3
		Macedonian	5.5
		Montenegrin	2.6
		Hungarian	1.8

Source: Adapted from Economist Intelligence Unit data

TABLE 2.3 Ethnic diversity in Yugoslavia, late 1980s

Although Albanians only constituted 7.3 per cent of the overall population of the former Yugoslavia, by 1991 they made up 90 per cent of the population of Kosovo as opposed to a Serb population of 35 per cent in Yugoslavia as a whole, but only 10 per cent in Kosovo.[11] Through a series of strategies Milosevic tried to hold on to power as Yugoslavia crumbled. But the collapse of communist order provided Milosevic and other Serb nationalists with the rationale for their actions, namely a desire to keep the Serb nation together and to restore its national identity.

THE IMPACT OF THE FALL OF YUGOSLAVIA AND MILOSEVIC'S RISE TO POWER

We shall win the battle for Kosovo regardless of the *obstacles facing us inside and outside the country.* (Slobodan Milosevic, 19 November 1988; my emphasis)

Milosevic's re-imposition of Serbian power in Kosovo sparked a cycle of competitive nationalisms, which by 1991, was to lead to the demise of Yugoslavia and to war.

(Judah 1999: 11)

Milosevic's rise to power from 1988, first as head of the Serbian Communist Party, then as president of Serbia, marked a return to a tougher policy on Kosovo. Sabrina Ramet refers to this process as the gradual 'Serbianization of the province [of Kosovo]' (Ramet 1997: 148). The Serbs were worried that the revolutions in east-central Europe in 1989 might lead to similar demands by Kosovo Albanians in Serbia. Therefore the iron glove was used once again. The most serious consequence was that Kosovo's autonomy was revoked in 1989. Milosevic sought to undo Tito's legacy by giving Serbs back what was 'rightfully theirs' – Kosovo. But he went much further than this. Milosevic and the Serbs exerted significant pressure to ensure that pro-Albanian leaders, such as Azmem Vliasi and Kaqusha Jashari, resigned; that the Academy of Sciences in Kosovo was abolished; that Albanian street names were changed to Serbian; that Serbs were allowed to enter the University of Pristina; that Serbs received preferential treatment; and, finally, Albanians were fired from their posts or lost their homes to Serbs (130,000 between 1990 and 1995).[12]

Despite this pressure and discrimination, Kosovo Albanians still demanded the right to secede from Serbia but *not* Yugoslavia in 1990. Moreover under Ibrahim Rugova's leadership Albanians by and large responded to this clamp-down with 'passive resistance'. For example, in 1992, ethnic Albanians set up a shadow government and various Albanian-language schools. This was the start of renewed tension between Serbs and Albanians in Kosovo. But it also had another key effect. Milosevic's policies, together with other factors, led to the collapse of Yugoslavia. Unlike the situation in other post-communist countries, such as the Czech Republic or Hungary, where the transition was relatively smooth, in Yugoslavia's case it was chaotic and difficult. Other republics, such as Croatia and Slovenia, now realized that Milosevic wanted to create a Greater Serbia, not a more multinational and tolerant Yugoslavia, so they quickly declared independence. They were the lucky ones; elsewhere in Bosnia the road to independence was far from easy and a hard-won peace was eventually

66 Milosevic's policies, together with other factors, led to the collapse of Yugoslavia 99

brought about by the Dayton Accord of 1995. Unfortunately, the Albanians received nothing because, in Rama's opinion, the Serbs 'vetoed any discussion on Kosova and the international community acquiesced' (Rama 2000). As a result, Kosovo remained part of Serbia.

In many of these instances, the leaders of former Yugoslavia played the 'ethnic card' and exploited it to the full for their political ends. This was also the case with the Serbs and Kosovo Albanians. Fearing that the worst was yet to come, many Kosovo Albanians fled. Thus, according to Ramet's calculations, 25,000 Kosovo Albanians fled to Italy between November 1994 and January 1995.[13]

Amid growing divisions within the Albanian community over how best to respond to Milosevic and the Serbs, things started to take a turn for the worse. Albanian loyalty to Yugoslavia was waning and the KLA was set up. According to some accounts, the KLA dates back to 1983, but most sources agree that it was established in the 1990s.[14] As for the reason for this change in attitude, Ramet comments:

it was Milosevic's adoption of policies of repression, apartheid and expulsion *that made separatism mainstream thinking among the province's Albanians.*

(Ramet 1997: 150; my emphasis)

This shift away from Kosovo Albanian loyalty to Yugoslavia and calls for greater allegiance to Albania were reflected in a late September 1991 poll which showed that 99.87 per cent of the Kosovo Albanians surveyed were in favour of Kosovo's merging with Albania (cited in Ramet 1997: 150). However, as Patrick Moore remarks, we must be careful not to read too much into this because a merger in theory was one thing; overcoming mutual suspicion, another:

Kosovars often regard Albanian citizens as backward people who lack a modern education or knowledge of the wider world; [while] people in Albania tend to view Kosovars as arrogant braggarts with questionable business ethics.

(Moore 1999)

Although these divisions subsequently disappeared as Kosovo Albanians fled Serb repression and went to live in Albania, Italy and elsewhere, such public opinion polls simply made the Serbs more determined to continue their hard-line approach and not grant any more concessions to Kosovo Albanians. Thus the same September 1991 poll showed that 83 per cent of Serbs were opposed to the idea of granting any concessions to Kosovo Albanians (cited in Ramet 1997: 150).

ETHNIC CLEANSING AND THE ABUSE OF KOSOVO ALBANIAN HUMAN RIGHTS

The recent Serbian campaign to drive a majority of Kosovar Albanians first from their houses and then from the province altogether has reminded the rest of Europe and the United States that this unsuccessful cleansing of 1999 was preceded by others that were more successful, from primarily Serb campaigns in Croatia and Bosnia to the Croatian cleansing of all the Krajina Serbs in 1995.

(Lampe, *Yugoslavia as History*: 367)

The Serb is the new Jew, the Jew at the end of the twentieth century.

(Dobrica Cosic, Serb intellectual)

Men like Milosevic did more than take the lid off some simmering pot of ethnic unrest. They *engineered that ethnic unrest by deliberately provoking hatred and fear among their people.*

(Cristina Posa; my emphasis)

Throughout the late 1980s and early 1990s, Milosevic and the Serbs continued to abuse the human rights of Kosovo Albanians. Their homes and businesses were looted and burned, they were illegally detained, raped or executed.[15] Using the myths referred to at the start of this chapter, Serbian nationalists argued that it was the Serbs who had been repressed and suffered most. Parallels were even drawn between the plight of the Jews and that of the Serbs, as the Cosic quote above shows. Drawing on the importance of the Kosovo mythology to Serb identity, Milosevic and others sought to justify the Serb policy of ethnic cleansing in Kosovo and elsewhere. As more Kosovo Albanians fled, the Serbs implemented a resettlement policy and preferential loans scheme and if the latter was not possible, Albanian property was simply confiscated and Kosovo Albanians were expelled from their homes. Albanian businesses were ransacked and Albanian journalists were unlawfully detained.[16]

> 66 Serbian nationalists argued that it was the Serbs who had been repressed and suffered most and parallels were drawn between the plight of the Jews and that of the Serbs 99

Judah shows how Milosevic exploited past historical myths to increase Serb fears, while at the same time furthering his own ambitions for greater power through a Greater Serbia.[17] Unfortunately, as Cristina Posa states:

... Serb politicians like Slobodan Milosevic and Vojislav Seselj turn to stirring nationalist feelings and finding ethnic scapegoats in order to gain power while *offering no real solutions to Yugoslavia's economic and political deterioration.*   (Posa 1998: 70; my emphasis)

It is clear from Table 2.4 that by the mid-1990s, both Albanians and Serbs thought that a war over Kosovo was likely sooner or later. This war could, of course, have been averted either if the West had kept the pressure on Milosevic or if the Dayton Accord had made the appropriate provisions for Kosovo. Unfortunately neither of these happened. Throughout the early–late 1990s while Milosevic and the Serbs hounded Kosovo Albanians, the USA and Western alliance opted in Ramet's words for 'minimal responses' (Ramet 1997: 156). In other words, they stood by and did nothing. As a result, Milosevic had a largely free hand in Kosovo and, if after Dayton was signed Western leaders thought that 'the Balkans wars were over' (Judah 1999: 12), they were seriously mistaken.

Throughout 1998 the situation in Kosovo went from bad to worse. In late March 1998, Kosovo's ethnic Albanians voted for their own president and parliament with the latter being inaugurated in mid-July 1998. But the Serb authorities refused to recognize the former political figures and used the police to disperse MPs and others. By this time, members of the KLA now reached the conclusion that because Kosovo Albanians had not achieved their goals in a peaceful manner and, because a Serbian crackdown was likely to be maintained unless something was done, it was necessary to take other radical steps. Thus in 1998, the KLA embarked on a series of insurgent operations against Serb officials and government structures in Kosovo. The Serbs defined KLA actions as 'terrorist' and responded by sending in tanks. Thereafter, the West, rather belatedly started to get involved and asked Milosevic to 'back off'. Milosevic ignored the West's warnings and sent 50,000 special forces into Kosovo.[18] But instead of taking the appropriate action the West 'backed down' (Ramet 1999: 314). Even at this very late stage the West, that is, the USA and Europe, was still clinging to the notion that independence for Kosovo was out of the question; instead it was preferable that the Albanians were granted 'broad autonomy' (Rama 2000).

> 66 Members of the KLA reached the conclusion that because Kosovo Albanians had not achieved their goals in a peaceful manner, it was necessary to take other radical steps 99

Sample = 200

Question/Answer	Albanian response (%)	Serbian response (%)
Is peace possible in a single state?	Yes, 19	Yes, 54.5
	No, 65	No, 40
How can the Kosovo Question be solved?		
Join Albania	43	
Create own state	57	
Make Kosovo part of Serbia	3	62
Do Albanian children in Kosovo have the right to be educated in their own language?	Yes, 100	Yes, 81.5
		No, 16
Whose human rights are violated – Serbs or Albanians?	Ours, 91 Both, 7	Ours, 52 Albanians, 1.5 Both – 23
Is a war likely?	Yes, 17	Yes, 42
	No, 37	No, 49
Who would start the war?	Albanians, 9	Albanians, 45.2
	Serbs, 71	Serbs, 4.8
	Foreigners, 15	Foreigners, 28.6

Source: Adapted from J. Mertus, 'A wall of silence divides Serbian and Albanian opinion on Kosovo', *Transition*, 22 March 1996, p. 51.

TABLE 2.4 Serbian and Albanian attitudes towards Kosovo, September 1995

ON THE ROAD TO WAR IN KOSOVO

In the past Milosevic's interest has been power, pure and simple. Perhaps he wanted glory too.

(Judah 1999: 14)

By late September 1998 Western anxieties about Serb actions in Kosovo had reached their peak. Thus on 24 September 1998 Nato issued an ultimatum to Milosevic asking him to stop the violence in Kosovo or face Nato air strikes. This did nothing to deter Milosevic because in Judah's words 'Milosevic [had] promised to secure Kosovo for the Serbs' (Judah

1999: 15). Following the massacre of Kosovo Albanians by Serbs in early October, the UN Security Council condemned Serbia and warned that air strikes would begin in two weeks unless all hostilities ceased in Kosovo. The reasons behind this strategy and the viewpoints of different countries within the Western alliance will be explored in the chapters that follow, so suffice it to say here that the West hoped this time that Milosevic would listen and that a military conflict could be avoided. It looked as if a compromise had been reached when the Holbrooke–Milosevic agreement was signed in October 1998, whereby Serbian security forces were withdrawn from Kosovo and Nato halted the threatened air strikes. But, although a small contingent of Organization for Security and Cooperation in Europe (OSCE) forces arrived in Kosovo in November, 1998 and it looked as though there would be a de-escalation of hostilities between the KLA and Serbia, the cease-fire did not last long. In early 1999, renewed fighting soon broke out and the Serbs also launched a clamp-down on the Kosovo Albanian mass-media, as journalists and broadcasters tried to tell the true story of events. This led to a military build-up on all sides (Serb, KLA, the West). An attempt was made at Rambouillet to defuse the crisis, but Milosevic refused to allow Nato troops in to 'police' Kosovo. Instead he provocatively declared: 'We will not give up Kosovo, even if we are bombed' (cited in *New York Times*, 19 February 1999). The Rambouillet talks subsequently collapsed and with them the prospect of a permanent cease-fire. With the failure of these diplomatic efforts, the West felt that it had no choice but to bomb Serbia. It is to the bombing issue, and the consequences for Serbia and Kosovo of Nato 'winning' the war that I now wish to turn.

> 66 Following the massacre of Kosovo Albanians by Serbs in early October, the UN Security Council condemned Serbia and warned that air strikes would begin in two weeks 99

THE END OF THE BEGINNING OR THE BEGINNING OF THE END: WESTERN INTERVENTION IN KOSOVO – THE MOTIVES

Each contributor will be exploring the different responses to Nato air strikes in their respective chapters, so I would now like to examine some of the debates surrounding Nato action in general and whether or not it was appropriate to use air strikes rather than other means to resolve the Kosovo crisis.

Without doubt Nato's air strikes on Serbia marked one of the most significant aspects of Western intervention in the Balkans at the end of the
twentieth century. It is beyond the scope of this chapter to explore in
great depth the question of Western intervention in the Balkans in the
late 1990s, but the key areas of concern and debate are:

- What were Nato's objectives?
- Why did Nato use force?
- Should Nato have used force?
- What other alternatives were available?
- What chance did Milosevic have of winning the war and, if he lost,
  would the West make him into a martyr and what would he/the
  West do next?

There are broadly two schools of thought on Nato action in Kosovo. The
first, which includes key policy and decision-makers and heads of state
throughout the Western alliance, believes that Nato actions against
Serbia were *justified*. As the American president, Bill Clinton, put it, by
bombing Serbia 'we are upholding our values, protecting our interests
and advancing the cause of peace'. He went on:

Had we failed the result would have been a moral disaster. The Albanian
Kosovars would have become a people without a homeland, living in
difficult conditions in some of the poorest countries in Europe.

(Clinton cited in Chomsky 1999: 3)

In addition to the above, the then UK defence minister, George
Robertson, declared:

Our military objective – our clear, simple military objective – will be to
reduce the Serbs' capacity to repress the Albanian population and thus
avert a humanitarian disaster.   (cited in Roberts 1999: 111)

Serbia, of course, would dispute the validity of this claim and, as we shall
see in this book, Milosevic was not alone in arguing that Kosovo was an
internal matter, and therefore no outside agency or country had the right
to interfere in its internal affairs. Debates on whether or not Nato was *justified* in its actions do not stop here. It has also been suggested in some
quarters that Nato had *no legal justification* for military intervention
because of the absence of UN Security Council authorization. However, in

the eyes of the 19 countries involved, some of whom are represented in this volume, the West was morally and militarily justified in taking action to protect 'the inhabitants of Kosovo' (Roberts 1999: 108).

But other thinkers, such as the British left-winger Tariq Ali, have concluded that, although the declared aim of the West was to defend the Kosovo Albanians, Nato action in the end failed to avert a 'humanitarian disaster' in Kosovo.[19] We shall explore the post-war repercussions below.

Other scholars believe that the 'humanitarian crisis' was merely a disguise for more sinister motives. On the latter, there has been a fierce debate in academic and other circles in recent years over American hegemony. As the only superpower that survived the Cold War intact, the USA is in a position whereby it can achieve its foreign policy goals via the 'use of force'. Tariq Ali, Noam Chomsky, Peter Gowan and others are all highly critical of Western actions. They argue that the West was either wrong to intervene at all or wrong not to consider other options, such as economic sanctions or blockades. The West was wrong because 'superiority' does not give it the right to do what it wants. As Chomsky points out:

Now freed from the shackles of the Cold War and old fashioned constraints of world order, the enlightened states [the US and its British associate] can dedicate themselves with full vigour to the mission of upholding human rights and bringing justice to suffering people, *by force if necessary*.

(Chomsky 1999: 4; my emphasis)

For this second group of scholars, the Nato mission in Kosovo had nothing to do with averting a 'humanitarian disaster'; instead the aim was to ensure that nothing challenged American hegemony and that the West retained its economic and political superiority in the post-communist new world order. There seems to have been an assumption on the West's part that it was now the arbiter of what constitutes 'goodness' 'justice' and 'civilization'. And through its new 'moral imperialism' or what Chomsky refers to as the 'new military humanism' the Western alliance supposedly had the right to stop those, such as Milosevic, who sought to undermine these cherished values. Only Johnstone argues that Western action was perhaps misguided because of confusion over the difference between 'national' and 'human' rights.[20] In order to deflect attention away from these other non-humanitarian

> **❝ The Nato mission in Kosovo had nothing to do with averting a 'humanitarian disaster' ❞**

reasons for the use of force, the Western media and senior political figures have, as Erin LaPorte points out, successfully 'demonized' and 'dehumanized' the Serbs.[21]

In addition to the human rights abuse aspect, the US and western Europe also feared that the violence in Kosovo might spill over into other former Yugoslav republics as well as other Balkan countries, such as Greece and Turkey.

THE CONSEQUENCES OF NATO ACTION

Tariq Ali argues that Nato action in Kosovo was evidence, first, of the breakdown of the system of collective security and, second, of 'hollow reasoning' on the part of the West.[22] In my opinion, Ali is incorrect on the first point because the collective security system had already effectively collapsed in the 1930s prior to the signing of the Nazi–Soviet Pact and had never really been reinstated. What Ali means perhaps, as Roberts notes, is that the Nato bombing 'marked a significant break from NATO's previous policy and practice' (Roberts 1999: 103). Even if Ali is referring to the West only, if anything, Nato action demonstrated the opposite. Not the collapse but a strengthening, albeit temporarily perhaps, of the collective security system. Once again Roberts argues that

> The fact that 19 states with multi-party democratic systems *did act collectively is impressive*, and the democratic nature of their systems may have helped to place certain constraints on the means used and on the goals of the military operation.   (Roberts 1999: 107; my emphasis)

Individual contributors will no doubt explore the validity of our claims. Ali is, however, on firmer ground in pointing to the West's 'hollow reasoning'. This is perhaps what Ted Galen Carpenter means when he uses the term 'NATO's Empty Victory' for the title of his edited collection. In this book, Carpenter and the various contributors highlight the fact that Nato's policy was 'ill-conceived' from the start: based on a biased view of the Kosovo crisis which, in its desire to oppose Milosevic, totally ignored the

66 According to some reports, the USA and some EU states, such as Germany, may have even helped finance the KLA 99

KLA's terrorist roots and tendencies.[23] Moreover according to some reports, the USA and some EU states, such as Germany, which have groups of at least 300,000 and 400,000 Albanians respectively, may have even helped finance the KLA.[24] Finally, Bandow points out that Nato and the Western alliance was hypocritical in so far as it ignored the abuse of Serb human rights until Nato bombing had finished and furthermore the West had failed to intervene on 'humanitarian grounds' in other wars earlier in the twentieth century, namely, conflicts between France and Algeria, Turkey and Cyprus and so on.[25]

The aforementioned discussion shows that the Kosovo conflict might have been avoided if the West had adopted a more conciliatory, less aggressive stance towards Milosevic. I am not condoning his actions towards the Kosovo Albanians, merely suggesting that the West backed Milosevic into a corner and failed to consider other alternatives. As Christopher Layne points out, Milosevic was forced to negotiate at Rambouillet with 'a gun at his head' (Layne 2000a: 16). Like any trapped rat, Milosevic had no choice but to try and fight his way out.

> 66 Like any trapped rat, Milosevic had no choice but to try and fight his way out 99

Thus through a series of 'miscalculations' and 'blunders' before, during and after the war – such as under-estimating Serbian resolve, favouring the KLA, assuming force would mean victory – the West secured a 'hollow victory'. Nato action did not restore peace in Kosovo, did not mean that Milosevic was immediately dislodged from his position of power and, finally, Nato's resort to bombing meant that other alternatives and possible solutions to the crisis were ignored.

THE PROSPECTS FOR PEACE IN KOSOVO AND THE BALKANS

> Good has triumphed over evil, justice has overcome barbarism, and the values of civilisation have prevailed.
>
> (Tony Blair)

Once the West, having overcome US Congress opposition, public ignorance and indifference, had launched air strikes and 'won' the war after seventy-eight days of bombing, it then had a series of tricky problems to address, such as justifying Nato action, dealing with atrocities and war crimes on all sides, disarming the KLA and neutralizing Milosevic and building a new Kosovo. These are by no means easy problems to resolve.

We concluded earlier that the West believed that a Nato strike was justi-fied to avert a 'humanitarian disaster' although the Serbs, Russians (see Chapter 11) and some sections of the American and UK left felt that the West was morally wrong to act in this way and should have pursued other avenues to resolve the crisis.

With regards to the second question, once the war was over, the Western alliance expressed its regret at the loss of civilian lives. As General Wesley Clark stated in the summer of 1999:

It was *not a campaign against the Serbian people*. It focused on the forces of repression from top to bottom to coerce a change in their behaviour or failing that to degrade and ultimately destroy their means of repression. Allied planners, targeters and pilots *worked diligently to prevent injuries and loss of lives among the civilian population and to prevent collateral damage*.

(cited in Roberts 1999: 115; my emphasis)

For the Serbs, however, this war was personal. It was as much against them – military and civilian alike – as it was against their leader Milosevic and other senior government figures. Although any loss of civilian life is to be condemned – and between 300 and 500 lost their lives[26] – it nevertheless remains true that the number of civilian deaths was far outweighed by the loss of life due to ethnic cleansing by all sides. In any case, it is estimated that at least US$195.8 million will be required in humanitarian aid for refugees over the next few years.[27] Of course, we must not forget the enormous refugee problem that lies ahead.[28] According to a recent Amnesty International report at least 250,000 ethnic Albanians are 'displaced', many others have disap-peared and at least 1,000 were detained on charges of 'terrorism' and 'armed rebellion' (Amnesty International 1999). Many Serbs too have been killed and harassed.[29] On top of the growing number of refugees, there is the issue of large numbers of asylum seekers from Kosovo. According to UNCHR statis-tics by mid-1999 at least 36,000 asylum seekers were located in 17 European countries awaiting the outcome of their applications.[30] If these refugees are to return to Kosovo unharmed, they need to be cer-tain that they have security, shelter and, above all, peace. But for reasons explained below, the situation in Kosovo, despite a Western presence, is far from stable.

> If the refugees are to return to Kosovo unharmed, they need to be certain that they have security, shelter and, above all, peace

General Clark also raised the important issue of 'collateral damage'. This is extremely difficult to quantify, but one Group 17 report suggests that the total economic damage caused by Nato bombing amounted to nearly US$30,000 million.[31] More specifically, various European Commission/World Bank reports claim that at least 30 per cent of housing, more than 50 per cent of agriculture and most of the communication system in Kosovo were destroyed before or during the war.[32] It is estimated that the reconstruction and recovery plan will cost between US$2.3 and 5 billion.[33]

A harder issue to resolve is that of atrocities and war crimes. The recent trials of Yugoslav 'war criminals' in the Hague are evidence of the West's determination to pursue this matter to the bitter end. The indictment of Milosevic and others, as Chomsky acknowledges, is 'warranted' and 'long overdue' (Chomsky 1999: 84), but the West must ensure that all those, including Kosovo Albanians, members of the KLA etc., who commit crimes are brought to trial and sentenced. We must be careful not to repeat past errors, as the West did when it employed Nazi war criminals after 1945.

The thorny issue of the need to disarm the KLA and neutralize Milosevic has proved to be particularly difficult. All sides are only slowly coming to terms with the war and its aftermath. The West for its part has had to continue dealing with Milosevic and was forced to include Serbia in the negotiations on the Balkans stability pact in 1999–2000. But as Georgieff and Blocker rightfully note: 'You must not penalise 10 million Serbs for the conduct of one man' (Georgieff and Blocker 1999). In the meantime, though, Milosevic for his part has been 'defiant in defeat' (although he would see the war as a victory).

In the aftermath of the war, the KLA was transformed into the Kosovo Protection Corps (KPC). Although 100,000 Serbs have fled, and many have been murdered, Nato estimates suggest that 97,000 Serbs still remain in Kosovo. It has proved extremely difficult totally to disarm the KLA which had approximately 10,000 members or its successor, the KPC with 3–5,000 members. The KLA/KPC as well as Serb paramilitaries, according to one late-1999 South Balkans report, are still seeking revenge and have even turned on other minorities in Kosovo, such as the Roma.[34] This is not just a security issue – many members of the KLA remain underground, others have turned to organized crime and still more have formed their own political party, the Party of Democratic Progress of Kosovo (PPDK).[35] All of these factors are likely to shape the political process and stability in the region for many years to come. Finally, there is the related issue of how to rebuild Kosovo and the Balkans. There is no consensus among experts about how to proceed here. According to Zoran Lutovac, possible options include:

- genuine autonomy
- regionalization
- the creation of a unitary state
- independence for Kosovo
- annexation of Kosovo by Albania
- the setting up of an international protectorate in Kosovo.[36]

Little did Lutovac know in 1997 the latter would become a reality in 1999–2000. From an Albanian perspective, Shinasi A. Rama believes that there are only three options available:

- independence
- partition
- a colony.[37]

Finally, Janusz Bugajski goes a little further arguing that we need to put the Kosovo Question in its broader Balkan and post-communist context. He argues that it is possible to characterize many post-communist Balkan regimes, including Serbia, as having authoritarian tendencies, stagnating economies, resurgent nationalism (based on what he calls 'ethnic collectivism') and strong nepotism, patronage, corruption and rising crime.[38] Bugajski suggests that in the future, there are two distinct possibilities: regional regression based on resurgent authoritarianism, political paralysis, social breakdown and an upsurge in populist-nationalism or greater security as a consequence of political and economic stability, strong institution building, the emergence of a civil society, regional cooperation and a sustained fight against organised crime and corruption.[39] In the case of Serbia and Kosovo the more pessimistic option looks likely in the short term due to a combination of Milosevic holding on to power and the fact that Western forces are now sharing power with the Serbs and Albanians in Kosovo. Finding a solution to the post-war crisis will be far from easy. One year after the Nato air strikes, it is

> 66 Getting Serbs and Albanians to trust each other will be difficult enough, but getting them to trust the West will be even harder 99

clear that Nato actions 'protected one minority' (the Kosovo Albanians) but in the aftermath created 'others' (Serbs). It seems as if 'the oppressed [has now] become the oppressor' (Snegaroff 2000). Getting Serbs and Albanians to trust each other will be difficult enough, but getting them to trust the West will be even harder.

CONCLUSIONS

This analysis shows that it is extremely difficult to determine the truth with regard to the origins of the war in Kosovo. Western perceptions of the war suggest that the Serbs are 'guilty' while the Kosovo Albanians are 'innocent'. This constitutes reductionism and historical oversimplification. It stems from a desire on the West's part to justify its military intervention and for this it is necessary to cast Milosevic in the role of 'villain'. We have also seen that both sides have, according to their respective version of events, equal 'claims' to Kosovo. But the West simply decided that Kosovo Albanians had the 'rightful claim' so it was their interests that must be protected, acknowledged and respected. The West reached this conclusion because only it knew what constituted 'good' and 'just'. In the process, the notion of 'other' was exploited to the full: the West was 'democratic', Milosevic and his supporters 'barbarian'.

In order to convince the general public of the correctness of its response on the Kosovo crisis, the Western media, counting on widespread ignorance or misconceptions of the Balkans in general and Kosovo in particular, presented Nato's actions as a 'just war'. This can be seen in BBC and other Western media coverage of the Kosovo crisis that tried to construct a view of the war that backed Nato's stance, and rarely sought to portray a more objective, balanced picture. The emphasis throughout was on the 'justness' of Nato's cause – to protect Kosovo Albanians – and the slant taken was largely anti-Serbian. Serbs were portrayed as either being exploited by Milosevic (such as the image of being used as 'human shields') or as accidental victims of 'collateral damage' during Nato sorties.

> **Through the distortion of facts and coverage, the West was able to justify its 'new moralism'**

Through the distortion of facts and coverage and the discouragement of any empathy with the Serbs (if Milosevic was 'bad' so were they), the West was able to justify its 'new moralism'. In taking this stance, however, the West has merely exposed its bias, lack of objectivity, tendency to manipulate public opinion and above all reproduced age-old prejudices and stereotypes about the nature of the Balkans, Kosovo and its peoples, of the type mentioned by Tomova above. In this sense the media was just as much an instrument of war as Nato planes. In order for the Balkans to be rebuilt upon new lines in future, there is an urgent need for government officials, scholars and journalists to escape from these biased, prejudiced and ahistorical viewpoints and instead to look at the Kosovo and Balkans Questions with fresh eyes. It is not the author's intention to condone Serb ethnic cleansing of Kosovo Albanians or the actions of Milosevic, but with generate a debate on the question of whether or not the Kosovo Albanians have simply swapped one master for another. The latter issue is closely connected with the need to foster a genuine democratic transition in Kosovo today. The key question now is: does the latter objective mean ousting Milosevic and, if so, how will this be done? Does it mean another war (so Kosovo will not be America's last war in Europe) or are there other means at the West's disposal, such as mobilizing opposition to his regime? Neither will be easy. But, now that the West has 'won' the war, can it 'win' the peace? To have any possibility of victory, the West needs to define its role in Kosovo more clearly and more carefully.

NOTES

1   Mazower 1997.

2   Vickers 1998.

3   Vickers 1998: 22–8.

4   Ramet 1999: 303.

5   Ramet 1999: 305.

6   Ramet 1999: 306.

7   Lampe 2000: 337.

8   Lee 1983: 67.

9   See Lampe 2000, Table 11.4: 340.

10 Lee 1983: 89.

11 See Table 2.3 in this book; Lampe 2000, Table 11.3: 337.

12 Ramet 1997: 148; Ramet 1999: 308.

13 Ramet 1999: 308.

14 See Sigler 1999.

15 US State Department report 1999.

16 Ramet 1997: 151–52.

17   See Judah 1997, Chapters 9–15.

18   Ramet 1999: 314.

19   Ali 1999: 65–6.

20   Johnstone 1999.

21   LaPorte 1999.

22   Ali 1999: 65–6.

23   Jatras 2000.

24   See Kosovar Albanians 1999.

25   Bandow 2000.

26   Layne 2000b: 55; Human Rights Watch 2000.

27   See Group 17 report 1999: 12.

28   UNHCR 1996.

29   Human Rights Watch 1999.

30   UNHCR 1999.

31   See Group 17 report 1999: 3.

32   See World Bank 1999a, 1999b.

33   UNHCR 1999.

34   South Balkans 1999.

35   IGC 2000.

36   Lutovac 1997.

37   Rama 2000.

38   See Bugajski 1999.

39   Bugajski 1999.

3

BRITAIN: TO WAR FOR A JUST CAUSE

STANLEY HENIG

THIS CHAPTER ADOPTS A TWIN-TRACK APPROACH. It offers a British view on Kosovo and Serbia: the nature, origins and development of the conflict. This view is necessarily subjective, but is probably broadly in line with majority opinion. Second, it seeks to follow the specific line adopted by the British government during the development of the crisis and the subsequent military campaign. In international politics a country is assessed by the actions of its government rather than by references to whatever national controversies those actions may occasion. The convention is followed in this chapter – in the late 1930s 'Britain' determined upon a policy of non-intervention in the Spanish Civil War and 'Britain' resolved to appease Hitler at Munich. Sixty years later 'Britain' joined others in military intervention in an internal conflict for what 'Britain' believed were overwhelming humanitarian reasons.

How horrible, fantastic, incredible, it is that we should be digging trenches … because of a quarrel in a far away country between people of whom we know nothing.'

(Prime Minister Chamberlain in 1938)

The state has to protect the interests of the nation, and in the Balkans a nation means one particular ethnic group. Keeping the peace in this region means that every minority has to be completely assimilated into the majority.'

(Nikolai Thodorov, Vice President of the Bulgarian Academy of Sciences and
Director of the Institute of Balkan Studies)[1]

We have learnt by bitter experience not to appease dictators ... We must act to save thousands of innocent men, women and children from humanitarian catastrophe, from death, barbarism and ethnic cleansing by a brutal dictatorship.   (Prime Minister Blair, March and April 1999)

Nato forces are in Kosovo with ambiguous objectives and inadequate resources.   (Liberal Democrat spokesman 1999)

THE CONTEXT FOR POLICY-MAKING

The latter part of the 1930s defined British foreign policy for the remainder of the twentieth century and, perhaps, into the twenty-first. After those much quoted words about far off countries, Neville Chamberlain went on to proclaim that 'war is a fearful thing, and we must be very clear before we embark on it, that it is really the great issues that are at stake'. A generation earlier Britain had entered a Great War occasioned by the politics of the Balkans. Eighty years later Prime Minister Tony Blair, speaking to the House of Commons in March 1999 offered a reminder:

We know from bitter experience throughout this century, most recently in Bosnia, that instability and civil war in one part of the Balkans inevitably spills over into the whole of it, and affects the rest of Europe too.

At one level the Great War was about protecting small states such as Serbia, a country about which Britain knew little. Such an assertion is proved rather than negated by the remarkable introduction to his book on Kosovo by Tim Judah.[2] He gives an account of events in Britain in the summer of 1916 on what was called 'Kosovo day'. It is not difficult to imagine that for the next eighty years most inhabitants of Britain would never hear any further mention of the province. Perhaps at the end of the twentieth century our knowledge of Serbia was not very much greater than it was in 1918.

66 Perhaps at the end of the twentieth century our knowledge of Serbia was not very much greater than it was in 1918 99

For generations of subsequent British political leaders, the key lesson to be drawn from the outbreak of war in 1939 was that appeasement did not work. This has become an absolute almost regardless of circumstances. It coloured Britain's post-war approach to the Soviet Union and the foundation and operation of Nato. Later the incantation against appeasement was solemnly intoned by Eden at the time of Suez and Thatcher over the Falklands. The issues at stake in Kosovo and, as will be shown, the 1999 definition of national interest were very different, but Blair's assessment of appeasement is traditional and his choice of words not just a matter of chance:

Some people argue that Kosovo is a far away place that has little to do with Britain. Why should we get involved? ... To them I say ... our responsibilities do not end at the English Channel.

(*Independent on Sunday*, 14 February 1999)

It may be worth pointing out at this stage that throughout the Kosovo conflict there were no real discernible policy differences between the major political parties. There were questions and debate in the House of Commons, but no attempt on behalf of either the Conservatives or the Liberal Democrats to distance themselves from the broad thrust of the Labour government's policies. If anything the Liberal Democrats were even more hawkish than the government and certainly more ready to consider use of ground troops to enforce rather than simply monitor a settlement. Most of the opposition to the government came, perhaps not surprisingly, from the left wing of the Labour Party and from other leftist groups. In a sense such critics could be said to be drawn from the 'usual suspects', those generally unhappy with any actions involving the USA and/or Nato from the Vietnam war through to the Gulf War.

If there is one common thread which runs through modern British foreign policy it is support for the *status quo* and the 'sanctity' of international frontiers. On a cynical view this may be attributed to Britain having been at the beginning of the twentieth century what is sometimes described as a 'satiated' power. Any alterations to either the global polity or its economic structure were likely to be to our disadvantage – as indeed events were to prove. It has been a cardinal principle of British foreign policy that change should only come about through inter-state agreements. We had no difficulty in signing up to codes of good conduct such as the Covenant of the League of Nations and the Charter of the United Nations on the basis that international order would continue to be determined by the behaviour and interaction of sovereign states. This in turn promoted an, at times, obstinate belief that internal events within an internationally recognized sovereign state must remain the affair of that state. From this emerged the doctrine of non-intervention which in the case of the Spanish Civil War facilitated the overthrow of a legitimate government through a military insurrection backed by Europe's fascist dictatorships.

The course of the Spanish Civil War offers a potent illustration of the way in which the late thirties defined future foreign policy and, at the same time, presented future governments with an irresolvable conundrum: at what point does or should an internal dispute or crisis become an international issue? At one level, it was recognition by the EU of the constituent parts of what had been Yugoslavia that offered the basis for external intervention in what would otherwise have been a series of 'internal affairs'. That recognition externalized and internationalized the ethnic conflicts and gave the Western world a legitimate basis – critics would say, a pretext – for intervention. Ironically it may also have given the Serbs a pretext and motive for enhancing the various conflicts in ways which would inevitably occasion external involvement. A further irony is that such recognition did not, and still does not, apply in the case of Kosovo which remains a recognized part of Serbia. Michael Ignatieff has pointed out that from a British perspective:

Kosovo broke new ground ... a war fought for a new end: the defence of a party to a civil war within a state.[3]

It may now be possible to offer one contemporary *de facto* answer to the question posed about the transformation of an internal dispute into an international issue. Where different nations or ethnic groups are in conflict within the boundaries of an internationally recognized state and either or both can look for support to co-nationals elsewhere, there is a potential threat to peace and security that may involve the international community. It is a condition which has characterized the Balkans. The gradual disintegration of the Ottoman Empire and the post-1918 dismemberment of Austria–Hungary facilitated the emergence of a series of successor states. There were few natural frontiers and no 'recognized' historic boundaries. There is a sense in which both Empires could claim to be genuinely multi-racial: throughout most of the Balkan region there was a complex mix of ethnic groups. National territorial claims were usually based on the 'best' historic moment from the past: and it was often not much more than a moment. The term 'ethnic cleansing' is relatively new, but not the process. The 1921 treaty of Smyrna which ended the war between Greece and Turkey authorized the transfer between the two countries of some two million people. There is a sense in which the post-1989 disintegration of Yugoslavia, held together by Tito as a genuinely multinational state, mirrors the earlier dismemberment of the Ottoman

> 66 The term 'ethnic cleansing' is relatively new, but not the process 99

and Austro-Hungarian Empires. In all three cases the implications and ramifications were perceived externally as going beyond the region, thus justifying further involvement by external forces which had helped to precipitate the collapse.

The recipe offered by Nikolai Thodorov is an attempt to legitimize ethnic cleansing. At the end of the process, the Balkans will consist of a series of nation states, while the number of co-nationals living in other states will be minimal. The gulf between the visions of Thodorov and Prime Minister Blair could not be greater. The very concept, let alone the practice, of ethnic cleansing is totally unacceptable in the EU which many of the Balkan states hope ultimately to join. Blair's moral imperative points to intervention and engagement in what he termed a 'humanitarian war'. His anonymous Liberal Democrat 'critic', cited at the beginning of the chapter, draws attention to the resulting impasse without perhaps spelling out the post-war detail:

- The bulk of the Serb population has left Kosovo and would not wish to return to be ruled by an Albanian majority.
- There is no prospect of the two peoples living together in harmony in a single entity in the foreseeable future.
- The province of Kosovo is legally part of Serbia and could not, under international law, be transferred to Albania without Serbian agreement.
- Kosovo could not form a viable state on its own and has no history as such.
- Serbia remains militarily much stronger than Albania and could readily reconquer Kosovo in the absence of foreign troops and any agreement to change frontiers.

Past external involvement in the Balkans has been both fleeting and spasmodic, usually to put together a patched-up peace settlement in one of numerous endemic conflicts which the West itself may have even encouraged. Withdrawal from Kosovo may not be quite so easy!

The introduction to this chapter is deliberately wide-ranging, its themes broadly based. It is commonplace among Balkan experts to base contemporary analysis on history, and any study of Kosovo is certain to pay attention or tribute to both the real and mythical battles of 1389. When he spoke at the Lord Mayor of London's banquet in April 1999, Foreign Secretary Robin Cook clearly felt that Belgrade was living in the past:

He [President Milosevic] began by saying that I could not understand what was happening in Kosovo unless I started in 1389. There was something tragic about such a deep history perspective on current events … nor is it in the interests of Serbia to live in the Middle Ages when the rest of the world is moving on into the twenty-first century.

The phrase 'could not understand' and the word 'tragic' convey a wealth of meaning. This was an iron curtain between quite different mind sets:

East is East, and West is West, and never the twain shall meet.[4]

However meagre the diplomatic results, the meeting clearly had an impact on Cook who envisaged 'two Europes competing for the soul of our continent.'[5] Significantly he linked Milosevic's Europe to the race ideology of the fascists and weighed against this the European Convention of Human Rights. Cook accepted that 'Europe is a continent thick with ghosts – shades of old disputes and forgotten hatreds buried in shallow graves' but concluded that: 'It is time we laid our ghosts to rest … to create a modern Europe which provides a common home for all its people, whatever their ethnic origin.'[6]

VIEWING THE BALKANS

All states are products of history, but awareness of this varies through time and place. As national consciousness developed in the Balkans during the nineteenth century, history was particularly important because of the lack of a present for most potential states. This was reinforced by the 'victim' status of many of the peoples involved. For a 'satiated' state like Britain, unconquered since 1066, this state of mind is inconceivable. Previous paragraphs offer a context for British foreign policy. It refers to the past but relates almost exclusively to the twentieth century: as background to British policy-making over Kosovo in the late nineties, I have mentioned just three specific previous events – the outbreak of the Great War, the Spanish Civil War and the Munich agreement. Quite apart from the fact that none of these had anything to do with Kosovo, it is worth reflecting that they all took place within a period of less than twenty-five years. Their impact remains even though Munich and Kosovo are separated by more than sixty years. Obviously, Czechoslovakia is not part of the Balkans but, like Kosovo, it,

> **❝ History was particularly important because of the lack of a present for most potential states ❞**

too, had been part of a multinational empire. Moreover, Czechoslovakia and Yugoslavia were the two post-1918 successor creations that were clearly based on multi-ethnicity and not constructed as one-nation states. Neither has survived the post-communist transformation: Czechoslovakia opted for peaceful dissolution while Yugoslavia has imploded. The language employed by British policy-makers at the time of Kosovo demonstrates the link with the Munich agreement, even if it is reactive rather than causative. Prime Minister Blair was in no doubt:

We have learnt by bitter experience not to appease dictators. We tried it 60 years ago. It didn't work then and shouldn't be tried now.[7]

World War II ended modern Europe's first brief experiment with a cluster of small, independent states replacing polyglot empires. It resulted in a divided continent with one half effectively part of a new Soviet Empire and the other dependent on the USA. Within a few years the demarcation lines were fixed, apparently permanently. Europeans had to know and accept their place in the new world order; Britain, France and Germany now had relatively subordinate roles; in effect brute force simply put in abeyance the old ethnic cleavages and conflicts in central and eastern Europe. Yugoslavia gained a special place in the new configuration but this too was in effect defined by the East–West conflict. Strong internal leadership checked domestic tensions and kept external enemies at bay. In western Europe, the creation and development of the European Community (EC) was in large measure a response to the East–West cleavage. The Community was very much a part of the Western world and in no sense any kind of third force. In an apparently permanent bipolar world, it reinforced the security and prosperity of western Europe in alignment with the United States.

The sudden collapse of both the Soviet Empire and communism shattered the basis for this ossified world. George Robertson as British Defence Secretary coined an evocative phrase – the bonfire of certainties. The vacuum in eastern Europe has been filled by the creation or re-creation of nation states. The death or absence of ideology has helped to ensure that many of the new political parties are nationalist or ethnic-based. Without external forces to sustain it, Yugoslavia simply imploded under the new pressures. For western Europe the original *raison d'etre* for the Community had disappeared to be replaced by a new imperative. The end of the Soviet Empire might signal the beginning of a gradual US withdrawal; Europe needed some over-arching structure to ensure economic and political stability, and perhaps ultimately security, throughout the continent;

the Community already existed and did not need to be invented; its major members would have to face the challenge of re-assuming leading roles in their own continent. Indeed, in most parts of the world, the West suddenly found itself predominant in military terms. *Prima facie* it had the power to intervene wherever and whenever it chose, even if the lesson for the USA in Somalia told otherwise. With power goes responsibility: in Britain at least there is a tendency to assume that the West should somehow become involved. At the same time the interventionist constituency was not always ready to meet the cost in resource terms. It is an interesting reflection on the national psyche that the left-wing critics of Nato and joint actions with the USA do not challenge the notion that Britain should be a player on the world stage: their disagreement is with the external policies actually pursued by successive governments.

EVENTS UNFOLD

By the time Tony Blair became prime minister, Yugoslavia was little more than a geographic expression. There was no longer any union of southern Slavs; the break-up seemed prolonged and messy with many attendant atrocities. In the long history of the Balkans, atrocities were hardly novel and the disintegration of Yugoslavia took barely a decade compared to the century needed for the dismemberment of the Ottoman Empire. However, media attention, photographs and television images riveted attention in the Western world and, consciously or subconsciously, promoted the view that the West had a responsibility to intervene, at the very least to stop the bloodshed, actual and potential. It is outside the context of this chapter to assess the extent to which the conflict in Bosnia was ended by external pressure or by sheer exhaustion of the participants. The conventional wisdom beyond Yugoslavia was that ethnic conflict and government-sponsored violence had no place in the modern Europe and that the international community had quite simply failed to meet the challenge by preventing war or ending it sooner. Both general public opinion and the elites with most influence demanded and expected that in the future the West would respond more quickly and more effectively. Tony Blair recognized the force of the criticism:

66 In the long history of the Balkans, atrocities were hardly novel 99

In Bosnia we underestimated what would be needed to halt the conflict, and we underestimated the consequences of failing to do so.

It was almost inevitable that the next crisis would be over Kosovo. Many commentators have traced the break-up of what we might term the Yugoslav concept to attempts to 'Serbianize' that province which, significantly, gathered pace at the same time as the Soviet Empire was beginning to wind down. Thereafter for both Serbia and the Albanians it was a question of waiting, albeit for different reasons. As the 1990s wore on it became ever more likely that failure on the part of the peoples involved to reach a solution would lead almost inexorably to some kind of involvement or intervention by external forces. There is a good deal of evidence that this was the medium-term goal of the KLA. In the longer term the KLA sought complete separation from Serbia. There is no problem about assessing the motives of President Milosevic, but it is somewhat more difficult to discern his long-term strategy. The usual assumption is that his goal was the emergence of a greater Serbia out of the ruins of Yugoslavia. He presumably reasoned that the Croats in Croatia and Bosnia were likely to be much more formidable opponents than Albanians in Kosovo. Dealing with the Croats and settling the status of Bosnia were higher up the agenda than Kosovo. Milosevic may also have simply assumed that whatever happened there would be no Western challenge to the continued inclusion of Kosovo within either a smaller or a greater Serbia. Either way his chosen tactics in Kosovo – gradual Serbianization and the effective ending of any real autonomy within the Yugoslav federation, followed by a period of relative inertia and then the brutal crushing of any revolt – encouraged the emergence and subsequent strengthening of the KLA and then served almost certainly to guarantee the attainment of the medium-term goal. In Britain virtually nobody took any notice of Kosovo in the early phases of the break-up of Yugoslavia. At the same time Serbian excesses during the wars against Croatia and inside Bosnia ensured that public sympathy and feeling were all on one side as Kosovo gradually came into public view and consciousness during 1998. As Milosevic moved away from the period of relative inertia and into the brutal crushing of any revolt, he handed the KLA the attainment of their medium-term goal. Indeed, the circumstances under which this happened, particularly the bouts of ethnic cleansing – first directed against the Albanians before and during the allied bombing and then against the Serbs after the cease-fire – may well have ensured that in the long run the only viable solution will be separation of Kosovo from Serbia: the attainment of the KLA's ultimate goal.

> **" As Milosevic moved away from the period of relative inertia and into the brutal crushing of any revolt, he handed the KLA the attainment of their medium-term goal "**

Rhetoric apart, there has always been much continuity and considerable bipartisanship in British foreign policy. The change from a Conservative to a Labour government in 1997 made, for example, no perceptible difference to British policy towards Iraq. It is interesting to note that in his comment about failure in Bosnia, Blair uses the pronoun 'we', even though Britain had a Conservative government at the time. The Blair government came to office with two broad external commitments: to take a lead in European affairs and to follow an ethical foreign policy. The Kosovo crisis offered an ideal opportunity for demonstrating both. Ever since joining the Community in 1973 Britain, as a once great power, had been interested in possibilities which could be opened up through European Political Co-operation (EPC). Prime Minister Thatcher had no problem in squaring her antipathy for European integration with seeking support over the Falklands through the intergovernmental mechanisms of the EPC. As a key player in Nato with significant military capacity for overseas intervention, Britain was in a position to take a leading role in the latest round in the death of Yugoslavia.

> ❝ As a key player in Nato with significant military capacity for overseas intervention, Britain was in a position to take a leading role in the latest round in the death of Yugoslavia ❞

The ethical dimension has perhaps proved rather more troublesome, and not just in Kosovo. The world does not always work on ethical principles either in inter-state relations or in the corridors of the UN. On the other hand it is not unusual for governments to claim a moral purpose, especially where war or military activities are concerned. Opponents of 'foreign adventures' sometimes berate a lack of moral purpose and claim that the policy is based simply on crude national self-interest. In one sense they may always be right. The pursuit of national interest is a natural function of government. In the early stages of the bombing campaign, Robin Cook was quite explicit about the link between warfare and national interest:

One should not commit servicemen to take the risk of military action unless our national interest is engaged.

Clearly, the way in which national interests are defined will vary from time to time and from country to country. It is easy enough to explain the war against Iraq by reference to Western economic interests – above all oil.

It is very much more difficult to discover anything as simple or crude where Kosovo is concerned. The Yugoslavia government has attributed Western intervention to geopolitical reasons and has also focused on Kosovo's largely untapped natural resources – particularly oil and lignite.[8]

Interestingly, the British Foreign Office has also recognised the valuable mineral resources in Eastern Kosovo and pointed out, in rather bland terms, their value to Serbia before concluding that 'on the whole the province is a poor, mainly agricultural region'. It is hard to demonstrate much linkage between relatively hidden wealth in Kosovo and Western action and it may be significant that the mainly left-wing opposition in Britain to military involvement made little or no mention of this. Prior to 1914 Britain did have broad economic, political and strategic interests in the Balkans. This is hardly the case at the end of the twentieth century. The enormously costly British military involvement in Kosovo could not conceivably be justified by any of these considerations. On the other hand, theoretically at least, Blair clearly believes that an ethical foreign policy, 'saying no to appeasement' and a willingness to intervene overseas for humanitarian reasons are in Britain's national interest. Cook widens this in the imaginative detail of the already quoted speech of 14 April:

Upholding international law is in our international interest. Our national security depends on Nato. Nato now has a common border with Serbia … Our borders cannot remain stable while such violence is conducted on the other side of the fence. Nato was the guarantor of the October agreement. What credibility would Nato be left with if we allowed the agreement to be trampled on comprehensively by President Milosevic and did not stir to stop him.

In a fascinating article written shortly after the launch of the Nato bombing campaign, General Sir Charles Guthrie, Chief of the Defence Staff recalled (slightly out of context) Hobbes' dictum that 'life is nasty, brutish and short' and suggested that war has a 'tendency to be nasty, brutish and long.'[9] He went on to point out that for the West

It involves fighting by the Queensberry Rules … against thugs who know little and care less about civilized behaviour.

The hyperbole in the language is unfortunate, but Guthrie places his finger on the heart of the dilemma about ethics in foreign policy. It is hard to believe that neither the Foreign Office nor the 'spin doctors' working for the Prime Minister and Cabinet Office had any advance knowledge of Guthrie's text.

COUNTDOWN TO WAR

The crisis in Kosovo developed gradually during 1998. It is difficult to discern specific British diplomatic activity outside of our membership of the Contact Group, the United Nations, Nato and the European Union. As the year wore on, the Foreign Office devoted more time and resources to the issue, but there was neither bilateral British involvement nor any high profile given to our role in the multilateral attempts to deal with the growing crisis. Tim Judah mentions a visit to Belgrade by political directors of the British, Austrian and German foreign ministries (on behalf of the EU of which Britain was the president in the first part of 1998). The British representative evidently told President Milosevic:

If you carry on like this the British government will take military action against you within six months.[10]

Presumably this was intended as an informal piece of advice rather than a threat of war. It is hard to envisage a civil servant, no matter how senior, being entrusted with the latter. It remains an enigmatic incident since, allegedly and not unsurprisingly, the Foreign Office was at the time adopting a relatively cautious approach to the possibility of external intervention:

Lawyers had argued that there was still no case in international law to use force.[11]

We will presumably have to wait many years for clarification as to whether ministers or events on the ground swept aside such reservations. International law can be a somewhat elastic concept. In June 2000 a House of Commons Select Committee concluded that:

NATO's military action, if of dubious legality in the current state of international law, was justified on moral grounds.

It may be appropriate to reflect that in international politics *de jure* often follows *de facto*. At the United Nations in September 1998 Tony Blair was emphatic that no action by the KLA could 'justify scorched earth tactics and forcible creation of hundreds of thousands of refugees'. At the same time a British statement to the Security Council was equally explicit as to the consequences: under article seven of the Charter this was 'a threat to peace and security in the region' and as such a justification for action by the international community. It is beyond the scope of this chapter to discuss the interrelationship of article seven to article two which precluded international intervention in the internal affairs of sovereign states. Where there is a political will, there is usually a legal means. It was a defining moment in British foreign-policy-making, one which led inexorably to military intervention in a civil war within the internationally recognized boundaries of a sovereign state. There are few references to the threat to peace and security in subsequent statements made by the British government: the justification for military action was to be couched overwhelmingly in humanitarian terms. Sixty years on, the script for non-intervention in the Spanish Civil War had been rewritten.

An assessment of Britain's role in the conflict with Serbia/Yugoslavia must also pay some attention to influence within Nato. Tim Judah cites an unsourced comment by US special envoy Richard Holbrooke to the effect that 'Britain is often the key to Nato decision-making.' Successive British governments have tended to imply that this is the case, but Holbrooke's meaning is unclear. Britain remains the closest European ally of the USA and the two countries work reasonably closely together on actual or potential military issues within and without Nato. It is inconceivable that the USA would be pressing for military action by Nato inside Europe in the absence of a direct threat to the territorial integrity of its members and in circumstances where its partners were ambivalent. As they staked out their various positions on Kosovo, there is no evidence that other European countries were necessarily following a British lead. Perhaps Holbrooke and, more importantly, Secretary of State Madeleine Albright were looking closer to home and the need to persuade others in the US government that military action might be necessary. The forthright British stance might have been helpful at a time when the president had other domestic distractions.

From early 1999 the conflict in Kosovo had a much higher profile in Britain. The agreement reached the previous October between Richard Holbrooke and President Milosevic which should have paved the way for a reduction in Serbian military presence in Kosovo and the beginning of negotiations simply did not work; with some difficulty a Kosovo verification mission was put in place; nonetheless, the KLA increased their activity, the Serbs responded and, on 16 January, the Foreign Office received 'reports of a massacre at Racak.' Quite what happened at Racak and, in particular, how many 'unarmed civilians' were killed will probably never be known, but it was to be a defining moment in the

> 66 Quite what happened at Racak and, in particular, how many 'unarmed civilians' were killed will probably never be known, but it was to be a defining moment in the countdown to war 99

countdown to war. The following day Robin Cook spoke to his opposite numbers in France, Germany and Italy and they agreed that their four ambassadors in Belgrade would demand the immediate removal from duty of the army and police units involved while 'these murders are investigated.' Robin Cook attributed what he described as 'a potential humanitarian crisis' to Serb repression. He argued that the Holbrooke package offered Kosovo the prospect of real autonomy and Serbia the opportunity to 'withdraw from an armed conflict that undermines its autonomy and its economy and isolates it from the world'. He blamed both sides for the fact that after three months there had been no meaningful talks and suggested that 'neither side can win this war.'

As the crisis over Kosovo developed, there were three major players in the British government – Prime Minister Blair, Foreign Secretary Cook and Defence Secretary Robertson. Their statements suggest that British diplomacy was 'twin-tracking' up to the very moment the bombing campaign commenced. The goal was an agreed settlement along the lines laid down by the Contact Group and endorsed by Robin Cook:

- substantial autonomy for Kosovo
- enshrined rights for the Serb minority
- reserved powers for the Federal government.

As the chances of reaching any such agreement became ever more remote, the British government continually reiterated Nato's willingness to monitor one. This was a key theme in a BBC interview given by Cook on 6 February. The previous week there had been bilateral discussions between Prime Minister Blair and President Chirac. Apart from the almost ritual condemnation of violence and a commitment to seek to prevent another humanitarian tragedy, they, too, publicly expressed willingness:

To consider all forms of military action, including the dispatch of ground forces, necessary to accompany the implementation of a negotiated agreement.

However, they went on to look at the alternative:

If an early political agreement proves impossible, the two leaders believe that all options will need to be considered.

Logically 'all options' would surely have to include military action of a kind very different from the use of armed forces as monitors.

If this last sounds like a message to Milosevic, it was considerably modified when George Robertson spoke to the House of Commons on 11 February. Decisions had been taken that day 'to ensure that British forces are immediately available in case a Nato force is required to deploy to Kosovo'. Most of the statement was devoted to discussing the concept of a Nato force to support a peace agreement. At the end, he also had a 'clear message' for the House (and presumably for anybody else paying attention):

we will deploy our forces only in support of a clear mission and clear objectives alongside our allies.

Writing in the *Independent on Sunday* just three days later, Blair was seemingly clear about the structure, purpose and objectives for the forces:

Only NATO has the necessary experience and capabilities to set up and lead such a force ... (it) is likely to be based on NATO's British led Rapid Reaction Force ... these troops are not going to Kosovo to fight the Serbs.

Much Western diplomacy was based on the assumption that Russia could bring pressure to bear on Yugoslavia. In a television interview two days after the start of Rambouillet, Robin Cook reiterated the importance of Nato, but went on to suggest that Russian forces could also be part of a peace-keeping force. If this was intended to be a conciliatory gesture, there was a mailed fist at the end of the interview:

As Belgrade contemplates whether it wishes to accept the whole package which embraces the international military presence to provide the stability for that constitutional settlement, Belgrade must remember that we have already taken a decision in NATO which empowers Javier Solana, the Secretary, to take air strikes if it is Belgrade that has prevented a settlement.

Ignoring the inherent absurdity of the notion that such a decision would in practice be taken by Solana, this is an even starker reiteration of the basic message in the Blair–Chirac statement.

The outcome of Rambouillet, organized by the Contact Group and held under Anglo-French chairmanship, was confused. Cook argued that a process had commenced that would be continued the following month. He also stressed the importance of an agreed external military presence – which Belgrade had not in fact accepted. The process of twin-tracking continued. Cook added an apparently unambiguous message to Milosevic:

> ❝ The outcome of Rambouillet, organized by the Contact Group and held under Anglo-French chairmanship, was confused ❞

> those red lines that we set in October, they are still in place, the military presence is still in place

and then equally robustly declined to comment when asked what would happen if the warning were ignored. Later the same day in the House of Commons Cook reported that

> all the Nato members of the Contact Group repeated their support for decisive Nato action if Belgrade makes a disproportionate response or takes violent reprisals against the civilian population.

Some pretence of even-handedness remained when he added:

> we also hold the Kosovo Liberation Army responsible for their part in maintaining the cease-fire.[12]

Quite how that responsibility would be enforced was never explained.

It is easy enough to understand how Yugoslavia came to feel that the dice were loaded against them at the two Rambouillet meetings. The over-arching conspiracy theory expressed by Foreign Minister Jovanovic that Western policy was entirely based on geopolitical considerations lacks supporting evidence, but the complaint of favouritism towards separatists has more than a ring of truth.[13] From the British perspective the problem of Kosovo could only be resolved through substantial autonomy which Yugoslavia was never going to yield. The breakdown of negotiations at the second Rambouillet conference, the failure of Holbrooke's last visit to Belgrade and the bombing campaign which followed were all now inevitable.

BOMBING AND BEYOND

The tone of Blair's lengthy statement to the House of Commons on 23 March was, in turn, emotional and austere. It is worth bearing in mind that this was the first occasion since 1945 when Western forces would be involved in military action in Europe. Much of Blair's speech revolved around allegations of Serb atrocities – Nato action would be 'primarily to avert what would otherwise be a humanitarian catastrophe in Kosovo.' In the light of ongoing debate throughout Europe about asylum seekers and economic migrants, it is worth noting that Blair drew attention to the presence in the EU of more than one million refugees from the former Yugoslavia. Belgrade had failed to fulfill commitments and was held responsible for the continuing violence. The emotional high-point of the speech came relatively early:

We must act to save thousands of innocent men, women and children from humanitarian catastrophe, from death, barbarism and ethnic cleansing by a brutal dictatorship; to save the stability of the Balkan region, where we know chaos can engulf all of Europe. We have no alternative but to act and act we will, unless Milosevic even now chooses the path of peace.

This is only one of a number of statements which demonstrate Michael Ignatieff's assessment that Tony Blair was 'the alliance leader most obviously animated by cold fury and relentless conviction.'[14]

Over the two-and-a-half months of the bombing campaign the language of condemnation was to remain a constant backcloth. From Blair there were references to Milosevic's 'killing machine'; 'people being massacred'; 'the appalling and evil policy of ethnic cleansing'; 'the butchers of Belgrade'; 'unimaginable horrors'. While Cook was rather more urbane in his phraseology he used the words 'fascist' and 'fascism' with some frequency – perhaps understandably but hardly an appropriate description of the Yugsolav regime. Linguistic excesses are normal in times of international conflict. In Blair's case these were more than counterbalanced by his view of the future:

> 66 Over the two-and-a-half months of the bombing campaign the language of condemnation was to remain a constant backcloth 99

We need to enter a new millennium where dictators know that they cannot get away with ethnic cleansing or repress their peoples with impunity. In this conflict we are fighting not for territory but for values. For a new internationalism where the brutal repression of whole ethnic groups will not be tolerated. For a world where those responsible for such crimes have nowhere to hide.[15]

It has been suggested that the West's political leaders anticipated that the bombing campaign would be short-lived and that Milosevic would rapidly give way. For his part Blair claimed that he did not expect Milosevic to be defeated overnight, but it seems unlikely that he anticipated a bombing campaign lasting seventy-eight days. From the outset General Sir Charles Guthrie had warned that wars were likely to be 'brutish and long'. As the conflict unfolded, government ministers had simultaneously to justify its continuation until Milosevic gave way, explain away such incidents as the bombing of the Chinese Embassy and justify the West's unwillingness to supplement the bombing campaign with a ground invasion. Milosevic's tactics made the first two relatively easy. In effect Yugoslavia was at war on two fronts. In the first it was clearly powerless to resist the Nato bombing so there was no engagement at all. Milosevic allowed foreign journalists and photographers to stay in the country and report on the havoc and destruction caused by Nato. Meanwhile in Kosovo his forces sought to remove virtually the entire Albanian population – thus satisfying his Serb nationalist constituency by creating at least temporarily a new reality on the ground. In terms of the impact on Western public opinion, this was playing for 'stalemate'. The impact of every untoward incident arising from the bombing was immediately countered by pictures and reports of wanton destruction in Kosovo and lines of refugees heading for the Albanian or Macedonian frontiers.

In a sense resisting the argument for use of ground forces was even easier. It might be logical, but there was no real groundswell in public opinion which clearly preferred a virtual war without casualties. Blair accepted that ground forces would be needed to monitor a settlement and to help refugees back to their homes, but this would be after Yugsolavia gave way and would be very different from 'fighting our way in'. He added that 'a land invasion would be a massive undertaking' and concluded that intensifying the air strikes was a better option.[16]

Even successful wars do not achieve all their objectives. During the course of the bombing campaign, ethnic cleansing had intensified and, with it, the systematic burning and pillage of much of Kosovo. Whether or not this had been planned in advance by the Yugoslav authorities is irrelevant to the fact. The agreement which ended the war included a ground force to supervize the 'peace'. That meant a leading role for Britain and some subtle diplomacy to avoid any armed confrontation with Russian forces, the Nato invitation to join having been finally accepted. When the long presaged ground force finally arrived its first job was to supervize the return of the Albanian population that had been driven out. It then watched helplessly as ethnic cleansing contin-

> 66 During the course of the bombing campaign, ethnic cleansing had intensified and, with it, the systematic burning and pillage of much of Kosovo 99

ued – in accordance with Balkan tradition – only this time it was the Serb population that was largely driven out. The West then found itself facing the tasks of helping in the establishment of what was in effect an exclusively Albanian civil administration and in the economic reconstruction of the entire province. By the end of 1999 the British government had contributed £90 million to the twin tasks of humanitarian relief and economic reconstruction. It was anticipated that for the year 2000 expenditure would be at least three times that figure.

Clearly there have already been various government reviews of lessons to be learned from Kosovo. In late summer 1999 it was announced that Robertson would become the new Secretary General of Nato. In a thoughtful speech to the Royal Services Institute, shortly before taking on his new role, he discussed some of the lessons of Kosovo, while recognizing that 'one should beware learning to re-fight the last war.' Robertson felt that Nato had quite simply underestimated the humanitarian suffering inflicted by Milosevic's forces and the resources needed to deal with it. Perhaps the most interesting part of the speech dealt with the issue of ground forces:

What lessons does this hold for future conflicts? That we can rely on air power alone? Certainly not. NATO knew from the start that we could only hope to limit or contain the sort of state run terrorism that was happening on the ground. As armchair experts did not cease to remind us, using precision munitions dropped from 15,000 feet is a very poor way to attack bands of murderous thugs who commit their crimes with knives and small arms.

At the time of writing, there is not even any speculation as to when Nato's military involvement might come to an end. Yugoslavia agreed to withdraw, but just as this was not a formal war so there is no formal peace. Perhaps a virtual war can only be ended by a virtual peace. There is no indication that Yugoslavia or Serbia has accepted what amounts to the secession of Kosovo. Notions of future federations in which the peoples of the region live in harmony are couched in good will, but at the present time are based on pure fantasy. The lesson of history is that in the Balkans nothing is forgotten and nothing is (accepted) for ever. It took more than a year of diplomacy, international pressure and bombing to place a ground force in Kosovo. On the assumption that Nato will not want a withdrawal to be followed by further conflict, it will take a lot longer to extricate the force. Such a judgement can only be reinforced by further reference to the House of Commons Select Committee Report on Kosovo. After rejecting a long-term solution based on independence for Kosovo, the committee was equally adamant in opposition to partition.

> 66 Notions of future federations in which the people of the region live in harmony are couched in good will, but at the present time are based on pure fantasy 99

We believe that the re-drawing of boundaries which partition of Kosovo would involve would be destabilizing for the region and a barrier to any idea of multi-ethnic states in the region.

In the light of the past experience of multi-ethnic states such a conclusion ranks higher in terms of good will and ethical principle than it does in terms of Balkan realities. Insofar as the report goes on to applaud the international community for not making any precipitate decision on the future of Kosovo, it is presumably accepting that the West is now there for the duration, which is likely to be a long time.

NOTES

1   Quoted in R.D. Kaplan 1994.

2   Judah 2000.

3   Ignatieff 2000.

4   Kipling, 'The Ballad of East and West', 1982. Probably not the favourite poet of any of the principles to the conflict!

5   *Guardian*, 5 May 1999.

6   *Guardian*, 5 May 1999.

7   *Newsweek International*, 19 April 1999.

8   Press release by Yugoslav Federal Ministry for Foreign Affairs, 18 May 2000, drawing attention to a survey by Amoco and also articles in the *New York Times* and *The Economist*.

9   *Evening Standard*, London, 1 April 2000.

10   Quoted in Judah 2000.

11   Judah 2000.

12   Statement by Cook to House of Commons, 18 January 1999.

13   Judah 2000

14   Ignatieff 2000.

15   *Newsweek International*, 19 April 1999.

16   *Newsweek International*, 19 April 1999.

4

ITALY: THE RELUCTANT ALLY

UMBERTO MORELLI

ITALY: AN UNDEPENDABLE COUNTRY?

During the conflict a number of authoritative political commentators, Brzezinski for one, accused Italy once again of being an undependable country. These accusations went beyond the habitual stereotypes, being based on a certain ambiguity apparent in Italian foreign policy, which wavered between a respect for the alliances bordering at times on the servile, and a tendency towards Third Worldism and anti-American feeling. These convictions seemed to be endorsed by the political and economic ties between Italy and Yugoslavia, by the ambiguity of certain attitudes demonstrated by Italy both prior to and during the Kosovo crisis, and by a history of association between Italian and Yugoslav communist leaders going back to World War II. To understand the contradictions inherent in Italian foreign policy, we need to bear in mind not only the political system and culture of the country (the importance both of the communist left and of the Catholic circles, the influence of the Vatican, the widespread pacifism and the reluctance to have to do with all things military), but also its history and geography, European and at the same time Mediterranean. A country tied to Europe but looking also towards the Mediterranean, with interests not only in the West, but also in the Balkans, the Middle East and Northern Africa. A country like so many others, with contrasting geopolitical and geo-economic interests, but Italy differs from other countries in that scant patriotic fervour and a certain lack of inclination to think in terms of national interest renders those interests difficult to reconcile. This means that it is not easy to inhibit centrifugal impulses, and to steer foreign policy in one sole and unequivocal direction.

It is no secret that the five Western countries in the Contact Group, although basically united in their pro-Nato stand, did not all take the same position with regard to Yugoslavia. The Americans and the British were the most determined on military intervention; the Germans, the French and, most of all, the Italians were the least convinced – the desire for war seemed, indeed, to be in inverse proportion to the distance from Kosovo. The Italians, in fact, held out to the very last at Rambouillet for a negotiated solution, showing an almost unbounded willingness to mediate. They were subsequently the most reluctant to consent to military intervention, hoping against hope that a compromise solution might be sought and found and continuing to put their faith in a last-minute change of heart on the part of Milosevic. Throughout the whole period of the bombing, the Italians actively continued the search for a peaceful solution, a fact that was to cause a certain amount of friction with the allies, actually giving the impression, in spite of official denials, that cracks had appeared within the alliance. These rumours were seized on by the media, and raised Milosevic's hopes of extricating himself from the impasse. In the end, Italy gave the impression of being the most pro-Serb of the nations (with the exception of Russia and Greece) intensifying suspicions about its traditional unreliability. Its geographical location placed Italy in the front line and it was once again to be the first country to suffer from the effects of yet another Balkan crisis. We must not lose sight of this basic premise, if we are to understand the position adopted by the Italian government throughout the war.

> 66 The Italians were the most reluctant to consent to military intervention, hoping against hope that a compromise solution might be sought and found and continuing to put their faith in a last-minute change of heart on the part of Milosevic 99

The government sought to safeguard the national interest, while still respecting the international alliances (Nato and the EU). However, a sort of bashfulness, unjustified but deeply rooted in its political culture, kept Italy from stating explicitly that its foreign policy decisions were dictated principally by the need to protect national interests; nor was the issue ever aired in public debate, tending rather to be concealed under a mantle of more acceptable idealistic motives: this was a humanitarian war.

The national interest, dictated by a combination of internal and foreign political considerations, lay principally in one direction: ensuring stability in the Balkans and defusing the time-bomb that had for years been threatening Italy – the refugee problem. Since the early nineties, a steady stream of fugitives – illegal immigrants – had continued to trickle into the country. To Italy, the Balkans are foreign territory, but close to home; a failure on Italy's part to ensure stability in the Balkans would mean the Balkanization of Italy. Awareness of this risk gave rise to the prospect of the Adriatic – the dividing line between the West and the Balkan crisis area – becoming no more than a European lake (Morozzo della Rocca 1998). The Italian approach to the disintegration of Yugoslavia over the last ten years has been one of the most well balanced in that it has aimed at preserving stability in the area, a strategy that would be doomed to failure if Serbia, the largest of the former Yugoslavian republics, and situated as it is in the very heart of the Balkans, the pivot-point for the equilibrium of the whole region, were to be made an outcast. With this aim in view, Italy has never adopted a coercive policy, choosing instead the path of political dialogue and, unlike Washington, had no particular wish for the removal of Milosevic from power, since in Italy's view the alternatives might well provide a greater risk. Staying on good terms with Serbia would also mean removing the Balkans from the sphere of influence of Germany, Serbia's other major economic partner, which would be to the advantage of Italy's economic and trade relations in the Balkan region and in south-eastern Europe. Italy's margins for manoeuvre, however, were limited by the need to reconcile the apparently irreconcilable – remaining on good terms both with Serbia and with her enemies – by the scanty resources allocated to foreign policy, and by the decided inadvisability of setting herself up against stronger allies and of jeopardising her role within the multilateral organization (Serpicus 1998). Italy took the line that the objectives of bringing stability and development to the Balkans could best be achieved by a process of economic, commercial and cultural integration, both within the region itself and in a wider, European context. The means to be employed would be varied:

> 66 Italy took the line that the objectives of bringing stability and development to the Balkans could best be achieved by a process of economic, commercial and cultural integration 99

- official diplomatic channels
- cooperation between governments
- economic investment

- commercial exchange
- the presence of Italian local administrative bodies with their own cooperation and development projects.

Crucial to Italy were the Euroslav axes,[1] multifunctional corridors – for the transport of goods, people, energy, communications systems, running all over the Balkan peninsula and linking Russia, the Black Sea and the Caspian with Italy and the West (Paolini 1998). Since the time of the Bosnian crisis, Italy had been committed to a stabilization project whose aim was to create the conditions necessary for the reannexing of the whole region to Europe.

Another crisis would jeopardize plans for peace and create a situation of permanent instability in the Balkans. It would put at risk what remained of Yugoslavia, with a devastating effect on neighbouring countries (Montenegro and Macedonia), and turn the Adriatic into a route for criminal traffic: arms, drugs, illegal immigrants. New waves of refugees, illegal immigrants and criminals amongst them, would invade Italy's beaches once again; criminal activity in and around the Adriatic[2] – Italian, Russian, various Balkan mafias, Islamic terrorism – would receive a shot in the arm, and there would be a proliferation of little ethnic-mafia states, with serious social, economic and political consequences for the peninsula as a whole.

> 66 The Farnesina had shown itself to be one of Europe's most tireless defenders of the privileged role granted Milosevic – and subsequently annulled by Albright – as guarantor of stability in the area 99

The Adriatic tourism industry would be seriously damaged and the risk of environmental pollution – black tides, toxic clouds – would be increased. The refugees in particular, tens and perhaps hundreds of thousands of them, would create enormous problems for Italy. What (military) means could be used to keep them out? What would be the consequences (destabilizing the country, outbreaks of racism, increased crime) of taking them in? And quite apart from the question of what to do with the refugees, military intervention would create other problems for the government: pacifist demonstrations, a renewed upsurge of anti-American and anti-Nato feeling, weeping mothers if casualties occurred, Vatican opposition to intervention, the possibility that the majority might break up, and the consequent risk of a government crisis.

Another conflict would put Italian diplomacy in a very awkward position. The past few years had seen an attempt on the part of the Italians to regain the credibility they had lost within the alliance because of the poor showing Italy had made at the time of the Gulf War. They had, for example, started to play a more substantial role in peace missions, in the Balkan area in particular. At the same time, the Farnesina, following the *realpolitik* line consolidated by Lamberto Dini at the Ministry of Foreign Affairs, had shown itself to be one of Europe's most tireless defenders of the privileged role granted Milosevic – and subsequently annulled by Albright – as guarantor of stability in the area. It followed that Italy was the country that showed itself most reluctant to toe the tough American line; if the situation came to a head, it would be embarrassing for the Italians to find themselves in the front-line of Nato forces, but well to the rear of Western diplomacy.

Anxious to put a stop to Serbian repression in Kosovo and at the same time to avoid war, Italian diplomats at Rambouillet directed their efforts towards persuading both sides to accept the agreement drawn up by the Contact Group (an autonomous Kosovo within Yugoslavia, and the deployment of an international military force) and considered by them an honourable compromise. To support independence for Kosovo would mean opting for an ethnic state, where it was important to encourage a multiethnic society, and would simply prepare the ground for future conflicts. Success at Rambouillet would solve more than a few problems for Italy and would ultimately be seen as a success for European diplomacy, which had solicited the summit; a compensation, in a way, for Dayton, which had been an all-American show. Italy felt that the military presence should not be limited to Nato troops, but that Russia and perhaps other non-Nato countries should be actively involved. It should also allow the OSCE mission to continue and it should be legitimized by the UN Security Council. Italy attempted to capitalize on the credibility it enjoyed with the Serbian government, to induce the Serbs to sign. (Italy was Yugoslavia's second most important trading partner and invested substantially in that country. In 1997, for example, Telecom Italia had invested in its Yugoslavian counterpart, a questionable move from an economic point of view, but politically vital for Milosevic, whose depleted finances received a much-needed boost.) The Albanians were urged not to waste an unrepeatable opportunity, and to accept a considerable degree of autonomy, giving up the idea of a non-negotiable independence. Dini promised them Euros rather than Nato bombs, and the prospect of a Marshall plan for the Kosovo. When, on 20 February, the ultimatum

> 66 While in Paris events were coming to a head, in Italy voices were beginning to be raised against the war 99

expired, and it was clear that the Kosovo Albanians were not going to sign, Italian diplomacy considered the Serbs and the Albanians equally responsible for the stalemate. And if both sides were to blame for the break-down in negotiations, the bomb attacks for which the KLA was hoping became less justifiable and the risk of war receded. According to Dini, the reaction was bound to be different depending on whether both sides refused to sign, or only the Serbs did.

And while in Paris events were coming to a head, in Italy voices were beginning to be raised against the war.

ITALY AT WAR: THE POLITICAL FORCES

Once war had been resolved upon, Italy, reluctant as it was, could hardly remain uninvolved, not only out of deference to international alliances, but also because it was anxious to avoid further marginalization and loss of credibility and influence; it could not afford to be cut off from an area strategic to its interests. If Italy refused to become involved, the country would no longer carry any weight, not only within Nato – which would in itself rule out any possibility of Italy's being a protagonist in post-war reconstruction – but also within the EU. It would therefore be denying itself any meaningful political role if the EU should decide that rather than continuing to exist simply on an economic basis, it would also assume an active role in foreign and military affairs.

It became necessary at this point to persuade political forces and public opinion in a tendentially pacifist country – a country softened up by fifty years of Nato-ensured peace – to accept the idea of military intervention. The Italian left, governing the country for the first time, found itself facing the harsh realities of foreign policy and war, and also the problem of its own legitimization on both a national and an international level. The official justification was that this was a humanitarian war: a concept which, calling as it did on idealistic considerations, was deemed adequate to persuade the country to consent to its first military campaign for fifty years. However, the fact that only an ethical justification was given, while no mention was made of other, perhaps equally legitimate reasons, left awkwardly unexplained why governments had failed to intervene on other occasions when human rights had been violated.

As war loomed ever closer, cracks began to appear in the solid wall of the government majority, and the feared government crisis seemed a real possibility. If it were to maintain international credibility, Italy could hardly afford to go into the war just as it was embarking on a government crisis. Like other European countries, Italy was going to war under a government of the centre-left, but unlike its allies, it had as premier a former communist, a man whose apprenticeship had been served in a party with a strong anti-American and anti-Nato tradition. The real problem Massimo D'Alema faced, however, was that of gaining credibility with the allies, and particularly with the Americans, not so much because he was a former communist converted to Nato, but as a leader strong enough to ensure that a country widely known for its political instability remained governable. Given its geographical location, Italy's strategic role was evident: Nato had to be able to bank on using the aircraft carrier *Italy*; and on government stability.

Here D'Alema proved to be adroit, not allowing himself to be conditioned by his ideological origins, curbing the various forms of pacifism – red, green, Catholic – and revealing himself to be an able tactician. If Italy was turning out to be surprisingly reliable, it was D'Alema the allies had to thank for it. The premier was assisted in his task by the foreign minister. The two of them were to stage a dextrous, if unscrupulous performance which, though it brought to mind all the clichés regarding Italian machiavellianism, was to guarantee that Italy took part in the war; at the same time it kept the government in power, and, last but not least, was to go a long way towards salvaging the country's image in the eyes of the allies. The premier, an ex-communist, undertook to guarantee Italy's loyalty to the Alliance; the foreign minister, a man of the centre, had the role of reassuring the anti-war elements in the majority that the country still retained its pacifist vocation. The humanitarian mission Arcobaleno (Rainbow) reassured public opinion that even though it was taking part in a war, the country still had a heart, and thus, with the help of the media, popular support for the military campaign was assured. The use of a few convoluted expressions and one or two convenient ambiguities, an omission here and there and the thing was done. The government survived and Italy made it through to the end of the war without plunging into a major crisis, notwithstanding the gloomy predictions made by certain political commentators at the beginning of the war.

> 66 If Italy was turning out to be surprisingly reliable, it was D'Alema the allies had to thank for it 99

The risk of war had been underestimated. The Nato activation order, which went out on 13 October 1998, had been designed to be a military tool whose objective was to put pressure on Milosevic, and had met with general indifference. Until the beginning of the bombing, the frame of reference had been the Bosnian scenario, where a show of force had put paid to the violence. A couple of nights of air raids, a pause for reflection, another diplomatic endeavour, and then the hoped-for negotiated solution.[3]

The policy adopted by the government was:

- not to distance the country from the international political scene, so that it would retain some political influence
- not to delegate responsibilities in which Italy had a rightful share, given its geographical location, interests and the prestige it had gained with operation Alba (Dawn)
- to make sure the country continued to adhere to the same diplomatic line as Europe and the West
- not to tolerate ethnic cleansing within Europe.[4]

In Italy, as in Germany but not in Britain, the government coalition was conditioned by the presence of pacifist elements within its ranks, and also by the fact that public opinion was not unduly enthusiastic about the war. In choosing, albeit reluctantly, to take part in the war, the government found itself facing the problem of a fragile majority coalition where the communists – inheritors of the left-wing tradition who saw in any military action the seeds of a new imperialism, and therefore opposed the war – kept company with the sceptical Greens, the uneasy Catholics and the pro-Nato supporters of the Centre parties. Conditioned by this diversity of positions, the government adopted an Italian-style compromise, a sort of tacit agreement according to which it fulfilled its normal obligations while still respecting allied agreements; but refrained from appearing unduly militaristic. Political forces felt themselves at liberty to act as they thought best, while keeping strongly pacifist impulses in check. For the Italian Communists and the Greens, causing a government crisis would have meant bringing down the first government to be led by a former communist, and this was another card played by D'Alema in averting a crisis. Though it was clear from the outset that the majority was a fragile one:

- The Partito dei comunisti Italiani (Italian Communist Party, PdCI) declared itself opposed to the bombings, threatening the resignation of its ministers
- The Greens expressed strong doubts about the effectiveness of the bomb attacks

- The ministers of the Partito Popolare Italiano (Italian People's Party, PPI) were divided, some for and some against

- Sceptics appeared in the ranks of the Democratici di Sinistra (Democratic Party of the Left, DS).

For the whole duration of the war the situation within the majority remained tense, and the threat of a government crisis was ever present. It was the premier's task to hold together this heterogeneous coalition and present to the allies the image of a united and dependable Italy.

D'Alema was explicit from the outset: Italy was part of Nato and would respect the commitments it had taken on in October 1998. His uncompromising attitude reflected the need to re-establish good relations with the US after the friction the Ocalan affair had caused. He was to stick to this line as long as the war lasted – except on the occasion of the gaffe he made on 26 March at the European summit in Berlin, after a day of bombings.[5]

One problem was the conceding of the military bases. Members of the parties in power had for years been requesting that the US bases in Italy be closed down and that the country resign from Nato. It was to avoid the danger of a parliamentary vote that D'Alema steered clear of the problem – a controversial move – claiming that membership of Nato implied sharing its responsibilities, and that therefore the bases should be conceded.[6] In a statement in parliament on 26 March, the premier declared the intervention to be necessary and legitimate, in that its objective was to put an end to the violence and reopen the path to negotiations. Belgrade alone was responsible for the crisis; Italy had become involved in the war for humanitarian reasons. The country could not remain indifferent to the mass killing of civilians, nor would it tolerate ethnic cleansing just a few kilometres from its borders. A catastrophe was taking place in Kosovo, and the West was under a moral and political obligation to put a stop to it.[7] The defence of human rights as a justification for Italy's activity on the world political scene brought the DS into line with Blair's New Labour, and was in keeping with the trend shown by Italian foreign policy since the mid-nineties.[8] The premier urged political forces not to take refuge in abstract pacifism and not to repeat the error committed in Bosnia, reminding them that the war had started not with the Nato intervention, but with Milosevic's ethnic cleansing policy. He assured them that the government would continue to seek a diplomatic solu-

> 66 Members of the parties in power had for years been requesting that the US bases in Italy be closed down and that the country resign from Nato 99

tion, while still remaining loyal to Nato, and expressed his hope that Russia would play a decisive role. The premier's speech showed a firm and resolved D'Alema, desirous of keeping open the dialogue with Belgrade, but categorical in his affirmation that Italy would not act except in the context of a coordinated effort by the allies. A refusal to take part in military operations, though it would set consciences at rest, would do nothing towards obtaining peace.

> 66 D'Alema was aiming for a different partnership with the superpower, rather than passive acceptance of its leadership 99

His motives were those of a political left which was determined to count for something, and hence not disposed to isolate itself simply to keep its principles unsullied. In endeavouring – to the irritation of the USA and Britain – to hold a special position within the alliance (support, but critical support: saying yes to the bombing, but at the same time refusing to abandon diplomatic channels; it meant keeping open the door to dialogue, and seizing every opportunity to let politics prevail over arms; involving rather than humiliating, Russia) D'Alema was seeking both to safeguard the principles, and indeed the very spirit, of the left and to assert that Europe was not the US, and was aiming for a different partnership with the superpower, rather than passive acceptance of its leadership.

Throughout the war, Italian diplomacy made every effort to smooth the way to renewed negotiations, conscious of the need to mollify the pacifist element in the majority and to abide by the suggestions put forward in the resolutions passed by Parliament.[9] It supported the Vatican in its endeavour to obtain a cease-fire over the Easter holiday. Convinced that Russia could persuade Belgrade to accept a diplomatic solution, it encouraged all attempts to bring that country back into the fray, backing Primakov's mission, supporting Yeltsin's request that the G8 be summoned, and finally pinning its hopes on the Chernomyrdin mediation. From the very beginning of the war, Italy had shown more foresight than the supporters of the Keep Russia Out theory, maintaining a more open-minded attitude towards that country's involvement in the negotiation. It was counting on the socialist governments in Europe to point out that Europe had a different role to play from that of America. Italy supported Kofi Annan's mission and finally, as the war was coming to an end, formulated its own solution – the D'Alema plan (which was to prove useless) based on the involvement of the G8 and the UN.

It was the foreign minister who made it clear, and sometimes in clamorous fashion, that Italy was different from its allies, and this was to cause friction with the allies, though its conduct was in line with parliamentary recommendations and contributed to the preserving of government stability. When Yugoslavia broke off diplomatic relations with Washington, London, Paris and Berlin, Italy was the only Western power not to close down its embassy in Belgrade, and this for the entire period of the crisis; a clear sign that it preferred to keep communication channels with Milosevic open. Dini held that the Serbian leader, even though responsibility for the Balkan crisis rested squarely on his shoulders, remained the only possible channel for negotiations. The Italian minister asserted that the Rambouillet agreement was unacceptable to Belgrade because it paved the way for an independent Kosovo – without actually putting this into words – and blamed both sides for the breakdown in negotiations, implicitly delegitimizing the military intervention. About ten days into the war, it was becoming clear to Dini that the bombings were having no effect. He felt that the attacks could hardly be continued indefinitely and that the path to lasting peace was that of negotiation, rather than the force of arms. He therefore proposed that the bombings be suspended and that Serbia be placed under total blockade, with only foodstuffs and medicines being allowed into the country. Dini also voiced publicly his disapproval of the bombing of the Serbian television company, referring to it as atrocious and creating a great deal of embarrassment during the Nato summit in Washington. During the teleconferences that went on daily throughout the crisis, Dini, who felt himself to be under increasing political pressure from within the country, on more than one occasion requested a pause in the bombing, although he was subsequently forced to admit that this was impossible without some significant gesture from Milosevic (Haski 1999). At the beginning of June a weekly magazine published a sort of diary kept by the foreign minister in which mention was made of the possibility of Italy's saying no to a land-campaign, an event which provoked further controversy. And it was Dini whom Milosevic telephoned to announce Rugova's arrival in Italy.[10]

This kind of stand could hardly be expected to go down well with the allies. The impression given was that Italy was seeking to differentiate itself from the other members of the alliance for reasons dictated by internal politics. D'Alema and Dini appeared to be following two distinct political strategies, to the extent that the newspapers wrote of disagreement, promptly denied, between Palazzo Chigi (the Prime Minister's office) and the Farnesina (the Italian Ministry of Foreign Affairs). The opposition criticized the government for pursuing a wavering foreign policy. In actual fact it may simply have been a question of sharing out responsibilities. It was the post-communist D'Alema's job to make sure that the country remained loyal to Nato, while it fell to the moderate Dini to play a delicate political game, touching on awkward issues that no one else had the courage to raise (responsibility for the failure of the Rambouillet agreement, ineffectiveness of the bombing, what could be achieved by continuing to talk to Milosevic). Dini's object, duly achieved, was to mollify pacifist elements in the government, thus preserving its stability, and perhaps also to endeavour to make sure that Italy enjoyed a privileged relationship with Belgrade when the war was over.[11]

In terms of sheer numbers, Italy's military participation was exceeded only by that of America and France: 54 aircraft by the end of the war, not to mention ships, airports, ports, supplies and logistical support. Italy's Ministry of Defence was the only one among those of the leading Nato countries not to hold a daily briefing to keep public opinion informed of how military operations were proceeding, since this would have had disruptive political consequences both for the government (the reaction of the Communists and the Greens could easily have been imagined) and for the relationship with Belgrade, which would in all probability have broken off diplomatic relations. It was deemed more appropriate to maintain a discreet silence on the subject of military operations, particularly those involving Italian forces. The government declared simply that Italian forces were responsible for 'integrated defence', a reassuring phrase that allowed people to make a pretence of believing that Italy was involved in a war for purely defensive reasons.[12] The fact that the government held up and Italy remained in the war right up to the end was due in part to ploys of this nature and to certain things left unsaid. Through political opportunism – perhaps justified – the country missed an opportunity both to open a serious debate regarding its own strategic interests and the resources needed to defend them, and to persuade public opinion to come to a more mature awareness of the realities of foreign policy and of the need to build security rather than simply reaping its benefits.

> 66 It was deemed more appropriate to maintain a discreet silence on the subject of military operations, particularly those involving Italian forces 99

One of the government's principal worries was how to deal with the mass exodus of the refugees. If even a tiny percentage of their number were to enter Italy, the impact on public opinion could not be predicted, with potentially devastating consequences for government stability. The solution was to assist the refugees *in situ*, so as not to uproot them from their territory, to facilitate their return to their homes when the war was over and to avoid the enormous problems Italy's taking them in would pose. Refugee camps had therefore to be set up in Albania and Macedonia, and this task was undertaken by the Arcobaleno mission, launched by the government on 29 March, an exceptional humanitarian operation to which the media devoted ample space. To gain support for the mission, a subscription fund was opened with the backing of the philosopher Norberto Bobbio and two well-known journalists (Indro Montanelli and Eugenio Scalfari[13]) who addressed an appeal to the Italian people. The population responded enthusiastically. Within two months, over 68 million Euros had been collected. The Arcobaleno mission, the brainchild of the government – as it proudly proclaimed – succeeded in winning over to the cause of military intervention a tendentially pacifist public opinion, rendered the war acceptable and to a certain extent caused a rallying to the government's side of Catholic and left-wing elements who were opposed to the war but saw the humanitarian mission as a noble cause to serve. The insidious pacifist distaste for the war was therefore turned to positive effect, in the form of aid for the refugees. There can be no doubt that the Arcobaleno mission provided very real humanitarian aid, yet it must also be seen as a massive and effective campaign to influence public opinion in favour of the war. The government made much of the leading role taken by Italy in aiding the refugees, and endeavoured to ensure, paying careful attention to the image it was projecting, that the refugee aid programme received maximum exposure. It handled the job with uncommon efficiency, and obtained an international sanction giving it the task, assigned by the Contact Group, of coordinating humanitarian assistance in Albania. The refugee aid programme was designed to redress the balance for the negative fact of the war; yes, there was bombing, but at the same time a humanitarian operation was being implemented on an enormous scale. To achieve this objective, direct intervention was required, for Italy's role would not be given sufficient exposure through United Nations High Commissioner for Refugees (UNHCR) channels alone, and the papers therefore put over the image of a country that was ministering to the overwhelming needs of the refugees virtually single-handed. Headlines were designed to be harrowing: 'In the valley of death', 'A daily death toll

> 66 There can be no doubt that the Arcobaleno mission provided very real humanitarian aid, yet it must also be seen as a massive and effective campaign to influence public opinion in favour of the war 99

of ten in the refugee camps', 'Serbian rape lager', 'Screams from the Kosovo hell'; but reassuring with respect to Italy's role: 'Italy first in the race to aid', 'Let's save these people', 'Wojtyla: congratulations Italy on Arcobaleno mission'.

The government was attempting to find an acceptable balance between military involvement, the search for a diplomatic solution and humanitarian aid, an endeavour which, for as long as the war lasted, was to meet the approval of a large proportion of the Italian public.

The anti-war front was a heterogeneous mix of pacifism, anti-capitalism and anti-American feeling. It ranged from the extreme left to the extreme right, and included the Northern League (LN), certain fringes of the Greens and the DS, the Church and the various Catholic organizations.

Particularly difficult was the position of the PdCI, caught between loyalty to its ideological objections to the very idea of war, and its governmental responsibilities, which limited its scope for independent action. The leader of this party was Armando Cossutta, a communist of long standing, with strong ties with the Soviet Union. Aware that a government crisis would benefit the right, Cossutta did not seriously entertain the idea of leaving the government, but he was harried from the left by competition from the other communist party, which formed part of the opposition, and from below by pressure from the militants. In theory, Cossutta adopted an unbending position: the war was inadmissible and Italy should have refused to be involved either directly or indirectly, and should therefore not have allowed its bases to be used. He declared military action to be an act of war contrary to article 11 of the constitution, as did Fausto Bertinotti, the other communist leader.[14] In practice, though, Cossutta took a more realistic stand: the communist ministers would remain in the government with the objective of bringing the war to an end, and would resign only if and when it became apparent that they were meeting with no success. This meant accepting compromises and going back on certain things said. The Communists began by tolerating the use of the Italian bases, and announced a new *sine qua non* for the PdCI's remaining in the government: the suspension of the air strikes. When it became apparent that the bombings were not going to stop, the new uncrossable boundary line became the non-utilization of Italian armed forces and aircraft. As soon as it became clear that Italian planes were involved in the bombings just like those of other nations, that boundary line shifted once again: now it was a land operation that would not be tolerated. In the meantime the controversial meeting between Cossutta and Milosevic in Belgrade at the height of the war served as a sop to the rank and file, increasingly unhappy about the PdCI's demeanour, and it also gained precious time. Hope remained that the war would end, thus resolving a situation that was becoming ever more untenable.

The Refounded Communists, in the opposition, were free to revive the anti-American and anti-Nato tradition. They condemned the presence of Nato bases on Italian territory and contended that the decision to use those bases should be Italy's alone, as the decision to take part in the war should be parliament's. They accused the government of riding rough-shod over the constitution; of sending the country to war without a parliamentary mandate, of subservience to the USA. The Communists, opposed to the new strategic concept of a global Nato, held that the American decision to go into Kosovo allowed the US to pursue three objectives: to marginalize Russia; to remove the UN from the scene; to impede the forward march of Europe – it had just launched the single currency – and inhibit its attempt to achieve political unity.

The Greens, a government party, found themselves in the awkward situation of having to reconcile two conflicting ideas: pacifism and interference, albeit on humanitarian grounds. Although unconvinced both of the effectiveness and of the legitimacy of the bombings (effectiveness because they would reinforce Serbian nationalism and Milosevic's leadership, and provide an alibi for ethnic cleansing; legitimacy because the UN had not given its authorization), the Greens were anxious to stop ethnic persecution, and to see the war end in an equitable peace, so that the refugees could go back to their homes in safety. With the pursuit of these objectives in mind, they chose not to take a moral stand or to make a symbolic gesture, and remained within the government. They proposed that a certain number of the refugees be housed in the former nuclear base at Comiso, that Rugova be granted Italian citizenship – to affirm the principle of non-violence – and that Serbian and Montenegrian deserters be allowed into the country as a way of demonstrating support for democratic opposition to the regime. A delegation journeyed to Yugoslavia and met not Milosevic but exponents of the opposition, with the aim of giving the dissenting voices a chance to be heard, and also of re establishing communications between Western democracies and the local population and opposition.

Against the war was the LN, a party that had pressed for an independent Northern Italy and supported independence for Slovenia and Croatia. Its opposition to the war was motivated by its objections to the globalisation the US was seeking to impose on the Balkans. The LN saw in this policy another form of American colonialism, a process that was bound to do away with the regional differences and the ideal of the ethnic state on which its own ideology was founded. Certain party leaders went so far as to pay a visit to Milosevic at the height of the war.

The parties of the centre-right pronounced themselves in favour of military intervention, whereas the extreme right-wing fringe opposed it in the name of its anti-capitalistic ideals. The unspoken pledge of the centre-right to vote in support of the government even if the Communists and the Greens should defect, gave these parties another reason not to provoke a crisis, and to content themselves with the compromises proposed by the government.

The Vatican, which was seeking to effect a reconciliation between Catholic Europe and the Orthodox Church, and was diffident about American capitalism, also took up position against the war. Early on, it embarked on a series of diplomatic endeavours which raised great hopes at top levels in Italy, since it was felt that these measures might contribute to increased support for the government. When Primakov's diplomatic mission failed, the Holy See sent a deputation to Belgrade with the proposal that all military action be ceased over the period of the Catholic and Orthodox Easter, and that negotiations be resumed in the UN. The idea of an Easter cease-fire arose out of an agreement between the Vatican and the Quirinale; the president of the republic, worried that the government might not survive, and personally drawn towards Catholic pacifism, supported the Vatican undertaking. But the mission was not well received in Belgrade, where the recollection of the role played by the Church of Rome in the secession of Slovenia and Croatia eight years earlier was still vivid. Upon the failure of the mission, the Vatican shifted its standpoint and put out a plea for an equitable peace, cautioning Europe not to look to the US to solve every problem which arose, but to assume a more active role.

> 66 The Vatican, which was seeking to effect a reconciliation between Catholic Europe and the Orthodox Church, and was diffident about American capitalism, also took up position against the war 99

ITALY AT WAR: PUBLIC OPINION AND THE MEDIA

During the war certain newspapers published the findings of opinion polls whose aim was to ascertain what the public felt about the war.[15] In March, at the beginning of the campaign:

- only 25 per cent of the population considered the attack to be justified
- 49.5 per cent felt it was unjustified
- 25 per cent had no opinion.

Italy went to war with a substantial proportion of public opinion against doing so, but in subsequent polls this tendency was to change, and the media was in large part responsible for this. The continuing sequence of horrific scenes that appeared on television and in newspaper photographs had the effect of reinforcing not pacifist feelings, as some had predicted, but rather the conviction that intervention was justified. By early April those in favour had risen to 37 per cent while those opposed and those who were uncertain went down to 45.6 per cent and 17 per cent respectively. The end of April marked a decided turning point, with 43 per cent considering intervention justified, 33 per cent unjustified and 24 per cent of don't-knows. Support for Italian military involvement was also up (from 30 per cent to 51 per cent), while fewer people now thought that the country should avoid any type of political or military intervention (from 14 per cent to 5 per cent). The percentage of those who felt that Italy should cooperate politically but abstain from military action was down as well (from 45.5 per cent to 35 per cent). April also saw an increase in support for the government. The situation changed once more in May. Now only 35.4 per cent favoured attack, while the percentage of those who considered it unjustifiable went up to 42 per cent, with 22 per cent being unable to give an opinion. The same tendency was apparent as far as Italian military involvement was concerned, with only 44.4 per cent now in favour; 7.5 per cent were opposed to any form of involvement, 40 per cent for political but not military collaboration.

By and large, these variations were due to the fact that people, particularly those closest to the war-zone, had had enough; the war had gone on too long. Noble ideals and the promise that the campaign would be quick and effective, had motivated consent to the war. After a few weeks of bombing, all certainties had evaporated. The obvious ineffectiveness of the bomb attacks, which were dragging on well beyond the time predicted, was a bitter disappointment. The longer the war lasted, the greater was the risk that support for it would disintegrate. Another reason for the loss of enthusiasm lay in the succession of errors, the collateral damage, which had caused civilian casualties to increase and faith in the military capacity of the alliance to diminish. Public opinion had gone through three phases: opposition in the early stages, then adhesion to the idea of humanitarian motives, and finally weariness, disappointment and fear, a result of the alarming number of civilian casualties and the dragging on of the war.

In any democracy, public support is vital if a war is to be embarked on and won, especially when the country is under no direct threat. Propaganda and the mass media therefore play a decisive role. In the Kosovo crisis the constantly shown scenes of the refugees' flight played a crucial part in generating a strong emotional involvement which in turn was to become consent. The military campaign achieved legitimization on humanitarian grounds: an act of reparation for an intolerable injustice. If the Gulf War had been fought in the name of *realpolitik*, the bombing raids over Serbia were a triumph for *idealpolitik*. The three leading daily national newspapers took a pro-war position and disseminated the idea of 'humanitarian interference'; the right of an unspecified international community to intervene to stop ethnic cleansing, so as not to 'do a Munich'. They also gave space to the dissenting views expressed by journalists and external collaborators and to pro-Serb opinions – including a letter from Milosevic to Vedrine and Cook[16] – and drew attention to the errors committed by Nato, whose strategy they considered superficial and inadequate. After over a month of bombings, they started to point out that in the democracies of continental Europe there was a tolerance limit beyond which public approval for a war which was in theory just, but in its methods and its consequences increasingly unjust, began to melt away and to turn to dissent, and that that limit had been reached and perhaps crossed. The two principal left-wing newspapers, *il manifesto* and *liberazione*, took an anti-war stand. Essentially, three different points of view emerged from the press:

> **66 If the Gulf War had been fought in the name of *realpolitik*, the bombing raids over Serbia were a triumph for *idealpolitik* 99**

- in favour of humanitarian intervention and of the strategy adopted
- in favour of the humanitarian motivation but opposed to military intervention and hoping that other solutions would be found
- against the humanitarian motivation and the war in general, which was considered merely a blind concealing other less legitimate ends.

Articles were in the main reasonably accurate, bulletins from the Balkans well balanced. They gave a realistic picture of the damage wrought by the air raids, and did not seek to sanitize the war, as the Nato briefings from Brussels were doing. Space was given to internal political problems (whether the majority would hold together; Italy's involvement in the war as proof of its being a 'serious' European country) and to the refugees; less space to the way the war was going and the military aspects. The numerous and varied commentaries touched on issues like the relationship between Europe and the US, the failure of Europe to play its part on the international scene, the need for an autonomous Europe, European defence, Italy's image and national identity, Nato's new strategy, the just war, pacifism, the right to intervene on humanitarian grounds. These particular sources of information were aimed at a select readership rather than the masses, who were interested more in emotional factors, in the human element, than in a critical analysis of the situation. It was true that the leading dailies gave space to dissident and pacifist opinions, but it was not the cultured, dissenting and academic commentaries that formed public opinion. The widely disseminated image of a monstrous regime tended to create a conventional view of the situation in Serbia, and served as a justification for the war. By turning Milosevic into a criminal, the media endeavoured to create in the collective imagination the image of a monster; to arouse horror and fear. Milosevic became the new Saddam Hussein. Other, clearly unfounded comparisons were made too: Milosevic was Hitler; Pristina, Auschwitz.[17] Much blame was attached to Serbia, but the fact that the USA, Europe, the Vatican, the International Monetary Fund (IMF) had shown themselves incapable of avoiding – or subsequently putting a stop to – a war which had been tearing Yugoslavia apart for the past ten years, was glossed over. The leading dailies were full of scholarly dissertations on pacifism and humanitarian war, but certain aspects were never really discussed: the integration of the Balkans into the globalization programme; Nato's expansion eastwards; the new strategy of the alliance; American unipolarism and its hegemony over Europe; the needs of the war industries; the economic opportunities offered by the reconstruction programme; the warning given to Russia and China. Few commentators realized that the situation was escalating dramatically when, because of the unanticipated resistance of the Serbs and the difficulty of neutralizing their army, it became

66 What had begun as a pressure campaign designed to drive Milosevic to the negotiating table was now not much short of total war 99

necessary to intensify the bomb attacks and increase the range of objectives. Now even civilian and economic targets were included. The refugee drama, the good reasons for intervening in the war, the monstrousness of Milosevic, the unacceptable comparison with Nazism and the Holocaust: these were the absorbing issues. It escaped people's notice that what had begun as a pressure campaign designed to drive Milosevic to the negotiating table was now not much short of total war.

The general public was on the receiving end of emotionally charged reports broadcast by the television. The plight of the refugees stole the show. In every living room in the country, people were sharing their sufferings. These were persuasive images that could not fail to convince people that the war was humanitarian, just, a necessity.[18] But ultimately, the endless repetition bred familiarity and saturation point was reached, as was demonstrated by the cooling-down of public opinion registered in May. Television services often opted for the studio debate formula rather than for documentary programmes, failing to fulfil the moral obligation of a news service: to document before it comments. The overdose of repetitious talk shows, often with belligerent, biased and incompetent participants, merely added to the confusion, and did nothing to promote reflection or in-depth analysis.

Though admittedly the newspapers and periodicals, perhaps more than television, did a fairly good job of keeping people informed, and of analyzing the information available, it has to be said that they did not do very much at all to foster serious thought about the Balkan tragedy and the historical reasons behind it. They did not help readers to reflect on the foreign policy and the strategic interests of the country, to consider war in rational and pragmatic rather than emotional and ideological terms; to see the link between the rediscovery of the principle of national interest and the fact that the country needed to provide itself with an efficient military machine; or the link between security and the use of military force as a deterrent and a potential solution to the crisis. The attention given to the refugee tragedy did to a certain extent distract public opinion from serious considerations of this nature, and it also served to put consciences at rest: the Italians could show solidarity.

CONCLUSIONS: ITALY, A DEPENDABLE COUNTRY

After fifty years, Italy unexpectedly found itself at war again and having to cope with the problems this entailed: airports near operative zones closing down, civilian flights disrupted, the tourist industry floundering, a ban on fishing on the Adriatic, etc. For the first time, people were realizing that the country could not shirk international responsibilities and continue to benefit from the security afforded it by others, but that it had to look beyond its own borders, play an active role in the international community and collaborate with the allies to build security, accepting the obligations this involved.

The country passed the test: Italy did its best at first to prevent the war, then refused to desert the alliance. It made a decidedly significant contribution to military operations and was an efficient front-line protagonist in the refugee aid programme; it made it clear that the way to peace lay in involving Russia and the UN in negotiations once again; it paid the considerable costs – direct and indirect – of a war it had not wanted and which Italian diplomacy had done its best to keep as short as possible; it now provides the KFOR with one of its largest contingents. Only a land offensive could have plunged the country into crisis and dealt a death-blow to a hard-won political equilibrium, but, if this had happened, other countries, too, would unexpectedly have found themselves in the same boat. In its search for a diplomatic solution, the government managed to combine loyalty to Nato and independent action. The communists, the extreme left-wing elements of the DS, the Greens, the PPI, uneasy as they were, still balked at causing the break-up of the coalition; the opposition showed a similar sense of responsibility; the pacifists demonstrated; intellectuals, opinion leaders and politicians engaged in civilized debate. Italy revealed itself to be no different from other countries; the accusations of undependability had been belied by the facts. But if Italy can be said to have put up a creditable performance during the war, in fact it achieved little. Italy had stood out in the alliance as the country most favourable to a political solution, but was absent from the final negotiation that put an end to the hostilities; here others took the stage. The innumerable compromises resorted to by the government took their toll and when finally the various international assignments for the administration of the Kosovo and the reconstruction of the Balkans were handed out, Italy found itself excluded.

> 66 In its search for a diplomatic solution, the government managed to combine loyalty to Nato and independent action 99

It might have earned the right to be called a dependable country, but Italy had not yet become entitled to play a significant role in the international alliances. It has often been said that the war was rendered possible by American strength and by the Italian bases. Never before had Italy played such a crucial role. D'Alema himself emphasized this, pointing out that Italy had been invited to Quint and had influenced Nato decisions, especially by vetoing the striking of certain objectives, so as to avoid civilian casualties.[19] (D'Alema, 1999: 38, 51–3) In actual fact, Italy did not count for quite as much as she imagined. The vetoes on those targets were circumvented unilaterally by the US through US European Command (EUCOM), the headquarters of the American forces in Europe; the operations involving secret American equipment were decided not by Nato, but by EUCOM, responsible directly to the Pentagon and the White House. The invitation to Quint must be seen in the light of the American distaste for war by committee. After the Cold War was over, Washington decided that when operations were conducted outside Nato territory, the Europeans would be involved in the operation itself, and in the subsequent onerous peace-keeping phase, but would not be involved, or as little as possible, when decisions were to be made. The fact that the Italians were invited to Quint, and their consequent conviction that finally their country counted for something in the alliance, were seen on the other side of the Atlantic merely as expedients to induce Italy to toe the line as far as Nato decisions were concerned. The D'Alema plan, officially rejected but in actual fact adopted, or so its originator contended, was considered useful by the Americans not because of what it proposed, but because it served to hold the government coalition together, and thus to maintain the efficiency of the war instrument which was Italy. (Fubini, 1999: 18–22)

Geostrategic position and rational proposals do not in themselves carry much weight if a country is unstable, and particularly if money cannot be found to invest in defence. This is where the concept of a united Europe comes in. Italy on its own counts for little; the other major European countries perhaps slightly more. But what the Kosovo crisis has once again made manifest is that a politically united Europe still remains only a theoretical concept. Italy, with her dual tradition – Atlantic and European – must put the experience gained from the war towards the creation of a common European foreign and defence policy. It is US military strength that makes it possible for Washington to carry out its military experiments, but, not infrequently, it is the Europeans who pick up the tab ('they play, we pay').

> 66 A politically united Europe still remains only a theoretical concept 99

NATO remains responsible for security in Europe, but to the east of Italy there has arisen an underdeveloped and unstable area that is looking towards the Italian peninsula as the first stage on the road to hope. A European state is not a question of choice, but of necessity. Only a European state can guarantee not only a military presence, but also a politico-economic framework in the Balkans. It can also provide a general strategy that will allow the Balkan peoples to imagine a future not tainted by nationalism, by underdevelopment and by dictatorship, but enhanced by democracy and unity among peoples. Without the existence of a European state, Balkanization will roll westwards, and south-eastern Europe could overwhelm the continent, beginning with Italy.

NOTES

1   World geostrategic and geoeconomic interests clash in the struggle to control the strategic axes which crisscross the Balkans and provide communicational links between the republics of central Asia, the Caspian Sea and the Caucasus; an area where water is plentiful and natural and energy resources abound (as does the opium poppy). These axes leave Russia out on a limb, and consolidate the position of America's main ally in the area, Turkey. Italy is particularly interested in corridor 8, running from the Black Sea to the Adriatic, opposite the Italian coastline.

2   Crime in the Balkans, at least as dangerous as local nationalism, has links with criminal organizations in Italy, and the Adriatic has become an open frontier, difficult to control adequately.

3   This error of judgement had its Serbian counterpart: the Serbs thought that the West would divide, and that Serbia, if it was attacked, would succeed in igniting the Balkans, destabilizing the neighbouring countries. Both sides, in fact, went to war under a misapprehension. (D'Alema, 1999:17)

4   A previous indication of the desire to play an active role had been the presence, not originally planned, of Italian soldiers in the Extraction Force stationed in Macedonia.

5   D'Alema declared that there seemed to be signs that Serbian troops were retreating and that it was time to go back to the negotiating table. This declaration, unfounded, as D'Alema himself admitted, gave the impression that Italy was ready to back out, and caused pointless ill-feeling with the allies.

6   Leading members of the premier's own party criticized this procedure, claiming that the bases should not just be handed over automatically, but that an act of parliament was necessary, in that Nato was an organization for international cooperation, not a supranational organization (see the letter from the president of the Foreign Committee Giangiacomo Migone to the President of the Senate, dated 11 October 1999).

7   Walter Veltroni, leader of the DS, the premier's party, spoke in parliament in defence of the war, and affirmed once again that the new international left should be concerned first and foremost with the defence of human rights, a

position which was in complete contrast with that taken by the party at the time of the Gulf war. Inheritors of the old communist party ideas, the DS did not find it easy to accept the Nato intervention. They were caught between a number of conflicting elements: their traditional pacifism, their anti-American and anti-Nato past, the conditioned reflexes of the rank and file, the new responsibilities – including military ones – that the government had taken on, and the need to fulfil international obligations and to make sure that the country did not lose face. The extreme left voiced strong objections, and a few days into the war, in a controversial move, made an appeal to the UN, which collected 150 signatures from members of parliament. This document was not intended to convey disillusionment with the government, but it was symptomatic of the fact that some members of the DS found it difficult to accept the war.

8   Commitment to the setting up of an International Criminal Court, the banning of anti-personnel mines and combating the exploitation of child labour.

9   On 26 March and 9 May in particular, when the government was urged by parliament to try and pursuade the Nato allies to take immediate steps towards the reopening of negotiations and the halting of the bomb attacks, and the hope was expressed that the EU and the UN would act to achieve this objective.

10 Rugova had been freed thanks to the intercedence of the Rome-based Community of Sant'Egidio, which had for years been an active presence in the Balkans.

11 Tactics that may have been partly motivated by a desire to put his own tiny party in the limelight and to help him up the ladder to the Quirinale.

12 At the beginning of the war, Italian aircraft were simply allotted the task of defending the national territory and the Nato bases, and performing escort duties. The government soon realized the inconsistency, and removed the political veto, bringing them into full use.

13 They write for the three most widely read Italian dailies: *La Stampa*, *Il Corriere della sera* and *La Repubblica* respectively.

14 The article states that Italy rejects war as a means of resolving international conflicts. The communists also held that article 78, which affirms that parliament decrees a state of war and confers on the government the necessary powers, had been violated.

15 See the Ispo findings reported in *Il Corriere della Sera*, 27 March, 2 and 26 April, 10 May.

16 In *La Stampa*, 24 March 1999.

17 Both sides resorted to comparisons with Nazism. In the West, ethnic cleansing awoke memories of the lagers; in Yugoslavia Western policy was termed neo-Nazi, and the Nato bombings brought to mind the exploits of the Luftwaffe during World War II.

18 There were exceptions, of course. Halfway through April, a private television channel put on a programme, as spectacular as it was controversial, which was broadcast live from a Belgrade bridge and gave the Serbs point of view. The RAI's correspondent in Belgrade, who sent in live reports every day throughout the war, was accused of being pro-Serb.

19 Both General Clark and Secretary of State for Defence Cohen had imputed these restrictions to two countries, Germany and Italy.

5

GERMANY: THE FEDERAL REPUBLIC, LOYAL TO NATO

SABRINA P. RAMET AND PHIL LYON

IN CONSIDERING THE GERMAN POLICY DEBATE ABOUT KOSOVO, and, indeed, Germany's entire engagement in the Yugoslav crisis since 1991, one needs to keep several factors in mind:

- in 1990 Germany had just overcome 45 years of division and was, therefore, inclined to feel that other nations should enjoy the prerogative of self-determination

- Germany's availability for combat operations outside its own frontiers had long been taken to be excluded by the country's constitution

- Germany has been a reluctant partner in the Balkans, having had to be pressed by Nato to contribute forces to the Bosnian peace mission for example[1]

- 'war guilt' in connection with World War II has continued to be cited as a limiting factor in German policy debates

- the deeply rooted pacifism of the left has constituted a non-negotiable impediment for those concerned, to any military action not of a purely defensive nature.

Already during the Bosnian war, inter-party dynamics reflected the influence of these five factors. In 1994, for example, the opposition Social Democratic Party (SPD) and the Alliance 90/Green Party registered their opposition to the proposed deployment of German Tornadoes in Bosnia. The SPD had also challenged the constitutionality of German involvement in the Nato/WEU naval embargo of the Federal Republic of Yugoslavia (FRY) and had joined the Free Democratic Party (FDP) in challenging the constitutionality of German participation in aerial surveillance over Bosnia and the Adriatic. In 1995, moreover, the Greens split down the middle over the issue of the government's agreement to send a 4,000-man German contingent to Bosnia as part of the 50,000-man Nato peace-keeping force known initially as IFOR (later SFOR). Party 'leftists' (isolationists, not internationalists), who predominated in the party ranks, opposed the German mission. Among them was Kerstin Müller, spokesperson for the Green 'fraction' in the *Bundestag*. Party moderates (called 'realists' in the German press) outnumbered 'leftists' in the Bundestag, however, and favoured German cooperation with the Nato mission. Their leading spokesperson was Joschka Fischer, chief of the Green fraction in the *Bundestag*. A Green Party congress held in Bremen in December 1995 actually handed the 'realists' a defeat, by a vote of 402 to 260[2], but the 'leftists' were not so amply represented in the *Bundestag* where the 'realists' carried the day on 6 December by a vote of 543 to 107, with six abstentions.[3]

KOSOVO HEATS UP

With the exclusion of Kosovo from discussions at Dayton in November 1995, local Albanians began to lose patience. Albanians had hoped that the policy of passive resistance, urged on them by their unofficial president, Ibrahim Rugova, a Shakespearean scholar, would impress the West, would prevent Western observers from treating Serbian security forces and Kosovo Albanian civilians as morally equivalent, and would somehow create a moral pressure that would force the Serbian president Slobodan Milosevic to restore the province's autonomy (which he had suppressed in 1989). Now, after Dayton, it became clear to most Albanians that the West was quite prepared to wash its hands of the whole Kosovo problem, on the basis that this was Serbia's 'internal affair'. Indeed, after Dayton, the EU extended unconditional recognition to the Federal Republic of Yugoslavia, ignoring protestations on the part of Kosovo's Albanians. Germany, for its part, immediately began to repatriate the 130,000

> 66 Now, after Dayton, it became clear to most Albanians that the West was quite prepared to wash its hands of the whole Kosovo problem 99

Albanians who had fled there from Kosovo, as if there were no unre-solved problems of any consequence in the province.[4] It was, thus, no coincidence that tension began to rise in Kosovo almost immediately the Dayton Peace Accords were signed. There were fatal shootings on both sides in early 1996, and in mid-January 1997, a bomb attack on the rector of the University of Pristina, Radivoje Papovic, left him wounded. The KLA, an underground organization whose very existence continued to be doubted for another 12 months or so, claimed responsibility for the action. In the early months of 1997, '.... in the wake of political unrest in Albania, more than a million fire-arms were stolen from [Albanian] Army warehouses.'[5] Put up for sale on the black market, many of these weapons ended up in the KLA arsenal. Meanwhile, a 1996 agreement between Milosevic and Rugova concerning the return of Albanian stu-dents to school proved stillborn. And when, in autumn 1997, a German–French initiative sought to obtain some improvement of Kosovo, on the basis of recognition of Yugoslav sovereignty in the province, then Yugoslav Foreign Minister Milan Milutinovic rejected the initiative, which he characterized as 'interference in the internal affairs' of Yugoslavia.[6] There were further attacks by the KLA in December 1997, striking at Serbian police and police stations. Early in 1998, the KLA pro-claimed an 'insurrection'.

As of March, 1998, there were probably only a few hundred KLA fight-ers, though their ranks were expanding steadily. By November of that year, the KLA

... claimed to have some 20,000 well-trained men under arms and to be train-ing an auxiliary corps of 150 Albanian women for secret service operations.[7]

Although Kosovo was, by this point, a combat zone, a situation report of the German Foreign Ministry dated 11 March 1998 dismissed the notion that Kosovo Albanians being returned to Kosovo would face any repres-sion on the part of state authorities.[8] Shortly thereafter, German Foreign Minister Klaus Kinkel told *Der Spiegel* that the German government rec-ognized Belgrade's sovereignty in Kosovo and could not condone either Albanian separatism or efforts to alter existing borders.[9]

As of February 1998, Belgrade had concentrated some 20,000 troops and special police in Kosovo. Then, after the killing of four Serbian police on 28 February, Belgrade sent its forces in strength to the Drenica region in central Kosovo; at the end of a week of bloodshed, 83 Albanians were dead.[10] The USA and Britain reacted with shrill rhetoric, while Italy,

France, and Russia sought to restrain the Americans and the British. The German government sought to keep channels open with both its more hawkish and its more dovish partners.

The USA now pressed forward with a diplomatic initiative which resulted in a meeting between Milosevic and Rugova on 15 May. The meeting had no practical impact, as Yugoslav forces pressed on with their counter-offensive. Combat activity in late May resulted in the flight of some 50,000 Albanians. As fighting continued during the summer months, Foreign Minister Kinkel began to reconsider the conservative stance which his and other Western governments had been adopting *vis-à-vis* Kosovo and criticized the Western alliance's erstwhile strategy, flying to Moscow in the hope of opening some 'creative possibilities' in talks with Russian Foreign Minister Yevgeny Primakov. Kinkel returned in a gloomy mood, warning darkly, 'It is five minutes to midnight.'[11]

By the time veteran negotiator Richard Holbrooke was back in Belgrade, 11–12 October, for intense discussions with Milosevic,[12] the Kohl government had been swept out of power. Gerhard Schröder (SPD) was the chancellor-designate, and Joschka Fischer, the incoming foreign minister. Milosevic was being given a series of sliding deadlines, while Nato officials threatened Milosevic with consequences if he did not accelerate the withdrawal of Yugoslav forces from the province. The Schröder government confirmed the Kohl government's commitment to provide as many as 14 German fighter aircraft and 500 troops in the event that Belgrade did not comply with the UN ultimatum and force was deemed necessary.

The 12 October agreement called for the stationing of 2,000 unarmed OSCE observers in the province. When, on 27 October, Milosevic was deemed to have belatedly met the 'spirit', if not the letter, of the terms specified for the 16 October deadline,[13] the unarmed observers (200 of them German) were brought into the province. As doubts began to arise concerning the wisdom of this unarmed 'deployment', German Defence Minister Rudolf Scharping said:

his country might contribute troops to an international 'extraction force' to rescue international peace observers in Kosovo if a truce in the Yugoslav province breaks down.'[14]

The German government also agreed to participate in Nato air-surveillance missions over Kosovo. By the end of 1998, it was obvious to all observers that the Holbrooke–Milosevic agreement was not being honoured by Belgrade. Americans sympathetic to Serbia and Milosevic sometimes point out that the KLA was, in the weeks following the October agreement, engaging in acts of military provocation against Serb authorities. Be that as it may, Milosevic had undertaken to withdraw his forces, and the sense of the agreement was that, at a minimum, he should coordinate with Western governments before undertaking any further military reprisals. Moreover, wholesale 'ethnic cleansing' was clearly contrary to both the spirit and the letter of the October agreement. And yet, to the contrary, Belgrade had drawn up a top-secret plan

> 66 Belgrade had drawn up a top-secret plan code-named 'Operation Horseshoe' which called for driving Albanians out of the province 99

code-named 'Operation Horseshoe' which called for driving Albanians out of the province; the plan was set into motion on 24 December. Some 20,000 Albanians were driven from their homes during January 1999 alone, and by the end of the month, some 200,000 Albanians were homeless as a result of Serb military operations.[15] The massacre of 45 Albanian civilians in the town of Racak on 15 January shocked Western capitals, and a last-ditch effort at orchestrating a negotiated settlement was undertaken, when the Western powers invited the Belgrade government and the Kosovo Albanians to send delegations to Rambouillet. Three political groupings of Albanians were represented at the Rambouillet peace talks:

- the Democratic League of Kosovo (led by Ibrahim Rugova)
- the KLA (led by Hashim Thaci)
- the United Democratic Movement (consisting of a number of smaller left-leaning Kosovo parties, chaired by historian Rexhep Qosja, one of the founders of the Albanian Democratic Movement, a constituent affiliate of the UDM).[16]

The Serbian side signalled its lack of interest in these talks by continuing to bombard Albanian villages in the areas surrounding Podujevo, Decan, Vushtrri, Mitrovica, Suhareka, and Orahovac. Between 1 February, and mid-March 1999, another 60,000 Albanians were driven from their homes.[17] Meanwhile, the Western mediators at Rambouillet hammered out a compromise: Yugoslav sovereignty over Kosovo would be confirmed, in exchange for a restoration of the autonomy abolished in February 1989, and Nato troops would enter Kosovo to guarantee compliance, with license to enter any part of Yugoslavia. The Albanian side accepted the agreement. Belgrade's rejection essentially guaranteed a military response from Nato. Later, in mid-April 1999, a controversy would break out as to whether Foreign Minister Fischer and his counterparts at Rambouillet had really 'exhausted all diplomatic possibilities.'[18] Some German politicians would also later question whether the German government and its partners had adequately informed their respective publics.

TILL IT'S OVER OVER THERE

Even before the alliance went to war, while Western governments still hoped for Belgrade's acquiescence to the terms of the Rambouillet agreement, there were already the ripples of discord in Bonn, where the Christian Demcratic Union/Christian Social Union (CDU/CSU) announced its unwillingness to go along with the commitment of German troops (3,300 envisioned in the Rambouillet peace agreement) to an eventual KFOR peacekeeping force. The reform communist Party of Democratic Socialism (PDS) also voiced its displeasure with the agreement. With the initiation of hostilities by Nato forces on 24 March, the lines of polarization cutting through the German political landscape would become all the more obvious. The decision to put troops in harm's way is a difficult one for any government, but for Germany, still tainted by memories of the barbarism of its armed forces during World War II, a call to arms could only provoke controversy. This legacy of the past is only one of a number of interrelated concerns that have absorbed the attention of Germans, perhaps especially of those left of centre. The key to legitimizing German involvement in the military campaign against Yugoslavia, however, was that it was to be within the context of a joint Nato campaign. Indeed, Wolfgang Schäuble, chair of the CDU/CSU Fraktion, stated that the decision to vote for Nato intervention stood on secure ground in terms of both constitutional and international law.

> 66 The decision to put troops in harm's way is a difficult one for any government, but for Germany, still tainted by memories of the barbarism of its armed forces during World War II, a call to arms could only provoke controversy 99

The SPD–Green coalition understood very well the gravity of the decision taken by Nato, in which Bonn had concurred. As Chancellor Schröder noted in his address to the nation on 24 March, it was the first time since World War II that German soldiers were involved in combat action. The justification, Schröder urged, lay in the history of 'systematic violations of human rights' by Belgrade authorities and in the looming 'humanitarian catastrophe' in Kosovo.[19] The following day, in an address to the *Bundestag*, Defence Minister Scharping reported that more than

400,000 Kosovo Albanians had, by then, been driven from their homes, some 250,000 of whom were still in Kosovo.[20] For Scharping, Nato's response was nothing less than an *obligation* 'to take care of the stability of the surrounding states' and 'to give the whole of the Balkans a European perspective.'[21] Arnulf Barung, in a column for *Die Woche*, reflecting on this giant step for German foreign policy, tied Germany's new role in the first place to the end of the Cold War and of the Soviet imperium in eastern Europe.[22] Only the PDS (led by Gregor Gysi) issued a blanket denunciation of the aerial strikes, while the leaders of the opposition FDP and CDU quickly declared their support.

Ironically, the first political tremors struck Schröder's own SPD, whose chairman, Oskar Lafontaine, made no secret of the fact that he was opposed to the Nato aerial campaign. The SPD was constrained to convene an extraordinary Congress (on 11–12 April) to discuss the Kosovo crisis. In the course of this Congress, as we shall note at greater length below, Chancellor Schröder was installed as chairman of the party by a vote of 370 to 102, with 15 abstentions and six invalid ballots. A decisive majority of the delegates voted in favour of a resolution offering broad support for participation in the Nato mission, though the party's left wing continued to insist that there be no use of German ground troops in any combat capacity.[23]

In theory, the Congress should have dampened dissent at least temporarily. But some SPD members, such as Hermann Scheer, on the party's left wing, continued to protest against the war.[24] Already at the end of April the district SPD organization in Saxony-Anhalt adopted a resolution demanding an immediate bombing halt. Just two weeks later, in mid-May, the Bavarian branch of the SPD adopted a resolution calling for 'immediate negotiations' concerning a cease-fire, effectively repudiating the policy line embraced by the head of the party.

There was also some uneasiness within CDU/CSU circles. As early as 12 April, Bavarian Prime Minister Edmund Stoiber (CSU chair), returning from a visit to Moscow, worriedly repeated what he had been told in Moscow – that a Nato land invasion of Yugoslavia could trigger World War III.[25] Nor was his an isolated voice within the joint party. Indeed, that same day, the CDU presidium adopted a resolution urging that there be no military escalation and specifically welcoming initiatives from the UN and/or from Russia.[26] In the same resolution, the CDU endorsed the Nato aerial campaign and German participation alike. Two weeks later, the CDU presidium adopted a further resolution, expressly rejecting a ground war in Kosovo. CDU General Secretary Geissler set the tone for the party's Congress in Erfurt, on 26 April, by pleading for a 'just war' in order to bring about world peace.[27]

Milosevic no doubt watched these gyrations with interest. On the eve of the inception of the aerial campaign, Foreign Minister Fischer had been in Belgrade for talks with a man later described by Scharping as 'a dictator from the Middle Ages.'[28] On that occasion, Milosevic had boasted to Fischer that Nato could not win:

I am ready to walk on corpses, and the West is not. This is why I shall win.[29]

The Greens, traditionally a pacifist party, were scarcely prepared to 'walk on corpses'. As early as 9 April, the Berlin district committee of the Alliance 90/Greens adopted a resolution calling for a halt to Nato aerial strikes to allow Milosevic time to reflect in earnest. Milosevic was, at that time, sending his forces on a rampage through Kosovo, tripling the number of homeless within a matter of a few weeks. However, uneasiness within the Green Party continued to grow. By the end of the third week of April, Fischer was warning the left wing of his party that the government coalition would collapse if the party withdrew its support for the campaign. Others worried that the party might split in two. Coalition loyalists, aside from Fischer himself, included defense expert Angelika Beer and foreign policy expert Ludger Volmer, while critics of the Nato campaign included Jürgen Trittin, Minister of Environmental Affairs, and Gila Altmann, parliamentary State Secretary for Environmental Affairs.[30] While Fischer pleaded for party unity, the Baden-Württemberg Greens held a district Congress in Ulm. One hundred and twenty-five delegates voted in favour of the peace conditions drawn up by Fischer, but 84 supported an immediate halt to the aerial strikes.[31] By contrast, some 150 delegates to the district party Congress in Uelzen, Lower Saxony, on 9 May demanded an 'immediate, unilateral, and limited bombing pause.'[32]

> ❝ The Alliance 90/Greens adopted a resolution calling for a halt to Nato aerial strikes to allow Milosevic time to reflect in earnest ❞

Under growing pressure from the rank and file, the Greens met in Bielefeld on 13 May for a chaotic and often stormy party Congress. At stake was not merely the preservation of the coalition government but, quite possibly, the very survival of the Green Party as a unified organization. Amid name-calling, jeers, shouts, and other displays of the complete breakdown of party discipline, those assembled voted 444 to

318 for a motion to support the Nato campaign. Some of the out-voted left wing immediately resigned from the party, while in Hamburg, the left wing split off to form a new 'Green Alternative List'.

The nature of the Nato campaign and the supposed lack of alternatives thus became subjects of intense debate over the course of the conflict, among Social Democrats and Greens alike. Yet Schröder, Scharping, and Fischer were men with solid anti-war credentials who felt that their experience gave them added insight into the current conflicts. As '68ers', they took their decision to participate in the Nato campaign with no trace of *hurra-Patriotismus*.[33] In short, the German troika was articulating a new position for the German left when the three men confidently conceived of a German military action without militarism.

Throughout all of this, perhaps only the strictly 'anti-imperialist' PDS showed no signs of fracture. Denouncing Schröder as 'the war Chancellor,'[34] the PDS thundered against the Nato campaign, demanding an immediate halt to the strikes, the initiation of peace talks under UN auspices, and the provision of material assistance to rebuild the economic infrastructure of Yugoslavia. For the militant left, whether within the PDS or outside it, the aerial campaign had nothing to do with any desire on the part of Western governments to help the Albanians of Kosovo; in the view of the hard left, the Nato campaign was unambiguously motivated by imperialist and capitalist interests.[35]

> 66 For the militant left, the aerial campaign had nothing to do with any desire on the part of Western governments to help the Albanians of Kosovo 99

GERMAN PUBLIC OPINION

The issue of state sovereignty added to the controversy. During the Bosnian War of 1991–5, it was possible to insist that Croatia and Bosnia were 'sovereign' states. In substantiation one could point to their recognition in the diplomatic community and to their admission into the UN. The self-declared government of Ibrahim Rugova – contested, in any event, by the rival government declared by 29-year-old KLA leader Thaci in mid-April 1999[36] – enjoyed neither diplomatic recognition nor UN membership. Controversy, both in Germany and elsewhere in the international community, centred on two questions:

- What conditions could legitimize a 'humanitarian intervention'?
- Could an alliance of states by-pass the deadlocked UN Security Council in meeting a perceived need?

Many Germans were inclined to agree with Reinhard Müller that only the desire to stop genocide could legitimate 'humanitarian intervention'.[37] As for the necessity of UN sanctions, public opinion was more divided.

As of April 1999, 63 per cent of Germans supported German participation in the Nato campaign, with 34 per cent opposed. Support for the campaign was strongest among SPD members, 71 per cent of whom registered their approval, and weakest among PDS members, only 27 per cent of whom supported the bombing.[38] There were also striking differences east and west. Whereas 68 per cent of Western Germans supported the Nato aerial campaign, only 38 per cent of Eastern Germans did so.[39] In Hamburg, a group of 41 lawyers decided to challenge the constitutionality of German participation and filed charges against Chancellor Schröder and Defence Minister Scharping at the Constitutional Court in Karlsruhe. The Constitutional Court would later dismiss the charges.

The Churches also became involved in the debate. The Evangelical Church proved to be internally divided, with Manfred Kock, chairman of the EKD Council, and Bishop Wolfgang Huber of Berlin-Brandenburg expressing firm opposition, the latter characterizing the Nato campaign as murderous. Other Evangelical bishops felt that only force held any promise of ending Serbian violence against the Albanians. The Roman Catholic Church, on the other hand, pointed to a well-established 'just war' tradition and, accordingly, in a statement released in the second half of April, the German Catholic bishops offered a qualified endorsement of the campaign, calling on Nato to minimize harm to innocent civilians and damage to non-strategic infrastructure.[40] Later, in February 2000, in the course of follow-up deliberations, the Central Committee of German Catholics adopted a resolution legitimating the concept of humanitarian interventions, calling their resolution:

a signal to dictators that the protection of human rights cannot be stopped in the name of national sovereignty.[41]

Meanwhile, although the coalition had weathered the political storms at Bielefeld and could even count the outcome of that Congress a qualified victory, public opinion was becoming increasingly impatient with the war, as it dragged into its second month. Milosevic had quite astutely calculated that the 'MTV generation' would have patience only for campaigns producing virtually instantaneous victory. Defence Minister Scharping therefore considered it appropriate, during a speech in Bonn on 14 May, to underline Nato's determination to continue the campaign until its demands were met; at the same time, Nato military spokesperson Walter Jertz advised, in a broadcast carried by Deutschlandfunk Radio, that the left-wing Greens' demand for a temporary bombing halt was 'not helpful'.[42] Calling the end of May for 'a little more patience,' Scharping promised:

> ❝ The 'MTV generation' would have patience only for campaigns producing virtually instantaneous victory ❞

Nato is able to win, Nato will win, and Milosevic knows we will win.[43]

Even as the German government thus reiterated its determination to put a stop to what Joschka Fischer called Milosevic's policy of 'aggressive nationalism,'[44] differences of opinion emerged among the Nato allies, with Britain beginning to advance the case for ground troops as an option, the US starting to waver in its earlier determination to rule them out, Italy urging a bombing pause, and Germany holding to a middle course. Sensitive to the parties' deep reservations about the wisdom of deploying ground troops and fearful that any agreement to go along with such a deployment would spell the end of the SPD–Green coalition government, Fischer (on 18 May) and Schröder (on 19 May) firmly ruled out any such recourse. In a strongly worded statement, Schröder declared, in Brussels, that not only would his country not contribute troops to fight in a land war, but his government would, in fact, veto any such operation, with or without German troops. Schröder explained:

The strategy of an alliance can only be changed if all the parties involved agree on it ... 'I am against any change of Nato strategy'.[45]

By late May, German public support for the war had declined to just 51 per cent (though in neighbouring France, public support for the air campaign remained at a robust 70 per cent, with 60 per cent of the French public even supporting the use of combat troops, in the event that Nato judged such a recourse necessary.[46]

Inevitably, Hitler's ghost haunted German policy debates throughout the Kosovo conflict. German participation in the Nato campaign necessitated overcoming two taboos in the post-war German historical experience. The first of these involved the use of German soldiers outside the Nato area. Such a deployment was originally forbidden by the German *Grundgesetz*. Following the Dayton Peace Accord, a German contingent was sent to Bosnia, bending this rule for the first time, but the Germans had never participated in actual combat since the silencing of Hitler's guns. The second taboo concerned the fact that German soldiers were being sent not just abroad, but abroad in combat to a region where the *Wehrmacht* had perpetrated some of its worst atrocities.[47] For many, this fact was further cause to reject the Nato campaign. Others, however, saw in the Kosovo crisis an opportunity to partly exorcize the demons of the past. They recognized in the Kosovo conflict an opportunity to make atonement for the sins of the previous generation through the vigilant defence of human rights. In Schröder's estimation, Germany had an obligation to return to the Balkans and combat the brutality of the Serbian military campaign against Albanian civilians.

> 66 Germany had an obligation to return to the Balkans and combat the brutality of the Serbian military campaign against Albanian civilians 99

The recognition of the Nato campaign served both as a means of atonement for Germans at home and as a legitimization of German foreign policy in Europe's diplomatic halls. It is essential to remember that Schröder, Fischer, and Scharping belonged to the activist core of a protest generation which had challenged not only the Germany of the 1960s and 1970s, but also the previous generation for its moral and political failures in the 1930s and early 1940s. In an interview with *Der Spiegel*, Schröder related the failures of the previous generation to his role and the responsibilities of contemporary Germany:

There was a very lively debate regarding Hitler's fascism in which children asked their parents: Why did you not do anything at the time? By which they meant, why did you do nothing to prevent it? I would not like to be in a situation in which I must answer similar questions with regard to the brutality in Kosovo. I would like to be able to say in such a situation that I did what was possible and rational.[48]

In sum, the SPD and Green leaderships justified German participation in the Nato campaign on several levels, but all were somehow imbued with Germany's 'special history' and the obligations which derived from it. Fischer even observed that for once in the twentieth century, the Germans were on the right side of a war.

THE SOCIAL DEMOCRATS

Germany's Social Democrats spent 16 years out of power, having lost to Helmut Kohl's CDU/CSU in 1982. When they returned to power in 1998, it was at a time when even many loyal CDU/CSU supporters had become convinced of the need for change in the national leadership. The Social Democrats inherited both benefits and challenges from the outgoing Kohl government. On one hand, Schröder would have the prestige of being the first post-war chancellor to sit in Berlin and manage the transition from Bonn to the Berlin republic. On the other, the costs of reunification had, by 1998, come to exceed a trillion Deutschmarks. Somehow, the Schröder government would have to take steps to increase government revenue while also reducing government commitments. Additionally, steps would have to be taken to make the economy more competitive. Essentially, this ostensibly 'social democratic' government was faced with the politically unenviable task of reducing social services. The SPD was therefore faced with profound internal division surrounding one central dilemma: What is *Sozialgerechtigkeit* in an age of globalization and tight budgets?

Serious tension over the nature and extent of the reforms needed and disagreement about how to handle the developing crisis in Kosovo led to a showdown of sorts between the SPD's modernizing chancellor and Oskar Lafontaine, the party's traditionally socialist chair and finance minister in the Schröder government. The two had long had a tense relationship, as befitting a reforming pragmatist and a more traditional progressive, and the Kosovo crisis contributed handily to the demise of their working relationship. Schröder had earlier articulated a willingness to follow America's lead in Kosovo, a policy which Lafontaine considered reckless. In a cabinet meeting shortly before his resignation, Lafontaine aggressively and relentlessly probed the chancellor as regards the costs, legal basis, and goals of his Kosovo policy. Soon thereafter, Lafontaine refused, as finance minister, to release funds requested by Defence Minister Scharping to cover costs associated with the *Bundeswehr's* activities in the Balkans. When Schröder sided with his Defence Minister and ordered Lafontaine to release the money, the finance minister abruptly resigned on 11 March 1999. He quit his post as party chair at the same time. Lafontaine's resignation was greeted with dismay by some at least. Economic reformers and those inclined to favour Nato's stance on Kosovo were relieved, however. Schröder now had a free hand to manage the government as he saw fit. With no apparent rivals, the chancellor also appeared likely to inherit the job of party chair, a party congress was scheduled with the aim of formally confirming the change in leadership, while allowing also for a discussion of the developing situation in Kosovo. In fact, Lafontaine's resignation had less to do with the administration's policies in Kosovo than it did with domestic and ideological matters. Kosovo served as 'the last straw' so to speak. Nevertheless, his resignation and subsequent withdrawal from public life were evidence of an extreme dissatisfaction among elements of the SPD with the Schröder government and its policies on Kosovo. Despite calls for party discipline, a perceptible grumbling increased in volume during the weeks preceding the party congress. Party leftists planned a series of resolutions against German military participation in the campaign. The Young Socialists led by Andrea Nahles let it be known that they would introduce a resolution 'in which the immediate end to the attacks would be demanded.' Benjamin Mikfeld, a left-leaning member of the party's executive committee demanded a truce from Nato. The party's leftist 'Frankfurt Circle' drafted a resolution demanding that the government end hostilities immediately and work toward a cease-fire. Others like Gernot Erler wanted the cessation of the attacks to be made contingent upon the ending of the expulsions of the Kosovo Albanians by Serbian forces. Finally, at the party congress itself, the party leftists and other opponents of the Nato campaign combined forces to produce a joint resolution.

> 66 At the party congress itself, the party leftists and other opponents of the Nato campaign combined forces to produce a joint resolution 99

Although a strong minority did work to halt the Nato campaign, ultimately neither left nor right proved to be so extreme at the congress. The resolutions originally planned by the left were toned down from demanding an unconditional truce to proposing only 'the immediate interruption of hostilities with a limited ceasefire, in order to negotiate a proper truce.'[49] This resolution was rejected by the delegates. Much of the party's left wing and other delegates inclined toward pacifism were simply overcome by the perceived impotence of the West to compel the Milosevic regime to respect human rights through negotiations, treaties, and OSCE observers. Iris Gleike, a former member of the East German opposition *Friedensbewegung*, is just such a person. In spite of her commitment to peace and notwithstanding her belief that war could not be a means to make policy, she declined to sign the resolution of the party leftists.

A Yugoslav army soldier guards a Russian made NEVA (SAM) anti-aircraft rocket system near Pristina. The deployment of this system obliged NATO to bomb from a minimum altitude of 15,000 feet. (March 1998. Photo by STR. © Reuters 1998.)

Members of the Kosovo Liberation Army (KLA) take cover in the village of Grabovac near Pristina. The KLA was increasingly active in attacking Serb military and paramilitary forces in the months leading up to NATO intervention. (25 June 1998. Photo by STR. © Reuters 1998.)

US envoy Richard Holbrooke (l) shakes hands with Yugoslav President Slobodan Milosevic before talks in Belgrade. Holbrooke and Milosevic plunged back into marathon and fruitless talks over the Kosovo crisis as NATO bombers were readied for a military action. (12 October 1998. Photo by Emil Vas. © Reuters 1998.)

REUNION DE RAMBOUILLET

Contact group ministers seen during the final press conference of the inconclusive Kosovo talks in Rambouillet, west of Paris. They are (l–r): Russian Vice Foreign Minister Alexander Avdeiv, German Foreign Minister Jochka Fischer, British Foreign Minister Robin Cook, French Foreign Minister Hubert Vedrine, US Secretary of State Madeleine Albright, Italian Foreign Minister Lamberto Dini and Dutch Foreign Minister Jozias Van Adsen. (23 February 1999. Photo by Jean-Christophe Kahn. © Reuters 1999.)

The Kosovo Albanians sign a symbolic international peace plan for the Serbian province, but without the Yugoslav delegation, at a ceremony at the Kleber conference centre in Paris. (l–r, front row) Albanian delegate and newspaper editor Veton Surroi, Political Albanian leader Ibrahim Rugova, Kosovo Liberation Army political director Hashim Thaqi and Albanian politician Rexhep Qosja. The three contact group members standing behind are Boris Maiorski of Russia, Christopher Hill of the USA and Wolfgang Petritsch of Austria. (18 March 1999. Photo by John Schults. © Reuters 1999.)

A USAF F-16 Falcon fighter takes off from Aviano's NATO air base 24 March, prior to NATO air strikes at Yugoslav military targets in Kosovo. The decision for the attack was launched by NATO Secretary-General Javier Solana after President Milosevic refused to resolve the Kosovo crisis. At bottom of the picture is a Boeing 707 Awac early warning plane. (24 March 1999. Photo by Vincenzo Pinto. © Reuters 1999.)

Belgraders hold banners and flags during a protest against NATO air raids on Yugoslavia in Belgrade's centre during the first week of the campaign. (30 March 1999. Photo by Petar Kujundzic. © Reuters 1999.)

Some 4,000 ethnic Albanian Kosovars walk on the railway line into Macedonia after disembarking from a train at the General Jankovic border crossing in Yugoslav territory. Eyewitnesses claimed that the Kosovars were forced into the train by Serbian forces in Pristina and transported with their few belongings at the Yugoslav-Macedonian border where they were deported. Pictures such as these were instrumental in maintaining public support in the West for NATO intervention. (1 April 1999. Photo by Yannis Behrakis. © Reuters 1999.)

After three hours of debate, delegates endorsed a resolution supporting the government's policy on Kosovo and laying down conditions for suspension of military measures against Yugoslavia. These included:

- withdrawal of military forces from the province
- stationing of international security forces in Yugoslavia
- return of refugees and international refugee organizations
- signing of a treaty based on the Rambouillet agreement.

Emphasizing the responsibility of the Yugoslav authorities, the resolution made clear that hostilities would be suspended only when they had fulfilled the conditions outlined.

Ultimately, Schröder and his backers carried the day at the party congress. The Chancellor's course had been contested but prevailed. Schröder spoke at length about Kosovo and German responsibility and sought to assuage his critics when he assured them that:

Whoever opposes war out of fundamental principle will continue to find a political home in the SPD.[50]

The Schröder-Lafontaine conflict appeared little in evidence and Schroder was elected party chair, as expected. But with a smaller majority than normal for such an election: indicating that real dissatisfaction with his government's policies persisted within his party.[51]

Shortly after the party congress, Lafontaine re-emerged from his self-imposed seclusion to grant several interviews and give a speech before an audience of 12,000. He emphasized that he did not exclude military attacks on Yugoslavia altogether, while objecting to the methods used. He condemned the labelling of Schröder as a 'War Chancellor' (*Kriegskanzler*) and to the comparison offered by one member of the audience, who likened Schröder to Hitler.[52]

THE GREENS

The Green Party is in many ways more of an alternative movement than a party. It has a rather non-traditional party structure and includes elements who challenge the notion of government entirely. These anarchistically inclined members, known as 'Fundis', are opposed by the more 'pragmatic' moderates, called 'Realos', who seek to advance the Green agenda through participation in government. Joschka Fischer, as noted earlier, belongs very solidly in the latter camp and, as foreign minister, was at the centre of the Green Party debate about Kosovo. It was his task both to represent Germany abroad and to lead his party at home. As a long-time pacifist, Fischer was himself beset by doubts and conflict over the best course of German action. Nonetheless, he was defiant enough in his support for the Nato operation that many speculated that he would even leave the Greens and join the SPD in the event that the party abandoned his line. Fischer dismissed such speculation as rubbish. When dissent and division in the Green Party came to a head at the party's extraordinary congress on 13 May, at stake was not only the future of the Red–Green coalition, but, quite possibly, the very survival of the Green Party as a unified organization. Challenges to Fischer's line came from many persons, among them Annelie Buntenbach, Monika Knoche, Steffi Lemke, Irmingard Schewe-Gerigt, Christian Ströbele, and Sylvia Voss. Many of these critics had voiced indignation at the onset of the Nato campaign, calling it a war of aggression and demanding a return of the monopoly of legitimate violence to the most legitimate international organization, the UN. Emphasizing that war could never be an alternative, *Bundestag* deputy Buntenbach objected that not all options had been exhausted before the onset of hostilities. In her view, the Nato action was incapable of achieving its stated goals, and bombing was only worsening the situation. Furthermore, she expressed fear of an automatic logic of escalation and advocated not merely a bombing pause, but a complete stop to the Nato campaign. Lastly, Buntenbach criticized the action as profoundly counterproductive in that it had rendered Nato an illegitimate mediator by suddenly making the alliance a warring party in the region. Christian Ströbele (another *Bundestag* deputy) and others seconded these concerns, but also concurred with Buntenbach's call to remain in the government in order to change its policies from within.

> 66 At stake was not only the future of the Red–Green coalition, but the very survival of the Green Party as a unified organization 99

Others at the congress, such as defence policy spokesperson Angelika Beer, defended government policies and emphasized contributions which Fischer and other parliamentary *Bundestagfraktion* had been able to make toward resolving the conflict, especially Fischer's insistence on keeping the door open to opportunities for negotiation. Favouring a cease-fire, Beer nonetheless concluded her address by calling on party members to support the resolution which upheld government policy, but also called on Nato to declare itself ready for a humanitarian cease-fire.

The resolution passed at Bielefeld largely, though not totally, reflected the views of Fischer, while also acknowledging the views of others. In broad terms, the document supports the Nato campaign, but with clear misgivings. It lays out the grounds and goals of the Nato campaign, pointing out that Milosevic himself could stop the war at any time. The resolution nonetheless criticizes Nato for not having exhausted all alternatives before resorting to war. Furthermore, it is critical of the alliance for having acted without a UN mandate, thereby, allegedly, undermining the organization while reinforcing suspicions that Nato would itself like to assume the UN's role as keeper of the peace in Europe. The resolution called on Nato to declare a cease-fire and return the monopoly of legitimate violence to the UN. Acknowledging that the Greens must ask themselves fundamental questions on the orientation of their foreign, security, and peace policies, it nonetheless rejects surrender of pacifism as a guiding Green principle.

The document is most notable where it acknowledges the fundamental conflict of principles faced by the Greens over Kosovo and where it outlines the lessons learned in Bosnia, particularly at Srebrenica. Although the resolution calls for the introduction of peacekeepers under a UN mandate, it specifically states that these peacekeepers must also have the task of 'peace enforcement'. As regards principles, it observes that many Greens had been confronted with one of the most difficult decisions of their lives: the apparent choice between the rejection of violence and the defence of human rights. The resolution observes that it must be a priority of the Green Party to find a means to combine these two objectives. How to resolve these two seemingly contradictory imperatives? At present, there seems to be no objective answer. Therefore, the party emphasizes the need for respect and dissent within the party, while recognizing the party's ability to cooperate despite differences.[53]

> 66 Many Greens had been confronted with one of the most difficult decisions of their lives: the apparent choice between the rejection of violence and the defence of human rights 99

All told, the Bielefeld congress was a victory for the 'Realo' wing of the Green Party. The resolution supporting the government's line was passed and the party held together.[54] That said, the Greens had to confront certain potentially contradictory, fundamental tenets of their ideology and their *raison d'être*. The party emerged from the congress with a louder voice, if not a unified one. Compromise became inevitable owing to the political realities of majority politics and the demands of existing in a coalition government. This has prompted at least one observer to wonder what the *raison d'être* for a Green Party stripped of its radicalism might be.[55] If participation in government means surrendering precisely those goals that define a particular party, then does it make sense for that party to enter into the government at all? This was a dilemma the Spanish Anarchists had confronted in the mid-1930s, when they joined the government of the Republic.

CONCLUSION

By 1 June, the war had cost the German Bundeswehr more than 400 million Deutschmarks (of which 288 million Marks was to replace the German 'harm' missiles used in Serbia).[56] With the negotiated settlement in early June, Germany stood prepared to enlarge its Balkan peacekeeping contingent to 8,500 men, at a total cost of 811 million DM for 1999 (in addition to the 460 million DM already spent on the German contingent in the Bosnian SFOR peacekeeping force).[57] As these forces moved to take up positions, German politicians began to discuss just when the roughly 194,000 Kosovo Albanian refugees in Germany might begin to return to their homeland.[58]

Nonetheless, the German coalition government, consisting of two parties, did not follow the exact line of the US. On the contrary, driven especially by Foreign Minister Joschka Fischer, Germany asserted itself as it never had before in international affairs, insistently working to keep the prospect of negotiations at least open, while simultaneously endorsing participation in Nato's aerial campaign. Foreign Minister Fischer promoted his peace plan in European capitals and in Washington, and eventually won the support of Nato and also of the G-8, whose chairmanship Germany held. This initially led to some tensions within the government, and Schröder at first distanced himself from, and then denied the existence of, a 'German peace plan'. In time, however, the double strategy of bombing while simultaneously working for peace was instrumental in bringing Russia to support Nato goals, at the same time that the Fischer plan was being widened to include Russia's perspectives and interests.[59]

Shortly after Martti Ahtisaari's announcement in Cologne of Belgrade's acquiescence to the revised Fischer plan, and with reference to Security Council Resolution 1244, which provided Nato with the UN mandate it had long lacked, the *Bundestag* formally approved the deployment of

Bundeswehr soldiers in Kosovo, with majority support from all parties except the PDS. As part of the Fischer peace initiative, a Stability Pact was envisioned for the Balkans which would address regional security problems as a package.

Except for the PDS, all parties became divided over the Kosovo crisis. The CDU and FDP suffered some doubts, as did the SDP. But the Green Party was brought face to face with the existential question of its very being and purpose by the Kosovo crisis and the 'Realos' endorsement of the Nato campaign. Throughout the crisis, and after, Foreign Minister Fischer made statements that would have been unthinkable for a Green leader only a few years earlier. Fischer came to recognize in Nato and the military a potential tool for humanitarian intervention, even as he and his party continued to warn against the self-mandating of Nato and feared the logic of automatic military escalation. At times, Fischer even sounded enthusiastic about Nato. Similarly, Schröder, who had once passionately opposed the defence policies of Helmut Schmidt, embraced an approach strikingly reminiscent of his political forebear.

> 66 Fischer came to recognize in Nato and the military a potential tool for humanitarian intervention 99

In October 1998, *The Economist* wrote:

as yet, there is no reason for other countries to fear a Schröder administration, even if its assessment of Germany's national interests may be far more jarring to its neighbours than Mr. Kohl's used to be. That, after all, will be evidence of normality.[59]

Any student of German foreign affairs cannot but be struck with the frequency with which the term 'normality' comes up, as a standard against which to measure Germany, generally with the unspoken assumption and implication that Britain, France, Greece, Spain, Italy, and perhaps also Canada and the US are all 'normal' countries. And this, in turn, is very much a legacy of World War II, the Third Reich, and notions of collective German guilt. More specifically, until the Bosnian War, the German government did not allow itself the 'luxury' of committing armed forces to any operations 'out of area', and played a distinctly self-effacing role in Nato councils.[60] With the German commitment in connection with the Dayton Peace Accord and with German participation in the Nato operations against Yugoslavia in 1999, one may well ask whether it is time to speak of the Federal Republic of Germany as having 'come of age', or, to put it in the more usual if also more problematic terms, whether Germany was now a 'normal' country.

'Normality' has been an elusive quality for Germany since World War II, both in terms of confidence towards its allies and in terms of its trust in itself. For many Germans, the *Grundgesetz*'s prohibition of the use of the *Wehrmacht* 'out of area' was merely the legal expression of an acknowledged sentiment, which derived from the horror of Nazi crimes during World War II. Although the German leadership has more than earned the trust of its allies, it was confronted during the Kosovo crisis with the need to take difficult and often unpopular decisions to demonstrate support for the Atlantic alliance.

In the midst of the Kosovo crisis, outgoing German president Roman Herzog observed a transformation among the German people who, only years before could never have imagined the deployment of the *Bundeswehr* abroad, and yet, in 1999, demonstrated support, with a heavy conscience, for such deployment in lands formerly occupied by the *Wehrmacht*.

❝ Germans have embraced human rights as a central doctrine of policy ❞

Nonetheless, Herzog locates the change not in a German perception that the country should play a normal role in international affairs, but in the fact that Germans have embraced human rights as a central doctrine of policy. In the willingness of Germans to use military power abroad, Herzog observes not the expression of a normalization process, but rather a resolute desire for peace and the recognition that one should not champion human rights only with mere words. There are situations in which the use of force is the only way in which to defend those rights.

Has Germany become a 'normal' member of the community of nations as a result of its active foreign policy? Wolfgang Ischinger, state secretary of the foreign office since October 1998 and one of Germany's most experienced diplomats, is pessimistic, but has recognized Germany's changed role:

We are not a totally normal country, and will not become one in the foreseeable future either. We must remain conscious of the fact that our neighbours and partners do not consider us an entirely normal country...That's simply the way things are. What has been accomplished, however, is that the Federal Republic of Germany can now make contributions towards answering the challenges, such as the search for a peace settlement in Kosovo, that are commensurate with its weight, its role, its economic standing, and its military structure. This means that we are now able to make 'normal' contributions.[61]

Clearly Kosovo stands as an important chapter in post-war German history. Germany may not have been 'definitively emancipated from its post-war pacifism', as Roger Cohen claimed following the first night of the Nato campaign.[62] However, Germany is hardly the same place it was before that night. Whether or not Germany is a 'normal' country, it has come a long way since the débâcle of World War II. When German troops returned to the Balkans, they did so with the express mission of preventing ethnic cleansing, not furthering it. The Bonn Republic has become the Berlin Republic – a state with liberal-democratic values and the self-confidence that goes with Nato membership.

NOTES

1 Details in Sabrina P. Ramet with Letty Coffin, 'German Foreign policy *vis-à-vis* the Yugoslav Successor States, 1991-99', manuscript under review.

2 *Neue Zürcher Zeitung* 4 December 1995, 1.

3 *Süddeutsche Zeitung* (Munich), 1 December 1995 on *Lexis-Nexis Academic Universe*; and *Deutsche Presse-Agentur* (Hamburg), 6 December 1995 on *Lexis-Nexis Academic Universe*.

4 Troebst 1998.

5 Jens Reuter, 'Die internationale Gemeinschaft und der Kreig in Kosovo', in *Südost Europa*, 47, (7/8) July–August 1998, 289.

6 *Ibid*. p. 284.

7 Sabrina P. Ramet 1999b, 67.

8 Stenger 1999: 143.

9 Klaus Kinkel 1999: 214.

10 Troebst 1999: 784–5.

11 Quoted in *ibid*.

12 For details see Ramet 1999: 313–14.

13 Details in *ibid*. p. 315.

14 Quoted in *New York Times* 4 November 1998, A10.

15 *Illyria* 27 January–3 February 1991, 1.

16 Lipsius 1999: 359–60.

17 *Frankfurter Allgemeine Zeitung* 16 March 1999, 1.

18 Quoted in Zumach 1999: 63. See also *Frankfurter Allgemeine Zeitung* 13 April 1999, 6.

19 'Erklärung von Bundeskanzler Gerhard Schröder der Lage Kosovo', Pressemitteilung Nr. 111/99 vom 24. März 1999, at www.bundeskanzler.de/13/13/.

20 'Der stellvertretende Parteivorsitzende, bundesverteidigungsminister Rudolph Scharping zur Krise im Kosovo', Rede vor dem Deutschen Bundestag am 25. Marz 1999, at www.spd.de/politik/kosovo/scharpinghtm.

21 *Ibid.*

22 Arnulf Barung, 'Aufgabe im Ostern', in *Die Woche* (Hamburg), 29 April 1999, 8.

23 'Beschluss des a.o. Parteitages zum Kosovo-Konflikt' (12 April 99), at
    www.spd.de/politik/kosovo/parteig120499.htm; and 'Gespannte Ruhe' in *Der
    Spiegel* (Hamburg), 29 April 1999, at
    www.spiegel.de/politik/deutschland/nf//0.1518,16770.html.

24 *Frankfurter Allgemeine Zeitung* 29 April 1999, 3.

25 *Frankfurter Allgemeine Zeitung* 13 April 1999, 7.

26 Neue politische Initiativen sind unverzichtbar, um das Leiden und Sterben im
    Kosovo zu beenden' (12 April 1999) at www.cdu.de/presse/archiv/pro47-99htm.

27 *Frankfurter Allgemeine Zeitung* (27 April 1999), p.3.

28 Quoted in *Süddeutche Zeitung* 19–20 June 1999, 13.

29 Quoted in Josef Joffe, 'A Peacenik Goes to War' in *New York Times Magazine*
    30 May 1999, 31.

30 *Die Welt* 21 April 1999, at
    www.welt.de/extra/brennpunkte/kosovo/artikel317.htm; and *Frankfurter
    Allgemeine Zeitung* 22 April 1999, 2. See also AND (Berlin) 21 April 1999 in
    BBC Monitoring Europe-Political 22 April 1999 on *Lexis-Nexis Academic Universe.*

31 *Frankfurter Allgemeine Zeitung* 26 April 1999, 5.

32 Quoted in *Frankfurter Allgemeine Zeitung* 10 May 1999, 5.

33 'Ich bin kein Kreigskanzler', in *Der Spiegel* 12 April 1999, 34.

34 *Frankfurter Allgemeine Zeitung* 26 April 1999, p. 8.

35 *Frankfurter Allgemeine Zeitung* (4 May 1999), p. 3. See also Elasser 1999.

36 *Frankfurter Allgemeine Zeitung* 13 April 1999, 2. For a history of the ministers in
    the Kosovo 'transitional government' as of mid-September 1999, see 1999b, 498.

37 Reinhard Müller, 'Ein Recht auf Unabhängigkeit', in *Frankfurter Allgemeine
    Zeitung* 9 April 1999, 5.

38 *The Economist* (London), 24 April 1999, 51.

39 Der Krieg spaltet die Deutsche in Ost und West', in *die Tageszeitung* (Berlin),
    13 April 1999, at www.pds-online.de/1/zukunft/9904/wittich.htm.

40 *Frankfurter Allgemeine Zeitung* 21 April 1999, 4, and 24 April 1999, 5; 'Papst und
    Bischofe: Frieden im Kosovo' in *Kirchenzeitung*, Bistumer Fulda, Limburg and
    Mainz 11 April 1999 at www.kirchenzeitung.de:81/kizartik; 'Bischofe: Nato soll
    Gewalt begrenzen' in *Kirchenzeitung* (23 April 1999) at
    www.kirchenzeitung.de:81/kizartik; and 'Zentralkomitee der deutschen
    Katholiken (ZdK) aussert sich erstmals zum Kosovo-Kreig' in *Kirchenzeitung*
    2 May 1999, at www.kirchenzeitung.de:81/kizartik.

41 Quoted in *Süddeutsche Zeitung* 25 February 2000, 6.

42 AND (Berlin), 14 May 1999, trans. in *BBC Monitoring Europe – Political*
    14 May 1999, on *Lexis-Nexis Academic Universe.*

43 Quoted in 'Yahoo! Headlines' (24 May 1999) at
    www.yahoo.co.uk/headlines/1999524/news/9275441000-3-1.html.

44 Quoted in *The Week in Germany* 28 May 1999, 2.

45 Quoted in *New York Times* 20 May 1999, A12.

46 *New York Times* 26 May 1999, A12.

47 Regarding the Wehrmacht's role in Serbia, see: Jonathan Steinberg, *All or Nothing: The Axis and the Holocaust, 1941–1943* (London and New York: Routledge, 1990); Karl-Heinz Schlarp, *Wirtschaft und Besatzung in Serbien 1941–1944* (Stuttgart: Franz Steiner Verlag, 1986); and Branko Petranovic, *Srbija u drugom svetskom ratu 1939–1945* (Belgrade: Vojnoizdavacki i novinski centar, 1992).

48 Schröder in "Ich bin kein Kreigskanzler', in *Der Speigel* 12 April 1999, 35.

49 *taz* 13 April 1999 on LNAU.

50 Quoted in *taz* 13 April 1999 on LNAU.

51 *Ibid.*

52 'Lafontaine kritisiert Kosovo-Politik', ZDF.MSNBC (25 April 1999) at w3zdf.msnbc.de/news/32906.asp.

53 *Ibid.*

54 In spite of some key resignations, such as that of Green Party's founder.

55 Sabine von Dirke, 'Where have all the flowers gone? The German Green-Alternative Movement between Utopian Idealism and Political Pragamatism', lecture at the University of Washington. Seattle (4 May 1999).

56 *Deutsche Presse-Agentur* 2 June 1999 at www.yahoo.de/schlagzeilen.

57 *Frankfurter Allgemeine Zeitung* 9 June 1999, 3.

58 180,000 had been in Germany for several years already; the other 14,000 had fled to Germany during 1999. *Die Welt* 18 June 1999 at www.welt.de/daten/1999/06/18/0618del118198.htx.

59 *The Economist* (London), 3 October 1998, 20.

60 *Der Spiegel* 5 April 1999, 30.

61 Interview with Wolfgang Ischinger, in *Deutschland*, August/September 1999, 18.

62 Roger Cohen, 'Half a Century after Hitler, German Jets Join the Attack' in *New York Times* 26 March 1999 at codoh.com/newsdesk/99326.html.

6

FRANCE: QUESTIONS OF IDENTITY

BERNARD LAMIZET AND SYLVIE DEBRAS

A CRISIS OF IDENTITY

The place of the Kosovo conflict within the long-term French memory of European history prevents us from considering it as a predominantly territorial or political war as in other cases of war in Europe. In France at least, it was viewed as a conflict centred upon the issue of identity where what was at stake was the expression of national identity, and of the recognition of this identity on the world stage. Thus in *Le Monde* of 1 April 1999, J. Viard points out:

> 66 What is at stake is the expression of national identity, and of the recognition of this identity on the world stage 99

The world of the southern Slavs is one of two nodal points – the other being Germany – connecting areas of large migrational activity and its accompanying myths which cross our continent.

The Kosovo conflict was not therefore viewed merely as a regional war which as such would have been of less interest to the media, but as a war of identity whose symbolic dimensions extend beyond the physical boundaries of the region to raise a series of wider political issues. This is why the Kosovo conflict was the opportunity for the French media to recall the history of the former Yugoslavia, reminding the French that the birth of this country formed part of the historical process of the development of national identities in Europe. As B. Feron writes in *Le Monde* of 17 April 1999:

The concept of Yugoslavia would not have taken root had not the Hapsburgs lost the war of 1914–18.

Thus the French media recognized that the Kosovo conflict was of a kind that distinguished it from other European wars: the birth of Europe as a political space lies at the very heart of the conflict. However, *Libération* of 23 April 1999 also locates the conflict in another domain of the French collective memory of the twentieth century, that of the Cold War between East and West and of which Nato is a dominant symbol. The conflict is therefore also located in the collective memory and discourse that springs from the division of the world between East and West following World War II.

The particular nature of the concept of identity formation, and the historic place that it occupies in media discourse and political communication is the key to understanding how the French media have reported the Kosovo conflict. The periodical *Cahiers de la Médiologie* of September 1999 stressed the importance of 'beliefs' in the ideological development of public opinion about the war in France. According to François Bernard Huyghe in the same issue:

War is located in a bizarre metaphorical place ... on one hand it reactivates the past ... on the other, one adversary produces its own symbolic accomplishments and signs which it sets within the reactivated historical context in order to invalidate the signs and symbols of the opposing foe.

War is thus removed to the symbolic setting of conflicting forms of identity. And in this respect, the representation of the conflict in the French media is not dissimilar from others such as the Vietnam War, which for much of the French media was the founding event in the representation of war in the post-1945 era. The French media represented the Kosovo war as the dramatization of a claim to identity, which explains, on one hand, the emphasis placed upon the conditions in which Yugoslavia disappeared as a nation (*Le Monde*, 17 April 1999):

Once upon a time there was a country called Yugoslavia

and on the other, the reaction of the media to the ethnic dimension given to the conflict by president Milosevic (*Le Monde*, 6 April 1999):

The allied dilemma is either to accept ethnic cleansing or risk destabilizing the host countries.

In the media-generated debate in France, the ethnic dimension to the national identity issue in Kosovo ran counter to the political and diplomatic ones of non-intervention and the recognition of the sovereignty of a country like Yugoslavia. That is why the French media insisted from the beginning on presenting two strands of opposition to the events in Kosovo. The first was political in nature and directed against the regime of President Milosevic, and the second was humanitarian aimed at saving the majority population of Kosovo. These two strands within the reporting of the war explain, among other things, the importance of the personalization of the conflict as being between the Serbian president Milosevic and the Albanian opposition leader Ibrahim Rugova, the latter's activities being compared with those of the French Resistance against the Nazi occupation of France during World War II.

The place of the identity issue in the discourse of the French media is a complex matter[1] because the history of France itself has seen its identity called into question on several occasions in modern times. This is why the conflict in Kosovo attracted so much attention in the French media and, more generally, in what one may call the ideological and political imagination of French consciousness. In its first aspect the identity issue relates to Kosovo itself, and the conflict between Serbs and ethnic Albanians was compared to that of the French Resistance against the occupier and to the role that this movement played in the sustaining of French national identity during World War II. In *Le Monde* of 4 May 1999, the Albanian writer Ismael Kadare writes:

After the holocaust against the Jews, this new foul deed weighs heavily upon people's consciences.

The second aspect of the identity issue relates to the attitudes of France, through the Kosovo conflict, to the period of decolonization and the Algerian war. Jacques Almaric and Jean-Francois Helvig for example write in *Libération* of 9 May 1999:

Using the Algerian analogy, is it not the case that the KLA is the expression of national feeling in a way similar to that of the FLN [Front de Libération Nationale]?

In this respect, the political culture of the media in France is widely dominated by the importance of the question of decolonization; a process which constituted the founding crisis of the Fifth Republic.[2] The third aspect of the media response to the identity issue is linked to the questions of the independence of France, and Europe generally, from the influence of the US. This gives the identity issue in Kosovo for the French an added international dimension. Pierre Haski in *Libération* of 26 April 1999, writes:

The nineteen [Nato allies] have succeeded in putting on a common front in the carrying out of military operations and expressed a strong solidarity with the countries of the region.

Also, Jean-Marie Colombani, the editor-in-chief of *Le Monde* writes in an editorial of 8 April 1999:

This is why this war is not, despite appearances of a unified command, an American war: it is about the future of Europe.

These three different approaches to ways of framing the issue of Kosovo identity illustrate the complexity of information on this topic in the French media. Indeed, this war was not merely the simple object of information and interest for the French; it was not a simple event on which the media felt obliged to report to their readers: it was a crisis that represented a symbolic condensation of identity issues which France has had to confront since World War II. In other words, the Kosovo crisis was the opportunity for the French media to recall the conditions in which French national identity and French political culture themselves were created in the second half of the twentieth century.

> 66 The Kosovo crisis was the opportunity for the French media to recall the conditions in which French national identity and French political culture themselves were created 99

THE PLACE OF THE BALKANS CONFLICT IN FRENCH POLITICAL CULTURE

The cultural heritage in the relations between France and the former Yugoslavia is particularly complex. On one hand, during World War I, France was, from the beginning, the ally of Serbia against Austria, on the other, in the post-1945 period,[3] French foreign policy of non-alignment in some ways resembled the policies of Tito after World War II. In these circumstances Yugoslavia has a special place in French political culture. This explains why the French media have been particularly sensitive to conflicts in the region. This sensitivity is well illustrated in the *Le Monde* editorial of 8 April 1999:

Why is France, along with others, going to war with Serbia? In what calling? And in the name of which vital interest in a region that the past has taught us to be cautious about, and against a country which historically was one of our staunchest allies?

By emphasizing the apparent rupture between French policy in Kosovo and its past policy towards Serbia, *Le Monde* shed light upon the special nature of the war in Kosovo for the French compared with other wars when France was on the Serbian side. For France to be such an active participant of an American-led alliance in the light of its past foreign policy of independence from the USA was also anomalous and these two factors caused considerable turmoil and rethinking of political positions within all the major political parties in France. We shall examine these realignments internal to French politics in a later section. At this point, however, we need to look more closely at the position of France with regard to Nato.

> 66 For France to be such an active participant of an American-led alliance in the light of its past foreign policy of independence from the USA was anomalous 99

FRANCE AND THE NATO ALLIANCE: A CHANGING RELATIONSHIP

It was in 1966 when on the initiative of De Gaulle, France withdrew from the integrated military command of Nato and, while it has never left the alliance completely, its relationship has been one of indirect association. In 1995 President Chirac proposed a closer link with Nato's military command structure and this initiative was interrupted in 1997 following the refusal of the US to 'Europeanize' the Nato Southern Command based at Naples. France therefore is not a full member of the integrated Nato military command structure. Incidentally, it is worth noting that it was within this kind of context that President Chirac along with other European leaders, notably Prime Minister Tony Blair, proposed the setting up of a European Defence Force and the development of a common European foreign defence policy.[4] This proposal however did not and has not prevented the French army from participating in joint military operations with Nato in special circumstances. One such occasion, of course, was the Gulf War: a military operation involving French troops under an overall American command. This kind of participation on the part of France is a long way from the Gaullist policies of the 1960s and 1970s where France studiously maintained a distance between itself and the USA. The presidencies of Giscard d'Estaing and Mitterrand, while wary of the Americans, were more 'Atlantic' in disposition, an attitude that gave rise to considerable political tensions within government in France during the 1981–95 period, particularly with the Communist Party.[5]

Arguably, the French acceptance of American supremacy in the Kosovo context could be explained by three factors. The first was the categorical rejection of the policies of Milosevic, in particular the perceived policy of 'ethnic cleansing' which reminded the French of the camps in Bosnia and which had as its objective the deportation of Kosovo Albanians out of Kosovo into the adjacent countries of the region. This policy was judged as separating the Serbia of 1999 from the Serbia (and Yugoslavia) of the past, which until 1999 had been supported by France, i.e. the Serbia of 1914 upheld against the Turks, that of 1940 against Germany, and of 1945 upheld in support of Tito's stand of non-alignment.

The second reason for the commitment of France to the American side, which also holds good for its commitment eight years earlier in the Gulf War, is the implicit 'rapprochement' between the two countries begun in the Giscard presidency and continued under those of Mitterrand and Chirac. These three presidents, having fewer reasons for maintaining a distance between themselves and the USA, were significantly more 'Atlantic' in outlook than either De Gaulle or Pompidou.

The third reason for the 'rapprochement' between France and the USA when confronting Milosevic is no doubt linked with internal ideological and political factors, the continued weakening of European communism generally, and the disappearance of the former Eastern Bloc. These factors too, brought about a narrowing of the distance separating France and American policies. From an opposite viewpoint, these factors also explain firstly, the support given by Jean-Marie Le Pen (leader of the original National Front Party) to the Serbs, and secondly, and apparently incongruously, the rejection of the anti-Serb and pro-American position of the government by certain politicians such as Charles Pasqua (former Gaullist and supporter of the traditional RPR) and J.-P Chevènement (former socialist and supporter of the Socialist Party).

Thus, for these and other reasons, in France and in French media culture, the Kosovo conflict represents a turning point because France, for the first time, is not a Serbian ally, but instead finds itself on the side of

Nato, the enemy of Serbia. Hence, the media were obliged to underline the difficulty of the French position and the particular nature of the latter compared with the positions of other Nato allies. For this reason, too, the French media frequently emphasized the common view held by both the French president and the prime minister, who belong to opposed political parties. A photo published on the front page of *Le Monde* of 9 April 1999 showed the two men in close physical proximity and was accompanied by this subtitle:

> 66 The Kosovo conflict represents a turning point because France, for the first time, is not a Serbian ally 99

Jacques Chirac and Lionel Jospin have displayed complete unanimity of views on military options, the refugee question and the way of dealing with Milosevic.

THE SPECIAL POSITION OF PRESIDENT CHIRAC

Again, we need to pause for a moment to examine the special position of the French President in the context of the Kosovo crisis. The complexity of the position of the president, and in a more general way, that of the neo-Gaullist party of which he is a key member, can only be explained by a contradiction. The Gaullist right in France does not share the commitments or the values of the European liberal right (these are more properly espoused by the UDF). In particular, as already intimated, the Gaullist right was characterized by a strong antipathy for the foreign policies of the USA and, during the period of the Cold War division of Europe, by a certain affinity with the views of the former Soviet Union and with those of the Eastern Bloc countries generally. But such a position runs counter to the needs of internal political development in France and in particular to the strategic need for a closer link between the Gaullist right and the liberal right in order to confront the Front National.

It could therefore be argued that the very anti-Serb position adopted by Chirac may be explained by a genuine rejection of the totalitarian tendencies of Slobodan Milosevic which was no doubt linked with a basic feeling of anti-communism causing him to repudiate everything remotely connected with the communist party, however deformed and delinquent as represented by the policies of Milosevic.

Beyond this, (and this is a matter of speculation on our part), we wonder whether in this rejection of Milosevic, Chirac is seeking to place his personal mark upon French foreign policy. The latter is a responsibility he shares with the prime minister and which is a domain, along with that of defence, where the president of France exercises a particular influence accorded to him by the constitutional provisions of the Fifth Republic. In order to make his mark (as Mitterrand had done on the left in the Gulf War), it is possible that Chirac had to break away from the traditional inclinations of neo-Gaullist foreign policy. We should add perhaps that with regard to Chirac, that his attitude may also be explained by the fact that he belongs to a generation that did not exercise power in the immediate post-war period, and which as a result does not feel bound by the same points of reference (such as, for example, the sense of national unity that prevailed at that time). For these reasons he did not hesitate to go on national television on 6 April 1999 in order to underline the identical views held by himself and the socialist prime minister, Lionel Jospin and the government:

The horror demanded and organized by Milosevic defies the imagination. Alongside the government, I say this again to you – it is unacceptable. I choose to believe that the Serbian people for whom we have nothing but respect and friendship, will open their eyes in order to see the reality of his regime.

The significance of Chirac's policies can be interpreted in the light of two important facts. Taking into account the internal state of French politics and in particular certain leanings within the RPR (neo-Gaullist party) towards a link with the extreme right, it is and was essential for Chirac to take up positions that were unambiguously and firmly distinct from the extreme right. Also, it should be said, despite our observations above relating to the demise of the power and influence of the Eastern Bloc, that the position of the French President was to some extent determined by the traditional 'entente' between French and Russian foreign policy, a point mentioned by J.-M. Colombani, the chief editor of Le Monde in his editorial of 8 April 1999. Jacques Chirac, when it suited him, was right to disassociate himself from Washington in order to try to ensure that Russia was associated with any international settlement. From a French point of view, to give credit to the Russians might have subsequent rewards if the aim was to ensure that western Europe remained on peaceful terms with Moscow.

THE IMPACT OF THE KOSOVO CRISIS UPON INTERNAL FRENCH POLITICS

Such a convergence of opinion of the kind declared between the president and prime minister was in keeping with the existing framework of events which required the presenting of a common front concerning French policy, particularly with regard to other countries, and with regard to French policy in the Balkans, a region in which France has always sought a political, cultural, economic and diplomatic presence. In these circumstances, as we have said, the place of the Kosovo conflict in the French media was one which, by calling Serbia's actions into question, also called into question a long-standing alliance with France. It was also a war which, by revealing underlying ethnic cleansing policies on the part of Serbia, reminded France of another memory, that of the Occupation. For these reasons the French media were obliged to become involved in a kind of cultural duality in their approach to Kosovo which was, in part at least, contradictory, and which had political repercussions.

> 66 It was a war which, by revealing underlying ethnic cleansing policies on the part of Serbia, reminded France of another memory, that of the Occupation 99

The Kosovo conflict not only took on an international and regional dimension in Europe, it also had a profound impact upon internal French politics. *Le Monde* of 2 April 1999 devoted a full page to the emerging sequence of political events in France which included Lionel Jospin imposing his will upon the communists; the recognition of the need for agreement between the president and prime minister on French involvement in Nato operations; the right seizing upon divisions within the government; and the plans of the French Communist Party for promoting agreement among the parties supporting the government.

Public opinion about the Kosovo crisis fell within the framework of a political realignment on the part of the principal political actors in France which can be illustrated with reference to an article, published in *Le Monde* of 11–12 April 1999, by a group of politicians from different parts of the political spectrum of the left in France, (a communist, a Trotskyist and a representative of the socialist movement) who claimed common political cause with regard to the Kosovo conflict:

It would be a good thing if, straightaway, men and women of opposing political horizons, without disguising their differences or antagonisms, together set out their common ground.

The Kosovo conflict divided the left in a different manner from that of the Gulf War: *Le Monde* of 9 April 1999 notes the difference:

The Gulf War is certainly an event of the past. Whereas in 1991 a whole section of the left joined up together with pacifist and Christian bodies in opposition to American intervention, the Kosovo crisis is dividing the radical left.

It is for this reason that the debate in France was not one in which the lines between the left and right were clearly drawn. The positions of the French left were much more complex with regard to the USA. The scholar, Paul Allies, a committed thinker on the left, was in no doubt when he wrote in *Le Monde* of 14 April 1999:

Whatever battles lie ahead in the development of relations between social and political power [in relation to the Kosovo crisis], a framework for action and a rationale along with a public sphere of reference based upon patriotism and basic human rights must be created within democratic Europe in order to deal with the Kosovo conflict.

So, the positions adopted in the public debate in France, both within the media and outside them, were extremely divided. Some, even those on the left and otherwise anti-Atlantic in attitude, supported military intervention. Even at the very heart of the PCF, which was in the process of refounding its ideological and political position, views were very complex and even contradictory with regard to which stance to adopt. According to *Le Monde* of 9 April 1999, the PCF found itself caught between the instinctive need to retain its identity, and a vague impulse to open up [politically] for the European elections, a move that required a development in the party's public position. In the same issue, *Le Monde* drew attention to the tensions associated with the PCF in consequence of the Kosovo crisis.

> **❝ The positions adopted in the public debate in France, both within the media and outside them, were extremely divided ❞**

There is *L'Humanité*, in its new role as the paper of the radical left, restricted to being the peacemaker.

The political dilemma of the PCF was further underlined by *Le Monde* when it bluntly pointed out the contradiction implicit in that party's continuing participation in the Jospin government and its rejection of Nato intervention in Kosovo. It concluded with continuing candour that:

If Nato sent ground troops into Kosovo, the unanimity of the government's position and the much vaunted 'usefulness' of the communist ministers would then be placed in jeopardy.

On the other hand, the realignments and restructuring also affected the right. Thus, *Le Monde* of 27 March 1999 also pointed out that the worries expressed by F. Bayrou of the Union for French Democracy, (UDF) traditionally sympathetic towards the USA, represented a new development in the position of the pro-American right which was distancing itself from US policy and regretting that France was so tightly committed in that direction:

A fact which is sufficiently rare to be noteworthy, M. Seguin seems to be in agreement with M. Bayrou who says that we are in the frame but not at the level [of influence] we deserve.

In France, as in Europe generally, the Kosovo conflict turned many political attitudes and frameworks upside down, a phenomenon illustrated by an article in *Le Monde* of 20 May 1999:

In the Balkans, France and Great Britain for a long time seemed resigned to the worst, to have abdicated before the indignity of the situation, preferring gesture politics to those of intervention. The criminals were to have a free hand. Impotence took its toll and was made worse by the lengthy deliberations of the UN.

In the same article, J.-P. Langellier asserts that the entry of the USA on the scene brought about a change in the attitudes of European powers and a reformulation of public opinion of the kind outlined above.

Not only was this phenomenon of political restructuring widespread in Western Europe, *Le Monde* also emphasized on 31 March 1999, that the unfolding war had led to a realignment of public opinion in eastern European countries too. In summary, as the direct result of the Kosovo crisis, French public opinion was reconstructed by the media and political parties within a framework of discourse[6] that simultaneously displaced and restructured the usual political oppositions and which prepared the ground for a public debate wherein new choices relating to French foreign policy would be available.

66 French public opinion was reconstructed by the media and political parties within a framework of discourse that simultaneously displaced and restructured the usual political oppositions 99

THE EUROPEAN DIMENSION

The European dimension of the Kosovo conflict was well represented in the French media, firstly as the consequence of the weight of history, as already mentioned at the beginning of this chapter, which located the conflict at the heart of Europe, and secondly, because of the growing importance of European affairs themselves as topics of information in the media. A good example of this European dimension may be found in an article by the left-winger, Regis Debray[7] of 1 April 1999, which provoked considerable comment in France for the sympathetic manner in which he represented Milosevic:

Between the superstitions of history which hold sway in the Balkans and the eradication of history which is rife in Western Europe, between the paranoia and the frivolity, we might have wished that the Old Continent could have put forward a just solution, because Belgrade and Pristina are still part of its own past by which it is being confronted: the Ottoman invasion, the eastern question and the Versailles Treaty.

There could be no question of the French media considering the Kosovo conflict without considering the importance of history in the fashioning of European identities that lie at the heart of the war. Moreover, the political importance of the EU is underlined in these media texts, particularly with regard to its relations with the USA and Russia. Thus *Le Monde Diplomatique* of September 1999 raised the need for a Marshall Plan for the Balkans, with the object of refounding territorial configurations and renewing economic flows in the region.

Indeed the need for such a plan had been mentioned earlier in the conflict when C. Lalumière wrote in *Le Monde* of 13 May 1999:

In the years to come, the European Union will be committed to a gigantic project that will recall the reconstruction which followed the Second World War. This project will embrace the Balkans but will also include central and eastern Europe and a large number of countries bordering on the Mediterranean.

Earlier still, in *Le Monde* of 11–12 April, former defence minister, Pierre Joxe, underlined the European nature of any future Balkans Plan:

It seems necessary to me … to relaunch the political and economic concept of a confederation of Balkan states which have as their objective not to join Nato, but the European Union instead.

Such a point of view represents the desire for the political, economic and military restructuring of Europe outside the Nato context and thus, by extension, free from the influence of the USA.

Finally, notwithstanding the long-term implications for European action, the intervention of Nato in the Kosovo crisis underlined the international dimension of the conflict and in particular the relationship to which Europe and the USA are committed in the Kosovo context and beyond. From the beginning of the conflict, news services which underlined the international dimension and international bodies – the UN and Nato – were present either as direct participants in the conflict or as mediators and negotiators. Thus *Le Monde* of 31 January 1999, emphasized the importance of the international mediation taking place under the chairmanship of Robin Cook and the participation of the rest of the Contact Group at Rambouillet. In the same edition there was an article that focused on the development and status of international forces. Indeed, a strong insistence on the international dimension of the conflict and its consequences for Europe and for the resulting relations between Europe and the USA can be perceived throughout the French media coverage of the crisis:

> **66** From the beginning of the conflict, news services were present either as direct participants in the conflict or as mediators and negotiators **99**

A platform of minimum common ground among the Kosovo Albanians is foreseeable. It will probably result in a [political] alignment of ethnic-Albanians with that of the most radical group whose views are riding high – total independence and nothing else, warned a western diplomat, something which the Serbs and the international community do not wish to hear.

MEDIA RHETORIC IN THE KOSOVO CRISIS

The media description of the space and territory of Kosovo placed the war in context by recalling both the historical formation of territorial boundaries in the region and by presenting the battle zones in both word and image. In this way the media developed a kind of spatial rhetoric in the representation of Kosovo. Thus *Le Monde* of 31 March 1999 published a sequence of maps of space and boundaries which formed the successive national frontiers of the countries of central Europe after the disappearance of the Ottoman Empire. This spatial analysis in *Le Monde* had a kind of double rhetorical function: it served, on one hand, to reveal the instability of the frontiers in the region in order, on the other, to better demonstrate the importance of the territorial issue in the foundation and expression of national identities, which are factors in the Kosovo conflict in particular and which underpin the political framework of central Europe in general. This spatial rhetoric, also had a dual function. Firstly, through maps and tables it showed how frontiers developed and also gave the positions of the opposing sides during the course of the conflicts. Secondly, through photographs and verbal accounts of the countryside, it gave a real, perceivable aspect to the countries it depicted in the news.

The media representation of the Kosovo countryside and that of the surrounding region complemented the political representation, discussed earlier, of the same space by making it more accessible and understandable to readers and viewers. For example, a photo in *Le Monde* of 3 April 1999 shows an old woman on horseback against a background of deserted mountains. This photo accompanies the account of the flight of Kosovo Albanians to Albania. The meaning of the text is clear: it seeks to depict the war as turning the Kosovo Albanians into nomads by making them flee the violence of the conflict. The former space of Kosovo changes in significance: whereas the territory in the past meant a place of life and security, after the outbreak of the conflict it became a desert where only displacement and nomadic movement allowed the inhabitants to survive.

In this case, the rhetoric of the picture and of the text in relation to the space consists of showing that the war had caused the territory of Kosovo to disappear and to be replaced by a desert where only nomadic wandering was possible and in which the roads and crossings now structured and organized the distribution of the population within the former space of Kosovo. So the media depicted a double disappearance of the space of Kosovo: they showed how the territory had disappeared as a space that offered identity to the inhabitants, and a settled living space, into one which transformed the Kosovo Albanians into nomads. This makes the representation and emphasis laid upon the significance of history by the media all the more important: the significance of history was to demonstrate that Kosovo only existed as a land and as a living space in the context of the past, which effectively had disappeared.[8]

> 66 The significance of history was to demonstrate that Kosovo only existed as a land and as a living space in the context of the past 99

CONCLUSION

Briefly, in conclusion, we can summarize the French position: for the majority of French public and political opinion, the Serbs seemed to be determined to ethnically cleanse Kosovo of Kosovo Albanians in order to recover a land of which they had been dispossessed by the Turks in the Middle Ages. The ensuing conflict and Nato intervention were interpreted as being events related to cultural determination and independence (for both Serb and Kosovo Albanian). In the light of France's own experience in the recent past, the ensuing war touched a sensitive nerve among politicians and media alike which led to singularly strange political contradictions and political rhetoric. In order to support the nationalist claims of the Kosovo Albanians it was necessary also for France to align militarily with the USA and abandon the more independent position of post-war French foreign policy. The internal political realignment is ongoing and, since it is highly unlikely that the Kosovo situation will be resolved in the short term, French political thinking and public opinion will continue to feel the repercussions of events in the Balkans for some considerable time ahead. No doubt there will be consequences for the presidential elections of 2002, which in turn will have a bearing upon internal French politics and foreign policy until 2007.

NOTES

1   See Lamizet 1998: 97, 179, 325.

2   The Fifth Republic was inaugurated in 1958 upon the adoption of the Constitution proposed by De Gaulle who became Head of State from that year until his resignation in 1969.

3   French policy of non-alignment was particularly apparent from the 1960s, the period when De Gaulle was distancing himself from the USA and involving France in the process of decolonization. The pro-third world policy of France was achieved by (political) distancing of itself from the USA and the Soviet Union, and the policy of cooperation embarked on with the emergent countries of the third world, notably in Africa (where French oil interests were strong).

4   A first attempt had failed in 1954 with the proposal of a European Defence Community.

5   1981–95 was the period of the Mitterrand presidency and during this time the government was headed by the socialists from 1981–6 and from 1988–93. The Communist Party formed part of the government from 1981–3 and supported it between 1983 and 1986 and between 1988 and 1993.

6   This recomposition of identities in France also expresses itself in the recomposition of political culture along lines of gender: a survey of daily newspaper readers in France revealed a public sphere where male and female readers appeared not to hear the same question. Males, for the most part, particularly older men, offered their opinions on the war itself, whereas women and some younger readers expressed their opinions in terms of the victims. Male readers remained detached with regard to the war and to the media. Women, on the other hand, were more subjective and stressed their emotional response to the media coverage of the war.

7   The scholar and intellectual, Regis Debray, is well known for his anti-American stance and his opposition to the Bolivian Junta along with Che Guevara in 1967. He subsequently became an advisor to François Mitterrand.

8   Another significance can be attributed to this event: Europe as a new political space is yet to be created.

7

THE EU: OLD WINE FROM NEW BOTTLES

JUAN DIEGO RAMIREZ AND MANUEL SZAPIRO

FEW EVENTS IN THE HISTORY OF EUROPEAN INTEGRATION have under-mined the EU's image as much as the member states' collective impotence in the Kosovo crisis. This inability to act, when faced with the necessity of imposing peace upon conflicting parties, brought to light a dissatisfying fea-ture of the consensual and civilian nature of the EU. This is particularly true as European public opinion expected more from the EU. European citizens, kneaded by the EU's humanistic principles, experienced a shock, probably even greater than the one they had felt during the dramatic dissolution of Yugoslavia, by witnessing – powerless – the flagrant violation of human rights through ethnic persecutions against Kosovo Albanians, taking place on their doorstep. Furthermore, the imbroglio of Nato's intervention made European policy-makers acutely aware of the consequences of their collective impotence. The failure of Operation Allied Force to produce a quick capit-ulation of the Serbs contributed to exacerbating the EU's moral responsibility for the crimes committed on the old Continent, in spite of the adoption of all the solemn declarations about 'never again'. The tragic experience in Kosovo thus shed a new light on the role and responsibility of the EU in European security. EU perspectives on the Kosovo conflict fundamentally reflected the need for a rejuvenated debate on *what the EU should/can do in order to restore its credibility as an international actor.*

> ❝ The Kosovo conflict reflected the need for a rejuvenated debate on what the EU should/can do in order to restore its credibility as an international actor ❞

First and foremost, the Kosovo crisis provided the EU with the opportunity to re-affirm, given the matter's urgency, its civilian role. Moreover, the conflict offered a window of opportunity for the EU seriously to contemplate the creation of a meaningful and operative ESDP, due mainly to the widespread perception that the EU would not be able to act effectively in international affairs unless it could use military instruments.

THE EU INTERVENED AS A CIVILIAN POWER: A STORY OF WINE AND BOTTLES

The EU's involvement in the various phases of the Kosovo conflict took different forms in the wide panoply that a civilian power has at its disposal. During the unfolding of the crisis and its military escalation, the EU resorted to its traditional economic and diplomatic tools, thus putting the 'old wine' of its civilian potential in the 'old bottles' of diplomatic missions, economic sanctions and mediations. These responses had little or no effect on bringing Serbian actions to an end. In the aftermath of the conflict, the EU thus took the lead in a reconstruction process, not only of Kosovo, but of the whole south-eastern European region. Hence, the EU chose to resort to its economic and political leverage (the old wine) to establish peace, security and stability for the region, while re-packaging its old products under novel co-operative frameworks.

Despite the fact that the conflict had been ongoing from the beginning of the twentieth century, and the dangerous potential of warfare risk and regional destabilization was known – Kosovo being the first study of the Conflict Prevention Network[1] (CPN), the antagonism between Kosovo and Serbia had not been the subject of any EU proactive measure. In the time period stretching from the abolition of Kosovo's autonomous status in March 1989, to the break-up of former Yugoslavia in 1991 and until the signature of the Dayton Peace Accords in 1995, the few initiatives that sought to impede the outburst of violence in that province were not the direct result of an EU initiative but rather an initiative of the UN[2] and the USA. A divergence of national interests that in turn led to a lack of political will, and the reliance on Washington's lead are the main reasons for this inaction. The EU's newly born commitment to contribute 'to preserving peace and international security' (article 11, Treaty on European Union), was therefore, in this case, inoperative from its inception. The West, including the EU, demonstrated once again its inability to foresee a crisis or to interpret correctly the warning signs of an emerging conflict at the Dayton peace talks. Here, mention of the situation in Kosovo was omitted and subordinated to the wider US and EU objectives of avoiding any confrontation with Belgrade that could hamper the smooth implementation of the agreement. Moreover, in the end, neither the international community nor the EU backed Rugova's peaceful and violence-free struggle for equal rights of the Kosovo Albanian population in the province. This resulted in the progressive withdrawal of popular support from this political leader, thus strengthening the less consensually

> 66 Neither the international community nor the EU backed Rugova's peaceful and violence-free struggle for equal rights of the Kosovo Albanian population 99

minded KLA. It was not until March 1998, after the indiscriminate attacks by Serbian forces on suspected KLA strongholds in the Drenica Region, when violence was at its zenith and serious concerns about the human rights situation and the potential of this crisis for the region's stability came to light, that the EU decided to take it to the fore of its political agenda.

THE EU *REACTED* AS A CIVILIAN POWER: 'POURING OLD WINE FROM OLD BOTTLES'

As was the case in Bosnia, the EU's role in the Kosovo crisis could be characterized as inconsequential. The EU also found itself sidelined by mainly supporting the initiatives of other participants. Nevertheless, the EU seemed to have tried to resort to the full scope of instruments available under its traditional role as a civilian power.

The primordial value for the definition of an entity as civilian power is its desire to preserve peace. Peace here is not simply based on the absence of war but also on democracy, economic growth and prosperity through free-market economics, social justice, regional cooperation and the respect of human rights and the rule of law (Farrell 1998). In its search for durable peace and stability in Kosovo, the EU's involvement made use of the different forms of the wide panoply of tools that a civilian power has at its disposal, pouring out its 'old wine' matured in experience of its 'old bottles' employing both diplomatic and economic instruments. The EU used the ammunition of its diplomatic civilian instruments, firstly, by, *inter alia*, issuing declarations/statements to express concern, condemn, announce punitive measures and encourage specific diplomatic activities. Additionally, on several occasions, the EU resorted to sending special representatives to the region: Felipe González, Wolfgang Petrisch, Panagiotis Roumelotis and Bodo Hombach. On 8 June 1998 the Council appointed Felipe González EU Special Representative for the Federal Republic of Yugoslavia. Mr González's mandate, which was to enhance the effectiveness of the EU's contribution to the resolution of problems in Yugoslavia, ended on 11 October 1999. Wolfgang Petrisch, Austria's Ambassador to Belgrade, was appointed EU Special Envoy for Kosovo on 30 March 1999. In the light of developments in the region, in particular the deployment of the UN Mission in Kosovo, Mr Petrisch's mandate terminated on 29 July. Panagiotis Roumelotis was appointed EU Special Representative on 31 May 1999 to support his role as Coordinator of the process of stability and good neighbourliness in south-east Europe (Royaumont Process). Bodo Hombach was appointed EU Special Representative on 29 July 1999 to carry out the tasks defined in the Stability Pact for south-eastern Europe of 10 June 1999 to help the countries concerned develop a joint strategy for ensuring the stability and growth of the region.[3] The EU also deployed the presence of the monitors of the European Community Monitoring Mission, as it had done earlier in Bosnia, to collaborate with the OSCE's Kosovo Verification Mission.

Finally, also in the field of political machinery and through the channels of multilateral diplomacy, the EU supported the efforts of other international organizations in its quest for a solution to the conflict. During the process of the internationalization of the crisis, between the Drenica incidents in March 1998 and the beginning of the bombing campaign one year later, the EU repeatedly backed the responses already given by other international actors. In this respect, the EU aligned itself with the OSCE in the latter's stance in the crisis, which advocated respect of the territorial integrity of Yugoslavia and recognition of regional, national and cultural identities. This was translated into the EU's Common Position of 19 March 1998 which supported the mediation of the OSCE representative, Mr González. Mr González was also nominated, with immediate effect, as EU Special Representative in order to increase the EU's effectiveness in contributing to resolving the crisis. The EU also supported the diplomatic efforts undertaken by the Contact Group to find a peaceful solution to the crisis. Here, the EU helped to secure endorsement by central and eastern European countries of sanctions and other punitive measures adopted by the Contact Group at its London meeting on 9 March 1998.

The EU also participated in the organization and sponsoring of peace conferences, such as the Rambouillet peace talks on 6 February 1998 under the auspices of the Contact Group. Through its representative, former Finnish President Martti Ahtisaari, the EU, together with Russia, was an active party in the negotiations that put a formal end to the hostilities on 9 June 1999.

As the world's largest economic block, the most powerful tool the EU has at its disposal is its enormous economic weight. The EU can wield a wide range of economic instruments in its response to crises. In this case, the economic instruments are oriented to the achievement of a determined political outcome. This is epitomized by the concept of political conditionality which can be defined as the linking of economic (and also political) benefits to certain political standards, relating particularly to democracy and human rights. Within the concept of political conditionality, a choice can be made between positive and negative conditionality. The former is a promise of certain benefits such as the conclusion of different types of trade agreements, the provision of aid, the award of loans, on the condition that specific standards are met, whereas the latter comprises measures such as sanctions, embargoes, boycotts and suspension or denunciation of agreements that involve reducing, suspending or terminating those benefits if the standards are violated.

> 66 As the world's largest economic block, the most powerful tool the EU has at its disposal is its enormous weight 99

The EU has thus made use of the various positive measures. As far as aid is concerned, the EU is by far the single biggest donor of aid to Kosovo and the western Balkan region as a whole:

Since 1991, not counting the contributions of member states, the EU has provided more than 4.5 billion euro to the region.[4]

The EU is also the most important international contributor in the provision of humanitarian aid. Through its European Community Humanitarian Office (ECHO), the EU invested a total of 370 million euro in Kosovo in 1999, having cleared another 50 million for the present year.

By engaging its negative measures, 'the EU took an early lead in applying economic sanctions' (Duke 1999). These were directed, in March 1998, to freezing Serb foreign assets, banning any new investment in Serbia and the prohibition of arms exportation to the Federal Republic of Yugoslavia,[5] to banning all flights from and to Yugoslavian territory, as agreed at the Cardiff summit on 15–16 June 1998 and prohibiting the supply and sale of petroleum and petroleum products in April 1999.[6] In all cases, the removal of the punitive measures imposed was explicitly subordinated to stated terms and conditions. The EU's common position of 19 March 1998 on the arms embargo against Yugoslavia clearly states:

The sanctions set out in the Common Position will be reconsidered immediately if the Government of the FRY takes effective steps to stop the violence and engage in a commitment to find a political solution to the issue of Kosovo through a peaceful dialogue with the Kosovar Albanian Community.

Out of all these possible techniques, there exists within the EU an innate preference for the use of those of a positive nature rather than 'sticks' (threatening or inflicting punishments):

Rather than coerce other actors, the EU tries to convince them, using persuasion or rewards, to behave responsibly, to cooperate with each other, or to democratise and respect human rights.   (Smith 1997)

Consequently, only in exceptional circumstances, such as the case in Kosovo, when all the other measures have failed, will coercive measures, such as sanctions, be envisaged. But even in Kosovo, where the EU was obliged to use coercive measures on several occasions, the calls for reconciliation, dialogue and cooperation were always present and can be traced in all the declarations and statements that the EU released during the crisis. The invitations on the part of the EU leaders, both to the Belgrade authorities and the leadership of the Kosovo Albanian community, to 'refrain from further violence'[7] and to engage in 'full and constructive dialogue'[8] in the search of a durable 'mutual agreement'[9] are recurrent in all these texts.

66 While the US believed in dealing with the conflict directly with armed forces, there was a consensus among EU leaders to prioritize instruments based on dialogue, diplomatic action and economic cooperation 99

European reluctance to use coercion contrasts with the American approach where force is used for conflict resolution. This contrast results in an implicit repartition of roles, also witnessed in the Kosovo conflict, that Jacques Rupnik very illustratively has characterized as 'le baton américain et la carotte européenne' (Rupnik 1998) (the American stick and the European carrot). This division of labour reflects the two different standpoints from which the US and the EU approached the conflict:

while the US believed in dealing with the conflict directly with armed forces, and made clear that the role of Washington in the area after the war would be limited militarily and financially, there was a consensus among EU leaders to prioritize instruments based on dialogue, diplomatic action and economic cooperation and to emphasize its role in the process of economic reconstruction during the post-conflict period.

However, this difference in approach, apart from being the result of the means respectively available to support a certain diplomatic campaign, also stems from much more profound differences directly related to the international identity and nature these two entities hold. As Nicole Gnesotto puts it, in the case of the EU, in line with the presumptions that characterize it globally as a civilian power, it regarded:

the bombing of Serbia not only as a means to weaken the regime in Belgrade, [but also sadly as] … the destruction of a part of our continent, the infliction of suffering on the lost members of the European family, which do not share anymore the values of democracy and tolerance.

That is why, once the military conflict was brought to an end, the EU fully recovered its protagonist role in the reconstruction phase.

We must help them to return to Europe: they could do so just by renouncing to president Milosevic and his regime. Only in this way they could become true European actors.   (Gnesotto 1999)

THE EU ACTED AS A CIVILIAN POWER: 'PUTTING OLD WINE IN NEW BOTTLES'

STABILIZATION OF THE COUNTRIES OF SOUTH-EASTERN EUROPE

The belligerent confrontation in Kosovo ended after 78 days of Nato's bombing campaign and peace was brought back to the region with the acceptance by Yugoslavia of the Military Technical Agreement of 9 June 1999. Nevertheless, the termination of the conflict left European governments confronted with two major challenges: first, that of de-Balkanizing the Balkans (Pierre 1999), trying to tackle the roots of the region's instability which, successively, had given rise to different episodes of military confrontation, economic crisis and political unrest, and second, that of avoiding the 'Balkanization' of both central and eastern Europe, still fragile in its development, and the EU countries themselves, confronted with serious risks of destabilization (including the massive flow of refugees resulting in social unrest).

Kosovo was not the first conflict in the area, but the fourth, and previous crises had already triggered off a response by the international community which had tried to realize the goal of 'never again'. The initiatives taken to redress the traditional lines of hatred and confrontation, according to which the history of the area has been written, are numerous: in 1995 the EU had launched the so-called Royaumont Process and was itself party to the South-Eastern European Co-operation Initiative and the Central European Initiative. However, in their inability to prevent the outburst of violence in Kosovo, the weaknesses of these initiatives became evident. In the words of German Foreign Minister Joschka Fischer:

The previous policy of the international community *vis-à-vis* former Yugoslavia had two severe deficits: it concentrated on the consequences instead of on the sources of the conflict, and it tackled the problems of the region individually and separately from the ones in other parts of Europe.[10]

Due to this failure, and the urgency of the matter, the EU, in its quest for a new solution:

could only look into the tool kit of the past and largely re-wrap an existing policy instrument – enlargement – as its main response.

(Friis and Murphy 1999)

Nonetheless, the lessons of Kosovo did not seem to be bygone, and the old wine of the EU with its traditional civilian values was being served this time in a new bottle: a broad regional and inclusive initiative, which tried to embed the countries of south eastern Europe in the organizational and normative structures of the Euro-Atlantic community. The aim was to bring long-term peace, stability and economic development to the region, by means of the perspective of membership as a key instrument. This initiative was launched in the form of the Stability Pact for South Eastern Europe and the Stabilization and Association Process, the EU's main contribution to the Pact.

> 66 The aim was to bring long-term peace, stability and economic development to the region, by means of the perspective of membership as a key instrument 99

THE STABILITY PACT FOR SOUTH EASTERN EUROPE

European leaders were convinced of the need to set up the Stability Pact for South Eastern Europe for two reasons: First, the external factors – the tremendous external pressure on the EU stemming from the conflict; and second, internal factors – the inadmissability of any kind of acceptance of the Kosovo situation for the EU as an organization promoting values such as peace, stability and democracy.

The Stability Pact for South Eastern Europe is reminiscent of previous initiatives, such as the Balladur Plan for Central and Eastern Europe (1993) or the Royaumont Process (1995), which served as inspiration. A short period of negotiations resulted in the integration of these traditional ideas into new frames, therefore putting the old wine of the search for a lasting peace and stability for the region in the new bottle of the Stability Pact for South Eastern Europe. The Stability Pact was adopted at a special meeting of foreign ministers, representatives of international organizations, institutions and regional initiatives, in Cologne on 10 June 1999 and was formally launched more than a month later at the Sarajevo conference on 29–30 July.

In this respect, the Stability Pact for South Eastern Europe is the first EU preventative, strategic and pan-continental action. It seeks to strengthen:

the countries in south-eastern Europe in their efforts to foster peace, democracy and respect for human rights and economic prosperity, in order to achieve the stability of the whole region,[11]

objectives similar to those mentioned in article 11 of the Treaty on European Union, by offering them the perspective of integration into the EU structures. Consequently, the EU has chosen the traditional tool of EU membership as the central element of its new response, being aware of its political, stabilizing, and strategic potential:

The idea of EU enlargement has acquired new impetus over the past year. One of the key lessons of the Kosovo crisis is the need to achieve peace and security, democracy and the rule of law, growth and the foundations of prosperity throughout Europe. Enlargement is the best way to do this. There is now a greater awareness of the strategic dimension to enlargement.[12]

Opening the bottle of this new instrument has given rise to a series of consequences that could run counter to its over-arching rationale: the provision of peace, stability and prosperity for the region. Indeed, the perspective of membership has transformed the enlargement process into an inclusive one extending as far as the Balkan Peninsula. As a result of this inclusivity, it was no longer justifiable to keep the so-called second wave countries, Bulgaria, Latvia, Lithuania, Slovakia, Romania and Malta, out of the start of negotiations, especially when some of them, such as Bulgaria and Romania had provided both direct and indirect assistance to the EU and to Nato forces in their campaign against the regime in Belgrade. At the Helsinki Summit, 10 and 11 December 1999, European leaders were forced to recognize this inclusivity, inviting the remaining applicants to start accession negotiations, as a way 'to lend a positive contribution to security and stability in the European continent'.[13] However, possible strains in the process's evolution could arise, since the hopes of those newly embarked on accession could become frustrated due to the discrepancy between the ambitious entry goals set and the slow rhythm of their own transformation process. This is added to the simultaneous high cost of the anxiety of the six front runners, Czech Republic, Estonia, Hungary, Poland, Slovenia and Cyprus, which fear further delays on their path to accession.

The negative potential for frustration with the present strategy might be even greater in the case of the Balkan countries. The Western countries are serious about sharing security and prosperity with them, but the task ahead is huge and the real chances of the south-east European countries being integrated are not encouraging for the moment. The failure of the EU to meet the south-east Europe countries' expectations could produce dangerous effects in the region. The EU has, through the Stability Pact, raised high expectations for Balkan countries and the possibility of disappointing them through lack of economic resources and security assurance is high.

> 66 The EU has, through the Stability Pact, raised high expectations for the Balkan countries and the possibility of disappointing them through lack of economic resources and security assurance is high 99

Finally, this new strategy brings forward far-reaching considerations that touch upon sensitive questions such as the geographical borders of the EU and even its place in the international arena. The membership prospect for the Balkan countries could be followed by a domino effect. If the door to membership is opened to Albania, Bosnia-Herzegovina, Croatia, Yugoslavia and Macedonia, on which basis could one exclude other countries such as Ukraine, Moldova and, eventually, Russia and those in the Caucasus from having the same opportunity?

THE STABILIZATION AND ASSOCIATION PROCESS

As the EU's main contribution to the Stability Pact, and in the wider context of the Stabilization of the Countries of South-Eastern Europe, the European Commission proposed on 26 May 1999 the creation of a Stabilization and Association Process[14] for Bosnia-Herzegovina, Croatia, Yugoslavia, Macedonia and Albania.

This initiative can be seen, first, as an additional effort on the part of the EU to favour regional cooperation in the resolution of these problems. For that purpose, it enhances the already existing regional approach of the EU *vis-à-vis* these five countries which was developed in 1996 with the prospect of EU integration for them all.

Second, it tries to upgrade simultaneously the relations with each country by means of a new type of contractual relationship, the Stability and Association Agreements. These take into account a country's individual situation, and require compliance with certain conditions to be monitored by the Commission:

- respect of democratic principles
- human rights and the rule of law
- protection of minorities
- market economy reforms
- regional co-operation
- in the case of Bosnia and Herzegovina, Croatia and Yugoslavia compliance with obligations under the Dayton and Erdut Agreements, the Peace Implementation Councils and with the Resolution UNSCR 1244).

The agreements also include the concept of closer integration with EU structures or 'light membership' through:

- consolidation of democratic reforms
- a framework for political dialogue
- the possibility of free trade
- justice and home affairs cooperation
- association-oriented assistance programmes in practically all fields of EU competence.

Even within this new framework, it is nevertheless obvious that the EU resorted to draw, once again, from the experience of past solutions. Indeed, in this case the combination of both bilateral and multilateral relations seems to echo the EU's contractual relations with central and eastern Europe, and the different sections of the Stability and Association Agreements reflect those of the Association or Europe Agreements.

CONCLUSION: A CIVILIAN POWER REVISITED

Although the civilian power has been labelled by many scholars as obsolete when it comes to intervention in the 'real wars' of post-bipolarity, the EU has shown on several occasions that 'civilianization' (Farrell 1998) or 'domestication' of external relations (Duchene 1973) convey a substantial potential for the EU to redress many of the security problems proper of the post-Cold War era. Indeed, in the period after 1989, security:

has acquired a much broader connotation than military security: threats to security within and between states arise from a variety of sources, including ethnic disputes, violations of human rights, and economic deprivation.

(Smith 1997)

Consequently, the EU's position as an acting civilian power involves the promotion of the:

principles of representative democracy, of the rule of law, of social justice – which is the ultimate goal of economic progress – and of respect for human rights.   (1973 Copenhagen Report on the European identity)

not only among its constituent states, but also defending them where they are threatened and promoting them where they do not exist. In the protection of these values the EU has found a role for itself. In this respect, the Heads of State and Government of the EU, at the occasion of the Berlin European Council of 24 and 25 March 1999, in their urge to 'the Yugoslav leadership under President Milosevic to summon up the courage at this juncture to change radically its own policy', declared that Europe could not 'tolerate a humanitarian catastrophe in its midst' and acknowledged their responsibility:

for securing peace and cooperation in the region ... This is the way to guarantee our fundamental European values, i.e. respect for human rights and the rights of minorities, international law, democratic institutions and the inviolability of borders.[15]

In the words of Jacques Delors, security is now an 'all embracing concept', which includes issues such as respect for the rule of international law, societal problems as well as defence (Delors 1991). It would seem that the EU is much better fitted than any other organization to address these types of problems. But as Nato entered into the fore and finally won the war, a new light was to be shed on the linkage between the limited diplomatic clout of the EU and its military impotence.

THE MILITARY REACH OF THE EU: OLD TRUTHS AND NEW DISCOURSES – OLD TRUTHS STILL HOLD

The EU very quickly found itself sidelined with the outbreak of hostilities thus illustrating the limits of 'civilian power instruments' such as diplomatic negotiations and economic sanctions. This crisis acted as a psychological catalyst, reviving *old truths* about the difficult role of the EU in international crisis management. These reminiscences led to *new political discourses* on the imperative of endowing the EU with a genuine European Security and Defence Policy (ESDP). Whether the reality of military action will ever match the rhetoric of ESDP remains, however, to be seen.

OLD TRUTH NUMBER 1: THE 'CAPABILITY–EXPECTATIONS GAP'

The crisis highlighted yet again the *capability expectations gap* of the foreign, and above all, security dimension of the EU's external reach. The hiatus between EU diplomatic and security ambitions on the one hand and the lack of an autonomous decision and action capacity on the other was made particularly apparent in the Kosovo crisis. Three months before Operation Allied Force began, the EU was still reaffirming its:

determination, as demonstrated by the active efforts of the EU special envoy Wolfgang Petrisch, to support the political process, to contribute to humanitarian efforts and, as soon as the parties have reached an agreement (on the future status of Kosovo) to assist reconstruction.[16]

However, unlike the US, which could legitimately use the threat of Nato's intervention, the EU's bargaining power could hardly be based on a military deterrent. Nato's Operation Allied Force effectively proved to be predominantly that of the US airforce: American aircraft carried out about 80 per cent of the air strikes against Serb targets and some 90–95 per cent of the precision-guided weapons and cruise missiles used were American. It thus became evident once again that the EU was, for various reasons,[17] lacking the key elements of an effective force, namely the logistics and the so-called C^3I: the command, control, communication and intelligence capacities (Duke 1999). The Kosovo conflict made the Europeans conscious of the need to remedy their material dependence on US military technology.

OLD TRUTH NUMBER 2: THE EU CANNOT AFFORD TO LEAVE THE SECURITY OF THE REGION IN THE SOLE HANDS OF THE USA

It is unreasonable to expect the US to hold a long-term interest in intervening wherever and whenever the EU, as a whole or some of its member states, sees fit. The assumption of continued convergence between the EU and the US security interests is quite naive, to say the least. In fact, the US has on several occasions shown a tendency to react late to emerging European crises (Bosnia), if at all (Albania) – (Hendrickson, 1999). In the Kosovo conflict, the Clinton administration experienced extreme difficulties in sustaining public support throughout the bombing, while vital US territorial interests were clearly not deemed to be at stake. What was at stake, however, thanks to the reiterated threats of force by US Special Envoy Richard Holbrooke, and US Secretary of State Madeleine Albright,[18] was the very credibility of the Atlantic alliance. Looking back, the Clinton administration may have drawn the conclusions that even the rhetorical – leaving aside the practical – involvement of Nato, and *ipso facto* of the US, in an external European crisis could prove an incautious strategy. The apparent US support for the development of an autonomous EU military capacity[19] stems partly from the subsequent realization that the alliance's founding principle of collective engagement does not apply under all circumstances (Gnesotto 1998).

> 66 The assumption of continued convergence between the EU and the US security interests is quite naive, to say the least 99

Even in such cases where the collectivity of engagements would be deemed as a necessity, one may question the suitability of the 'zero-casualty' doctrine that seems to have dictated the modalities of the US approach to international crisis management (notably the strategy of gradual escalation, air intervention as opposed to ground and the mandate of US aircraft to fly above 15,000 feet to reduce the risk to American pilots). This principle has been highly criticized for having sustained rather than terminated Milosevic's humanitarian exaction: the premature statement on the part of the US that no ground forces would be used undoubtedly encouraged Milosevic in his sins (David 1999). Hence, although airpower alone was seen by the Pentagon as *the* means to intervene in peripheral conflicts, the absence of additional commitment of ground troops was considered as a strategic error (Gere 1999). However, this option remains anathema to the US military doctrine, still experiencing the aftermath of such traumatic experiences as Vietnam and Somalia. Thus one of the lessons that the EU will have learnt from Kosovo is that such war is not only fought with American capability but also with American doctrine.

> 66 Although airpower alone was seen by the Pentagon as *the* means to intervene in peripheral conflicts, the absence of additional commitment of ground troops was considered as a strategic error 99

OLD TRUTH NUMBER 3 – THE COST OF NON-EUROPE[20]: THE EU CONTINUES TO FINANCE THE POLITICAL ADDED-VALUE OF NATO AND THE US

The cost of military presence and reconstruction in Kosovo[21] is a reminder to the EU that an autonomous security and defence capability, acting as a visible and effective deterrent might have reduced the present and future costs of stability and economic rebuilding:

As the EU faces the costs of assimilating or repatriating refugees, those of reconstruction in Yugoslavia, and policing any eventual settlement, the economic and political costs of creating a genuine CFSP may seem rather affordable.   (Duke 1999)

It is worth noting at this stage that the rejuvenation of the Common Foreign and Security Policy (CFSP) 'bare necessities' was only made possible via the convergence of national positions *vis-à-vis* the creation of an ESDP. The British reversal constitutes, in that respect, a determining element, which created momentum for the development of European 'defence' capabilities.

NEW DISCOURSES: ACTIONS SPEAK LOUDER THAN WORDS

The Saint-Malo Summit (4 December 1998) crystallized the Franco-British leadership, thus contributing to the reinvigoration of a vision for the EU's external ambition. The two countries displayed the need for the 'European Union [...] to be in a position to play its full role on the International stage' notably by acquiring a:

capacity for autonomous action backed by credible military forces, the means to decide to use them and a readiness to do so, in order to respond to International crises.

This formulation pragmatically recalls the conditions to be satisfied in order to develop a genuine common foreign and security policy, namely (De Schoutheete 1997):

1 formulating ambitions/objectives

2 endowing the EU with the relevant instruments to realize those objectives

3 showing the political will to use those new instruments.

Whereas the last point will remain for some time in the ambit of the unknown, many steps have been taken so as to meet the second requisite, by making Europe more effective in its defence capabilities.

THE OBJECTIVES: DROPPING THE 'D' IN ESDP?

The many different European Councils (Cologne, Helsinki, Feira) that followed the Saint-Malo Joint Declaration all explicitly referred to article 5 (collective defence) of the Nato treaty, thus restricting the 'Europe only' defence option to Petersberg tasks missions[22] (collective security). The Cologne Presidency Conclusions ruled out the full integration of WEU in the EU to avoid providing the EU with a collective defence clause. The option of converting the EU into a collective defence community would be anathema to the US as it would create a strategic rival to Nato. This outcome thus confirms the view that the EU heads of state or government gathered in the European Council to deal with CFSP issues often

> 66 The option of converting the EU into a collective defence community would be anathema to the US as it would create a strategic rival to Nato 99

had the US as 'an invisible guest' (Sloan 2000) at their negotiating table. All in all, collective defence will remain Nato's primary responsibility. In the EU context, it is therefore highly understandable that the emphasis in developing an autonomous capacity for military intervention has been placed upon crisis prevention and crisis management.

THE INSTRUMENTS OF ESDP: 'A CAPACITY FOR AUTONOMOUS ACTION' – TOP–DOWN, BOTTOM–UP

For the first time in the fifty years of the EU's development, *all* member states have taken a serious interest in agreeing exactly on what capability Europe needs. Building on the guidelines established at the Cologne European Council (3 and 4 June 1999), the EU heads of state and government thus agreed in Helsinki (10 and 12 December 1999) that in:

cooperating voluntarily in EU-led operations, Member States must be able, by 2003, to deploy within 60 days and sustain for at least 1 year military forces of up to 50,000–60,000 persons capable of the full range of Petersberg tasks.

Further to the setting up and progressive implementation of these 'headline goals' for the development of EU's military crisis management capability, steps have also been taken to develop common equipment requirements and programmes. The coming into existence of OCCAR (Organisation Commune de Coopération d'Armements) paves the way for the creation of a genuine European armament agency, based on pragmatic and improved defence cooperation. OCCAR was launched in November 1996 by the UK, France, Germany and Italy (the Netherlands having applied for membership) to manage defence procurement collaborations. One interesting feature of OCCAR is the renunciation of the 'juste retour' (whereby each country would get a share of work in proportion to the equipment it buys), so as to promote choice based on competition. Such a European agency would eventually have extensive responsibilities for all factors affecting the definition of the demand for armament products, thus facilitating in turn restructuring and consolidation on the supply side of the defence industry. This restructuring is already taking place: the European Aeronautic, Defence and Space (EADS)[23] constitutes, from that perspective, an oligopolistic attempt to foster concentration on the part of the Governments' demand. These recent undertakings are consistent with the view expressed by Lenzi (1997) that:

Pan-European security cannot be bestowed or imposed from above: it must be built from the bottom up by interlinkage and interaction of organisations and national efforts.

However promising the restructuring of the defence industry might be, it is difficult to dissent from the opinion that the acquisition of high-tech intelligence, airlift capacities and cleaver weapons will be a costly business. An enhancement of the member states defence expenditures is, however, highly unlikely, especially in view of the budgetary discipline imposed by the Stability and Growth Pact (Luxembourg 1997) for EMU members and foreseen in the Maastricht criteria for 'pre-ins'. As Hoffmann (2000) suggests:

Here there is a conflict between the commitment to a common defence and the commitment to a stable common currency.

'WHAT WE NEED IS THE WILL, WITH THAT ALL THINGS ARE POSSIBLE'

A clear conception of 'shared security interests' (Duke 2000) is still missing.

There are questions which arise from the apparently growing convergence in ESDP between France and the UK. France sees ESDP as a goal in itself, giving a very strong meaning to the word 'autonomous' in 'capacity for *autonomous* action' (cf. Saint-Malo and Cologne declarations mentioned above). Nato is, from that standpoint, the one (temporary) instrument that France has no option but to use in its quest for a genuine European Security Policy. France is therefore resolved to make every effort to bridge the technological capability gap between the EU and the US. As for the UK, on the other hand, ESDP is primarily a means to reinforce the relevance of the Atlantic alliance and the guarantee of the American engagement in Europe on a differentiated basis. ESDP thus allows the British to keep their entrenched attachment to the alliance while sustaining their new European 'enthusiasm'. Hence the question arises as to how long the Franco-British seemingly converging stance on ESDP can be maintained, notwithstanding the risk of a change of government in the UK (mainly) bipartite political system, which would probably undo what Blair's reversal has achieved so far. Furthermore, the use of military instruments is anathema to the EU's political culture.

> 66 France is resolved to make every effort to bridge the technological capability gap between the EU and the US 99

Another aspect deserves attention in this context. When faced with a crisis, EU member states will need to show the will to use force and to determine common objectives for military action. Without the political backing of the US and given the absence of any precedents in the EU's political culture, the decisiveness of such intervention may indeed remain diluted in the polity of the EU for some time. The EU's history is primarily one of profound aversion to using coercion, preferring instead the use of internal compromises and external dialogue. All the statements and instruments in the world may not be able to alter this entrenched feature of European construction. The EU has been so (purposely?) absorbed by the discussion of *how* to enhance its coercive influence that it has neglected the all-the-more-necessary debate on *whether* the member states will ever be willing to actually use its new military capabilities for coercive purposes. In the meantime, the EU's military reach constitutes a fundamental culture shift or revolution for the Union, which recalls what Davies (1996) referred to as the EU's 'profound crisis both in terms of identity and intent'.

> 66 EU member states will need to show the will to use force and to determine common objectives for military action 99

CONCLUSION: A DEFENCE IDENTITY FOR THE EU? DEBATING DEMOCRACY AND THE USE OF FORCE

The institutional problems and political uncertainties concerning the 'progressive framing of a common defence policy' (article 17 of the Treaty of the European Union as modified by the Treaty of Amsterdam) thus throw us into the quest for a European defence identity. If the tragic experience in Kosovo proves anything, it is precisely the need to clarify the role and responsibility of the EU in tomorrow's Europe. Can the Union, which is not a state proper but still a *sui generis* political concept/reality in the making, pursue anything like a foreign and security policy, let alone a common defence? The EU's moving borders, make the very concept of 'foreign policy' a blurred one, thus highlighting in a way the inextricability of internal and external EU politics. From that standpoint one may in fact wonder how the EU might reconcile its internal foundations based on the principles of tolerance, compromise and humility with the external use of violence. In other words, can the EU legitimately continue encouraging others to renounce, like it did, the use of force, while paradoxically making use of coercive instruments against third parties? As Andreani (1999) puts it:

Europe cannot, without contradicting itself, indulge in the crude power projection elsewhere in the world.

Should the EU rather remain true to its core characteristics of a 'civilian power', and nothing else? The understandable current euphoric stance on the EU's autonomous defence capability conveys the risk of confusing the centrality of military capacity with the definition of the EU international identity. The inclusion, following a Finnish–Swedish initiative, of non-military crisis management goals at the Helsinki and subsequently Feira European Councils, partakes of this need to de-sanctify the military dimension of power. Behind the issue of legitimacy, lie the questions of efficacy and willingness. Will member states accept to delegate authority to the EU in the security and defence arena? When called upon to fulfil the missions of peace enforcement, member states may be able to do so, thanks to the current ESDP developments. Whether they will be ready is a different story.

NOTES

1 The CPN is a network of academic institutions, non-governmental organizations (NGOs) and independent experts and was initiated by the European Commission in January 1997. The overall aim of the CPN is to provide both analytical and operational input to the EU system, thus contributing to preventing or alleviating violent and costly conflicts and crises.

2 The UN Security Council proved to be efficient in this respect by authorizing a Preventive Diplomacy Operation (UNPREDEP) in March 1993 on the border between Kosovo and Serbia.

3 Further information on the mandates and activities of the EU's special envoys may be obtained from http://ue.eu.int/pesc/defult.asp?lang=en.

4 http://europa.eu.int/comm/xeternal_relations/see/kosovo/1_year_on.htm. As far as member states' contributions are concerned, they are estimated to amount broadly to the same sum.

5 EU's common position of 19 March 1998.

6 Common Position 1999/273/CFSP defined by the Council on 23 April 1999.

7 Declaration by the presidency on behalf of the EU concerning the upsurge of violence in Kosovo, 3 March 1998.

8 *Ibid.*

9 Declaration of the General Affairs Council of 23 February 1998.

10 Speech of the German Foreign Minister, Joschka Fischer, at the Conference of the Foreign Ministers concerning the Stability Pact for South-Eastern Europe, Cologne, 10 June 1999, quoted in Biermann R. 1999.

11   Stability Pact for South-Eastern Europe, Cologne, 10 June 1999, http://europa.eu.int/comm/dg1a/see/stqpqct/10_june_99.html.

12   *Composite Paper, Regular Reports from the Commission on Progress Accession by each of the candidate countries*, 13 October 1999, European Commission, DG Enlargement, http://europa.eu.int/comm/enlargement/.

13   Presidency conclusions, Helsinki European Summit, 10 and 11 December 1999.

14   For more information, check http://europa.eu.int/comm/external_relations/see/sap/index.htm.

15   Presidency Conclusions, Appendix 2, Part III, Statement by the European Council concerning Kosovo.

16   Presidency Conclusions, Vienna European Council, 11 and 12 December 1998.

17   Among which: the comparatively modest defence budget in the EU member states; the allocation of public spending to oversized armies rather than to targeted investment in high-tech military equipment; the lack of cooperation between member states' defence industries (article 296 of TUE still provides exemptions from the rules of the common market for armament industries); the resulting 'Balkanization' of supply and demand in armament, at the expense of the much needed economies of scale.

18   For a selection of statements, press conferences, and other documentary material on the outbreak of conflict, see 1999.

19   'We want to see a Europe that can act effectively through the Alliance, or, if Nato is not engaged on its own, through the European Union', Strobe Talbott, US Deputy Secretary of State, at the Nato Ministerial Meeting, Brussels, 15 December 1999, http://www.nato.int/usa/states/s99121c.html.

20   The title 'the Costs of non-Europe' refers to Paolo Cecchini's 1988 *ex ante* evaluation of the benefits of further European integration (that of the Single Market Programme), which he carried out notably by looking at the *opportunity costs* of such an undertaking.

21   In 2001, for instance, the EU (not counting bilateral contributions by its member States provides 360 million Euros for Kosovo alone.

22   Adopted at the June 1992 WEU Ministerial Conference and incorporated into the Treaty of Amsterdam, the Petersberg tasks include humanitarian and rescue tasks, peace-keeping tasks and tasks of combat forces in crisis management, including peacemaking.

23   EADS company founded by DASA (D), CASA (E) and Aerospatial Matra (F) on 10 July 2000. The EADS will cover all transport capacities, ranging from C-212 to the A400M project and the entire panoply of high-tech missile systems.

8

THE MEDIA: INFORMATION AND DEFORMATION

ANTHONY WEYMOUTH

THE HISTORICAL CONTEXT: A COLLECTIVE MEMORY OF WAR

Western media coverage of the civil war in Bosnia–Herzegovina and of the Kosovo crisis emerged from and was fashioned by previous experience of war in the twentieth century. In particular it took World War II as its frame of reference and the ensuing confrontation between the East and West which was to last for nearly half a century after 1945.

Looking back at the twentieth century, it is possible to distinguish between two phases of media activity within Western liberal democracies. The first dates from 1945 and reaches a climax of sorts in 1989 with the fall of the Berlin Wall. The second phase begins in 1989, is marked significantly by the civil war in Bosnia in 1994, then by the Kosovo crisis in 1999, and continues into the new century. Identifying the political role of the Western media in the first phase will, I hope, throw some light on the new direction it may be taking in the second.

> 66 Looking back at the twentieth century, it is possible to distinguish between two phases of media activity within Western liberal democracies 99

The need for Western democracies to reassert their liberal ideologies upon the turbulence, created by the defeat of fascism and by the onset of the Cold War, offered a major role to the post-war media in the creation of the new world order. For over forty years the media actively represented to the peoples of Europe images of themselves as nations existing on one side of the Iron Curtain within a new world configuration, dominated by the two superpowers of the United States and the Soviet Union. Notwithstanding the different and conflicting political opinions, emanating from the extreme right and hard left within Western society relating to the North Atlantic Treaty, which were represented in some parts of the media, it is clear that the majority of the press and broadcasting sectors and, by extension, their readers, listeners and viewers, have either acquiesced to or positively supported the American-led alliance. There were times when this support for Nato and American domination in the West faltered and indeed, it reached its lowest ebb in the late 1960s when demonstrations against the war in Vietnam received sympathetic treatment in the mainstream media. Hobsbawm 1994: 244 describes American isolation thus,

The Vietnam war demoralized and divided the nations amid televised scenes of riot and anti-war demonstrations; destroyed a president; led to a universally predicted defeat and retreat after ten years (1965–75); and what was even more to the point, demonstrated the isolation of the USA.

At the end of the Vietnam conflict, a time when the economic prospects in the West promised greater material wealth than ever, despite the oil crises of 1973–4, the anti-American demonstrations receded without disappearing altogether. But, importantly, the Western media which had sympathetically represented the anti-Vietnam movement were less sympathetic in their reporting of other anti-American political groupings such as those campaigning for nuclear disarmament or for the removal of American troops from European soil. The general acquiescence to and support for the *Pax Americana* re-established itself and strengthened from the mid-1970s culminating in the extraordinary scenes of rejoicing at the fall of the Berlin Wall in 1989, an event wherein the majority of the Western media along with Western governments were among the principal celebrants. But with the Eastern Bloc crumbling literally before their eyes, governments in the West, their people and the media who served them, have had to reinterpret a world in which state communism was absent and where only one truly superpower remained – the USA.

It could be said, therefore, that 1989 marks the beginning of the second phase of Western media activity, one in which a new representation of society dominated by 'humanitarian' principles of liberal capitalism is proposed. The story has yet to be told, but the media coverage of the Kosovo crisis, with the emphasis on humanitarian values, is an indication of how the narrative may unfold over the longer term. If the Nato alliance needed to redefine itself in the post-Cold War period, it could be argued that the Kosovo crisis provided an ideal opportunity. As it had in the earlier phase, the media played and will play its part. By adopting a moral perspective, Western media coverage of the most significant displacement of people since the 1940s was made in a spirit of 'a plague on both your houses'. It simultaneously identified currents of both fascism and communism in its interpretation of events and, distanced itself from both. By drawing such direct and emotive parallels with the past, the media succeeded in stirring the collective memory of both Europeans and Americans in effective ways. The way was clear to present Nato on the world stage in a new light.

> 66 By adopting a moral perspective, Western media coverage of the most significant displacement of people since the 1940s was made in a spirit of 'a plague on both your houses' 99

With one or two spectacular exceptions the media do not create events.[1] Natural catastrophes on one hand and human malice on the other provide between them ample material for media reports without the need for confection on the part of journalists. But, while they do not create events, it can be argued that the media do make the news in the sense that they draw attention to specific issues at the expense of others, interpret them in certain ways, and are able to sustain public interest in them, influence opinion or terminate it, almost at will. At the time of writing, for example, barely six months after the cessation of hostilities, the allied follow-up to the crisis is mostly relegated to the occasional report in the Western press and is entirely absent in some sectors. Given the importance claimed for the allied intervention in Serbia at the time, the billions of dollars expended in the name of Western humanitarian values, and the social, economic and political consequences for Europe of a prolonged occupation of Kosovo, this dwindling in media attention is regrettable but not untypical. Commercial and political interests simply combine to point public attention in a different direction.

THE MEDIA NEVER TELL THE TRUTH

What motivated us to maintain the resolve of the alliance was our values: freedom, justice, compassion – basic human decency...

(Robin Cook, British Foreign Secretary)

You can't believe a word you're told ... truth is the first casualty of war ...

(Tony Benn, Member of Parliament)

When in the future, historians peer back through that dark prism of time to examine the twentieth century, they will have been bequeathed at least one unique and illuminating gift. Our century was the first to perfect and use the moving image to create a comprehensive visual history of the time in which we live. It will hand down to all who wish to know a vivid and moving documentary of all its great achievements as well as of its frequent acts of unspeakable cruelty. In our own time, we can only speculate upon the extent to which film has influenced public opinion and shaped the course of events, but it clearly has done so with increasing effect since the 1940s. Few observers doubt that the filming of the Vietnam War and its daily distribution on Western TV networks was instrumental in galvanizing public opinion against the continuing involvement of the USA in military conflict in south-east Asia. Equally, few can doubt that the 'management' of the media during the Gulf War demonstrated that the American military had drawn lessons from the media disasters of Vietnam by doing everything in its power to offer the public a sanitized version of events. It is highly likely that the distinctly unsanitized pictures coming out of Kosovo of alleged Serb brutality in attacking the civilian population in 1998 and in the spring of 1999 were instrumental in forcing the hands of Western politicians to take action against Milosevic. It is equally *un*likely that the action of the allies was motivated by public opinion alone. There were and are political objectives central to American and Nato policy that were triggered by the threat of further destabilization in the Balkans (see below). But throughout the summer of 1998, the Western media were focused less upon the increasing violence and persecution of ethnic-Albanian civilians in Kosovo than they were upon the impeachment proceedings against President Clinton in the so-called 'Lewinsky affair'. In the summer of 1998, as part of Europe literally

> **❝ It is highly likely that the distinctly unsanitized pictures of alleged Serb brutality were instrumental in forcing the hands of Western politicians to take action against Milosevic ❞**

burned, the world was invited by the media to speculate upon the nature and provenance of a stain upon a young woman's dress. However, widely televised footage and press coverage of the alleged massacre at Obria of twenty or more civilians – men, women, children of all ages on or about the 24 September 1998 – wrested the voyeurism of the Western media away from the impeachment proceedings and back to the Kosovo crisis. According to both Madeleine Albright, the American secretary of state and Richard Holbrooke, the US special envoy to the Balkans, the pictures of this massacre, attributed to the Serbs, were instrumental in provoking public outrage in America and in prompting President Clinton and his advisors into a new sense of urgency in relation to Milosevic (see below).

The media of Western, liberal societies share many features in common, the most striking of which being:

- they are frequently inaccurate in reporting events
- they are always biased.

Curiously enough, for reasons we have discussed elsewhere,[2] both these characteristics are admissible within the accepted norms of media performance in Western democracies. In the reporting of war, arguably the least rational and most terrible of human activities, it is hardly surprising that these two features become acutely more pronounced and distorted. The Kosovo war was no exception. Inaccuracies in the reporting of events were legion, and the range of opinion relating to the rights and wrongs of the war was extremely wide, albeit within the context of an ideological position which was predominantly pro-Western and anti-Serb.

THE ALLEGED SERBIAN VIOLATIONS OF HUMAN RIGHTS PRIOR TO 24 MARCH 1999

The series of events leading up to the military intervention by Nato in March 1999 can be traced in the medium term to July 1990 when the Serbian parliament suspended the Kosovo parliament and dismissed most Kosovo Albanians – teachers, police, civil servants – working in the state sector. In response to this Serbian reaction to their demands for greater autonomy, Kosovo Albanians increasingly rallied around the Democratic League for Kosovo which, under the moderate leadership of Ibrahim Rugova, set up a range of 'parallel' institutions – health clinics, schools, university institutes – paid for out of a voluntary tax by his own people. The early period between the suspension of the Kosovo parliament in 1990 and 1994 was characterized by police violence which Amnesty International describes as follows:

The most obvious targets of police violence have been ethnic Albanians, who by their political or other activity in the organisation of the 'parallel' society ... created outside official state structures. They included political activists ... members of the Democratic League of Kosovo, members of other ethnic Albanian political parties, teachers and academics; trade unionists, those involved in the organisation of humanitarian aid to families in need; ... local sports leaders. Journalists, former police officers and former military also appear to have been targeted.

(Amnesty International, 1998: 41–2)

The period between 1994 and the military intervention of Nato in 1999 is marked by a spiral of violence between the Serbian security forces and the newly formed KLA in the course of which the Kosovo Albanian civilian population was apparently attacked indiscriminately along with the KLA. It has to be said that there were also acts of extreme violence committed by the latter upon Serbian civilians not directly involved in the fighting. However, because 90 per cent of Kosovo is made up of Kosovo Albanians, they suffered the brunt of the violence. By August 1998 it was estimated by Amnesty International that more than 170,000 people had been forced by Serbian intimidation to flee their homes in search of safety in the countryside or across the frontier in adjacent countries such as Albania, Montenegro and Macedonia.[3] It is important that this situation of violence and high level of displacement of Kosovo Albanians prior to the bombing campaign is noted here, because once the bombing started, the blame for the flight of refugees was laid, by opponents of the bombing, at Nato's door.

The Western media widely represented the pre-intervention hostilities in a pro-Kosovo Albanian light, and the Serbian security forces, apparently unaware of the cameras, obligingly continued to shell civilian centres of population in broad daylight and in full view of the world's media. I spoke earlier of how in this gathering madness the pictures of the civilian dead in the village of Obria which appeared both on television and in the *New York Times* on 30 September 1998, concentrated the minds of the Americans on the need for direct action of some sort. Richard Holbrooke describes the effects of the pictures as turning the dialogue decisively in the direction of military action:

66 The Serbian security forces obligingly continued to shell civilian centres of population in broad daylight and in full view of the world's media 99

The *New York Times* sat in the middle of the oak table in the middle of the situation room ... terrible photograph of that dead person in that village [Obria] was a reminder of reality and it had a very positive effect upon the dialogue.[4]

A second alleged massacre of civilians was widely screened throughout the West on 15 January 1999 at Racak where there had been a confrontation between the Serbian forces and the KLA. Again, the Serbian military was obligingly on hand with tanks and artillery to demonstrate its skills upon the largely civilian population of the village. Subsequently, 45 bodies were found of persons whose dress and apparent circumstances in which they met their deaths strongly suggested that they were civilian farm workers[5] killed at close range by Serbs, just outside the village. As we have seen in other chapters, the Contact Group's attempts in January 1999 to bring order into the rapidly deteriorating situation on the ground failed at Rambouillet where both Serbs and Kosovo Albanians refused to sign an agreement, and failed again when in Paris the Albanian delegation signed up to the agreement but where the Serbs walked away, because, it was subsequently alleged, of the late addition of an appendix to the document that guaranteed its non-acceptance by Belgrade.[6]

Against this background of recrimination, alleged procrastination and rejection of the Contact Group's terms, the massacre at Racak was to prove the straw that broke the impatience of the West. The reasons for this refusal seemed clear to Nato: all intelligence reports suggested that the Serbs were intending to launch a new spring offensive against the Kosovo Albanians. The Western allies were coming round to the idea that a solution to the problem of Kosovo might not be negotiable after all. It has been argued by opponents of Nato's intervention that the media coverage of the events in Kosovo in the period that preceded the bombing was exaggeratedly anti-Serb and deliberately placed the ethnic cleansing policy of Milosevic within a context of renascent fascism which, they argued, it clearly was not. There can be little doubt that some film coverage for television audiences in the West certainly played on its audiences' recall of European fascism of the 1940s and so the question remains as to whether or not the references to fascism were justified. This issue will be raised again towards the end of this chapter and in the conclusion.

THE REPORTING OF THE ALLEGED SERBIAN
VIOLATIONS OF HUMAN RIGHTS POST-MARCH 1999

As reported by the Western media there was much variation on certain key issues:

- the evaluation of the numbers of displaced persons, both Albanian and Serb
- the extent of alleged massacres
- the alleged systematic rape of Albanian women by the Serbian paramilitaries
- the damage inflicted upon the Serbs by allied bombing.

This variation can be illustrated by examining one issue, the number of Kosovo Albanians thought to have been killed by the Serbian military. For example, the front-page headline of the *Independent* of 12 April 1999 asserted that,

Nato hits Serbs as fears rise for 100,000 'disappeared'...

On 18 April 1999 an American government official claimed on ABC television that:

Tens of thousands of young males have been executed ...[7]

On 19 April 1999 the US State Department announced that:

500,000 Albanian Kosovars ... are missing and feared dead ...[8]

Western television and radio also put out what in retrospect appear to be grossly inflated figures of Kosovo Albanian casualties resulting from Serbian violence.

On 20 and 21 April 1999 TF1 (French Television) estimated that the death toll was between 100 and 500,000.[9] Where did these figures come from? The answer would seem to be from no single source. Sometimes the politicians led the way with exaggerated and ill-judged references to 'genocide'. Prime Minister Blair, two weeks into the bombing campaign, spoke of the Serbian situation thus:

66 The politicians led the way with exaggerated and ill-judged references to 'genocide' 99

I pledge you now, Milosevic and his hideous racial genocide will be defeated ...

(Speech to Roumanian Parliament, 4 May 1999)

And the same term was repeated both by the German Foreign Minister and President Clinton to describe events in Kosovo between November 1998 and April 1999. Whether or not the media took their cue from this kind of extreme language is a matter for speculation, but in April 1999, as the bombing intensified, the European and American media were representing the possible loss of life in terms of the hundreds of thousands mentioned above.

In the aftermath of the conflict, such assertions were found to be significantly exaggerated. On 17 June 1999, the British Foreign Office, for example, announced that:

Ten thousand people had been killed in more than 100 massacres.[10]

At the time of writing, the forensic investigations of the International Criminal Tribunal for the former Yugoslavia (ICTY) have exhumed 2108 bodies.[11] Although this ICTY figure is by no means a final count, and is in any case appalling, the numbers represented in the media justifying Nato action in the height of the crisis were clearly, by ignorance or design, grossly exaggerated.

Inaccuracy in news representation of this kind is the consequence of many factors frequently operating simultaneously. There may be incompetence on the part of journalists who, lacking the necessary knowledge or failing to check verifiable events properly, file misleading reports. There may also be deliberately misleading press briefings from 'reliable sources' of the kind mentioned above which are too readily accepted by reporters hard pressed by editorial deadlines. This was a common criticism made of Nato briefings by the political left as well as by some of the more scrupulous members of the Western press corps during the conflict. There is also the element of bias – the deliberate ideological skewing of information – present in all media reporting, which I shall deal with in more detail below. But, in addition, superimposed on these mostly obvious and all-too-human reasons for inaccuracy in the reporting of the war, is what may be called the 'existential dilemma', the *angst* all journalists experience when having to report on the lack of reason and the violence of human conflict: the need to decide what is actually happening at a minute's notice for an audience, which, literally, in the case of the broadcasting media, is just the flick of a switch from the events as they unfold. The bombing of the Chinese Embassy on the 7 May 1999 is an example of this dilemma. Was it an error of tragi-comic proportions on the part of the American intelligence services? Or had the Pentagon made a cynical calculation to bomb – given the alleged evidence of Serbian military transmissons from the building – on the basis that the end justified the means and that, after the predictable protests from China, the incident would recede from public attention? No one in the press corps knew the answer to this question (even if Nato plausibly claimed it was an accident), and few can claim to know it today.[12]

On the issue of Western media bias, the reporting of events as they unfolded was, as we have noted above, almost by definition, predominantly pro-Western and anti-Serb. This particular ideological current in the media is not new; indeed it has its origins in Western perceptions of the Balkans dating from the beginning of the century, and was reinforced by World War II and the anti-communist Western stance which dates from the Cold War of 1947–89. In an interview with George Robertson, the British defence secretary at the time of the Kosovo conflict, Sir David Frost's question offers a good example of the Cold War ideological framework (i.e. references to allied zones and the partition of Germany) in which the crisis was often represented:

DF: I thought you were slightly softer there about no partition, ... no Russian areas of control ... So it's 100 per cent 'no' to Russian zones ?
GR: I'm saying it's 100 per cent 'no' to partition.

(Frost Interview, 13 June 1999, BBC2)

In addition to this kind of language which recalls the East–West divisions of the Cold War period, there was the rhetorical imagery in which the events of the Kosovo crisis were presented to viewers in the West as acts of neo-fascism. The disturbing scenes of makeshift tractor convoys filled with the old and women and children and endless files of distraught and frightened peoples making their way on foot to the borders of Kosovo in an attempt to escape Serb persecution, chillingly (and deliberately) recalled the Nazi persecutions of the mid century. Both before the allied invasion and during its course, pictures of the emaciated Albanian dead, killed in massacres attributed to the Serbs, further underscored the parallel drawn by the media with Nazism.[13] On the basis of this media reporting, it is not surprising that public indignation and outrage in the West was aroused to back Nato intervention and the bombing campaign which began on 24 March 1999.

> 66 The disturbing scenes of distraught and frightened peoples making their way on foot to the boaders of Kosovo chillingly (and deliberately) recalled the Nazi persecutions of the mid century 99

NATO STRATEGY: THE AERIAL CAMPAIGN

The Kosovo war was unique in one sense at least: it was the first in history to be won by air power alone without a single fatality being suffered by the airborne power in the battle zone. This was an extraordinary outcome, all the more so because the strategy was far from ideal in the eyes of the military planners. The 'bombing only' policy was largely the result of two factors. First it emerged from US domestic politics – a beleaguered president at loggerheads with both Senate and House of Representatives in the aftermath of the Lewinsky affair – where both upper and lower houses would have strongly opposed any suggestion of commitment of ground troops. Thus at the outset, the president went on television to announce to the public and to the Serbs that there would be no commitment to ground troops. The second factor was that, despite opinion polls in the UK and France indicating that a majority of people there were in favour of a land invasion, many other Nato allies, Germany and Italy in particular, were against any intervention by ground troops. A 'bombing only' campaign therefore was the only option available at the time, being the highest common denominator upon which all Nato countries could agree.

The bombing, when it started, was reported in the West with varying degrees of authenticity and detail. Aerial shots taken from the bombers themselves, clinically destroying Serbian targets made good television since the damage they inflicted was indicated by explosive clouds rather than by shattered buildings and civilian casualties. Although some images of civilian dead did get through, they were fewer in number and for the most part dried up when most Western journalists left Serbia in April 1999. Images of civilian casualties were presumably available to the West via footage taken by the news teams from other countries who were allowed to stay, but few such pictures were shown in the West. So, for the most part, unless the event was too important to ignore, such as the bombing of the Chinese Embassy in Belgrade or the alleged targeting of a civilian train at Lescovac, this kind of footage showing civilian dead was not widely distributed on the major channels.[14]

Thus, the war as seen on Western television was very much a war fit for Western eyes, where the awesome power of Nato's intervention, including its bombing 'errors', were off-set (and justified) by alleged oppression, torture and killing of civilians and by a calculated campaign of ethnic cleansing resulting in the displacement of hundreds of thousands of Kosovo Albanians. The pictures of the constant stream of refugees on the roads prior to the commencement of the bombing became a flood in the days that followed – the vast refugee camps, where few of the victims appeared to blame Nato for their plight, gave ample support to the West's insistence upon its humanitarian credentials.

WESTERN MEDIA REPRESENTATIONS: CONSENSUS AND DISSENT

In the UK, and to some extent elsewhere in Europe, the media reporting of the crisis from the onset of the bombing campaign until the cessation of the bombing in June 1999 can be summarized as falling under three categories. First, there were the majority voices of the 'humanitarian cause' advocated by Robin Cook, the British foreign secretary, the British prime minister, Tony Blair, President Clinton and the heads of other Nato member countries. There was general support for military intervention in Kosovo on humanitarian grounds in the mass media, although the nature of this intervention, i.e. Nato's legal rights and military strategy, were questioned and frequently found wanting. This majority position of the media may be deemed effectively to have been supporting the evolving allied position under American and British leadership.

Second, there were in both the press and broadcasting what may be termed the dissident voices of Western liberalism; voices which also in the name of non-ideological[15] humanitarian values took issue with the alleged high-mindedness of the American /British position by pointing out the contradictions in its implementation. Such voices were in the minority but widely disseminated when they belonged to such eminent and respected journalists as the BBC's John Simpson and Robert Fisk of the *Independent*.

Lastly, there were the voices of the far left, for whom the Nato intervention in Kosovo was an inadmissible act of aggression upon a sovereign state and the extension of American foreign policy objectives in central Europe. In Britain as elsewhere in Europe, the voices of the far left, were loud and forceful at their point of expression; but, unlike in France and Italy, in Britain they were not widely disseminated since they were restricted to the pages of the minority press and also received scant air time.

THE HUMANITARIAN CAUSE

At the end of a particularly inhumane century, to claim that intervention in the internal affairs of a sovereign state can be justified on humanitarian grounds may perhaps be applauded as both shrewd and appropriate reasons for action by the Nato allies. It was shrewd because the people needed little convincing; the evidence – the shattered villages, the streams of refugees, the dead and the accounts of atrocities related to the cameras by distraught civilians – was all too clear. Rarely has a humanitarian cause been supported by such an immediacy of apparent documentary proof. If there were other reasons for the intervention by Nato of a more complex nature, and there is ample evidence that there were, there was little need for them to be explained to the public. The newsreel footage that concentrated on the human disaster, widely distributed throughout the world, said it all. Understandably, given the events of a similar nature that had occurred fifty years earlier in Europe, to many it was both appropriate and sufficient justification for action.

However, motives other than humanitarian can be discerned in the public declarations of some European politicians. In his speech at the Lord Mayor's Banquet, on 14 April 1999, Robin Cook asserted that the events in Kosovo were, in part at least, unacceptable because of their geographical location:

… it is … a Europe that represents the equal rights of every citizen regardless of ethnic identity … a Europe that does not just tolerate cultural difference but treasures them as part of the richness of our community …

Any alert observer will have noted that the new humanitarian role claimed for Nato is linked to the geopolitical sphere of Europe and its freedoms historically guaranteed in the twentieth century by the Atlantic alliance. While the principal and driving reason offered by the media for Nato intervention in Kosovo was indeed a humanitarian one, others were not entirely ignored by the British press. The *Guardian* leader of 26 March 1999 takes specific issue with the 'single justification' argument, pointing out that the West had political and economic reasons in plenty for moving against Serbia:

> 66 While the principal and driving reason offered by the media for Nato intervention in Kosovo was indeed a humanitarian one, others were not entirely ignored by the British press 99

National, American and European interests are inevitably involved ...
regional stability in the unstable Balkans, allowing a start to be made on the
vital economic reconstruction ... The Italians don't want Albanian refugees
clogging up Brindisi harbour ... Nato 'needs' to be tested in its new guise
and this conflict will do as well as any other.

For the politically alert at least, the reasons beyond the humanitarian
were available although not always well represented in the mass media.
As will be noted later, it was these political and other reasons which were
the focus of attention of the far left in both British and continental
European politics. However, as we shall see in the next section, in which
we examine some of the mediated events in Kosovo, these other political
and economic reasons did not make the headlines. It was enough for
Nato to allow the pictures of apparent unspeakable acts of cruelty to
speak for themselves. Thus, intervention in the name of humanitarian
values such as 'justice, compassion and basic human decency' of the
kind referred to by the British foreign secretary, Robin Cook, found a
general consensus of support among the majority of the European and
American media. Within this framework of consenting voices there was
plenty of scope for argument about the means of achieving Western
objectives, but the objectives themselves, the halting of the perceived
Serb oppression of the Kosovo Albanians and the punishment of
Milosevic, were not in question. Thus in the period leading up to the
bombing and during the Nato operation itself, we can identify major
themes (not all dealt with here) of the mass media as follows:

- humanitarianism: definitions and justifications
- alleged Serbian crimes against humanity
- Milosevic, the untrustworthy and ruthless dictator
- role and strategy of Nato
- role and strategy of the UN
- American and allied response to the crisis: motivation and respective
  roles of President Clinton, Prime Minister Blair and other European
  players
- European unity over foreign policy and defence
- role of Russia
- the KLA as pro-Nato defenders of the Albanian population
- war damage, and casualties both military and civilian.

DISSIDENT VOICES IN THE MAINSTREAM MEDIA

While the course of the bombing campaign was reported in the main from a pro-Nato perspective in the West, there were dissident voices. In the UK these dissenters fell, as previously indicated, into two groups: high-profile media critics whose reporting was widely publicized in the press and on television, and critics of the far left whose opinions were much less reported by the mainstream media. Of the first group, the opinions of Robert Fisk of the *Independent* and John Simpson of the BBC are good examples of a kind of criticism of the campaign which while representing minority voices in the media and in the country generally, was triply effective in its impact, first, because of the distinguished sources of origin, the *Independent*, the *Sunday Telegraph* and the BBC; second, because these outlets commanded mass audiences, and finally because these journalists saw fit to challenge Nato's motives on the very humanitarian grounds it had itself claimed as the reason for military intervention. Robert Fisk, in a relentless series of articles criticizing Nato throughout the campaign, persisted in revealing to the British public the costs in terms of civilian lives which Nato and some other media coverage referred to as 'collateral damage'. His reports were shocking in their detail and a direct challenge to Nato's insistence that it was not targeting the civilian population. When the studios of Serb Television were bombed in late April 1999, Fisk wrote a stinging, shocking account of the loss of life resulting from the attack:

> **Robert Fisk persisted in revealing to the British public the costs in terms of civilian lives which Nato and some other media coverage referred to as 'collateral damage'**

Hanging upside-down from the wreckage was a dead man, in his fifties perhaps, although a benevolent grey dust had covered his face. Not far away also upside down – his legs trapped between tons of concrete and steel – was a younger man in a pullover, face grey, blood dribbling from his head onto the rubble beneath. Deep inside the tangle of cement ... was all that was left of a young woman, burnt alive when Nato's missile exploded in the control room ...

John Simpson, the world affairs editor of the BBC, also challenged the humanitarian claims for Nato's aerial bombardment by focusing on the human contradictions on the ground. At one stage during the bombing, his reports so discomforted the British government that unnamed sources were suggesting that he was himself the victim of Serbian propaganda and that his nightly reports from Belgrade to the BBC's *Nine O'Clock News* were being supervised by the Serbs.

An extract from an article written for the *Sunday Telegraph* early in the bombing campaign well illustrates the kind of scepticism that Simpson brought to his reports in the subsequent weeks. Here he suggests that Nato tactics are backfiring:

The differences between the Gulf War … and the war against Yugoslavia now are instructive. Iraq is essentially one man governing as a despot. Here, although President Milosevic has skilfully used his powers under the state of emergency to strengthen his political position and silence his critics, he does not need to urge his forces against the ethnic-Albanians in Kosovo: they are fully prepared to take the initiative there.

… the bombing here is supposed to show the Serbian people that Slobodan Milosevic has led them astray. It isn't working.

(*Sunday Telegraph*, 28 March 1999)

Both during and after the cessation of hostilities, Simpson strongly defended the candour and the nature of his reporting:

There's a depressing pattern: when things go wrong British governments tend to lose their nerve. They get frightened at the thought of people getting independent, objective information so they start a whispering campaign about the personal abilities of the broadcasters. Anonymously of course. (*Sunday Telegraph*, 18 April 1999)

In the cooler light of retrospect, an examination of the reports filed by Fisk and Simpson clearly shows that their candour is even-handed and applied to both sides. The offence in the eyes of British politicians was presumably a simple one: these journalists persistently reminded the British public of a truism that lay half concealed behind the military euphemism of Nato briefings, namely that 'collateral damage' meant civilian deaths. I shall return to this issue in the conclusion of this chapter.

DISSIDENT VOICES ON THE FAR LEFT

The dissenting voices of the far left, in contrast with those of Fisk and Simpson, did not receive wide media coverage in the UK, although they did receive wider coverage elsewhere in Europe. This will come as no surprise to anyone familiar with media politics in Britain which are dominated by the voices of the right and centre. While sharing the horror of the effects on the civilian population of bombing, groups of the far left imposed a familiar interpretation of huge and sinister proportions on Nato's intervention in Kosovo. According to this account, the campaign was perceived as an act of capitalist aggression on behalf of the IMF and Central Intelligence Agency (CIA). Its strategic objectives were economic and four-fold:

- former Yugoslavia was seen a gateway to European eastern oil supplies
- the natural resources of Kosovo itself offered a rich and coveted supply of raw materials to the West
- the reconstruction of Kosovo represented potentially very lucrative contracts for Western companies
- the West, and the IMF in particular, were eager to accelerate the privatization of the Serbian economy thereby opening it up to the global market, a desire the Serbs had vigorously resisted.[16]

This overtly ideological, and some might say, familiar interpretation of perceived Western military aggression by the far left, while vociferously proposed, received scant public attention outside the very limited circulations of its own media for the reasons already stated.

CONCLUSION

Halimi and Vidal (2000), in an impressively documented article, argue persuasively that Western media grossly exaggerated the scale and nature of Serbian brutality against the Kosovo Albanians. They point particularly to the charge of genocide that underpinned some essential arguments for Nato's intervention on humanitarian grounds and which in retrospect must be judged to be exaggerated.

While liberal observers in the West may share a sense of anger at this kind of disinformation, it would be disingenuous to be wholly outraged by the media reporting at the time. There are, in the West, ideological assumptions founded on concepts of democratic freedom, free trade, and free movement of capital, as well as a sense of military supremacy, to which certainly the majority of the people of the member states of Nato either subscribe or aspire. The historical opposition of liberal capitalism to both fascism and communism in the second half of the twentieth century has predisposed the people of Western democracies to perceive post-war conflicts as resurgences of the earlier struggles between the extreme left and right. Such perceptions run deep in the ideological consciousness of the West and greatly influenced the media in their interpretation of Serbian activities in Kosovo. With hindsight it is becoming clear that the Western media's representation of events did indeed significantly exaggerate the numbers of Kosovo Albanian dead and play down the damage inflicted on the civilian population of Serbia by the Nato bombing campaign. Can such distortions be justified?

> 66 The Western media's representation of events did indeed significantly exaggerate the numbers of Kosovo Albanian dead and play down the damage inflicted on the civilian population of Serbia by the Nato bombing campaign 99

The answer to this question may be 'yes, but with extreme difficulty' with regard to the reporting of Serbian brutality, for the following reasons. First, in the chaotic exodus of Kosovo Albanians in April 1999, calculations of the dead and missing were difficult if not impossible to make with any accuracy. Although it was incautious of the media to report hearsay or be influenced by the rhetoric of politicians or Nato briefings, in the absence of hard figures and in the context of a news-hungry public impatiently waiting in the West, inaccuracies were as inevitable as they were inexcusable. Second, there is the issue of a higher order begged by this question that relates to the Western experience of violence in the last half of the twentieth century. Genocide, even if it was a major political objective of Nazism in the immediate pre-war period, was, for obvious reasons, never publicly declared. It was insidious and incremental, beginning with verbal then physical abuse and social exclusion, and the rounding up of people which only later developed into their systematic destruction.

The problem for Western democracies and their media confronting the events in Kosovo was, among others, knowing how to interpret the violence in terms of the intensity of its racial underpinning and predicting where the violence was leading. The Holocaust was not merely the logical extension of the insanity of fascism, it represented the failure of Western values to prevent it. In Bosnia in 1994 and in Kosovo in 1999, the West was again confronted with the spectre of massacre and ethnic cleansing, this time not in Cambodia or Rwanda, but in its own back yard. Haunted by the mistakes of the past and fearful of the outcome of this new calamity as it unfolded, politicians and the media may well have engaged in a feeding frenzy of rumour, conjecture and ambiguous information, and exaggerated the nature of Serbian brutality. But it is conceivable at least that this overreaction occurred more out of ignorance (in the absence of verifiable information) than out of a primary desire to mislead the public.

With regard to the so-called 'collateral damage', the killing of Serbian civilians, and the tactical targeting of electricity supplies, bridges and oil refineries that affected the whole civilian population including the sick, the elderly and the very young, the downplaying by the media of the damage was an act of disinformation. But at the heart of this shameful act lies yet another mediated self-deception to which the West has succumbed. While an aerial campaign waged from a height of 15,000 feet may well have ended without a single fatality for the airmen of Nato, the same altitude factor and the lethal cargoes of state-of-the-art bombs guaranteed the loss of civilian lives. It would have been more honest of the politicians, the Western media and their audiences, to have publicly acknowledged from the outset, the inevitability of civilian casualties. To have done so would probably not have changed the decision to launch an air attack. But if, having confronted the certainty of civilian casualties, the West had still been resolved to go on, it would at least have prevented the charges of hypocrisy and deception-by-euphemism that passed for facts as the bombing took its toll.

> 66 It would have been honest of the politicians, the Western media and their audiences, to have publicly acknowledged from the outset, the inevitability of civilian casualties 99

NOTES

1 Some readers will have heard at least of the notorious radio hoax played on a terrified American audience by Orson Welles in 1938 announcing an impending invasion from Mars.

2 See Weymouth and Lamizet 1996 Chapter 1.

3 See Amnesty International 1998 Chapter 2.

4 Interview, *War in Europe* Channel 4 (30 January 2000).

5 OSCE 1999.

6 Critics of the drafting of the Rambouillet document point out that additional clauses were appended by the Contact Group (referred to as Appendix B) which ensured Serb non-cooperation. These clauses conceded to Nato 'free and unrestricted passage and unimpeded access throughout FRY, including associated airspace and territorial waters'. These clauses were abandoned in the negotiations that continued after the bombing had begun. The content of the Rambouillet document was not made available in the UK until 1 April 1999 when a single copy in the House of Commons (see Noam Chomsky, 'Another way for Kosovo' in *Le Monde Diplomatique*, March 2000, English edition).

7 See Halim and Vidal 2000.

8   *Ibid.*

9   *Ibid.*

10   *Ibid.*

11   OSCE 1999.

12   It was claimed subsequently in at least one British newspaper that the Chinese Embassy was deliberately targeted for alleged assistance given to the Serbian military (*Observer*, 28 November 1999).

13   'I was determined to shoot it as well as I could and try and get the most emotional pictures possible' (TV journalist, interview in *War in Europe*, Channel 4 (31 January 2000)).

14   Martin Bell, MP and former reporter for the BBC suggests that television's motives for not showing casualties is determined by self-censorship in the name of protecting its audiences from the horror of war: 'There is certainly a resistance to showing things as you find them because the editors believe you shouldn't upset people at home.' *Between Ourselves*, BBC Radio 4 (13 June 2000).

15   The term 'non-ideological' is used here loosely to denote non-identifiable, non-doctrinaire attitudes or beliefs which by definition cannot be attributed to a political party or creed. We are aware of the specialized meaning of 'ideology' used in Critical Linguistics which purposes that *all* language has ideological content.

16   Benn 1999.

THE USA: TO WAR IN EUROPE AGAIN

SABRINA P. RAMET

CONSTITUTIONAL CONCERNS

In late March 1999, the USA joined its Nato allies in launching a two-month-long aerial campaign against Yugoslavia. The campaign provoked widespread controversy in the media, in policy circles, and in the US Congress itself. Constitutional concerns quickly came to the fore as some legislators claimed that the president of the United States, although bearing the title Supreme Commander of US Forces, had no constitutional right to commit American forces to combat without prior Congressional approval. This in turn implied a review, and possibly revision, of the War Powers Act of 1973 (50 USC 1544) under which the president had been authorized precisely such a right, for a period of up to 60 days.

Several points may be stated at the outset. First, the constitutional framework for foreign policy-making was crafted, quite consciously, with an eye to obstructing and impeding the commitment of American forces and resources abroad – the very phrase 'foreign entanglements', favoured by the Founding Fathers, is redolent with disapproval. Although the office of the president represents the country as a whole, the individual congressmen, congresswomen, and senators represent severally the sectional interests of their districts or states. It was with these considerations in mind that Congress was given authority to approve or disapprove commitments to war.

Second, the US government, rather obviously, does not function like a think-tank, much less like a university. Legislators cannot afford to specialize in any particular area of policy-making and, as the congressional record amply illustrates, cannot even take such advantage of their research staffs as might permit them to make balanced, reasoned judgements on all subjects to come up for discussion. The Congressional debate about Kosovo, in particular, reveals an appalling level of ignorance about Kosovo on the part of a number of representatives. While ignorance on one or another subject may be excused, energetic representations and remonstrations on the basis of complete ignorance are less excusable, especially when they carry the risk of crippling vital foreign policy endeavours.

Third, the executive branch itself may be ill equipped to act fully 'rationally' to employ that fashionable buzz-word, on any but a few issues at a time. Crisis-overload is part of the explanation. But beyond that, there are two procedural biases that subvert the possibility of rationality in foreign policy. The first is that, although provided with formidable staffs of researchers, decision-makers in the departments of State and Defence often fail to heed the recommendations of their support staffs. The insistence on keeping the arms embargo in place against the Bosnian Muslims, 1991–5, is one example of this procedural myopia. The claim by Warren Christopher, President Clinton's first Secretary of State, that German advocacy of recognition of Slovenia and Croatia was somehow 'responsible' for the outbreak of war is another example of the failure of expertise to percolate to the top.

Fourth, within the Congress, as among the American public at large, there has been a tendency to downplay recognition of the fact that the USA, as a full member of Nato, might have some obligations towards that body. Hence, for example, we find Representative Horn from California telling his colleagues in the House of Representatives on 28 April 1999 that:

If the Europeans have a European problem, they ought to be making the decision and they ought to be sending their own ground troops.[1]

But if the USA, as the strongest power in Nato, were to tell its allies that it was unwilling to participate in Nato's first operational campaign, at a time when the leading European Nato allies shared a view that Milosevic's repressive policies were threatening European stability, would that not spell the end of Nato? Perhaps Congressman Horn would in fact advocate the dismantling of Nato, but, if so, he did not indicate in his comments on that day, what benefits he believed might accrue to the USA, if any, from the dismantling of Nato.

'Realist-solipsists' often construe American national interest as if it some-how existed in a vacuum, divorced from the rest of the world. Solipsists sometimes refer the question to the observation that, in the absence of a frontal assault on American soil or property abroad, no vital US interests should be thought to be threatened. Along these lines, we find Congressman Metcalf from Washington state advising his colleagues:

I have opposed US military action in the Balkans without a declaration of war. There are no vital US interests now being threatened anywhere in Europe, certainly not in the Balkans, worthy of a declaration of war. We really have no business there militarily. We should not be committing acts of war there.[2]

Or again, Representative Ganske of Iowa, construing national interest narrowly, urged that:

while the American public is rightly concerned about the human rights violations in Kosovo, few believe that our own country's interests are at risk.[3]

Fifth, the process of policy-making in conditions of crisis must endure elements of distortion that routine policy-making is spared. The media, with their openness to 'everything-experts', 'overnight experts', and colourful personalities who offer advice on subjects remote from their areas of specialization (for example, novelist Norman Mailer offering advice on Kosovo),[4] and with their heavy reliance on government sources for information, both inform and disinform, sowing confusion even while providing, in scattered fragments, the raw material for a critique of the media's own confusion. The media figure as mediators between the government and the public, passing along the prejudices and dispositions of the policy-makers for the public to ingest and regurgitate in public opinion polls, in turn 'justifying' the policies already devised by the government. As James Sadkovich notes:

> ❝ The media figure as mediators between the government and the public, passing along the prejudices and dispositions of the policy-makers, in turn 'justifying' the policies already devised by the government ❞

The media are part of a feedback loop that includes their sources, their audience, and themselves. They mediate information from their sources, they define what is newsworthy, and they distribute it in the form of news. The audience then mediates and legitimates by consuming the news and feeding it back in various ways, including public opinion surveys. Raw material from sources is thus processed by journalists, consumed by the public, analysed by pollsters, and recycled by political advisers.[5]

This loop breaks down from time to time. In the Vietnam War, for example, as in the Watergate crisis, the media, or at least a portion of the media, defected, in the process undermining the government's capacity to maintain its monopoly of mainstream discourse. This loop also broke down during the Nato aerial campaign against Yugoslavia in 1999; personal foibles, knee-jerk opposition to any and all military ventures, paranoid fears about conspiracies, and wild comparisons of Milosevic with either Ho Chi Minh or Davey Crocket, Tony Blair with Benito Mussolini, and Bill Clinton alternately with Neville Chamberlain, Winston Churchill, Mexican General Santa Anna, or even Adolf Hitler, all played their parts in a largely fruitless debate about the venture in Kosovo.[6]

But on the whole, as Sadkovich notes, journalists are eager to preserve their contacts with policy-makers and to avoid being excluded from access. The result is that the media all too often treat policy-makers, or even indicted war criminals, with deference and respect, even where a more critical orientation might seem to be indicated.

And sixth, in the policy debate concerning Kosovo, there has been a double polarization at work, subverting 'rational' discourse and, in the case of one leg of the polarization, making discourse hostage to purely partisan interests. Here I am thinking of the tendency of the Republican legislators to adopt a posture of knee-jerk 'nay-saying' to whatever policies Democratic President Clinton might adopt. In the case of the Bosnian War, for example, when President Clinton prioritized coordination with America's Nato allies and agreed to leave the controversial arms embargo in place, moving all too slowly to make an effective military response, Republicans expressed outrage and demanded the immediate lifting of the embargo. Republicans wanted decisive action against Milosevic, or so they said, and professed to be unimpressed by considerations of the unity and coherence of the Nato alliance.

> 66 The Republican legislators expressed outrage and, in some cases, demanded the immediate cessation of any decisive action against Milosevic's regime 99

In 1999, when the president, again acting in coordination with America's Nato allies, agreed to cooperate in a joint Nato campaign, the Republican legislators expressed outrage and, in some cases, demanded the immediate cessation of any decisive action against Milosevic's regime. Representative Tom Campbell (R – California), espousing this line, opined that

'... it is fair under the Constitution for us to declare that war if we are at war, and if we do not wish to engage in the war, to withdraw from that war.[7]

Since the Congress had already agreed that none of America's Nato powers wanted to see war declared against Belgrade, the conclusion followed inevitably, for Campbell, that America should withdraw from the engagement haste-post-haste.

As for the other leg of the 'double polarization' in American policy-making, I am referring here to the irresoluble conflict between a camp that might variously be described by the terms *idealist*, *internationalist*, and *Wilsonian*, and a camp that might be designated alternatively by the terms *materialist*, *isolationist*, and – albeit contentiously – *solipsist*, and which rallies its forces under the banner of supposed *'realism'*. Insofar as these camps subscribe to fundamentally opposed premises, it is an unusual event when they can agree on matters of grave importance.

CONGRESSIONAL PERCEPTIONS

There had been Congressional hearings on Kosovo since at least the mid-1980s,[8] but it was perhaps not until the election of Ibrahim Rugova, a Shakespeare scholar, as president of the opposition government of 'the Republic of Kosova' in May 1992 that the Congress began hearing testimony to the effect that the situation in Kosovo was in need of urgent remedy. On 21 October 1992, for example, Dr. Bujar Bukoshi, Prime Minister of the opposition government of Kosovo, spoke before the National Press Club in Washington DC, and warned those present of 'an alarming and very dangerous situation in Kosova'. He told the press club of his government's continuing efforts to persuade American 'officials to undertake something urgently to stop the aggression in Kosova ...'[9] Two years later, Bukoshi was back on Capitol Hill to give testimony before the House Foreign Affairs Committee. Warning that the systematic repression of the Albanians of Kosovo had escalated in the preceding months, Bukoshi called for the internationalization of the Kosovo crisis, echoing Ibrahim Rugova's call for an international protectorate for Kosovo.

However, the USA and other Western powers declined to act on Kosovo's behalf or even to put Kosovo on the agenda for the Dayton peace talks, in spite of Kosovo president Rugova's pleas to that effect. Rugova had persuaded the Albanians of Kosovo to practise a Gandhi-like passive resistance against the Serbs and, in the absence of major conflict locally, the Western powers were disinclined to act. Yet the scale of human rights violations in the province, well documented by Amnesty International and Human Rights Watch Helsinki, was staggering. In 1997 alone, more than 10,000 Kosovo Albanians suffered injuries at the hands of Serbian/Yugoslav authorities, according to the Kosovo Albanian Committee for the Protection of Freedom and Human Rights, based in Pristina.[10] By the end of that year, the KLA was claiming credit for attacks on Serbian police installations, in a clear reflection of growing disillusionment among Albanians with Rugova's pacifist tactics. But American officials were slow to take the KLA seriously. In February 1998, in particular, Robert Gelbhard, then American chief mediator in the Balkans, characterized the KLA as 'a small, irrelevant terrorist group.'[11] Gelbhard would have to eat his words: at the end of June, he joined special envoy Richard Holbrooke for a meeting in Switzerland with two ranking KLA figures. As of June 1998, the KLA controlled about 40 per cent of the territory of Kosovo.

> 66 Rugova had persuaded the Albanians of Kosovo to practise a Gandhi-like passive resistance against the Serbs 99

However, on 29 June, Serbian forces launched a massive counteroffensive against the Albanian insurgency and, at a cost of US$2 million per day, pushed back the KLA, torching Albanian villages in the process. By mid-September 1998, some 700 Albanians were dead and another 265,000 homeless.[12]

On 17 September 1998, the OSCE held a hearing on atrocities in Kosovo, with co-chairman Christopher H. Smith (R – New Jersey) presiding. In testimony before this commission, Assistant Secretary of State John Shattuck described the situation in the province as 'a humanitarian emergency and a human rights crisis, and a very serious catastrophe in the making,' noting that some 18,000 homes had been totally or partially destroyed in the course of the Yugoslav Army's counteroffensive.[13] Shattuck concluded that

... only the establishment of a democratically elected government that reflects the will of all the people of Serbia and respects civil society, opposition voices, and an independent press will end this larger crisis.[14]

As concern for the plight of the province's now-homeless Albanians escalated, the Western powers reflected that a failure to act early might risk a
replication of the sanguinary pattern of events already witnessed in
Bosnia. Accordingly, in the course of late September and early October
1998, Nato brought pressure to bear on Belgrade, eventually obtaining
an agreement between Yugoslav president
Milosevic and US envoy Holbrooke; the
Albanians were not party to this agreement.
Under the terms of this agreement, Milosevic
agreed to pull most of his forces out of
Kosovo by 16 October, reducing their
strength to the pre-28 February level. In fact, Milosevic withdrew what
was considered an 'acceptable' portion of his forces only by 27 October,
but subsequently reversed his marching orders. By 23 December,
Yugoslav Army troop strength in the province had actually increased
from 18,000 as of October (pre-agreement) to 23,500. As of 24 March
1999, Milosevic had some 29,000 troops in Kosovo.

> 66 Milosevic withdraw what was considered an 'acceptable' portion of his forces but subsequently reversed his marching orders 99

The Commission took up questions of Balkan instability again in a 10
December 1998 hearing, with Representative Smith once more presiding;
Smith's comments on this occasion reflected some 'Wilsonian' sympa-
thies. After noting that

human rights abuses in one country are not an 'internal matter' but a
legitimate concern for this country and all others

Smith confessed that he and other congressmen were 'disgusted' by the
history of Western collaboration with Milosevic in the quest for Balkan
peace. Reinforcing the conclusion already drawn at the earlier hearing,
Smith called democratic change in Serbia the key to long-term Balkan
stability – a view echoed by Daniel Serwer, a Senior Fellow at the United
States Institute of Peace.[15] Serwer offered the commission a detailed
plan for promoting democratization in Serbia, urging the USA to
increase its spending to assist democratization in that country from
US$18 million (the level of such aid for 1998) to US$53 million in
1999. His budget called for US$10 million in assistance to independent
media, US$7 million in assistance to opposition political parties, US$5
million in assistance to alternative education networks, and US$5 mil-
lion earmarked for indigenous NGOs (among them, the Serbian
Orthodox Church), with the remainder of the funds to be dispersed for
other purposes.[16]

At this time, unarmed international observers attached to the OSCE Kosovo Verification Mission (KVM) were witnessing some 'strange' developments, incompatible with the spirit and letter of the October agreement. As Ambassador William Walker, head of the KVM, testified the following April:

We saw by mid-December increasing evidence of civilian quote, unquote 'home guards' being armed by the security forces, weapons being handed out. We saw increasing evidence of the paramilitary forces. The famous Arkan and his people started making their appearances in mid-December. We also saw a very disturbing trend, which was an increasing arrogance by the troops, by the army, by the MUP [security forces of the Ministry of Internal Affairs]. They would shell villages, they would loot, they would torch villages. They would routinely beat people in the villages, in front of the media – apparently with no shame as to what they were doing. Another disturbing trend in mid-December was that the violence moved into the population centres, moved into places such as Pristina ... We were denied access to trouble spots, we would hear there was shooting going on or a village was under attack. We would try to get our people out there, and most often the MUP or the VJ [the Army of Yugoslavia] would stop us from going in. And since they were armed and we were not, it was very difficult to push forward. And occasionally, the KLA also denied us access. There was also an increase in physical threats, abusive behaviour becoming normal against our people. And the risk of serious injury to unarmed verifiers in fact became a statistical likelihood.[17]

The Serbian massacre of 45 Albanian civilians in the village of Racak in mid-January 1999 proved to be a turning point in terms of congressional perceptions and understandings of the situation. Already in early February, senators Richard Lugar (R – Indiana), Joe Lieberman (D – Connecticut), and Chuck Hagel (R – Nebraska) wrote a letter to President Clinton, pressing their belief that:

... only the threat of military force will bring at least [at last?] Serbian attention to the situation .... The United States has to be prepared with military force, including bombing of all parts of Serbia, if necessary, to try to bring Milosevic to the [negotiating] table.[18]

This was a bold summons, involving unprecedented use of Nato resources in the European theatre.

Meanwhile, Western-mediated peace talks between delegations from Belgrade and the KLA got underway on 6 February. The KLA delegation eventually signed the compromise plan on 18 March, but the Yugoslav delegation balked. On 20 March, the KVM was pulled out of Kosovo, and Belgrade, which had been beefing up its military presence just north of the provincial border since late February, dramatically escalated military operations against Albanian civilian settlements.

Later, Milosevic would argue that there had been no refugees before the inception of Nato's aerial campaign on 24 March.[19] A number of gullible persons, some of them making uncritical use of internet sources, accepted Milosevic's claim, conveyed by sophisticated Serb lobby groups and their web sites, at face value, even agreeing with the official Serbian line that the refugees were fleeing *from Nato bombardment*. Why the Serbs were not fleeing from Novi Sad and Belgrade and other areas which were being directly targeted, while the Albanians were fleeing from areas not being targeted by Nato was of course, not explained. But the facts are, in any event, different. Between Christmas 1998 and the end of January 1999 alone, some 45,000 Kosovo Albanians were driven from their homes by Serbian forces[20] and as of late February, some 300,000 Kosovo Albanians were homeless, according to Associated Press (AP) writer Anne Thompson, though Amnesty International reported that 170,000 were homeless at the time.[21] As of the eve of the air strikes, Serbian depredations had already reduced some 450,000 Albanians to refugees, according to US Representative Christopher Smith.[22] It was, thus, on the basis of quite adequate documentation that senator Orrin Hatch (R – Utah) told the Senate Subcommittee on Immigration, on 14 April,

We have plenty of evidence that these genocidal plans [by Belgrade] were already in place and, in fact, were being slowly [sic] implemented before March 24.[23]

Meanwhile, the publication in *The Washington Post* on 17 March of an article by R. Jeffrey Smith added to the growing sense of urgency in Washington. Inserted into the *Congressional Record* the same day, the article reported that an independent team of Finnish forensic experts had completed its investigation into the Racak killings and had concluded that

... the victims were unarmed civilians executed in an organised massacre, some of them forced to kneel before being sprayed with bullets ...[24]

By this point, the Republican Party was becoming internally divided, with senator John McCain (R – Arizona) and former senator Bob Dole (R – Kansas) urging military action against Belgrade and senators Trent Lott (R – Massachusetts) and Kay Bailey Hutchinson (R – Texas) expressing misgivings. On 18 March, as the Rambouillet peace talks collapsed, Senator Lott claimed that the Senate did not have sufficient information to suggest that military action was advised,[25] while Senator Hutchinson told reporters, that same day:

I have been very concerned about the United States and Nato getting involved in Kosovo, particularly with the volatile situation, with no clear peace agreement. And I am more convinced than ever that this is a mistake at this time ... So I am very firm that I will oppose action in Kosovo until there is a clear peace agreement ...[26]

The evident confusion in phrasing suggests that the senator had not thought out her statement in advance.

THE AERIAL CAMPAIGN

The aerial campaign launched on 24 March was a Nato operation, not a unilateral US operation. This deserves emphasis, because Republican legislators repeatedly demanded that the USA pull out of the campaign and let its European partners continue the campaign on their own, if they so chose,[27] and issued categorical statements that the campaign had been conducted 'disastrously' or had already failed when it had barely begun,[28] or asserted that national sovereignty took precedence over human rights as the supreme principle in international law[29] – an assertion contrary to the spirit of the Universal Declaration of Human Rights, among other covenants.

> **Top military advisers found themselves having to repeat that it was unrealistic to expect instantaneous results and that one needed to be patient with the aerial campaign**

In late March, 41 senators (38 of them Republicans) opposed using force against Belgrade, in a surprising vote against Nato councils. Meanwhile, top military advisers found themselves having to repeat that it was unrealistic to expect instantaneous results and that one needed to be patient with the aerial campaign.

For a number of Republicans, the crisis in Kosovo figured, in the first place, as an opportunity for a fresh offensive against President Clinton. Conservative Republicans, whose loathing of Clinton began already in his first term, with the president's defence of gay rights and advocacy of health care reform – if not earlier, with the discussion of Clinton's adolescent opposition to the Vietnam war – fell into harsh criticisms of the US engagement in the Nato campaign, even while voting generously to fund that very engagement. Republican Stephen Buyer (R – Indiana) is a case in point. On 9 April, in the course of a news conference, this congressman extrapolated from the sex scandal over Monica Lewinsky to declare:

I prosecuted this man, so I can say it – he lies.[30]

In this way, Buyer offered the president's misleading (though not strictly mendacious) comments about his private life as if they constituted proof that the president would also lie about the public affairs of the nation or, to put it another way, that the president's treatment of embarrassing information having no connection with the national interest should be seen as *necessarily indicative of, if not identical with*, his treatment of matters of national interest having no conceivable potential to cause embarrassment. But the congressman's confusion extended also to history. Specifically, in his recollection, the Austro-Hungarian Monarchy of 1867–1918, which included the *Kingdom* of Hungary, became 'the Hungarian Empire of World War I'.[31]

Almost as soon as the aerial campaign began, discussion began about the possibility of arming and training KLA forces. Senator Mitch McConnell (R – Kentucky) advocated this option in a public statement on 13 April, but conceded,

There's apparently still a good deal of negative reaction to any proposals to arm the KLA, which I find totally mysterious, since they are the only people on the ground inside Kosovo willing to fight the Serbs.[32]

Critics of this proposal, citing reports that the KLA received some of its funding from 'drug barons',[33] characterized the KLA as 'narco-terrorists' (a term favoured by the Serb lobby) and declared that the largely secularized Albanian Muslims *and Catholics* of Kosovo, who in any case enjoy friendly relations,[34] might well set up a 'Taliban-style' fundamentalist Islamic state if given the chance. That such paranoid utterances could even enter into the debate at high levels suggests that infirmity of judgement may be far from exceptional among policy-makers. Meanwhile, the KLA was, in fact, receiving military assistance from a number of US-based private military companies, according to retired Army Colonel David Hackworth. Hackworth alleges further that a company called MPRI (Military Professional Resources, Inc.):

... used former US military personnel to train KLA forces at secret bases inside Albania.[35]

Appeals to undertake an open programme of arming and training the KLA, like grumblings about President Clinton's exclusion of the use of ground troops for combat in Kosovo,[36] reflected some genuine anxiety that the war might drag on beyond the limits of congressional and public patience. In an effort to address such concerns, General Henry H. Shelton, chairman of the Joint Chiefs of Staff, read a prepared statement to the Senate Armed Forces Committee on 15 April. In this statement, General Shelton explained that:

This substantial, sustained air campaign was designed to establish the conditions for success, isolate the military and security forces in Kosovo, and systematically reduce the ability of President Milosevic to sustain his operations. Our attacks have inflicted considerable damage on the Yugoslav military and security forces. We began by degrading the robust, multi-layered integrated air defence system in Yugoslavia – the first step in reducing the risk to pilots and aircrews in subsequent operations. We have effectively isolated the forces in Kosovo by disrupting command, control, and communications links, attacking POL facilities, and severing lines of communication. There are increasing indications of fuel and supply difficulties and we will continue to reduce the Yugoslav capabilities. They will continue to get weaker by the day.[37]

There were complications nonetheless. To begin with, Milosevic sent a delegation to Iraq to confer with Saddam Hussein and his advisers; as a result of Baghdad's advice, Belgrade kept its radar equipment turned off during Nato raids, except for very short intervals, thereby denying Nato the opportunity to destroy Serbia's radar capability.[38] Second, there was concern among Pentagon officials that the Yugoslav Army had stocks of lethal and non-lethal chemical weapons, including 'weaponized CS', BZ (an agent said to induce hallucinations), mustard gas, and sarin gas. Fearful of the impact on civilian populations in the event of a direct hit on a chemical plant producing such agents,[39] Nato forces specifically avoided targeting installations suspected of producing chemical agents. And third, Milosevic caught at least some observers off guard by being willing to absorb Nato strikes, using them as an excuse to intensify his own campaign against the Albanian population. At its peak, Milosevic's forces had driven some 850,000 Albanians out of Kosovo.

> 66 Belgrade kept its radar equipment turned off during Nato raids, except for very short intervals, thereby denying Nato the opportunity to destroy Serbia's radar capability 99

Although, as already noted, the 1973 War Powers Act[40] had authorized the sitting president to commit US forces to a combat situation for up to 60 days without obtaining Congressional approval, 26 legislators, led by Republican Tom Campbell (R – California), filed a lawsuit against President Clinton at the end of April, just 37 days into the Nato campaign. In their lawsuit, the legislators contended that the president's commitment of military force to the Nato mission was illegal under the War Powers Act. In filing prior to the expiration of the 60-day 'grace period', the anti-war legislators violated the spirit and letter of the Act. In any event, their lawsuit was dismissed on 8 June, just as the aerial campaign was ending.

> 66 In their lawsuit, the legislators contended that the president's commitment of military force to the Nato mission was illegal under the War Powers Act 99

Republican Campbell also filed two legislative proposals just three weeks into the aerial campaign, offering Congress a choice between demanding that the US forces be withdrawn from the Nato operation and declaring war. Both measures were tantamount to a repudiation of the concept of collaborative, consensual decision-making within Nato councils, and would have signified the *de facto* 'secession' of the US from the Nato campaign. This argument may seem paradoxical where the option of a formal declaration of war was concerned. But no other Nato power was considering a formal declaration of war, and such a declaration would have risked committing the USA to fight for Belgrade's unconditional surrender, thereby establishing more ambitious goals than those endorsed by Nato. And this, in turn, would have entailed the risk that Germany, Italy, Greece, Hungary, and perhaps other Nato allies as well would have distanced themselves from the operation, possibly denying the use of their facilities and air space for military operations. Campbell himself hoped for a vote to withdraw, urging that, in the event of such a vote, 'I don't think that any tyrant will take comfort or any ally need be disconcerted at the exercise of our constitutional processes and our democracy.'[41]

The House of Representatives declined, with a 213–213 tie vote on 28 April, to endorse the American participation in the Nato mission, but simultaneously voted some US$12.9 billion in emergency funding for the Balkan operation, more than doubling the amount requested by the president. By the time the bill passed the Senate three weeks later, the tab had risen to US$14.9 billion (against the US$6 billion originally requested by the president) and included US$2.9 billion in assistance to the victims of tornadoes in the Midwest and hurricanes Mitch and George in Central America. The bill also cut some US$2 billion in funds which had already been appropriated for food stamps, housing subsidies, and community-development block grants.[42]

In fact, votes taken in the House of Representatives on 28 April displayed a strange inconsistency. Within the space of a few hours, the House voted 'no' on ground troops (249–180), 'no' on requiring the unilateral withdrawal of all forces within 30 days (290–139), and 'no' on declaring war (427–2), while deadlocking, as already mentioned, on a resolution passed by the Senate four weeks earlier, which would have authorized the president to continue the air strikes.[43] One congressman, Republican Rod Blagojevich (D – Illinois), had travelled to Belgrade in April, accompanying the Reverend Jesse L. Jackson in his (successful) effort to obtain the release of three American soldiers kidnapped in Macedonia by Serbian/Yugoslav troops. Blagojevich returned to Washington DC under Milosevic's spell, and late in May, organized a group of 26 House Democrats to appeal for a 72-hour cease-fire in the campaign against Yugoslavia.[44] Blagojevich even volunteered that the indictment of Milosevic and four of his aides for war crimes did 'not change anything.'[45] Blagojevich did not explain why he believed that Milosevic could reach new conclusions in a bombing pause which he could not reach in conditions of continued bombardment.

But Blagojevich was by no means alone in his confusion. Republican Randy 'Duke' Cunningham (R – California), sporting the same sobriquet favoured by Serbian right-winger Vojislav 'Duke' Seselj, told the House on 5 May that he was worried about Albanian expansionism and extrapolated from his childhood experiences with cats that did not get along conclusions about the difficulty of returning Albanian refugees to Kosovo.[46]

In the Senate, Republican John McCain introduced a resolution authorizing Clinton to use 'all necessary force' to win the conflict in Kosovo. But the Senate proved unable to agree that victory deserved prioritization, and tabled the measure by a vote of 78 to 22.[47] Unimpressed by expert testimonies about human rights violations in Kosovo and elsewhere in the Republic of Serbia, senator Tim Hutchinson (R – Arkansas) confessed that he was unaware that the USA had *any* national security interests in the Balkans, come what may. Even the White House displayed some confusion in the early stages of the campaign, declaring against independence for Kosovo. On the other hand, it is possible that the White House was adopting a tactical ruse here, in order to keep the Nato coalition on board.

POST-VICTORY ATTITUDES

Ultimately, the aerial campaign ended far more quickly than perhaps most people had imagined. With warnings about a long 'quagmire' *à la* Vietnam commonplace,[48] some observers had clearly feared that the USA might find itself bogged down in the 'jungles' of Kosovo for a decade or more. Yet on 28 May, the day after his indictment by the UN War Crimes Tribunal, Milosevic announced that his government would accept the principles for a peaceful resolution of the crisis which had been prepared by the Group of 8. Yugoslav forces began their withdrawal from Kosovo thereafter, and Nato and Russian peace-keepers moved into the province.

Ironically, even after this rather unambiguous victory, the partisan squabbling continued. While Republicans John McCain and Dennis Hastert (House Speaker, R – Illinois) congratulated Clinton on the victory, senator Don Nickles (R – Oklahoma), who had earlier made a name for himself by declaring that no action was required on the part of Nato or the USA, because, allegedly, the 'ethnic cleansing [in Kosovo] hadn't reached the level of genocide,'[49] now claimed that it was the Nato mission which had produced the 'humanitarian disaster' in Kosovo in the first place.[50]

> 66 On the day after his indictment by the UN War Crimes Tribunal, Milosevic announced that his government would accept the principles for a peaceful resolution of the crisis 99

Evidently agreeing with Milosevic's account, Nickles was, it seems, unaware of the fact that between 250,000[51] and 450,000 Albanians had already been driven from their homes before Nato responded and that a full-scale military operation against Albanian civilians in Kosovo had been ordered by Belgrade long before Nato acted. Where was senator Nickles when senator Hatch had testified?

'Why are we so eager to say a victory has been achieved?' asked the aforementioned Republican Buyer of Indiana, a sworn enemy of Clinton, while his colleague, Republican Mark Souder (R – Indiana), offered, 'This is certainly no victory.'[52] Herbert London, the John M. Olin Professor of Humanities at New York University, argued in an article for the *Ventura County Star* that as long as Milosevic remained in power, one could not justify characterizing the campaign as 'victory', regardless of the close correspondence between the results achieved and the publicly declared objectives of the campaign.[53] Yet the Republicans had been quite prepared to declare 'victory' in the Desert Storm campaign in 1991, even though Saddam Hussein was allowed to remain in power.

The *Seattle Post-Intelligencer* was more sober, and urged that the success of Clinton's (and I would add, Nato's) strategy be recognized,[54] while the House of Representatives voted on 10 June to cut off further spending in Kosovo, in a move interpreted as aiming to deprive Clinton of success in peace. Sadly, though not surprisingly, the Kosovo crisis demonstrated the inability of many members of Congress (including most Republicans) to rise above partisan politics. For the partisans, Enemy No. 1 was not Milosevic but Clinton, and debates had to be tailored to defeat the 'people's enemy' on Pennsylvania Avenue, rather than the indicted war criminal in Dedinje.

> 66 The Kosovo crisis demonstrated the inability of many of Congress to rise above partisan politics 99

The record also shows that both parties remained internally divided, even in so significant an undertaking as a belated, long-overdue effort to stop a despot who had already brought great suffering to Slovenes, Croats, Bosniaks, Hungarians of Vojvodina, and Muslims of the Sanzak, who was now extending his programme of systematic house-burning, murder, pillage, rape and expulsion to the Albanians of Kosovo, who had in any event also brought much misery to Serbs, and who had been championing, for more than a decade, the supposedly superseded concept of a racially pure state. That so many in Congress preferred ambivalence or even appeasement prompts some uncertainty as to the lessons some of our officeholders have drawn from the historical record of other attempts at creating racially pure states.

Debates in both houses of Congress also show a marked tendency among America's elected officials to discuss America's military contribution in abstraction from its context, i.e., as if it had not been a Nato operation, or even as if there were no Nato. And this, in turn, reveals again the profound isolationism, bordering on agoraphobia, which afflicts all too many officeholders in the USA.

Finally, endless denials that the systematic murder and expulsion of Albanians could be compared to the Holocaust in any significant aspect[55] together with recurrent denials that Milosevic did anything deserving even of censure, let alone of an unarmed response (such as Geoff Berne's description of Serb atrocities in Kosovo over a period of more than a decade as 'a pogrom against an ethnic minority that was never committed', which Berne calls 'an unproven genocide'),[56] raise questions concerning the moral fibre of the international community. Debates about what constitutes and does not constitute 'genocide' in particular seem driven, at times, by the desire to avoid responsibility. Under the Geneva Conventions, the pulping of Albanian-language books from the Pristina National Library by Belgrade authorities in the mid-1990s, insofar as it was aimed at erasing the cultural and historical memory of Albanians in Kosovo, was already an act of 'genocide'. Again, under the Geneva Conventions, Operation Horseshoe, the military operation launched by Belgrade on Christmas Eve 1998 to drive Albanians out of Kosovo, was 'genocidal' in intent, whether or not Albanians would be killed. The fact is that most people do not bother with the specificities of the Geneva Conventions and prefer to think of genocide in the less legalistic, more 'commonsensical' manner of dictionaries. The definition offered by *The Oxford English Reference Dictionary*, for example, defines 'genocide' as 'the mass extermination of human beings, esp. a particular race or nation'[57] while *The American Heritage Dictionary of the English Language* defines 'genocide' as 'the systematic, planned annihilation of a racial, political, or cultural group'.[58] And, in fact, most, if not all, denials of genocide in the area have been based on dictionary understandings of genocide, rather than on the Geneva Conventions.

It is within this context that some observers have embraced the term 'ethnic cleansing', in spite of its Nazi origins and its linkage to notions of racial and ethnic 'purity'. In fact, the term 'ethnic cleansing' is much more of a hot potato than 'genocide'; the major advantage enjoyed by policy-makers in admitting that 'ethnic cleansing', but not 'genocide', has been practised in one or another country is that, unlike the case of 'genocide', it does not require any response under the Geneva Conventions. Amid these and other (related) debates, some analysts have speculated that the campaign in Kosovo might prove to be a major turning-point for American military and security policy. This notion seems dubious to the present writer. Be that as it may, a year after the end of hostilities, the US House of Representatives voted overwhelmingly to require that US troops begin to be phased out of Kosovo by April 2001, unless the sitting president should prove able to certify by then that America's Nato allies[59] are shouldering a larger portion of the costs. Less than 24 hours later, however, the Senate voted 53 to 47 to reject the House initiative, thereby sparing the White House the embarrassment of being forced to let down the Nato allies. As of May 2000, some 5,900 US troops were in Kosovo as part of the Nato-led, 37,000-strong peace-keeping force.

NOTES

1   In debate at the House of Representatives (28 April 1999), at thomas.loc.gov/cgi-bin/query.

2   *Ibid.*

3   *Ibid.*

4   Norman Mailer, 'NATO Fell into Milosevic's trap', in *The Irish Times* (26 May 1999) at www.ireland.com/newspaper/opinion.

5   James J. Sadkovich, *The U.S. Media and Yugoslavia, 1991–1995* (Westport. Conn.: Praeger, 1998), p. 2.

6   Regarding this debate, see Sabrina P. Ramet, 'The American Debate about Kosovo: Hawks, Doves, Kiwis, Falcons, and Nightingales', forthcoming.

7   In debate at the House of Representatives (28 April 1999) at thomas.loc.gov/cgi-bin/query.

8   I took part in one such hearing in autumn 1986.

9   News briefing with Bujar Bukoshi, Prime Minister, Republic of Kosovo, 21 October 1992, *Federal News Service* in *Lexis-Nexis Congressional Universe*.

10 Rub 1999: 50.

11 Quoted in Zumach 1999: 65.

12 *International Herald Tribune* (Tokyo ed.), 30 June 1998, p. 1; *The Daily Yomiuri* (13 September 1998), p. 3.

13 'Atrocities in Kosovo', Hearing before the Commission on Security and Cooperation in Europe, 105th Congress, 2nd session, 17 September 1998 (Washington DC: US Government Printing Office, 1999), p. 12.

14 *Ibid.*, p. 14.

15 'The Milosevic Regime versus Serbian democracy and Balkan Stability', Hearing before the Commission on Security and Cooperation in Europe, 105th Congress, 2nd session, 10 December, 1998 (Washington DC: US Government Printing Office, 1999), pp. 1–3.

16 *Ibid.*, pp. 41–5.

17 Ambassador William Walker, in testimony before the Commission on Security and Cooperation in Europe, chaired by Rep. Christopher Smith (R – New Jersey), Rayburn House Office Bldg., 6 April 1999, *Federal News Service* in *Lexis-Nexis Congressional Universe*.

18 Senator Richard Lugar, in a news conference in the Senate Radio/TV Gallery (2 February 1999), *Federal News Service*, in *Lexis-Nexis Congressional Universe*.

19 Slobodan Milosevic, interview with UPI (Belgrade, 30 April 1999), *Federal News Service*, in *Lexis-Nexis Congressional Universe*.

20 Rub 1999: 60–61.

21 AP (26 February 1999) on *Lexis-Nexis Academic Universe*.

22 Representative Christopher Smith (R – New Jersey), Rayburn House Office Bldg., 6 April 1999, *Federal News Service*, in *Lexis-Nexis Congressional Universe*.

23 Senator Orrin G. Hatch, in testimony at the US Senate (14 April 1999), *Federal Document Clearing House Congressional Testimony* in *Lexis-Nexis Congressional Universe*.

24 *Washington Post* (17 March 1999) as inserted into the *Congressional Record*, in testimony in the House of Representatives (17 March 1999) at thomas.loc.gov/cgi-bin/query.

25 Senate Majority Leader Trent Lott, press statement outside closed Senate foreign policy briefing (18 March 1999), *Federal News Service*, in *Lexis-Nexis Congressional Universe*.

26 Senator Kay Bailey Hutchinson, press statement outside closed Senator foreign policy briefing (18 March 1999), *Federal News Service* in *Lexis-Nexis Congressional Universe*.

27 For example, Republican Dana Rohrbacher, before the House International Relations Committee, 21 April 1999, *Federal News Service*, in *Lexis-Nexis Congressional Universe*; Republican Tom Campbell (R – San José), as reported in *Copley News Service* (16 April 1999) on *Lexis-Nexis Academic Universe*; and Republican Steve Chabot (R – Cincinnati) as reported in *The Cincinnati Enquirer* (22 April 1999) p. A2 on *Lexis-Nexis Academic Universe*.

28 See comments by Republican Tom Campbell as reported in *Wisconsin State Journal* (18 April 1999) p. 2B; on *Lexis-Nexis Academic Universe*; Republican Steve Chabot as reported in *The Cincinnati Enquirer* (22 April 1999) p. A2 on *Lexis-Nexis Academic Universe*; Republican Curt Weldon (Pennsylvania), in a statement issued on 13 May 1999 at www.house.gov/curtweldon/pr; and Senator Pat Roberts (R – Kansas) as reported in *Chicago Sun-Times* (20 May 1999), at *www.suntimes.com*.

29 See the comments by Republican Ron Paul (R – Texas) in press release (26 May 1999) at www.house.gov/paul/press/press99.

30 Republican Stephen Buyer, in a news conference in the House Radio/TV Gallery (9 April 1999) *Federal News Service* in *Lexis-Nexis Congressional Universe*.

31 *Ibid.*

32 Senator Mitch McConnell, press statement on the White House driveway (13 April 1999) *Federal News Service* in *Lexis-Nexis Congressional Universe*.

33 See *Sunday Times* (London) reprinted in *Illyria* (The Bronx), 19–21 May 1999, p. 3.

34 See Albanian TV (Tirana), 20 July 1999, trans. in *BBC Summary of World Broadcasts* (22 July 1999).

35 Madsen 1999: 29.

36 For an example of such grumblings, see the comments by Senator Mitch McConnell in debate at the US Senate (21 April 1999) at thomas.loc.gov/cgi-bin/query.

37 General Henry H. Shelton, Chairman of the Joint Chiefs of Staff, in a prepared statement before the Senate Armed Services Committee (15 April 1999) *Federal News Service* in *Lexis-Nexis Congressional Universe*.

38 Republican Stephen Buyer, in a news conference in the House Radio/TV Gallery (9 April 1999) *Federal News Service* in *Lexis-Nexis Congressional Universe*.

39 See the detailed report in *New York Times* (16 April 1999) p. A13.

40 *Las Vegas Review-Journal* (30 April 1999) p. 3A on *Lexis-Nexis Academic Universe*.

41 Quoted in *Copley News Service* (16 April 1999) on *Lexis-Nexis Academic Universe*.

42 *Star Tribune* (Minneapolis) 28 April 1999 p. 6A on *Lexis-Nexis Academic Universe*; *Seattle Post-Intelligencer* (29 April 1999) p. A1; *New York Times* (29 April 1999) p. A28; *The Austin American-Stateman* (21 May 1999) p. A3 on *Lexis-Nexis Academic Universe*. See also *New York Times* (7 May 1999) p. A14.

43 Jake Tapper 'Declaring war on undeclared war' in *Salon.com News* (6 May 1999) at www.Salomag.com/news/feature/1999/05/06/war/index.html.

44 *Chicago Sun-Times* (28 May 1999) at www.suntimes.com/output/special/cong28.html.

45 *Ibid.*

46 Republican Randy 'Duke' Cunningham in debate at the House of Representatives (5 May 1999) at thomas.loc.gov/cgi-bin/query.

47 *Copley News Service* (4 May 1999) on *Lexis-Nexis Academic Universe*.

48 See for example, Irving Louis Horowitz 'The Vietnamisation of Yugoslav' in *Society*, Vol. 36, No. 5 (July–August 1999) pp. 3–10.

49 *Las Vegas Review-Journal* (15 June 1999) p. 7B on *Lexis-Nexis Academic Universe*.

50 *Ibid.*

51 The figure of 250,000 is the official German government figure, cited by Chancellor Gerhard Schröder in an address to the Council of Europe on 26 March 1999 as posted at www.eupraesidentschaft.de/03/0302/0075/index.html.

52 Both quoted in *Lewiston Morning Tribune* (13 June 1999) p. 1F on *Lexis-Nexis Academic Universe*.

53 Herbert London 'Vague peace deal validates Milosevic's bloody campaign' in *Venture County Star* (13 June 1999) p. B9 on *Lexis-Nexis Academic Universe*.

54 *Seattle Post-Intelligencer* (15 June 1999) p. A11 on *Lexis-Nexis Academic Universe*.

55 See, for example, Deb Reichmann 'Jewish leaders say ethnic cleansing in Kosovo differs from Holocaust' in *Star Tribune* (Minneapolis), 15 May 1999 at www.startribune.com.

56 Geoff Berne 'Yugoslavia: A Holocaust Denied' in *SpinTech* (12 February 2000) at www.spintechmag.com/002/gb0200.htm.

57 *The Oxford English Reference Dictionary* (OUP Press, Oxford, 1996).

58 *The American Heritage Dictionary of the English Language* (Boston and New York: American Heritage Publishing Co. & Houghton Mifflin Co., 1970), p. 550.

59 *Süddeutsche Zeitung* (Munich), 20/21 May 2000, p. 10.

10

AIR STRIKE: NATO ASTRIDE KOSOVO

PETER J. ANDERSON

THERE IS NO EASY ROUTE TO UNDERSTANDING the nature of Nato's involvement in Kosovo. Despite this, simplistic views exist on all sides of the political spectrum. For some on the left, for example, the whole point of the pre-conflict diplomacy and of the bombing campaign that followed was to expand aggressively the role and influence of an American-dominated Nato further into the largely vacated sphere of influence of the former Soviet Union. However, this view of things starts to run into difficulties when, for example, the variety of influences and opinions within and around the Clinton administration of the time is taken into account. There was certainly no unanimous agreement, at the highest levels of the American military elite, for example, as to how far Nato should be prepared to go over Kosovo.[1] Most troubling to this conspiratorial view is the personality and history of the then secretary of state, Madeleine Albright, who played a leading role prior to and throughout the military campaign. Rather than being an 'American imperialist' of long-standing, she is in fact of Czechoslovakian birth and has suffered the life-determining experience of having been one of the many European refugees from Hitler's Nazis.[2] Whatever her stance on other matters of American foreign policy, it might be reasonable to assume that such a background would give her a perspective on events in Kosovo that is less self-interested and 'imperialist' than Tariq Ali in Britain and others on the European far left seem prepared to allow (Ali 1999: 62–72; Gowan 1999: 83–105).

In addition, the extent to which Nato could be 'aggressive' was limited clearly by the domestic political agendas of such Alliance members as Germany (with, for example, the strong influence of the Greens), Italy and Greece (the latter with its long-standing popular resentment at anything that smacks of US 'imperialism' in consequence of its people's memories of the period of the military dictatorship). While, on the admission of Wesley Clark, Nato's 'political' generals did in fact manage to pursue a broader bombing campaign than some Alliance members felt they had signed up to,[3] it is very obviously the case that hawks such as the British, or Albright and Holbrooke within the Clinton administration, were in many ways constrained in their impact by the doves within Germany, Italy, France, Greece and, ironically, given the perspective of some critics, the Clinton White House. While the Nato bombing campaign might indeed have been substantial in terms of the ordnance dropped on Serbian targets, the alliance in fact was relatively restrained in terms of the level of 'aggression' it could have unleashed but chose not to. Equally, when Russian forces made their dash for Pristina airport at the conclusion of the campaign, those within the alliance who allegedly wished Nato forces to confront them were cancelled out by those who did not wish to see this happen. In short, the lead-up to the campaign and the military phase itself were characterized by a continuous struggle between hawks and doves – and the intervention of such unpredictable events as the Monica Lewinsky affair – within and across alliance member states, and it would be a mistake to assume that there was any one over-arching agreed military strategy *that found consistent support from every key member state*. It is perhaps also not entirely frivolous to mention at this point that it is a sign of how little has changed since the time of the ancient Romans that the most powerful alliance in military history found its possibilities for decisive 'aggressive' action severely restricted as a result of the exotic sex life of the president of the US.

> 66 The alliance in fact was relatively restrained in terms of the level of 'aggression' it could have unleashed but chose not to 99

Bearing in mind, therefore, that accusations of Nato 'aggression' or 'imperialism' need, at the very least, to be treated with care, it is necessary to do several things here if a useful understanding of the Alliance's involvement in the Kosovan conflict is to be achieved. First, this chapter will analyze briefly the way in which Nato's role has developed and changed since the end of the Cold War, in order to put its decision-making over Kosovo into context. Second, it will look at the reasons why

Nato chose to use force in Kosovo. Third, it will attempt to explain why Nato chose to rely on an air campaign and to rule out the use of ground forces until after a peace agreement had been signed. Fourth, it will look at the lessons and implications of the Kosovo campaign for Nato. Finally, it will discuss the legality and ethics of Nato's actions over Kosovo, and will examine the success/failure debate concerning the above involvement. It is simply not possible in a brief chapter to examine every relevant aspect of Nato's involvement in Kosovo, but it is hoped that an analysis of the above issues will give the reader an insight into the dark and complex heart of the matter.

NATO'S CHANGING ROLE SINCE THE END OF THE COLD WAR AND THE DECISION TO USE FORCE IN KOSOVO

Since the demise of the Cold War previous relative certainties in the relationship between the USA and its European and Canadian Nato allies have been called into question. The disintegration of the USSR began a period of prolonged soul-searching as to precisely what the alliance's role should be after the fall of its principal opponent, Soviet communism. This period of questioning and self-examination was tied into obviously related processes of re-thinking about questions of European defence and security within the European Union, the USA and the UN. One chain of events that followed from this was mainly limited in its scope but highly symbolic in its nature, and is particularly important with regard to the shape of Nato policy towards eastern Europe, and the former Yugoslavia: it was the incremental improvement in military-security relations with the former Soviet Union. This started modestly with the North Atlantic Cooperation Council in 1991, then began in earnest with the launching of the Partnership for Peace in 1994. In the words of Nato:

Through detailed programmes that reflect individual Partners' capacities and interests, Allies and Partners work towards transparency in national defence planning and budgeting: democratic control of defence forces: preparedness for civil disasters and other emergencies: and the development of the ability to work together, including in NATO-led PfP [Partnership for Peace] operations.   (Nato 1999a)

However, Western aims in all of this have been perceived as less than benevolent by a number of commentators. Steele, for example, claims that after the collapse of the Soviet Union, one of the USA's main goals was:

...to weaken Russia strategically to prevent any chance of a revival of the Soviet Union, but without provoking resistance and turning the country into an enemy again.   (Steele 1999)

Part of this process involved Nato's enlargement into eastern Europe, and in Steele's view and that of others, the purpose behind the partnership arrangements with the Yeltsin administration was to contain and reduce Russian anger at this prospect. They did indeed help oil the wheels of progress towards the most truly mould-breaking event in all of the above, which firmly underlined the shift in the balance of power and spheres of influence within Europe that has occurred since the end of the Cold War: the formal accession to the Nato alliance of three of the former Warsaw Pact states, Poland, Hungary and the Czech Republic, in 1999, with the Russian government's reluctant acceptance. When linked with the EU's rapidly developing plans for enlargement into the East during the same year, the scale of Russia's loss of influence to its former Cold War opponents during the 1990s can be seen in its startling enormity.

This loss created a problematical vacuum in the Balkan region which Nato chose to fill. The context in which it decided to do so was one in which the several previously mentioned processes of re-thinking (within the UN, the USA, Nato and the EU) all interlinked in the first major challenge in Europe since the end of the Cold War: the various disputes and wars that started to erupt as the former Yugoslavia began to disintegrate. The crises that followed from this process began to expose the extent to which American thinking about European problems can diverge from that of the Europeans themselves in the post-Cold War order.

Why precisely Nato chose to intervene first in Bosnia, and later in Kosovo, is a question that has been examined already in some detail within this and other works. It is not intended here to exhaustively re-visit ground that has been well covered already. The views of the far left have been mentioned already at the beginning of the chapter, and indeed, if one wanted to advance a traditional Marxist view of Nato as being an instrument through which the interests of the dominant capitalist states could be pushed forwards, then there is plenty of evidence that could be offered in support of this perspective. For example, it could be argued that tying as much of eastern Europe as possible into Nato membership and/or the EU, or Nato/EU influence, would serve the economic interests of Western bourgeois elites by not only facilitating the creation of new markets for their goods, but by also securing the cheap labour for industrial production that powerful Western corporations such as Volkswagen have found attractive. Equally, if one were trying to construct a traditional 'balance-of-power-politics' interpretation about what has been going on in the former Yugoslavia in recent years, then there is certainly a strategic logic behind the view that Steele alleges drove the American government in its attempts to reduce and contain the power of nuclear-armed Russia, after the end of the Cold War (Steele 1999: 16). An expansion of the Western sphere of influence right into the heart of the Balkans would further help to secure that goal.

There are, however, also other grounds which one could argue were more credible candidates for explaining Nato's actions in deciding to take the high risks (relating particularly to Alliance unity) that were involved in deciding to go into Kosovo. First, both the USA and some of the former European colonial powers had previously been embarrassed politically and made to look ineffective and uncaring over the mass slaughter in Rwanda, and had been seen also as slow to react effectively while the atrocities during the Bosnian War continued to grow in number. The Bosnian situation was particularly poignant, given the relatively recent history of the Nazi genocides in Europe, and the fact that they had extended into Yugoslavia, primarily through the actions of client political groups. The EU had been made to look woefully clumsy during the Bosnian conflict and some of its leading members, with their dual role as members of Nato, were anxious not to be seen to be ineffective twice over when the Kosovo situation started to become critical during 1998/99. In the USA, one figure in particular has stated that she was keen to get things right second time around. Madeleine Albright, being originally a Czech refugee from the Nazis, had a unique status amongst the proponents of the bombing campaign, in so far as she could claim a degree of moral authority for her actions derived directly from her own personal experience and history. A less charitable view of Albright's motives is offered by Gowan, who observes that a:

> **❝ The EU had been made to look woefully clumsy during the Bosnian conflict and some of its leading members were anxious not to be seen to be ineffective twice over ❞**

successful military operation against Milosevic before the Washington summit to agree Nato's new role would have been a stunning political triumph for Madeleine Albright, whose term of office had, hitherto, been marked by a long catalogue of failure, most notably in the Middle East.

(Gowan 1999: 102)

Indeed, from an overall American perspective, he argues:

Success would decisively consolidate US leadership in Europe ... And it would seal the unity of the alliance against a background where the launch of the Euro ... could pull it apart.

(Gowan 1999: 102)

Another leading alliance figure who shared 'hawk' status with Albright, Britain's Tony Blair, was compelled to seek an effective solution to the Kosovan situation that put human rights at the top of the agenda by his own government's very public commitment to the notion of an 'ethical foreign policy'. A more cynical, although not necessarily unjustified perspective on Blair, given his well-documented concern with media 'spin' and image, and his past deference to Margaret Thatcher on some issues, is that he remembered well how she had played the 1982 Falkland/Malvinas war to her advantage. It is striking how much the image of strong leadership that he conveyed through the presentation of his role in the war echoed that of his part-mentor. Both have been accused of striking Churchillian poses and it is interesting that one American Nato insider referred to 'that Winston Blair'. [4]

There was also the whole business of Nato's search for an enduring post-Cold War role, and the way that this had developed into a debate over collective defence versus collective security. For those most concerned to build up the latter role, Kosovo was an obvious opportunity to extend this aspect of its new activities. There was also an interest on the part of those within the USA who wished to see Nato's role extended 'out of area' in expanding its military involvement in eastern Europe.

66 While there is now much information concerning the Kosovo campaign available within the public domain, it is still insufficient for a firm judgement to be made about the real reasons behind Nato's decision to use force 99

All of the above begs an answer to the question concerning which set of motives and interests were most crucial in provoking Nato intervention in Kosovo. However, it is the belief of this commentator at least that, while there is now much information concerning the Kosovo campaign available within the public domain, it is still insufficient for a firm judgement to be made about the real reasons behind Nato's decision to use force. Too many serious doubts can be raised against each alternative view as things stand and it is necessary for more 'deep background' (as opposed to superficially credible evidence offered by leading players via TV interviews) to come to light before anything resembling a final verdict can be reached. Any assessment of the motives of the USA, for example, is complicated greatly by two factors:

- the previously mentioned personal experience of Madeleine Albright during the Nazi regime
- the fact that the consequences of Bill Clinton's sexual adventures were so preoccupying him during the months preceding the Rambouillet talks that it is very clear that his mind was frequently distracted from detailed contemplation of the Kosovo problem.[5]

What can be said is that there appears to have been a decisive moment at Rambouillet beyond which it was not really possible to pull back from some kind of substantial military action against Milosevic. Many commentators – the Russian foreign minister of the time among them – have stated that, in their view, a diplomatic solution to the crisis could have been pushed through at Rambouillet and the fact that such a solution was not possible was the consequence of Nato laying down terms it knew were too humiliating for the Serbs to accept. Albright has been accused of being the leading hawk who pushed the Serbs into a corner with no way out. Her actions and those of the politicians and diplomats who formulated the Western position at Rambouillet have been explained on several grounds. One suggestion is that the Americans relied too much on the memory of the Dayton Agreement and believed that Milosevic could be pushed into agreements with harsh terms, if he could be persuaded that there was no realistic alternative. In this case, what was not taken into account was the very different political, historical and cultural significance of Kosovo for Serbia and the fact that Nato had been less than convincing in its previous attempts to convey an image of determination to take truly effective military action over Serbia's conduct in the province. A second view sees Nato's demands for apparently draconian rights of military access and immunity within Serbia itself as realistic, given Milosevic's long record of duplicity and barbarism. From this point of view, the time for respecting Serbian national sensitivities had passed, and appropriate measures had now to be taken to try and bring a decisive end to officially conducted ethnic persecution in Kosovo and the problem this was causing for the major powers. Anything less would simply allow Milosevic and his henchmen to find a new way to pursue their deadly mischief.

On the other side of the coin it has been argued that there were those within Nato who, by the time of Rambouillet, wanted to see Milosevic punished, or, at least, who believed that any diplomatic solution would be unworkable unless the Serbs were first shown in decisive fashion that Nato could act firmly against them over Kosovo. There is, too, the previously mentioned view of Gowan that Albright needed a war to boost her personal success ratings. It could also be argued that by this stage Nato had allowed its bluff to be called too many times previously and that, whether or not there was a workable diplomatic solution on the table, it now needed to show that it retained its ability to use force in order to retain military credibility for future collective security or even collective defence crises. From these perspectives, Rambouillet was an agreement deliberately designed to fail.

> 66 Rambouillet was an agreement deliberately designed to fail 99

Whether or not one accepts the validity of any of these views, the fact is that once the Rambouillet terms had been formally turned down by the Serbs, diplomacy had to enter a military phase if Nato's credibility was to be retained. There can be little doubt that one more failure to deliver on a military threat would have made Nato a spent force. More dangerously, from the point of view of some strategists, it would have created a risk: in any possible future confrontation with a less friendly, nuclear-armed Russia, the Russian military might have taken Nato threats to be a bluff, leading to unnecessary and serious conflict. That such situations are possible, even within the relatively improved overall atmosphere of the post-Cold War world, ironically was demonstrated by the Kosovan conflict itself, when Russian troops raced Nato to Pristina airport and effectively confronted Nato forces. In this case, the problem was resolved peacefully, but, it could be argued that the possibility of such peaceful resolutions requires first that Nato has military credibility. That credibility had been acquired to a degree as a result of Nato's air campaign, but the fact that the Russians initially retained doubts about it, might be seen as the result of the ambiguous message that Nato sent to Moscow as a result of its fear of committing ground troops prior to a peace settlement.

THE GROUND FORCES PROBLEM AND THE DECISION
TO RELY ON AN AIR CAMPAIGN

The reasons why the alliance was unable to deploy ground troops prior to a peace agreement being in place obviously require some examination here. The American position is particularly crucial, given the continuing role of the USA as Nato's premier member state. In order to understand its stance, it is necessary to remember that it was not a new development and that when the Clinton administration finally accepted the need to intervene militarily in the Bosnian quagmire earlier in the decade, it then had agreed to do so only on the clear understanding that American ground troops would not be deployed until a peace agreement was in place. The American insistence on this was to a degree determined by apparently significant changes in US economic interests. In the early years of the Clinton presidency, there had been an emphasis on the economic potential of the New Pacific at the expense of America's European concerns, and, now that the Cold War was over, there seemed to be a feeling in some key Washington quarters that, if ground troops were required to deal with 'brushfire' conflicts in post-Cold War Europe, then it should be the Europeans' responsibility to provide them. Relatively 'minor' problems in Europe, such as the Yugoslavian problem, were now a second order US concern. More important, however, was US domestic public opinion. While there were loud Congressional voices and highly vocal relevant ethnic groups within the electorate shouting in favour of an effective American response to the Bosnian situation, it needs to be remembered that there were also very loud voices raised against it. Furthermore, there are large sections of the US electorate who are little interested in foreign affairs as a whole, let alone those concerning far-away Europe. Given the lessons of the Vietnam War in the 1960s and the 1970s, and of the later *débâcle* in Somalia in the early 1990s, the last thing that Clinton wanted was to have prime-time television news pictures of US bodybags coming home from a war that many of the public would not deem as being sufficiently important to merit the loss of American lives. Only a major war in Europe or elsewhere, in which core US interests were clearly involved, could merit such a level of American intervention, and such a war would not be in place unless the Bosnian conflict triggered a wider Balkan conflagration. This conclusion remained dominant in White House thinking during the crisis over Kosovo during 1998–9, despite the presence of dissenters such as Albright and Holbrooke.[6]

Different messages have come out of the USA government and military, and close allies in other states, since the conflict, about whether or not the USA ultimately would have been prepared to deploy ground troops in the event of Milosevic's non-capitulation and withdrawal from Kosovo. But what is certainly very clear, as in the case of Bosnia, is that President Clinton's strong preference was for ground deployment to occur only after a peace agreement was in place. This was a consequence of several factors, including the continuing dominance of the above-mentioned post-Somalia doctrine, strong advice coming from some key military advisors in the Pentagon, the knowledge that the deployment of combat ground troops would arouse some powerful criticism within Congress and sections of the electorate, and the president's weakness *vis-à-vis* Congress following the lingering fallout from the Monica Lewinsky affair.

The British prime minister, on the other hand, made no secret of his preference for ground troops to be used, if that was necessary to force Milosevic into submission. It has been claimed that initially France supported this view also, but to a lesser degree.[7] Both Britain and France were limited in their ability to secure this objective, not only by Clinton's reluctance to agree with it, but also by the failure of their own and other European governments to maintain a level of military equipment, organization and preparedness that would have permitted them to execute such an option without substantial American assistance. The domestic political situation of both the German and Italian governments, on the other hand, was one that permitted them to go no further than agreeing to an air campaign until a peace agreement was in place, when they, like the Americans, would then be prepared to supply ground troops. For one of the smallest alliance states, Greece, the situation was even more problematical. Continuing popular distrust of the USA since the days of the military dictatorship, together with religious and cultural ties with the Serbs, meant that it was difficult enough for the Greek government to remain attached to the air-strike option, let alone risking domestic political suicide by contemplating supporting the use of ground forces in an offensive capacity.

> 66 The bombing of Serbian civilian targets was adopted by Nato for the simple reason that there was a clear and powerful majority in favour of air strikes 99

The Greeks were unable to ensure that their particular ethical position on such matters as the bombing of Serbian civilian targets was adopted by Nato for the simple reason that there was a clear and powerful majority in favour of air strikes. The British, on the other

A Kosovo Albanian boy peers through the door of his family tent covered with a poster reading 'Kosovo' in the refugee centre in Rakovica near Sarajevo. Almost 13,000 Kosovo Albanian refugees in Bosnia arrived before NATO started air strikes against Yugoslavia on 24 March. The significance – political and emotional – of this carefully composed photo is clear. (12 April 1999. Photo by Danilo Krstanovic. © Reuters 1999.)

Dramatic video from the nose of a NATO missile shows a train on a Yugoslav bridge moments before the weapon struck, killing 10 people. NATO supreme commander General Wesley Clark, expressing profound regret for the civilian deaths, said the train moved into the NATO pilot's vision when it was too late for him to stop the missile. In what he called 'an uncanny accident', the pilot circled for another strike at the end of the target bridge but the crippled train had slid forward and was struck again. (12 April 1999. Photo by HO. © Reuters 1999.)

Residents of Novi Sad look at the remains of the last standing bridge destroyed by NATO planes. (26 April 1999. Photo by STR. © Reuters 1999.)

A Chinese man looks at the destroyed Chinese embassy during the anniversary of its destruction in Belgrade, 7 May. The bombing, which killed three Chinese people and sparked anti-NATO demonstrations across China, took place on 7 May in Belgrade, or early on 8 May, Beijing time, 1999. (7 May 1999. Photo by Goran Tomasevic. © Reuters 2000.)

A soldier smokes a cigarette in front of an appropriately named cafe at the US Army's Task Force Hawk Base in Albania. More than 5,000 army personnel were deployed with the force, which was assisting NATO's air campaign against Yugoslavia. (2 June 1999. Photo by Pool. © Reuters 1999.)

Russian troops block British forces on the road leading to Pristina airport. A 200-strong Russian contingent temporarily took control of the airport and forced the NATO peacekeeping force to alter plans to set up its headquarter there. (13 June 1999. Photo by Pool. © Reuters 1999.)

Kosovars show victory signs as they pass by a group of German tanks in Prizren, in June 1999. This was the first time that German troops had operated outside their national frontier since 1944. (14 June 1999. Photo by Peter Mueller. © Reuters 1999.)

A grave containing the bodies of four ethnic Albanian men allegedly killed by Serb soldiers in early April, were discovered by German soldiers in the village of Zagradska Hoqa in western Kosovo. The four men were buried in the shallow grave following the killing; their ages ranged from 68 to 73 years. (26 June 1999. Photo by Peter Mueller. © Reuters 1999.)

hand, had to accept a situation in which the prime minister's emphasis on the need for effective action to stop ethnic cleansing could only be realized via a strategy deemed unlikely to do the job, in time, on its own. These two positions represented the polar extremes within Nato at the time of the Kosovo conflict. Both came from diametrically different interpretations of the role and guilt of the Serbs in what was happening in Kosovo. Equally, both embodied radically different views on the limits to which Nato should be prepared to go in the use of military force. Most Nato states opted for the median position between these two poles, the air-strike option, as their declared first preference once all the proverbial boats had been burned at Rambouillet. However, in doing so, they also effectively ceded a key part of the decision-making about the conducting of the campaign to the USA since they had not maintained the appropriate quantity and range of immediately usable air power that would have enabled them to exercise greater influence. The US provided most of the manned aircraft, missiles and bombs, a position that inevitably gave them a key hold over many aspects of the strategy employed. This does not mean that the other member states were entirely unable to constrain the USA in how far it went with the use of air power – key American commanders have stated publicly since the conflict that their freedom of manoeuvre was constrained severely by European attitudes on what was permissible.[8] But what it does mean is that there were limits as to how far the Europeans could try and influence the nature of the American-dominated air campaign if they did not wish to risk biting the hand that was feeding them and suffering consequences that might have threatened the future of the alliance. Some of the European member states' tacit tolerance of Nato's transition to attacking what critics felt to be civil facilities in addition to clear military targets, might be explained in these terms. The question of how successful Nato's strategy was will be addressed later.

THE LESSONS AND IMPLICATIONS OF THE KOSOVO CONFLICT FOR NATO

The conflict in Kosovo was revealing of the problems and prospects of Nato in a number of respects. First, as implied above, the Clinton administration's refusal to commit ground forces prior to the cessation of active hostilities during the Kosovo campaign, as in the Bosnian conflict, reinforced emphatically the USA's post-Somalia doctrine: that American forces will only engage in ground operations in Europe, or indeed, any-where, prior to the conclusion of hostilities, in contexts where vital goals of US foreign, defence or economic policy are perceived to be threatened. This doctrine can significantly reduce Nato's chances of achieving suc-cess in military campaigns, given the well-established European reluctance to fill the capabilities gap by significantly higher levels of defence spending. This situation may improve during the next few years as a consequence of post-Kosovo declarations by the European military powers of their intention to enhance their capabilities and effectiveness within the context of both Nato and the EU. Equally, however, it might not, given the unpromising track record of European states with regard to defence-spending and burden-sharing.

Second, the alliance's intervention in the conflict over Kosovo demon-strated some of the likely factors that would limit the effectiveness of even a well-resourced future European military force, operating, as cur-rent plans suggest, either within the overall context of Nato as an European defence 'identity', or as an EU force. The difficulties several European governments had with the idea of a combat ground force in the Kosovo context demonstrate that increasing the roles and capabili-ties of European states (in addition to their existing access to US capabilities) within Nato would not in itself guarantee that the alliance would be able to agree to deploy ground forces in future situations where the American government refused to co-operate. Equally, the virulent domestic opposition within Greece and Italy, in particular to the bomb-ing of 'civil' targets, such as power stations and non-military industrial plants, as opposed to military targets, reveals severe problems in getting agreement within the alliance, even on military strategies that do *not* include ground troops. Third, the fact that the alliance has now increased in size to nineteen members, and includes a variety of non-complementary interests, concerns, sensitivities, imperatives and 'bottom lines' deriving from differences in political perspective, geo-graphical locations and proximities, cultures, ethnic linkages and commercial interests, means that, not only is it enormously difficult to get agreement about what to do concerning specific problems, but should agreement ultimately be achieved, it is just as difficult trying to hold it together in a solid alliance front, even over a relatively short period in time of conflict. It has been revealed since the end of the Kosovo campaign that some within the American government, Strobe Talbot among others, had serious doubts that Nato could have kept its united front intact had the conflict gone on for very much longer.[9]

Fourth, the conflict exposed embarrassingly the inadequacies of the European majority within the alliance with regard to readily deployable military hardware. As pointed out already, most of the air strikes were carried out by American aircrews or missile crews, and the Europeans were also greatly dependent on them for airlift capabilities and intelligence. While there have been statements of intent to do something about this deficiency since the end of the conflict (see, for example, NATO 1999a), there seems little reason to doubt that, as in the past, the Europeans will not be prepared to risk damaging electorally significant domestic policy programmes by redirecting the full amount of necessary resources into their military budgets.

> **The conflict exposed the inadequacies of the European majority within the alliance with regard to readily deployable military hardware**

The bombing campaign also demonstrated graphically the limitations of air power as an effective military tool when used in isolation, despite all the wonders and promise of modern technology. It has become apparent since the end of the conflict that very few Serb military vehicles, for example, were hit within Kosovo, despite the substantial quantities of bombs and missiles that were used. It seems reasonable to conclude that it was only when Nato turned instead to attacking the civilian infrastructure of Serbia itself that Milosevic began to fear that the economic and human consequences would be so severe as to turn the population against him in sufficient numbers to secure his overthrow. It is a possibility, too, that he assumed wrongly that a ground invasion of Kosovo was increasingly imminent, and that this further undermined his resolve. He was most certainly unnerved by the Russian government's decision to give its backing to the peace proposals that finally heralded the end of hostilities.

Overall, the Kosovo conflict was something of a shock to the system for several of the leading European Nato governments. For example, Prime Minister Blair discovered that his much-vaunted personal and political links with the Clinton administration were not strong enough to change the president's unwillingness to authorize ground troops prior to a peace agreement. He also came under considerable fire from isolationist politicians (the right-wing nationalist, Pat Buchanan, famously referred to him as, 'the mouse that roared') and from some within the American military (one of whom referred to him as 'that Winston Blair'[10] while another is alleged to have observed that Blair 'would have fought to the last American'), and from other Nato allies who found his 'hawkish' sentiments inconvenient or annoying.

All of the European allies discovered that the small proportion of their overall forces and capabilities that were readily deployable in Kosovo meant that whether individual governments wanted to strengthen the air war with a ground campaign or not, the option was not feasible without the Clinton administration agreeing to participate. Furthermore, reliance on American air power also emphasized that it was difficult for European governments to act at all in such a context without the USA at least agreeing to prosecute an air war. This vividly demonstrated that their current weakness meant that they remained almost as unequal in their partnership with the USA in the post-Cold War world as they had been during the Cold War. The new secretary general of Nato, Lord Robertson, stated when taking office, that:

... the Kosovo campaign has ... taught us that to remain effective in future, Nato's Allies must make efforts to improve their cooperation and their contributions. They can only be sure to be able to defend their interests if they acquire the right capabilities: interdependence means accepting responsibilities not relying on the overwhelming might of a single ally.   (NATO 1999b)

It was in part as a reaction to this kind of sentiment that progress towards a European Defence Identity gathered pace during 1999, with (since the second half of 1998) the added element of the strong and positive participation of the Blair government.[11] By the end of the year the drive to expand the capacity of European states to act more effectively had resulted in the solidification of the commitment to produce an EU military identity as well as a 'European' Nato one. However, given that the individual in charge of producing the new EU military identity was the previous Nato secretary general, it is perhaps unsurprising that he should portray it in terms that are more suggestive of a strong degree of complementarity, than a challenge to Nato. He stated, for example, that:

Helsinki ... makes clear that the Union has as its objective the capacity to conduct EU-led military operations in response to international crises, but only where Nato as a whole is not engaged. This will remain a guiding principle...

Most importantly, we have made clear that ESDP is not about collective defence. Nato will remain the foundation of the collective defence of its members ... Nor does ESDP attempt to undermine the right of Member States to retain their own specific security and defence policy ....

(European Union 1999)

The EU's military role would be restricted to the tasks first set out in the Petersberg Declaration of 19 June 1992. These encompass humanitarian and rescue tasks, peace-keeping tasks and crisis management military operations, including peacemaking. Given the continuing uncertainties about the long-term future of an economically enfeebled but still massively nuclear-armed Russia, it is not surprising that the European Nato members were not anxious to undermine the key leading role that the USA continues to make in collective defence.

THE ETHICS AND LEGALITY OF NATO'S ACTION IN KOSOVO

In its Strategic Concept document of 1999, Nato stated that:

The United Nations Security Council has the primary responsibility for the maintenance of international peace and security and, as such, plays a crucial role in contributing to security and stability in the Euro-Atlantic area.

(NATO 1999a)

It is ironic, therefore, that Nato should choose to take major military action over Kosovo without authorization to do so from the UN Security Council. Under the UN Charter Nato is indeed entitled to use force as an agent of the UN, but specific authorization from the Security Council is necessary before it can do so. The alliance came under serious criticism as a result of its decision to 'authorize itself', an action that many critics saw as flying in the face of the legal international order. Furthermore, Kosovo was still a part of Serbia, and recognized as such by Nato among others within the international community. Thus, because Nato attacked Serbia without having first been attacked by it, the Alliance was accused of aggression against a sovereign state. The question, therefore, is one of whether or not Nato's actions can be defended in legal or ethical terms.

> 66 Because Nato attacked Serbia without having first been attacked by it, the alliance was accused of aggression against a sovereign state 99

As far as Security Council authorization is concerned, it has to be acknowledged that Nato was faced with considerable problems. Key Nato governments clearly felt that international law had been developing in such a way during the 1990s that it had become legitimate for UN authorized external parties to use force on the territory of a sovereign state in order to stop human rights abuses of the kind that were occurring in

Kosovo. However, they were aware also that the interests and composition of the Security Council meant that such a view could be upheld within the UN on no more than a case-by-case basis. As far as Serbia was concerned, it was very clear that, for differing reasons of their own, neither China nor Russia would be prepared to approve the use of force over Kosovo. Russia, for example, not only had close cultural and ethnic ties with Serbia, (both are seats of Orthodox Christianity and both are dominated by Slavic peoples), but also had a strong interest in preventing Nato from using force in Kosovo. This was because, in theory at least, the Balkans had been part of the sphere of influence of the former Soviet Union. Russia had little interest in seeing the USA and Nato use military force so uncomfortably close to its own borders, and public opinion polls during the conflict were to show that many ordinary Russians feared that Russia itself might be a future target of Nato aggression, if the Kosovo campaign succeeded. For Russia, it seemed, the question of human rights abuses in Kosovo by Serbs must take second priority to the wider challenge to Moscow's remaining influence in eastern Europe, and possible future threats to its security, if Nato continued to expand its military power close to Russian borders. There was therefore no prospect of securing UN authorization for the use of military force.

Nato also found the second major potential source of legitimization for its actions closed to it. The OSCE is a truly pan-European organization with over fifty members, including both Russia and the USA. It, too, could have authorized Nato to use force. However, the fact that such an authorization would have required unanimity, and that Russia would be guaranteed to block it for the reasons stated above, meant that the alliance was left without any legitimizing body for the use of force.

Nato was therefore faced with a stark choice. Once it had been decided that only force could control the situation in Kosovo satisfactorily, it could either leave Milosevic with freedom of manoeuvre, in which case he might continue serious human rights abuses whenever he chose to do so, or it could use force to constrain him permanently. If it chose the latter course, it would be acting within what key members now felt to be the *spirit* of international legally acceptable practice, even if (for reasons beyond its control) it could not comply with the *letter* of the same by obtaining a formal UN Security Council authorization. It is on the latter ground that Nato's actions can be defended although, very clearly, the alliance's most severe critics do not accept the validity of this defence. In order to defend itself further against accusations of being in breach of international law and the UN Charter, Nato was careful not to suggest that Kosovo should become independent of Serbia. It thereby accepted Serbia's continued legal right to exercise sovereignty over Kosovo, *but only after it had gained its credentials as a civilized, even handed, and competent authority to do so.*

Law and specific systems of ethics, of course, often do not coincide. This means that it is necessary not just to view Nato's actions in Kosovo from a legal point of view, but also from an ethical perspective. Whatever the doubts and debates on the left and right and among some of those in-between, about the underlying motives behind Nato's actions, it could be argued that a clear set of conclusions can be drawn. In short, a firm judgement can be made with regard to the ethical questions involved, paradoxically without worrying too much about the motives behind the alliance's campaign. While the success of Nato's action ultimately in dislodging Serb forces from Kosovo did not stop ethnic cleansing there, it did at least make it clear that the racial mass murder that had begun in Bosnia and spread over to Kosovo would not be tolerated within modern post-Nazi Europe. The Nato campaign did not, and quite possibly cannot, stop the two ethnic groups distrusting and hating each other, and indeed, killing each other, but, *whatever* views we take of Nato's real motives, it at least made it clear that the mass atrocities that have so stained European civilization during the twentieth century must not be allowed to become the pattern of the new millennium. On this ground it could be said to be justified ethically in terms of its results.

> **The Nato campaign at least made it clear that the mass atrocities that have so stained European civilization during the twentieth century must not be allowed to become the pattern of the new millennium**

However, such a suggestion might be unacceptable to many ethical purists, who remain persuaded that Nato's real motives for its action in Kosovo were neo-imperialist, and take the view so well expressed by T.S. Eliot (1970) that:

The last temptation is the greatest treason,
To do the right thing for the wrong reason …

It could be contended that the fact that Nato's action succeeded in making a forcible statement about the unacceptability of mass murder in modern Europe outside of Russia's 'near abroad' is all that needs to be noted from the viewpoint of ethically evaluating the rights and wrongs of its basic decision to intervene militarily. The effect, which emerged from the alliance's tortuous decision-making systems, was in this sense 'good', insofar as it helped realize a value that is common across several of the world's most widely influential ethical systems (mainstream Christianity and Islam, for example): the taking of innocent human life is not permissible. It should be recalled that the alliance's decision-making system ultimately involved inputs from nineteen individual states with a range of different nuances in their interpretations of the rights and wrongs of the situation in Kosovo and a range of different degrees of personal commitment to the notion that politics should be about morality as well as pragmatics. In this context, it would be impossible to pronounce judgement on the motives behind Nato's decision as moral or immoral in any valid sense anyway. There were simply too many different people and opinions going into the alliance's decision-making process to make such an exercise feasible. One way around this problem of evaluation would be to try and establish that the USA dictated the motives behind and the nature of the final policy. However, it has been pointed out already that, while the USA undoubtedly is the alliance's dominant player, even it has to compromise and modify its decisions if alliance unity is to be maintained. Furthermore, a great deal of the available evidence suggests that much of what went on in Nato's decision-making processes involved hawks and doves cancelling out the relatively extreme positions of each, leaving the centre ground as the dominant influence by default on the choices that the alliance made.[12]

It is much easier to try and make moral judgements about the rights and wrongs of the means used to realize objectives once a military strategy had been set in place. From this point of view it is possible to take issue with the particular forms that the air-strike strategy took from a number of viewpoints. Most obviously, initially, it greatly worsened the plight of the Kosovo Albanians insofar as the Serbian reaction was severe and resulted in a mass flight of the population across the borders of neighbouring states. On the other hand, the fact that Nato ultimately prevailed seems to have been a very substantial compensation to many Kosovo Albanians: they were able ultimately to return to a province from which their perceived Serbian military oppressors had been evicted. The decision to extend the targets of the bombers and missiles to economic sites of an environmentally hazardous nature is much more problematic. The bombing of petrochemical plants in particular was a tactic that was well understood to carry long-term health risks both for the population of Serbia and for those of states downwind and downriver from the consequent fires and explosions. Known and suspected carcinogens undoubtedly would be released into the environment on a significant scale and would probably cause non-combatant civilians affected by them to have significant health problems in the future. To target such facilities is effectively to wage chemical warfare on the civilian populations and not just to engage in 'conventional' warfare. These kinds of consideration mean that, even if it is accepted that Nato's decision to intervene militarily in Kosovo was morally 'good' in itself, it was compromised by some of the specific means used to implement that decision. In terms of the traditional Christian-derived laws of war, Nato could be accused of transgressing in several key respects. For example, it could be accused of having lethally targeted innocent non-combatants within and beyond Serbia by attacking chemical facilities.

While it is relatively easy to advance a justification for Nato's overall decision to use force over Kosovo in terms of both common ethical systems and evolving norms of international law and behaviour, the waters become more muddied when the nature of the means used are considered. To the author's knowledge, the alliance has not yet offered a convincing justification for what appear to be clear breaches in the conduct of its campaign of some of the laws of war long accepted in the West.

WAS NATO'S ACTION IN KOSOVO A SUCCESS?

The alliance defied many predictions and succeeded in hanging together, despite the problems which, to varying degrees, the governments of such states as Greece, Italy and Germany experienced domestically as a result of the conflict. It succeeded in securing:

- its declared aims of a Serbian military withdrawal
- the insertion of a Nato-dominated peacekeeping force into Kosovo
- Russian agreement to, and participation in, the same
- the return of most of the Kosovo Albanians who had been forced to flee their homeland
- an end to the massacres that had threatened to escalate to the horrific levels experienced during the Bosnian conflict.

In these respects it can be said to have been successful. However, the bombing campaign has since been shown to have been much less effective in terms of military targets damaged than was suggested at the time,[13] and it is a common belief that it was 'touch and go' as to whether it would actually succeed in helping to force Milosevic to comply with the West's demands. The key military strategy employed, in other words, was only partially successful if measured in terms of its originally anticipated effectiveness. As key US policy player Strobe Talbot has since admitted, had Milosevic's nerve held for a few more weeks, it is quite possible that Nato unity would simply have started to fall apart and that no agreement to try and resolve the situation by raising the stakes to the committing of ground troops would have been reached.[14]

> 66 It was 'touch and go' as to whether the bombing campaign would actually succeed in helping to force Milosevic to comply with the West's demands 99

As far as the post-conflict situation is concerned, it is hard to be optimistic. While mass killings have been brought to an end, low-intensity conflict continues and people are still being killed, albeit in small numbers. For the most part, Kosovo Albanians and the province's remaining Serbs clearly are not showing any signs of learning to live with each other and there seems to be little that the UN administration and the KFOR peacekeepers can do other than to try to contain the situation. Critics have argued that Nato governments in particular must accept some of the blame for this in so far as they appear to have decided simply to live with things as they are, instead of applying any imaginative effort to encourage and secure any significant, albeit medium- to long-term, improvement in the situation. However, those with knowledge of how long it has taken to improve significantly the situation in Northern Ireland might be a little more charitable in their judgement, although it would be somewhat complacent not to argue that more needs to be attempted than is currently the case.

Overall, however, Nato should be credited with a major success, and one that is easy to forget now that the Western media's attention has largely shifted elsewhere. In a region where the ambitions of the Milosevic faction in post-Tito Yugoslavia provoked and unleashed all the worst traditions of barbarism and historical hatreds among the peoples of the former Federal Republic, the alliance has succeeded in saving the lives of hundreds and possibly thousands of civilians and soldiers. For those who believe that key Nato states were themselves responsible for helping create the conditions within which Milosevic-inspired violence could prosper (Gowan 1999), however, this can be regarded at best as the partial righting of past wrongs for which Western states share responsibility.

Whether Nato will succeed in keeping the lid on the situation in the longer term will depend upon the commitment of its politicians and electorates to remain involved in, and to work at the problems of this troubled region. Only time will reveal whether that commitment is there.

NOTES

1 *War in Europe*, Channel 4, 1999.

2 See, for example, the interviews with Albright on *Newsnight*, BBC2, 1999.

3 *Newsnight*, BBC2, 1999.

4 *Newsnight*, BBC2, 1999.

5 *Newsnight*, BBC2, 1999; *War in Europe*, Channel 4, 1999.

6 *Newsnight*, BBC2, 1999.

7 Marshall, 1999.

8 *War in Europe*, Channel 4, 1999; *Newsnight*, BBC2, 1999.

9 *Newsnight*, BBC2, 1999.

10 *Newsnight*, BBC2, 1999.

11 See, for example, Foreign and Commonwealth Office 1999.

12 For example, see *Newsnight*, BBC2, 1999.

13 NATO 1999c.

14 *Newsnight*, BBC2, 1999.

11

RUSSIA: WALKING THE TIGHTROPE

CHRISTOPHER WILLIAMS WITH ZINAIDA T. GOLENKOVA

The Balkan tragedy (Kosovo) was provoked by NATO aggression against Yugoslavia

(Igor Ivanov, Russian Foreign Minister, May 1999)

Few Western politicians and journalists really understand the background issues and actions that led to the appearance of another hot spot on the map of Europe. The roots of the crisis and tragedy lie much deeper than a superficial glance would have us to understand. Now, over one year on from what, in Russian eyes, was perceived as Nato aggression against Yugoslavia, it is clear that this conflict was by no means just regional in character. It was one of the most crucial moments in world history at the end of the twentieth century. Nato military intervention against Yugoslavia had adverse consequences for the post-Cold War system of international relations. The military might used against Yugoslavia was second in its intensity and power only to that used during World War II. This intervention was launched by a Nato alliance of 19 countries, 10 of whom were active participants in this operation. Nato forces used 11,000 air-

> 66 Nato forces used 11,000 aircraft, carried out 25,200 sorties over the territory of Yugoslavia, and dropped approximately 25,000 tonnes of bombs 99

craft and other cutting-edge military technology, carried out 25,200 sorties over the territory of Yugoslavia, and dropped approximately 25,000 tonnes of bombs. Nato seemed to show no discrimination in its choice of victim. Women, children and the elderly, mothers with babies, the seriously ill, queues of refugees, journalists, peasants in the fields, traders in the markets, train and bus passengers and all sections of society were affected. In all EU countries, under the influence of Nato, fiercely anti-Serb and anti-Yugoslav propaganda was put about in the media, the aim, from a Russian perspective, being to conceal mass crimes against the civilian population. The Kosovo crisis set an important precedent in the system of post-Cold War international relations as Nato launched an armed strike against a sovereign state. From a Russian viewpoint this was provoked not by Serbia's aggression against the Kosovo Albanians, but by the intention to interfere in Yugoslav affairs by meddling in Serbia's own internal ethnic conflict.

This chapter will view the Kosovo crisis from a Russian viewpoint by examining the following issues:

- the Russian reaction to Nato actions including an assessment of the views of the Russian president, Duma, political parties and the media
- the consequences of Nato's actions for Russia's relations with Washington, Nato and the EU, on the one hand, and with Serbia, on the other
- the effects on Russia's international standing in the new world order.

RUSSIA'S REACTION TO NATO ACTIONS

This is the most dangerous crisis between Russia and the US since the Cuban missile crisis   (Alexei Arbatov, moderate Duma MP)

One indicator of the significance of the Kosovo crisis for Russia can be gleaned from a Russian Centre for Public Opinion research (VTsIOM) survey of the ten most important events of 1999. VTsIOM found that Russians rated Kosovo the third most important issue of that year. Only the terrorist acts of autumn 1999 and the ongoing Chechen war were viewed as more important (VTsIOM public opinion poll cited in Levada 2000).

Although it is acknowledged that the West's alleged reason for aggression towards Serbia was to protect the human rights of ethnic Albanians in the region, the real reason, from a Russian point of view, was to curb the power of Slobodan Milosevic. In addition, Russian analysts believe that the USA used the Kosovo crisis to try and sustain and strengthen cooperation between America and its Nato allies.[1] It is also widely believed in Moscow academic circles that the Kosovo crisis was a testing ground for the EU too, insofar as responses to the crisis put EU unity, individual member nation states relations with Nato, EU/US relations, and Europe's role in world affairs at the end of the twentieth century to the test.[2] These issues have been addressed elsewhere in this book.

From this brief summary, it is clear that Moscow was aware that the Kosovo crisis was a highly complicated issue that could not be easily resolved. Although Moscow sided with Belgrade's view of the crisis, Russia's reaction is much more complicated and nuanced than most Western politicians and journalists would have us believe. True, Yeltsin and Milosevic both tapped into the long-term close ties between Russia and Serbia, but Russian specialists acknowledge that what was perceived as Nato aggression may have exacerbated matters. However, the origins of the crisis go much deeper than this. According to Yelena Guskova, the recent crisis between Serbs and Albanians in Kosovo is not simply the product of Milosevic's abuse of ethnic Albanians. It also reflects manipulation of the national question under Tito, long-standing socio-economic problems prevailing in Kosovo yet to be resolved, current problems stemming from the unprecedented growth in the number of Albanians in Kosovo, and outside support for their desire for independence.[3] Most Russian scholars side with the Serbian version of the Kosovo problem and few have examined the situation from a Kosovo Albanian viewpoint. On this matter, one dissenter, Nina Smirnova, has recently pointed out that Albanians, both inside and outside Yugoslavia, tend to see Kosovo as an area of importance to the origins of their culture and as a centre of the late ninteenth-century Albanian national liberation movement. Although Smirnova stresses that Serbs and Kosovo Albanians have not always been in conflict with one another, pointing in particular to past cooperation and interaction between them, she attributes the current conflict largely to Belgrade's use of force to keep Kosovo in Yugoslavia. However, Smirnova also blames Albanians inside, as well as the diaspora outside for failing to agree on a compromise before things got badly out of hand.[4]

66 The consensus among
Russian scholars, politicians
and the mass media was that
Serbia had every right to act
as it did towards Kosovo 99

Nonetheless, the consensus among Russian scholars, politicians and the mass media was that Serbia had every right to act as it did towards Kosovo. As Kosovo was part of Yugoslavia any ethnic conflict was an internal matter for the Serbs.

THE ATTITUDES OF RUSSIA'S POLITICAL ELITE TOWARDS KOSOVO

The bombing of Yugoslavia could turn out in the very near future to be just a rehearsal for similar strikes on Russia.   (General Viktor Chechevatov)

An assessment of the reaction of Russia's political elite, government and MPs to the Kosovo crisis needs to take into account past Russian responses to crises in Yugoslavia, such as that in Bosnia, and the domestic context in Russia itself. Ever since Tito's split with Russia in 1948, relations between the two countries have been 'precarious and oftentimes conflictive' (Cichock 1990: 53). According to Cichock, Moscow's policy towards Yugoslavia up to the mid-1980s was geared towards minimizing the impact of Yugoslavia on the socialist bloc, but between 1985 and 1990, there was some improvement in relations and greater cooperation between the two countries.[5] However, the collapse of both countries at the end of the 1980s–early 1990s meant that they focused on their own internal problems and paid less attention to each other.

Although Russia was slow to formulate its new post-communist foreign policy in general and its Balkan policy in particular, Russia was soon involved in Balkan affairs from 1991 onwards. In terms of the current chapter, it is evident that there are some similarities in Russia's response to Bosnia and Kosovo. Thus according to Bowker, during the Bosnian–Serb war and allied intervention of 1992–3, Russia took a pro-Serbian stance, opposed Western air strikes, voted against the use of an arms embargo and used a special envoy (Vitalii Churkin) to get the Serbs to agree to Western demands. This culminated in the Dayton agreement.[6] What Moscow wanted was to be consulted. Furthermore, although Russia sympathized with the Serbs and 'the Russian parliament articulated a more pro-Serb stance than the Yeltsin government' (Bowker 1998: 1258), on balance, as Voronkov (1998: 9) points out.

The priority of Russian foreign policy...was the normalisation of relations with the US [and] Western Europe...to the detriment of relations with the Balkans.

All in all, during the Bosnian civil war Moscow helped the West reach a settlement, its efforts were acknowledged by both sides and Russia ensured that Serb interests were recognized at an international level via the UN and Contact Group.[7] As we shall see below, this broad stance was adopted towards Kosovo.

As Williams shows elsewhere, during the Kosovo war, Russia's transition from communism to capitalism meant that its economy was in an extremely weak position and political instability and inertia were widespread (as indicated by numerous shifts in senior government officials).[8] Russia also had a range of social and ethnic issues of its own to deal with, particularly in Chechnya.[9] This situation meant several things in relation to Kosovo. First, most Russians were more interested in their own domestic situation than in crises elsewhere: 61per cent of those surveyed in March 1998 stated that they were *not interested in the Kosovo crisis* (cited in Davydov 1999: 252; our emphasis). Second, Russia's loss of superpower status, its economic collapse, political instability and growing reliance on the West throughout the 1990s for financial aid and technology, left Russia little room for manoeuvre and virtually powerless. Finally, despite Yeltsin and others voicing their discontent with perceived Nato aggression against Serbia, public opinion surveys show that both president and politicians manipulated public opinion: in March 1998, 83 per cent of those surveyed were *in favour of Russia remaining neutral during in the Kosovo crisis* (cited in Davydov 1999: 252; our emphasis). For all these reasons, Russia was powerless to influence Nato and especially US actions, and also had, as Davydov points out 'no influence with Milosevic' (Davydov 1999: 253). However, because Western policies were not bearing fruit, anti-Western views quickly gained ground in Russia during the Kosovo crisis. Such views were nothing new. For instance, Russia viewed Nato expansion and the eastern enlargement of the EU as a serious threat to its security interests[10] and the West's actions during the Kosovo conflict merely led some Russians to conclude that the West could not be trusted and that Nato might interfere with Russia's actions in Chechnya next. It was therefore high time, so some people argued, that Russia put its own national interests first and stopped bowing down to the West.[11]

The Kosovo/Balkan crisis in 1998–9 proved to be a turning-point in Russian–Western relations. The West's heavy-handed reaction to the Serbs' treatment of the Albanians in Kosovo led to increased Russian criticism of the West and growing sympathy for the underdog – the Serbs (see Table 12.1). As the newspaper *Sovetskaya Rossiya* put it:

The US missiles exploding in Yugoslavia had very loud and unexpected repercussions in Russia … The United States has suffered a massive political defeat in Russia.

(cited in Johnston 1999: 4)

It is clear that the West made a grave mistake in almost totally ignoring Russia before Nato decided to bomb Serbia. Thus in March 1999, 48 per cent of Russians blamed the USA and Nato for the Kosovo crisis and 90 per cent believed that Nato was not right to bomb Serbia for its treatment of Albanians. Finally, 74 per cent of those surveyed thought that this would have an adverse affect upon Russia's relationship with Nato in the future.

> 66 It is clear that the West made a grave mistake in almost totally ignoring Russia before Nato decided to bomb Serbia 99

It is possible to interpret this survey in three ways:

- as some Russians showing sympathy for their old ally, Milosevic and Serbia
- as part of the anti-Western camp in Russia
- as a growing realization that the West was not as civilised and democratic as many Russians initially thought.

Besides a purely emotive response at the early stage of the Kosovo crisis, what else could Moscow do to stop the West from continually bombing Belgrade? The answer, in short, is that Moscow was forced to walk a tightrope that involved criticizing Western actions and demonstrating its discontent in a number of different ways:

- holding protests against Nato and the USA outside the American Embassy in Moscow
- pulling out of the Partnership for Peace programme with Foreign Minister Yevgeny Primakov calling off a visit to the US in late March
- not taking part in the Nato summit in April 1999 (CNN 1999; Izvestiya 23 April 1999b: 1)
- offering to act as an intermediary in order to resolve the crisis and stop Nato bombing as soon as possible.

Question/answer	Answers as per cent of sample of 1,600	
	March 1998	March 1999
What do you think about the plight of the Albanians in Kosovo?		
Internal Yugoslav issue	26	64
Concern of the West	46	22
No answer	28	14
What caused the Kosovo crisis?		
Albanian separatism	13	
Serbian cruelty	7	
Aggressive response by USA and Nato	48	
No answer	32	
Do you agree that Nato was right to bomb Serbia?		
Yes	2	
No	90	
No answer	8	
What do you feel about Nato's attack on Yugoslavia?		
Indignation	52	
Anxiety	26	
Fear	13	
Understanding	2	
Approval	1	
Indifference	2	
No answer	4	
Did Nato have the right to attack Serbia without UN sanctions?		
No	90	
Yes	2	
No answer	8	
In what way do you think the Kosovo crisis might influence Russia-Nato relations?		
Increase tension	41	
Start a new Cold War	33	
No answer	26	

Source: VTsIOM survey of 27–30 March 1999 on Russian attitudes towards Kosovo cited in *Russkaya Mysl'* 8–14 April 1999, 1).

TABLE 12.1 Russian attitudes to the Balkan crisis, March 1999

ANTI-WESTERN STANCES

Divided over every other issue, Russian politicians have come together to challenge NATO intervention in Serbia   (Global intelligence update 1998: 1)

From a Russian perspective, the West failed to give Serbia time to reach a compromise with the Kosovo Albanians. Instead, the West tried to force all parties to sign the February 1999 Rambouillet agreement. When this strategy failed,[12] Nato increased the stakes and amidst allegations of increased Serb atrocities towards Kosovo Albanians, a decision was made to launch an air strike on Serbia. Russian Foreign Minister Yevgeny Primakov was due to meet US Vice-President Al Gore in late March 1999, but he cancelled because if Nato bombed Serbia while Russia was meeting the Americans, it might appear that Russia had abandoned its 'Slav Brother' Serbia, or, worse still, that Russia condoned American and Nato actions.[13]

> 66 From a Russian perspective, the West failed to give Serbia time to reach a compromise with the Kosovo Albanians 99

Meanwhile, the European Union and the USA pursued their own aims – they wanted a radical solution – to return the 'powder keg' of the Balkans to what it used to be (i.e. to integrate the region into the new post-Cold War Europe). Of the five countries in the region, Albania, Bosnia, Croatia, Macedonia and Yugoslavia, the latter was the hardest nut to crack (*krepkii oreshek*) for the West. Economically, Yugoslavia was the strongest country in the Balkans; this coupled with Serbian patriotism, its pro-Russian stance and the independence of Milosevic's government made Belgrade an unpredictable player in the late 1990s.

Nato's hard-line reaction received a cold reception from many quarters in Russia. Thus various national-patriots ranging from Zhirinovsky's LDPR through to Zyuganov's CPRF, whose parties had dominated Russia's parliament (Duma) for many years prior to the crisis, used the events in Kosovo to whip up further anti-Western sentiments.

Shortly after Nato started the bombing, Russian MPs called for several things: a halt to the air strikes on the basis that Nato had acted without UN Security Council sanction; increased military preparedness and a freeze on the ratification of the START II nuclear arms reduction treaty. This was followed by the withdrawal of the Russian ambassador to Nato, the expulsion of prominent Nato representatives from Moscow and the postponement of Russia's involvement in the Partnership for Peace programme. At the same time, various Duma decrees 'On Nato action in Kosovo' expressed solidarity with Belgrade's position and heavily criti-cized Nato policy on Serbia (Davydov 1999: 265–6). Some MPs even went as far as to advocate a Union between Russia, Serbia and other Slavic nations, such as Belarus. Thus when Milosevic visited Moscow in June 1998, the Head of the Russian government stated:

We have not forgotten that we must serve Slavic governments and others

(cited in Davydov 1999: 258)

The Union issue was discussed in the parliaments of all three countries in mid-late April 1999 and approved in each case. The aim, according to *Moscow News*, was to

take joint measures to avert any threat to the sovereignty and independence of each of the member states of the Union; to co-ordinate defence matters and Armed Forces and take other measures to sustain defence capacity (and to) supply and sell arms and military equipment (to each other).

(Lukyanov 1999: 1)

Once again, however, only a minority of Russians wanted such a Union. Thus according to an *Eko Moskva* poll of April 1999, 23 per cent of Russians were in favour and 77 per cent against any Union between Russia and Serbia and Belarus (cited in Davydov 1999: 259). Hence the views held by some Russian MPs were far from typical. Nevertheless, if such a Union had materialized then it would have seriously damaged Russia's relations with the West and also re-shaped the entire new world order. The creation of the Union was deemed necessary, according to some analysts, first, to protect Russia's national interest; second, to restore its damaged national pride, to enable Yeltsin to help the Serbs by overcoming the West's military blockade; and finally, to serve as a counter-balance to Western foreign policy (Davydov 1999: 259). According to this camp

The Serbs are now the downtrodden nation, and all talk about Milosevic's atrocities will fall on deaf ears in Russia as long as the Serbs are outnumbered, bombed, humiliated and insulted as they are today – in a patently unfair and cowardly fashion   (Roy 1999)

At this stage, Prime Minister Yevgeny Primakov stated that Russia was considering re-evaluating its relationship with Nato. The West therefore risked severing ties with Russia and forcing Moscow to resume full military co-operation with Belgrade and to seek new alliances elsewhere if Nato bombing continued. As Duma chairman, Gennady Seleznev, put it, Nato's actions might also give 'impetus to the start of a new phase in the old Cold War' (cited in Global intelligence update 1998).

Such an anti-Western stance was heavily promoted by the CPRF, for instance, who saw US and Nato actions in Kosovo as evidence of 'Western imperialism' and as an attempt by the West to achieve global hegemony. CPRF leader Gennady Zyuganov using highly emotive language, saw 'the (Nato) attack on Yugoslavia as the equivalent on declaration of war on Russia' (cited in Global intelligence update 1998). Aleksandr Pomorov, a Communist Party MP, echoed these sentiments. He used Reagan's 1983 statement to refer to Clinton's US as the new 'evil empire' (quoted in Davydov 1999: 269).

> **The West risked severing ties with Russia and forcing Moscow to seek new alliances elsewhere if Nato bombing continued**

Many CPRF MPs called for Russian troops to be sent to Yugoslavia, not to keep the peace, but to help Serbia against its Nato aggressor (*Sevodnya* 1999). Others, such as Zhirinovsky's LDPR, used the Kosovo crisis for its own party political ends, namely as a pretext for building closer ties with Saddam Hussein or Jean-Marie Le Pen, as well as Milosevic as they had similar objectives – one to build a 'Greater Russia'; the other a 'Greater Serbia' (Davydov 1999: 269).

Finally, as one might expect, Russian liberals occupied the middle ground. Hence, Yavlinsky's Yabloko recognized that both sides had legitimate concerns – Russia wanted to protect its national interests, while the West wanted to prevent further Serbia human rights violations of Kosovar Albanians. Yabloko was, therefore, not in favour of sending Russian troops to Serbia as this would mean that 'Russia entered the war' (*Vremya* 1999).

Criticism and the break with Nato were logical responses given growing anti-Western feelings in Russia and a desire to demonstrate solidarity with Milosevic's Serbia. They failed to have a major impact on Nato policy and were somewhat counterproductive because Western officials and analysts viewed Russia's initial responses as an attempt to divert attention away from Russia's domestic problems (the nature and aftermath of the economic meltdown of August 1998) and as an effort to try to recover lost status in the international arena. All in all, when Russia stood up for Milosevic, it effectively 'damaged' its 'national interest abroad and at home' (Goldgeier and McFaul 1998). It is for this reason perhaps that Russia's stance on Nato and Kosovo gradually shifted as the Kosovo crisis deepened.

MEDIATION IS PREFERABLE TO CONFRONTATION

There seems to be a shift. Russia appears more conciliatory and moderate to us now.   (Western diplomat, 21 April 1999)

Although some sections of Russia's political elite and the military saw Nato's response as an act of aggression and sympathized with Serbia over Kosovo because it saw parallels with Russia's stance on Chechnya (see Malashenko 1999), not everyone in Russia favoured a hawkish stance on Nato action in Kosovo. There were other groups in Russia who favoured a more cautious approach and one in which Russia should act as a mediator to try and resolve the conflict as quickly as possible. This stance, for example, was favoured by Andrei Kozyrev, the former Russian Foreign Minister,[14] and Viktor Chernomyrdin, former prime minister and head of 'Our Home is Russia', who later became Russia's special envoy to Yugoslavia. It was natural that Russian official pronouncements on the Kosovo crisis displayed a mixture of resignation, frustration and outrage over Nato action. If Russia went too far in criticizing the West, it risked cutting off its nose to spite its face, namely, pressure would be brought to bear on the IMF from the international community to halt aid to Russia.[15]

Even though earlier Russian missions by Boris Nemtsov and Primakov to Belgrade tried to resolve the Kosovo crisis and failed, Yeltsin nevertheless tried to keep the pressure on the West. On 1 April 1999, he called upon the G8 to devote greater attention to Kosovo.[16] However, the West, despite Russian military manoeuvres in the Mediterranean area, rejected Russia's demands for more diplomatic efforts rather than continued bombing. The USA and Nato rightly knew that Russia was not in a position to intervene militarily over Kosovo

66 To neutralize and soften Russia, the Clinton administration sanctioned an IMF loan of US$4.8 billion in early April 1999 99

(first, because it had no desire to do so, and second even if it did, the underfunded, divided and poorly led Army was still coming to terms with the first Chechnya fiasco (1994–6) and in the midst of trying to win in its second conflict over Chechnya). Therefore, Russia was too busy at home to go to war over Kosovo. In reality, in the early stages of the Kosovo crisis Russia could do little more than loudly criticize Nato and the West. To *neutralize* and soften Russia, the Clinton administration sanctioned an IMF loan of US$4.8 billion in early April 1999. This was designed to ensure that Russia did not supply military weapons and other war material to Serbia.[17] Yeltsin realized he was in an unwinnable position when he stated:

Our fundamental position is not to get sucked into a big war and not to deliver arms ... Russia will not get involved *if the Americans don't push us.*

(cited in Johnston 1999:3, our emphasis)

Shortly after this statement was made, events took a nasty turn. On 9 April 1999, President Yeltsin stated that Russia would not allow Nato to 'seize' Yugoslavia and turn Kosovo into a protectorate. If this occurred, he suggested, then a third world war might ensue.[18] It is probable, however, that Yeltsin was just trying to appease national-patriots at home rather than provoke a war. In the end, this proved to be the case, as senior Russian officials quickly assured Washington that rumours (allegedly spread by Duma speaker Seleznev) to the effect that the Kremlin had ordered missiles to be pointed at Nato/EU member states in the West were untrue and that Russia had no intention of getting involved in the war on Serbia's side against Kosovo Albanians and their Western supporters.[19] Although for a while, things were as tense as during the 1962 Cuban missile crisis, this knee-jerk response marked a turning-point in Russia's stance on Kosovo. From this moment on, Russia, in Matloff's words, 'made a more concerted attempt ... to resolve the (Kosovo) conflict' (Matloff 1999).

Realizing that Nato was unlikely to end the bombing or even grant a cease-fire, Russia adopted another tactic. This took the form of Russia acting as an 'intermediary' between the West and Milosevic from April 1999 onwards using Chernomyrdin and others (such as the new Russian Foreign Minister Igor Ivanov) as go-betweens. This also meant that Russia was drawing closer to the USA on Kosovo and it also enabled Russia to re-open its dialogue with Nato. According to VTsIOM data, of 1,600 people surveyed, 41.5 per cent thought that Russia should try to find a resolution to the conflict in Kosovo by working together with the two sides while 33.4 per cent thought that it should follow its own line.[20] This role was by no means an easy task. Special Envoy Chernomyrdin declared that the situation was 'serious', 'complicated' and 'very difficult to resolve'.[21] He had been favoured over Primakov because the latter was a threat to Yeltsin, whereas the former was close to US Vice-President Gore, Western political leaders and to Milosevic. Chernomyrdin flew regularly between Europe and Serbia trying to keep the dialogue open. Matloff summed up its significance thus:

At stake is not just finding a solution to the Yugoslav conflict, but preserving what's left of the delicate security partnership crafted after the Cold War's end.   (Matloff 1999)

and Clinton added on 26 April 1999:

Our Alliance (Nato) recognises the tremendous importance of Russia to Europe's future and we are determined to support Russia's transition to stronger democracy and more effective free markets, and to strengthen our partnership with Russia.   (cited in Csongos 1999)

In one Bonn meeting, Chernomyrdin tried to get Nato to stop the bombing while he negotiated concessions from Milosevic[22], although the West refused the question of having UN peacekeepers in Kosovo and the possible composition of international forces in the region was discussed in another meeting between Chernomyrdin and Milosevic held in late April 1999.[23] Slow but steady progress was being made. By late April 1999, Russia and the West were gradually developing 'shared objectives' (Lagunina 1999; Partridge 1999). By early May, Chernomrydin and Clinton met in Washington and Russia was optimistic that a solution to the crisis would soon be reached. The stumbling block was the withdrawal of Serb troops and their acceptance of international peacekeepers in the province.[24] However, by 6 May 1999, Russia had succeeded in getting Russia and the Western G8 powers to discuss a peace plan. As Ivanov noted: 'it would be premature to speak of a breakthrough, but progress has been made' (cited in ABC News broadcast 6 May 1999). From this moment on, the difficulties were first, getting Milosevic to accept a Serb withdrawal, the deployment and composition of peacekeeping forces and providing safeguards for 840,000 returning refugees;[25] and second, preventing the partitioning of Kosovo (USIS 1999) while Nato continued its bombing campaign. Although the latter almost led to Russia abandoning its diplomatic efforts,[26] and meant that little progress was made throughout May, the stalemate was eventually broken in early June. At a meeting between Chernomyrdin, Milosevic and Finnish President Ahtisaari in Belgrade on 3 June 1999, it was agreed that Yugoslav forces would leave Kosovo in exchange for a Nato halt to bombing, the introduction of peace-keeping forces (including Russia) and most of all, for Kosovo remaining part of Yugoslavia.[27] The threat of more air raids on Serbia acted like the sword of Damocles; in order to escape it Milosevic had to sign an agreement with the USA that involved the withdrawal of Serbian forces from Kosovo and the stationing of 2,000 OSCE observers there.

> 66 The treat of more air raids on Serbia acted like the sword of Damocles 99

ASSESSMENTS OF RUSSIA'S ROLE

Although Chernomrydin's role as a 'channel' between opposing sides was viewed as 'positive' and 'fruitful' by the US administration,[28] and the West thanked Chernomyrdin for his hard work, the reaction in Russia was totally different. Thus on 9 June 1999, a Duma resolution 'On measures aimed at resolving the Balkans crisis' stressed that Chernomyrdin was a 'poor choice as envoy' and a further resolution on the same issue dated 16 June criticized Chernomyrdin for 'pursuing a policy which violates Russia's national interests' (*Izvestiya* 1999d: 1). Most Russians concurred with this view. Thus by June 1999, 37 per cent of those surveyed thought Russia was unsuccessful in its 'mediator role', compared to only 26 per cent who viewed it as a success (VTsIOM poll 1999). On balance, though, it seems unlikely that without Russia's assistance, Milosevic would not have accepted the ten-point peace plan in the second week of June. Although Nato saw this as evidence that its bombing had succeeded, Serbia and Russia for their part viewed the settlement as a victory for them because as one Stratfor report put it: 'it was the Russians not the bombing campaign that delivered the Serbs' (Stratfor 1999). Most Russians surveyed by VTsIOM on 5 June 1999 agreed by a narrow margin (33 per cent no to 37 per cent yes) that Yugoslavia was right to give in to Nato demands (VTsIOM poll 1999). Shortly after an agreement had been reached, the Russian President and Prime Minister Sergei Stepashin discussed the use of Russia troops and other issues, such as Serb safety after the return of Kosovo Albanians.[29] At a USA–Russia meeting in Helsinki, two days later, Russia finally agreed to send in a Russian peace-keeping force.[30] Yeltsin agreed to send up to 3,616 troops until 10 June 2000

(*Izvestiya* 10 June 1999: 1). The goal of the Russian contingent and mission, according to *Parlamentskaya Gazeta*, was the 'preservation of Yugoslavia's territorial integrity on the basis of Kosovo's self-determination' (*Parlamentskaya Gazeta* 24 June 1999: 1). Although most Russians were not in favour of sending peacekeepers to Kosovo (34 per cent for; 51 per cent against), they nevertheless recognized that a Russian presence was more important for Russia (45 per cent) than Yugoslavia (34 per cent). Presumably, by this, respondents viewed a Russian presence positively in terms of Russia's increased international standing (VTsIOM poll of 1,500 respondents on 3 July 1999). Despite negative public opinion, the first Russian peacemakers flew to Kosovo on 6 July 1999, and 200 Russian troops arrived in Pristina airport, much to the delight of the Serbs and the dismay of Kosovo Albanians who viewed them as pro-Serbian.[31] However, the USA viewed a Russian presence as 'crucial' in allaying 'Serb fears when Albanian refugees started coming back' (RTR news 14 June 1999). Reinforcements of over 500 were sent later.[32] Later it was widely acknowledged in the West that:

> 66 Although most Russians were not in favour of sending peacekeepers to Kosovo, they nevertheless recognized that a Russian presence was more important for Russia than Yugoslavia 99

It was payoff time for Russia's reformers. At great risk to themselves, they delivered Milosevic to the bargaining table and delivered Kosovo to NATO. Without the Russians … NATO would still be drawing up plans for impossible ground attacks.   ('Russia in Cologne' 1999)

Although Yeltsin told senior Russian military personnel that 'Russia will not quarrel with NATO *recklessly* but we will *not flirt* with it either' (*Izvestiya* 9 July 1999: 2; our emphasis), Prime Minister Stepashin later told Vice-President Gore and the managing director of the World Bank, James Wolferson that 'what happened in Yugoslavia and Kosovo will *not force us back into the times of the Cold War*' (ORT news 27 July 1999. Our emphasis).

As we shall see below, Russia's role in the Kosovo affair has had both short- and long-term implications for pro-Westerners in Russia and for Russia's relationship with the West on one hand, and with Serbia on the other. But before we explore this issue, it is useful to examine how the Russian media viewed the Kosovo crisis.

THE RUSSIAN MEDIA AND KOSOVO

Ninety per cent of Russians are against NATO's actions in Yugoslavia. Russian reporters and editors share the opinions of their fellow Russians.

(Masha Lipman, Deputy Editor, *Itogi*)

Russians are ignorant about the roots of the conflict.

(Andrei Piontkovsky, political analyst)

In Russia, after the bombardment of Yugoslavia by Nato, public opinion was divided. As Table 12.1 showed earlier, most Russians thought that Nato and the USA, rather than the Kosovo Albanians and/or the Serbs, were to blame for the development of the conflict. As far as we are aware few studies have been carried out of Russian media coverage of the Kosovo conflict although some are pending. We have already touched on this topic indirectly in the previous analysis, so here we would like to offer a brief preliminary analysis of Russian newspaper and TV coverage of the Kosovo war from March to July 1999 (i.e. the time when the Nato intervention was in full swing).

The difference between Russian media coverage of Kosovo and, say, that of Chechnya throughout the 1990s is that, whereas in the latter there was a diversity of opinion and even some criticism of Russian official action,[33] with regard to Kosovo, the vast majority of Russian media was highly critical of Nato's military action. As Stuart Stein notes:

Papers of all stripes – official, neo-communist, centrist and reformist – excoriated NATO's bombing campaign on the grounds that it was *an aggression against a sovereign state, a violation of international law* and [that] NATO was [used] *as an instrument to establish Pax Americana in Europe and beyond.*

(Stein 1999; our emphasis)

More specifically, our analysis of the Russian press shows that *Rossiiskaya Gazeta*, the main governmental newspaper, equated its position to that of the Federal authorities, and criticized Nato's decision to use force, demonized Nato and presented the Russian government as the defender of the Serbs against the Nato aggressor. *Krasnaya Zvezda*, the official newspaper of the Ministry of Defence, devoted attention to the hostility, and evaluated events from a military-tactical viewpoint. This newspaper pointed to Nato incompetence, Serb casualties and the hardships encountered by the Yugoslav Army. The communist newspaper, *Pravda*, added its weight to the largely Russian media critique of Nato and the West by highlighting its opposition to Nato's actions, encouraged anti-Western feelings and sided with the Serbs. During the first month (March 1999) all the papers devoted favourable and widespread coverage to protest meetings in support of Yugoslavia and to the horrors of the continuing Western bombing of the Serbs.

Very few newspapers took a more balanced view. The exception was *Izvestiya*, a liberal reformist daily, which tried to discuss Kosovo in a more open-minded fashion by criticizing Russia's indirect involvement in the crisis. Thus on 9 April 1999 *Izvestiya*, while criticizing Nato's use of force against Serbia, shifted the focus instead onto the need for democracy, humanitarianism and the protection of human rights of both Serbs as well as Kosovo Albanians. It also criticized Russia for consistently siding with Milosevic and for ignoring ethnic cleansing in central Europe. Analyzing the results of the conflict, *Izvestiya* stressed its impact on USA–Russian relations (increased strain) and on the further disintegration and destabilization of Yugoslavia, together with the enormous human and material losses on the Serb and Kosovo Albanian side (*Izvestiya* 1999a). Furthermore, *Moscow News* argued that Russia's hysteria towards the West was due, first, to 'slanted news reports' and, second, to the lack of coverage of the humanitarian catastrophe in Kosovo which 'makes NATO air raids look like a senseless and absurd aggression' (cited in Stein 1999).

These were the exceptions, however. In most cases, there was a consensus among the Russian press that Nato was enacting 'terror' and 'massacring innocent Serbs'. Nato was labelled as the 'aggressor' and 'oppressor'. This accounts for Piontkovsky's and Lipman's comments above.

A similar approach prevailed with regard to television coverage. Most Russian TV stations took a favourable stance identifying with Russia's critique of Nato bombardments and portraying Russia's mediation role in a positive light. Only NTV's Itogi and Sevodnya, like their newspaper namesakes, offered a more balanced approach towards Kosovo. For example in early April 1999, NTV tried to allow its TV audiences to reach their own independent conclusions by familarizing them with the latest trends and different opinions of the conflict (Russian and Western alike). NTV also reported Serb atrocities and the plight of the Kosovo Albanians.[34] The Serbs for their part responded badly to NTV's balanced coverage. In fact, its reporter Vyacheslav Grunsky was expelled for no clear reason after being in the region for six weeks.[35] It is probable, however, that Milosevic did not want Russians to hear the other side of the story as represented by NTV's coverage.

The West viewed Russia's coverage of the Kosovo war as biased in favour of Serbia and against Nato. Despite this, a VTsIOM April 1999 survey pointed out that only 7 per cent of respondents thought that the Russian media *was reporting Kosovo with a pro-Milosevic slant* compared to 44 per cent who thought that Russia *was reporting the situation objectively* (cited in McLaren 1999). However, Russia's MPs and Duma disagreed. Thus on 12 May 1999, one Duma report stated that:

> The biased coverage of the Balkan conflict by the leading Russian TV companies reflects an attempt to use the Russian mass media to carry out propaganda in the Russian Federation in order to justify the [Nato or western] bloc's aggression towards the Republic of Yugoslavia
>
> (Teleskop No.17 (157), 19 May 1999)

In the event, 260 out of 450 Russian MPs recommended that the Russian government and president place severe restrictions on the inclusion of Western perspectives in Russian TV and press reports on Kosovo (Teleskop No.17 (157), 19 May 1999). Yeltsin and his government were too weak to effectively censor the media, only TV or newspaper owners really had the power to change things. Nevertheless this Duma vote showed the strength of feeling in Russia regarding Kosovo.

66 Russian MPs recommended that the Russian government and president place severe restrictions on the inclusion of Western perspectives in Russian TV and press reports on Kosovo 99

Katherine L. Starr argues that the Russian media's coverage of Western stances on Kosovo from late March to early July 1999 was designed to achieve several objectives:

- to point to the dangers of growing American power and influence
- to criticize Western intervention in the Balkans
- to highlight the flaws in Nato's new supposedly post-Cold War military strategy
- to show that the West (and especially Nato) had ignored the UN
- to illustrate that Russia no longer had any major international standing
- to show that Russia was no longer an equal partner with the US and Nato in policing the new world order.[36]

While some of the above anti-Western stances are hardly surprising given

Russia's difficult transition to democracy in the last decade, we must also not forget that the Russian press and TV operate under severe economic constraints. Journalists are poorly paid and newspapers struggle to retain readers as the costs of buying, producing and supplying papers increase. As a consequence, most newspapers and TV stations do not have the money to send reporters to the war-zone so, for this reason too, coverage is not as even or informed as it might otherwise have been. From the above brief overview, it is possible to reach the conclusion that most Russian newspapers and TV news programmes emphasized the senselessness of the use of Nato force over Serbia's actions in Kosovo. They also stressed the human costs – growing numbers of casualties, the deficiencies of Nato military operations (on innocent civilian targets) and the West's lack of political will to pursue diplomatic means to resolve the conflict. Hence an 'us-versus-them' dichotomy seemed to be operating in which the West was the 'enemy' and negatively portrayed for its brutality, destruction and grief inflicted whereas the Russians and Serb 'Slavic allies' were seen as 'heroes' and 'warriors' fighting their Western oppressor. In this context, President Yeltsin, Chernomyrdin and others were generally portrayed in a positive light for their anti-Western stance.

WINNERS AND LOSERS: THE LESSONS OF KOSOVO

Sure, NATO can triumph over Yugoslavia by assaulting it with everything it has in its arsenals ... [but] Europe will surely enter the next century without any respect for democratic values   (*Nezavisimaya Gazeta*, 5 May 1999)

Over one year after the war in Kosovo, it is now possible to review some of the short-, perhaps even long-term, implications of the war for Russia's relations with Washington, Nato and EU, on the one hand, and Russia's relations with Serbia, on the other.

With regard to the first variable, while the USA and western Europe are relieved that a peace agreement was reached and feel that their actions were morally justified, as the above quote shows, the outcome in terms of Russia–US/Nato/western European relations is far from clear. Thus Russia–US negotiations over START II arms reductions, nuclear cooperation, Nato expansion and the comprehensive test ban treaty are all at stake.[37] Moreover, the war has led to uncertainty about European security post-Kosovo in general[38] and as a result in January 2000, Russia revised its national security concept and strategy to broaden the situations in which Russia might deploy nuclear weapons, criticized Western attempts to go from a multipolar to unilateral solution to global problems, and Russia now describes America as a threat.[39] Future Russia–Nato relations, Nato's new 'strategic concept' and Nato expansion to the East will probably prove to be more difficult in the future.[40] As Antonenko points out, various myths regarding Russia's integration into the new world order, its *equal* partnership with the West and Russia's cooperation with Nato, have now been exposed for all to see.[41]

Although Nato has secured the departure of Milosevic, it has not broken Serbian national pride and the KLA remains a strong force in Kosovo.[42] More importantly, for future relations, Russia now has stronger ties with Serbia. Thus in mid-May 2000 Russia hosted an alleged war criminal (General Dragolub Ojdanic) and agreed to provide loans to Yugoslavia.[43]

Beyond this legacy of tension and frustration, there are also implications for Russia itself and its standing in the world. Despite the Russian response on Kosovo outlined above, and in particular Russia's role in negotiating a peace settlement, Russia's influence over Serbia and the West, as during the Bosnian crisis, is exaggerated. In both crises – Bosnia and Kosovo:

despite all the rhetoric, *the Russian government acted cautiously and within the generally accepted parameters of the international consensus.*

(Bowker 1998: 1259; our emphasis)

This refers to Bosnia but is equally applicable to Kosovo. For Alan Rousso, this continuity, and desire to work with the West on the Balkans and other security issues, demonstrates 'its standing and utility in international diplomacy' because Russia is *'becoming* a player in Europe' (Rousso 1999: 3). However, some Russian analysts, such as Oleg Levitin, believe that Russia suffered a major 'fiasco in the Balkans' because of:

Russia's weakness, inconsistencies in its foreign policy on the Balkans and above all Moscow's tendency to ignore Kosovo from Kozyrev through to Primakov until the problem got out of hand.   (Levitin 2000: 130)

Following Rousso, then, Russia managed to walk the tightrope and get from one side of the rope to the other; but for Levitin, Russia walked the tightrope, almost fell, regained its balance and just managed to get to the other side. The question now is what long-term implications will the Kosovo crisis have? Before Russia falls from the tightrope and there is no safety net underneath because the West has taken it away, it is likely that President Putin and anti-Westerners (read largely anti-American) around him will seek to restore 'Russia's strength' and this may in the years to come lead to a 'new assertiveness in [Russian] foreign policy' (Levitin 2000: 139). If this proves to be the case, the West may have won the battle for Kosovo but inadvertently opened up a new chapter of the Cold War.

NOTES

1   See Stenova 1999.

2   Rubinsky 1999.

3   Guskova 1999.

4   Smirnova 1999.

5   Cichock 1990.

6   Bowker 1998.

7   Bowker 1998: 1258.

8   Williams 2000.

9   See Williams, Chuprov and Staroverov 1996; Williams and Sfikas 1999.

10   See Black 2000.

11   Truscott 1997; Trofimenko 1999.

12   See Weller 1999.

13   CNN 1999.

14   See Karpov 1999.

15   'Russia's dilemma' 1999.

16   See 'Russia political and military posturing' 1999.

17   *Irish Times* 1999.

18   BBC News 9 April 1999.

19   BBC News 9 April 1999.

20   *Monitoring Obshchestvenmoe Minenie* 1999.

21   See RTR News broadcasts on 4–5 May 1999.

22   *Moskovskii Komsomolets* 30 April 1999: 2.

23   Stratfor Commentary Archive 1999.

24   RFE/RL Report 1999.

25   Frost 1999; Hughes 1999; *Izvestiya* 7 May 1999: 1.

26   Hoffman 1999.

27   ORT News 3 June 1999.

28   See TR News 4 May 1999.

29 ORT News 15 June 1999.
30 RTR News 17 June 1999.
31 Balkan Report 1999; RTR News 6 July 1999.
32 RTR News 15 July 1999.
33 See Vinokurov 1995.
34 See McLaren 1999; Pounsett 1999.
35 *Russia Today* 11 May 1999.
36 Starr 1999.
37 See Piyakev 1999.
38 Dannreuther 1999–2000; Vershbow 2000.
39 Hoffman 2000.
40 Dannreuther 1999–2000.
41 See Antonenko 1999–2000.
42 Hedges 1999.
43 Williams 2000b.

12

KOSOVO: THE DESECRATED ICON

JOHN SIMONS

MYTHS AND MANIPULATION

Here are some voices from Kosovo:

Weave a church on Kosovo,
build its foundation not with marble stones,
build it with pure silk and with crimson cloth,
take the Sacrament, marshal the men,
they shall all die,
and you shall die among them as they die.[1]

Unhappy! Evil luck has come on me.
Unhappy, if I were to grasp a green pine,
even the green pine would wither.[2]

These two quotations are taken from the great complex of poems and ballads about Kosovo that form the bedrock of medieval Serbian literature. Serbs who are now in their thirties would have learned many of these by heart while at school. In the first, Tsar St Lazar is given a choice by the prophet Elijah who comes down from heaven in the form of a grey hawk bearing a letter from the Mother of God. As the reader can see this letter offers a grim but glorious future which has had far-reaching consequences for the Serbian understanding of Kosovo and, therefore, for any outsider's understanding of the position which Kosovo occupies in the Serbian national myth. The second quotation is from a shorter poem usually given the title *The Kosovo Girl*. This work was given visual form in a 1919 painting by the Serbian artist Uros Predic´, much reproduced as an image of patriotic sacrifice.[3] The poem tells of a young girl who crosses the battlefield of Kosovo and comes upon the dying knight Pavle Orlovich. He tells her about the defeat at the hands of the Turks and the heroic death of the Serbian nobility. The quotation above records her reaction and ends the poem.

In a chapter that seeks to explore the current situation in Kosovo and the surrounding region it may seem odd to begin with some fragments of poetry that have their origins in the fourteenth century (although their current form dates from the early nineteenth century when they were collected, along with many others, by the scholar Vuk Karadzhich as part of the project to define Serbian national identity in the context of the struggle for independence from the Ottoman Turks).[4] However, I hope that it will be seen that these beautiful old verses are of the utmost importance in understanding the tragic events of the last two years. I want to suggest that in the attack on Kosovo the West simply did not understand the cultural complexity that binds the region to Serbia and therefore should not have been surprised at the obstinacy with which the Yugoslav government conducted itself throughout. In some ways, of course, this obstinacy was also a construction that was the result of the unacceptable clauses of the Rambouillet document.

> 66 In the attack on Kosovo the West simply did not understand the cultural complexity that binds the region to Serbia 99

At the Rambouillet conference Yugoslavia would have had to agree to a referendum on Kosovan autonomy, to allowing Nato troops unrestricted access to Yugoslav territory (not just Kosovo), and to a protocol that exempted those troops from any jurisdiction of Yugoslavian law. I believe that no country in the world could reasonably have been expected to agree to such terms and it seems now that they were incorporated late into the document with the specific intention of getting the previously recalcitrant KLA delegation to sign up to the agreement. From that point on it did not matter whether or not the Yugoslavs signed. A mandate for war was now available. We may, however, note that in the aftermath of the war neither of these two conditions has been achieved and that the occupying power (UN/KFOR) has shown no desire to press for them. These coercive clauses and their hasty abandonment are of the greatest importance in understanding both the pressure that the Western alliance had incautiously placed on itself in the preliminaries to the conflict and its conduct in acting as a force of occupation of Yugoslav sovereign territory in its aftermath.

In drawing the reader's attention to medieval Serbia I do not wish to argue that the Yugoslav reaction to the Kosovo crisis was motivated by national myth. The clauses in Rambouillet make this reaction very easy to understand in the simplest terms of practical politics. However, we need to consider this history for two reasons. The first is that Slobodan Milosevic's rise to power and continued control has been accompanied by a canny manipulation of the anxieties that arise out of that history and its associated nationalist myth. The second is that in the aftermath of the war the depredation of the Kosovan landscape has been very carefully targeted to destroy the history and culture that the myth of Kosovo so movingly articulates.

In fact, in my limited experience, some Serbs (I cannot say most) don't really care much about Kosovo or about Albanians. Nor are they much impressed by Mr Milosevic's less than outstanding record as their leader.[5] In practice, many seem to have a view of the region that is not unlike that which many British people have of Northern Ireland: it isn't worth the trouble. Furthermore, in spite of their dislike of Mr Milosevic it is hard to see how they could replace him and, even if they did, whether the Yugoslav opposition, which is fragmented and often characterized by self-seeking infighting, would throw up an alternative who would be much better. Indeed, some possible candidates would bang a nationalist drum that would be more dangerously divisive at home and more alarming abroad than the instrument played by Slobodan Milosevic. What is clear though is that the Yugoslav people, many of whom get their information not from local sources (which they see as government controlled) but from international ones such as CNN and Sky News, have suffered greatly. This is not only because of internal repression but also because of the extraordinarily crude measures the Western alliance has deployed to break Mr Milosevic's hold on power. Economic sanctions, for example, succeed in making the already difficult lives of the ordinary people more difficult while Mr Milosevic

66 It is difficult to see what sanctions are meant to achieve except to drive more people into believing the myths of heroic defeat on which Mr Milosevic thrives 99

appears to build his personal wealth. Meanwhile, the criminal elements that mar civil life in Yugoslavia and which have been consistently present in the Yugoslav conflicts of the past decade prosper under his regime. As the Yugoslav people do not have a choice in their government (or at least no *good* choices it would appear) it is difficult to see what sanctions are meant to achieve except to drive more people into believing the myths of heroic defeat on which Mr Milosevic thrives. It should also be said that while the Yugoslav people may live in this state of political aporia few, if any, of them would feel that their country should have been subject to a full-scale aerial bombardment. This will have helped to harden the very attitudes which the Western alliance had hoped to defeat.

Here are two more voices:

Watch what happens in Kosovo next week.

There is no law in the new world order.

The first of these quotations records something that was said to me on a street corner in Tirana in February 1998. I was saying goodbye to an Albanian friend after we had been out for dinner. I had been in Albania several times and had witnessed the outbreak of the rioting, ostensibly over pyramid saving schemes but, more likely, an orchestrated attempt to reverse certain shifts in the traditional north–south balance of power that had been in train since the fall of the Communist dictatorship. It

> 66 The KLA initiated the offensive that led inexorably to the provocation that drew Nato Into a war on the KLA's side 99

will be remembered that these riots culminated in the looting of the Albanian arsenals and, I am fairly certain, a consequent improvement in the then virtually unknown KLA's ability to conduct a large-scale terrorist campaign. Now in the much less pleasant atmosphere of Tirana after the chaos (which still afflicted much of the countryside) I was suddenly told something which I could not understand. A few days later I understood very well. The KLA initiated the offensive that led inexorably to the provocation that drew Nato into a war on the KLA's side.

What this chance remark shows is that the planning for the conditions under which the KLA would inaugurate its campaign was both sophisticated and hardly secret. In fact, events have shown that the KLA was fully in control of the media campaign from a very early stage and manipulated experienced Western politicians and diplomats in a manner that consistently cut off their escape routes. It should be remembered that both the state department and the foreign office were, at this time, clear that the KLA was a terrorist organization of a kind that put it beyond the pale of Western support. Indeed, there are rumours that some KLA funding came from Osama bin Laden whose various enterprises have provoked the USA to bombing raids elsewhere in the world. But in these few late-night words we can see just how careless the West seems to have been in its approach to the war and how unreflective on the wider issues its policy was to become.

The second quotation came from a Serbian friend who had just taken me to an art exhibition. It was in April 1998 and worrying news was filtering from Kosovo. In Belgrade it was rumoured that large sums of money were being offered to criminal elements to join paramilitary police forces in the province and it takes little imagination, given the previous Yugoslav conflicts, to think that these sums would have been readily supplemented by loot. But what was I being told? Here was someone who carried no particular political brief but was proud of his country and extremely knowledgeable about its history. The view that he was expressing may be glossed as follows: in order to demonstrate the role of the West in the world that has followed the Cold War, pariah nations are necessary. In the Middle East, Iraq fits the bill. In the West, Serbia has been selected. This is particularly puzzling to many Serbs as they are very conscious that Western leaders will shake hands with the Chinese or allow the Turks into Nato while permitting them to kill Kurds at will. In other words, my friend was saying that he felt himself to be the victim of a bully. The chain of events that had led him to suffer through several winters of sanctions and to see his earnings become worthless was linked in his mind to a global pattern in which the West seeks to justify itself through the selective punishment of nations that have little capacity to fight back. This was before the Kosovo war so I can only imagine, as my links with Yugoslavia have been relatively limited since the end of hostilities, that he is now even more convinced that he is right. What has happened to prove him wrong?

How many Serbs share his view? It is difficult to tell. I was once driven from Belgrade to the Macedonian capital Skopje. My driver was articulate and amusing and gave me some insight into what ordinary Yugoslavs think. I am increasingly convinced that the gap between the position of Western leaders and the reality of the Yugoslav situation in the late 1990s was created by a discursive gesture akin to that imposed on the countries of the Middle East and referred to, in academic circles, as Orientalism.

The discourse does not survive even limited exposure to ordinary people but world leaders do not meet ordinary people. The West tends to see Europe as based on the Rhine and the traditional nations of the Mediterranean and has little grasp of the other Danubian Europe and the Balkan peninsula even though it played such a decisive role in the history of the previous century. We might see in the attitudes expressed towards this region a process by which a discourse has been formed and it is against this discourse, and not against the thing itself, that Western policy seems to have defined itself.

66 The Yugoslav situation in the late 1990s was created by a discursive gesture akin to that imposed on the countries of the Middle East and referred to, in academic circles, as Orientalism 99

Having invoked the idea of Orientalism I think it would be right to suggest that the Balkan situation can also be understood as post-colonial. In their haste to castigate their own cultures Western commentators often appear oblivious to the fact that the most successful imperial project yet seen in the modern world (i.e. since 1400) was not the outcome of European/Christian capitalism but of Turkish/Islamic expansionism. The role of the Ottoman Empire in determining Serbian consciousness and in conditioning the complex relationships that obtain both within the various Balkan countries and between them should not be underestimated but it is often ignored. One cannot justify atrocity by an appeal to history but one can begin to understand how to deal with other cultures by understanding their view of the past. Serbia did not win full independence from Turkey until 1878 and Kosovo was not regained until 1912. That is not very long ago. If Serbia struggles both to live out its national myth and to escape from it, it is hindered in the attempt by the rest of Europe, which imposes a myth of its own yet seems reluctant to subject itself to critical analysis.

This reluctance is not surprising as the myth conveniently forgets western Europe's own complicity in the events which tore Yugoslavia apart in such a disastrous manner during the 1990s.[6] The hasty recognition of an independent Croatia by Germany was a moment of alarm and dismay in Serbia.[7] But this should have been perfectly understandable to anyone who thought even for a few moments about the history of Serb-Croat relationships during World War II. Croatia was a puppet state of the Nazis and, although there may be quibbles about the numbers who died, no one of any reputation denies the existence of concentration camps, especially that at Jasenovac, where Serbs were tortured and murdered by the Ustase militias.[8] The recognition of Croatia by Germany brought back all the nightmares of this nightmarish past. It is astonishing that no serious attempt was made in the EU to tone down or contest this recognition and that little consciousness of its import seems to have marked subsequent responses to the various Yugoslav conflicts.

SERBIAN PERSPECTIVES AND WESTERN COUNTER-PERSPECTIVES

So what views might Serbs have had in the run-up to the war and what counter-views were imposed by the West? On the extreme nationalist side it might be said that Serbia is a bulwark of Christendom holding back the expansion of Islam on behalf of the rest of Christian Europe. There certainly is a religious character to ideas of Serbian-ness. It would seem almost impossible for a Serb to conceive of a claim to Serbian identity that is not defined by Orthodoxy.[9] However, it is not the case that the conflict within Yugoslavia and, especially, Yugoslav domestic policy in Kosovo during the 1980s and 1990s, was explicitly configured by religion and, specifically, as a clash between Islam and Orthodoxy.[10] Kosovo occupies such a prominent place in Serb mythology not only because it was there that Serbian nationhood was submerged in an imagined defeat (which was, almost certainly, actually a military victory).[11] It is also because it is in Kosovo that the most holy sites of Orthodoxy are to be found.[12] In the myth of Serbia, Kosovo therefore represents both a secular and a spiritual heartland. This is so holy that when, in 1915, the Serbian army retreated after its initial successes the exhausted soldiers are said to have removed their boots when crossing the field of Kosovo Polje so as not to desecrate the sacred earth. In 1896 the painter Paja Jovanovic´ depicted, on an epic scale, the emigration of 1690 when Patriarch Arsenije led his people out of Kosovo to escape the Turkish armies which were seeking revenge for a failed rebellion against their rule.[13] However, in 1998 the matter was not one of Orthodoxy versus Islam but of how to respond to the well-armed terrorist army operating within the province. The heavy-handed response of the Yugoslav government and the atrocities committed by paramilitary criminal gangs gave credence to the West's discourse of the Balkans as a space of blood, violence and seething nationalist hatred.

> 66 Atrocities committed by paramilitary criminal gangs gave credence to the West's discourse of the Balkans as a space of blood, violence and seething nationalist hatred 99

In fact, there are Serbs who would argue that much of the past decade should be understood as an unleashing of gangsterism within a regime of legitimization that suited a government that had no taste for democracy and, indeed, feared it. I think it certainly the case that few Serbs who had grown up in a Yugoslavia that enjoyed relative prosperity, stability and, as far as this can be said for a Communist country, individual freedom, looked with any pleasure on the disasters of the 1990s. In 1995 a Macedonian engaged me in conversation as we were waiting for a bus on the steps of a hotel in Skopje. He lamented the break up of Yugoslavia and then said what I think is one of the saddest things I have ever heard:

We didn't know we hated each other.

I am sure that many Yugoslavs think this or similar things and that this idea applies to Kosovo as much as to anywhere else. At the same time, I don't believe that one can attribute the excesses of the last few years simply to criminals. It is clear that official forces were also involved and that many atrocities happened with the connivance, if not the participation, of local populations. The question though is how this came about and why the West failed to do more to support more moderate opinion or at least to demonstrate its readiness to back democracy rather than simply punish repression. In Kosovo it was noteworthy that, having re-designated the KLA as freedom fighters rather than terrorists, the Western powers marginalized the pacifistic 'official' leader of the Kosovo Albanians, Dr Ibrahim Rugova. By this means, assuming that Dr Rugova could have asserted any authority, a much more violent future for the province was ensured.

So we have two different stories. One speaks of a glorious past that must be defended at all costs to preserve the integrity of Serbian identity. The other speaks of the forces of lawlessness which have been allowed to prosper under legal protection. There is also another view and that is that Yugoslavia is, left to itself, a European country like any other, and that the common culture and common interests that link it to the West mean that it deserves better treatment. The first two have some elements of truth but are, in the final analysis, myths, in that they make history meaningful to those who are haplessly trying to understand its effect on their everyday life. The third seems to me to be true, and yet because the Western powers have imposed their own myth of the Balkans on the current situation it has no forum in which to be heard. Certainly many Serbs are puzzled as to why their staunch and extremely costly support of the allied cause during both World Wars has been forgotten. They are puzzled as to why the huge loss of life among the Serbian people during World War II (maybe as many as one in six lost his or her life, making Serbia one of the great victim nations of the conflict) has been forgotten.[14] They are puzzled as to why the non-aligned status of Yugoslavia and, therefore, its exemption from the ranks of the traditional enemies with the Soviet bloc has been forgotten. Frankly, I am puzzled by this too. Why have these things been forgotten? Why was it so easy to demonize Serbia? Was it just Milosevic? Or were other forces at work, some mythic, some grounded in the pragmatism of the new world order? Certainly when some Serb friends found themselves stranded in the UK during the war and desperate to go home they were concerned, seeing the press reports, that people would find out that they were Serbs and seek to harm them. At least one contact in Belgrade has said to me since the end of the war how difficult it feels to be known in Europe as a Serb. How can it have come about that a decent person leading a professional life not so different to that led by a person of equivalent status in London, Washington, Paris or Berlin should have been made to think such a thing?

REPERCUSSIONS FOR MACEDONIA

Before suggesting some answers to this question there is an important digression to be followed, if only briefly, and that concerns the nature of Macedonia and the involvement of that country in the events that unfolded before and during the Kosovo conflict. An enduring sight on our television screens during the war was that of streams of refugees fleeing the conflict in Kosovo and attempting to enter Macedonia. Whether they were fleeing Nato bombing as Mr Milosevic claimed, Yugoslav atrocities as Nato claimed, or the KLA's tendency to do business by provoking attacks on villages after they had evacuated them and thus leaving the locals to the mercy of the Yugoslav military and paramilitaries (as notoriously seemed to have happened at Racak) is not relevant here. What is relevant is that they were refugees, mostly, if not all, Albanians, and they were trying to enter Macedonia. Now, until Mr Milosevic's decision to gain power by manipulating and creating ethnic tension in Yugoslavia, the area where such tension existed between Slav and Albanian populations was not only Kosovo but also Macedonia. So the Slavonic people of Macedonia, who already perceived themselves to have a chronic and difficult 'Albanian problem', were now in the odd position of having to show that they deserved recognition as a state of the new Europe by opening their doors to columns of the very people that many of them feared. In addition, Greece, a Nato country abominates the very idea of Macedonia (because of its own minority group of ethnic Macedonians). Greece with an Albanian minority which it views with some unease, had to watch while Macedonia strengthened its claims to Western aid and acquired significant military strength as it hosted the Nato army which was to form the core of the KFOR occupation force.[15] As a Nato member Greece did not, however, use its position to stop the war in spite of the pro-Serb rhetoric of its leaders.

These events will have stirred up not only the ongoing antagonism between Greece and Macedonia but also revived old fears of the project to create a Greater Albania by bringing together Albania, Kosovo and the Albanian-dominated regions of Macedonia and even Greece. In joining the Kosovo insurgency on the KLA side – that is what both the KLA and the Yugoslav government plainly believe happened – Nato was running the risk of dividing itself and of laying the foundations for much worse conflicts in the future. Both of these risks may yet become horrible realities. In fact, it is my understanding that, apart from in the minds of KLA ideologues like Jakup Krasniqi, the idea of Greater Albania is not one that has had much currency. Kosovo Albanians relish the prosperity that comes from being part of Yugoslavia – and this could still be enjoyed even if they had a measure of autonomy – while they look with some dismay at the poverty and, to their eyes, primitive conditions that obtain in Albania proper. In my experience, Albanians take a realistic view too. They realize that the history which led to their ethnic group being scattered across borders cannot easily be reversed, if at all, and look solely to ensure that the prejudice and persecution, which obtains in all states – including Italy – where Albanians constitute a minority, should cease. That is a perfectly reasonable requirement and one that Nato should seek to support even if this means reprimanding its own members or potential members.

> 66 Kosovo Albanians relish the prosperity that comes from being part of Yugoslavia while they look with some dismay at the poverty and primitive conditions that obtain in Albanian proper 99

Another facet of the involvement of Macedonia in the conflict and particularly the representation of Macedonia in the context of the refugee crisis during the war, is the position of Bulgaria, a suitor for membership of the EU.[16] The relationship between Bulgaria and Macedonia is complex and interesting. Many Bulgarians seem to look on Macedonia as the lost province of a Greater Bulgaria. Unfortunately, many Macedonians seem to look on Bulgaria as the lost province of a Greater Macedonia. As far as I can tell, they are both correct: it depends where you stop reading the history. These mutually opposed perceptions do not appear, however, to resolve themselves in a friendly recognition of a shared past and a happy cooperation. Instead, they have become the occasion of great hostility and distrust. An example of this may be found in the fact that Bulgarian and Macedonian are very similar languages. It might be said that they are dialects of the same language and even this might overstate the differences. They are mutually intelligible yet, at a conference in Macedonia, I once witnessed a Bulgarian and a Macedonian speaking to each other by using a multilingual Albanian (who plainly found the idea hugely amusing) as an interpreter. This tells us a great deal about tensions in the region that remain largely invisible to the West and yet create a real threat of the widened conflict any local war is likely to spark off.

NATO: THE WRONG STRATEGY?

What this sad history has to do with Kosovo is that by engaging in a war to protect Albanians and, possibly, to enable the creation of an autonomous Kosovo, Nato was recklessly ignoring these collateral problems. In addition, the wrong sort of heart was almost certainly being given to persecuted Albanian minorities elsewhere. Not only this: the KLA and their potential imitators were taught that terrorism would be rewarded if only the West could be manipulated in the correct manner. Can we look to the formation of similar organizations in Greece and the FYROM? Just before this chapter was written I saw a report of a KLA operation in Serbia (i.e. outside of the borders of Kosovo).[17] It is often forgotten that the Albanian community in Serbia is not just confined to a concentrated group in Kosovo. Is the time coming when KFOR will be forced to carry out joint counter-insurgency operations with the Yugoslav army? Neither Nato nor the UN would ever have sought to create a position where the occupation of Kosovo resulted in the *de facto* creation of a safe haven for terrorists raiding into Serbia and, possibly, Macedonia. Yet that is precisely the predicament in which KFOR now finds itself.

Until the war in Kosovo the biggest verifiable refugee problem in Europe was probably that of the some 170,000 Krajina Serbs who, in 1995, had been driven out of what became Croatia by a Western-armed Croatian army.[18] The silence of the Western media on the plight of these people, who were not recent immigrants but had occupied this region since the sixteenth century, is another of the puzzles of Yugoslavia. The silence of the media, which had plenty to say during the Kosovo war itself, about events that are currently unfolding in the region, will be the focus of the next part of this chapter. The discussion of various aspects of Yugoslav, Balkan region, and Western attitudes conducted above forms a framework within which the difficulties of the Western media in reporting on Kosovo since the withdrawal of Yugoslav forces and the arrival of KFOR may be understood. The complexities of the situation and the many competing myths which I have tried to tease out above are not conducive to suppression by a narrative which shows a good, liberal, democratic Nato engaged in a humanitarian campaign to help an oppressed people against a bad, authoritarian, undemocratic dictator.

This narrative could be sustained during the war and, indeed, there is no doubt that the Kosovo Albanians were the victims of oppression and atrocity although the extent of this atrocity has yet to be measured, as has the role of the KLA in deliberately provoking it. At the same time Western leaders were guilt-ridden by their failure to act in Bosnia (and Croatia?). However, what they forgot is that not acting in Bosnia also meant that they did not have to hold together whatever state emerged in the wake of military intervention. Indeed, they seem to have forgotten that this was largely the reason they did not intervene in the first place. In Kosovo things would be different: they would not only act to end the oppression, they would also continue the intervention after the last bomb had fallen. It is this position that does not allow an easy co-option into a moral narrative and that is why the press is silent. It was easy to bomb the Yugoslav army out of Kosovo by attacking civilian sites in Serbia. At least it was after Russian diplomatic intervention meant that Slobodan Milosevic realized that the game was up. But the complexities of history and culture that created the

❝ It was easy to bomb the Yugoslav army out of Kosovo by attacking civilian sites in Serbia ❞

Kosovo crisis in the first place now have to be managed and this is not proving so easy. The public opinion that could be marshalled to support a war in which no Nato soldier would die from enemy action, in which casualty figures among civilians could be tallied off against the greater good of preventing alleged massacres of Albanians, and where the retirement of the Yugoslav army in good order and with equipment and morale apparently intact could be ignored, cannot be so easily co-opted behind an expensive, dangerous and morally grey long-term occupation of a foreign country about which most people don't care.

MEDIA COVERAGE

So what has the British media said about events in Kosovo since the war? There have been newspaper reports of late concerning the stand-off in Mitrovica where a sizeable Serb population is separated from the neighbouring Albanian community by a bridge now defended by KFOR troops. There have been numerous minor reports of intimidation and murder. From Serbia itself there was some reporting of the murder of the notorious paramilitary leader known as Arkan and several politicians. What has not been reported in any detail is the effect on the Serb population of the new regime in Kosovo. It is likely that about 150,000 Serbs have fled into Serbia.[19] This represents about 75 per cent of the original Serb population and if one of the aims of the war was to enable the displaced Albanians to return to their homes what, if anything, will be done to help this community? Furthermore there has been a wholesale desecration of Orthodox churches and cemeteries. I will return to this subsequently but I have yet to discover any significant reporting of this attack on Serbian culture in the mainstream media.

There have been some television programmes. Not long after the war Michael Ignatieff was filmed glumly traipsing round the rubble in Belgrade and learning that the effects of bombing civilians are more traumatic when viewed up close than through the lens of a hawkish article in *Prospect*. There was an audit of the war that told us just how much it cost the Western tax payer to blow up, *inter alia*, the bridges across the Danube at Novi Sad. But even this did not tell the full story. It did not mention for example that those bridges were the site of a terrible atrocity during World War II when large numbers of Serbs and Jews were murdered by being pitched into the icy water.[20] Nor did it tell us of the collateral damage to the University of Novi Sad that was caused by the flying debris. We can pay to mend bridges (in fact, the Yugoslav government has already done so) but the cost in history levied by the assault on a place of great emotional significance and the future cost levied by the damage to a liberal institution is higher and, perhaps, beyond our reach. However, none of this has been reported, as far as I know. Nor am I aware that any accurate tally has yet been made of the civilian casualties of the bombing offensive. I have seen estimates that vary between 500 and 2000. I am inclined to think that the likely sum is somewhere around 1500.[21] This does not include, of course, any subsequent deaths caused by long-term damage from depleted uranium warheads, if these were used as has been alleged. Furthermore, we have yet to know just how many Albanians were murdered before and during the war. I have seen a figure of 2000, based on excavations carried out in the six months or so immediately following the war. If this is true then it is a disgrace to the Yugoslav government. It is also far lower than the figures suggested by Nato as it prepared for the campaign, but forensic investigations have yet to be completed so the figure may well rise and, unfortunately, probably will. If the figures on Serb civilian deaths are in the 1500 region then we may well wonder whether a war that may have simply matched one set of civilian deaths with another was quite as just as we were encouraged to think. In the long term we will also need to add on the civilians, maybe as many as 1400 to date (the figures vary from 500 upward), murdered or abducted by the KLA since the beginning of the KFOR occupation and also the Serbs who died in the KLA campaign that provoked the war. We can add in, for example, the six Serb teenagers who died in Pec when the Panda Bar was sprayed with gunfire by masked men who, presumably, came from the KLA. The grave of at least one of these boys has now been desecrated.[22]

> 66 We may well wonder whether a war that may have simply matched one set of civilian deaths with another was quite as just as we were encouraged to think 99

I want to concentrate on two programmes. The first is *A Kosovo Journey*, subtitled *A Personal Report by Jonathan Dimbleby* (ITV, 16 January 2000). The second is *Moral Combat*, subtitled *NATO at War* (BBC2, 12 March 2000). In the first of these programmes Mr Dimbleby travelled round Kosovo carrying out interviews and interspersing human interest stories with political comment and analysis. What was noteworthy about this programme was the effort made by the broadcaster to place a *cordon sanitaire* around the whole enterprise. There is the subtitle, which put the responsibility for the film squarely at Mr Dimbleby's door. In addition, the announcer told us before the titles rolled that 'This programme is his [i.e. Mr Dimbleby's] personal view.' Why was this effort made? After all Mr Dimbleby made no effort to hide the horror that had been visited on the Albanian population before and during the war. What he did do, however, was point to the political inconsistencies that would, had they been more carefully resolved, have made the war difficult to justify. He referred to KFOR as 'the military wing of a colonial governor' (i.e. the UN Security Council) and as 'a colonial dictatorship'. He reminded us that the Western media has 'averted its gaze' from 'the ethnic cleansing' of Serbs and Gypsies (who are forgotten victims of the conflict) that has gone on since the end of the bombing and that the resolution under which KFOR is mandated to keep the peace in Kosovo makes no reference to any future autonomy for the province.[23] He also pointed out just how vicious the KLA terrorist campaign of 1998 actually was.

All these things – except the view that the UN has colonized Kosovo – are incontrovertible facts so why did ITV feel the need to distance itself from them? It surely comes down to the question of narrative that was briefly discussed above. The fall-out of the war has not delivered the resolution of the morally polarized story that we should have expected. The Albanians are now behaving just as badly as the Serbs were supposed to have done. KFOR spends its time protecting not Albanians but Serbs, and though I have no doubt that the soldiers are carrying out this task with the greatest integrity and diligence, they have an impossible job. What we have in Mr Dimbleby's journey is a subversion of the entire reporting effort that went into the presentation of events just before and during the war. It is not the case that ITN was telling lies but it is surely at least credible to think that its journalists had become caught up in a piece of story-telling that reflected not the complexities of the situation but a simplified narrative that articulated the Nato position. If this is true, then Mr Dimbleby's report could justifiably be seen as compromising and fundamentally challenging to the claims for impartiality that must characterize the news media of any democracy. Perhaps this is why his programme was so hedged about by disclaimers.

> 66 Journalists had become caught up in a piece of story-telling that reflected a simplified narrative that articulated the Nato position 99

The second programme was an in-depth account of the events leading up to the war and of the way in which the war was conducted. All the major players (except Mr Clinton, Mr Milosevic and Dr Rugova) were interviewed and the effort was made to demonstrate the difficulties that all encountered in trying to square the situation as they wished to see it with the situation as they actually found it. There was analysis of the problems faced by military leaders in running a war while trying to meet the impossible demands of their political masters. We were reminded of the North Atlantic Council's identification of the KLA as 'the main initiator of the violence' and of Ambassador Walker's (the head of the KVM, the group that was sent into Kosovo to verify adherence to the cease-fire which was meant to avoid war) view that most violations were the result of KLA activity. All this served to support the examination of the proposition that it is possible to fight a moral war. What became clear was the way in which the state department sought to woo the KLA at Rambouillet and thus create the case to fight that was then accepted by the Western allies. As I said above, this was partly achieved by the marginalization of Dr Rugova and, in the programme itself, he was often seen sitting at the top table with the other Albanian delegates. Viewers may have wondered about the identity of this somewhat eccentric figure, with a silk scarf tightly knotted around his neck at all times. The report chose however not to interview him (to be fair he may have refused) and instead concentrated on the sharp-suited and photogenic Mr Thaci, the KLA leader who now unofficially runs Kosovo. Dr Rugova was never even mentioned and although it is true that his reputation seems to have waned as local Albanians looked to the KLA for protection – a word of sinister ambiguity – it is still the case that his policies may have represented a very different future for Kosovo.

In making *Moral Combat* the BBC mounted a challenging exploration of the many-levelled debates and decisions that prepared public opinion for war. However, the conclusions that the viewer may have drawn from this lengthy and painstaking account have to do more with a moral question than with what is now happening in Kosovo. Although the BBC journalists asked many difficult questions and exposed embarrassing inconsistencies in the political process that created the war, they were unable to open up a space in which the plight of Kosovo now could be represented. On the one hand, this is because the programme sought simply to analyze the events of the war and those immediately preceding it. On the other, the problem of narrative again raises its awkward head. The journalists who made *Moral Combat* were plainly capable of confronting the situation in which Kosovo now finds itself. However, their programme concentrated instead on the war. This enabled them to confront the narrative of the just war with a dispassionate analysis in which the protagonists (including a senior Yugoslav general) were permitted to

> 66 The programme failed to look beyond the just war to the unjust peace 99

speak for themselves. This strategy unsettled a pre-existing story, much as Jonathon Dimbleby's programme had done but it did little to present the alternative story that is now unfolding virtually unreported in Kosovo. In other words, the programme failed to look beyond the just war to the unjust peace. This peace does not allow easy incorporation into story nor into an ethical debate and appears to deflect articulation within the discourse of the Yugoslav conflict which both the Western media and the Western allies have now developed.

CONCLUSION

This chapter has been about silence and has, to some extent, attempted to replace that silence by engaging in a quasi-journalistic activity of its own. In conclusion I will consider some of the events that have gone unreported in the West to try not only further to illustrate how difficult it is to speak of Kosovo within traditional journalistic categories but also to draw attention to atrocities that are happening now without KFOR intervention. The Orthodox Church is, as I said above, a pole around which the very notion of Serbian identity circulates, and Kosovo is at its heart.

> ❝ The Orthodox Church is a pole around which the very notion of Serbian identity circulates, and Kosovo is at its heart ❞

While most Serbs are broadly secular in their outlook, many are nonetheless concerned to protect the Church and the culture for which it stands. Throughout the war the Church attempted to press for peace and called for a cessation to violence on all sides, Yugoslav army and paramilitaries, KLA and Nato. These pleas were ignored. Indeed, Bishop Artemije did attempt to join the delegates at Rambouillet but was refused admission to the conference. Since the end of the war the Church's reward for this principled stance has been the destruction or desecration of at least seventy churches in the diocese of Raska and Prizren.[24] Many of these, such as the frescoed church of the Presentation of the Virgin in Dolac or the church of St George at Rudnik, were major pieces of medieval art. More modern churches have also been destroyed, for example, the church of the Holy Trinity at Grmovo (newly built) and the Holy Trinity church at Petric (1992). Some churches, for example St Jeremias at Grebnik (1920), have been so completely demolished that it is no longer possible even to tell where they stood.

This assault on the monuments of medieval Serb culture and on the Orthodox Church is a direct attack on the very idea of Serbian-ness. What it tells us is a story of an ethnic cleansing that far exceeds anything previously seen in the province and which has a religious character that was not, as far as I know, present in the Yugoslav government's offensive into Kosovo in late 1998 and early 1999. In addition, cemeteries are being destroyed and graves desecrated. To an Orthodox population this is a particularly painful matter as the resting places and bodies of loved ones are much cared for in Orthodox culture. One prayer that was used by the Serbian Patriarchate during the war specifically petitioned God to spare cemeteries from the Nato bombing.[25] Yet now cemeteries are being destroyed and worse, and KFOR seems unable to act. This is going largely unreported. I suspect that the reason for this silence is partly to do with the problem which Western media seem to have had with the articulation of an Orthodox viewpoint throughout the Yugoslav conflicts. It is noteworthy, for example, that while the most recent large-scale bombing of Iraq was held off so as not to offend Islamic sensibilities by waging war during Ramadan no such sensitivity was shown during the Kosovo campaign. The bombing was shamefully continued throughout Holy Pascha, the most important religious feast in the Orthodox calendar.

In September 1999 Bishop Artemije of Raska and Prizren said:

If Serbia continues with the democratic process, by the removal of president Milosevic, who is responsible for everything that has happened in the last ten years to the Serbian people, then Kosovo would be a part of those changes ... If by some chance, God forbid, this regime continues with its 'loser governing' of Serbia, then Kosovo would move towards Europe through Tirana, and it would be lost forever for the Serbian people.[26]

These words and the Bishop's proposal for a provisional 'cantonization' of Kosovo do not fit well with the views we have been taught to hold about Serbs and Serbia. But until a different set of reporting strategies emerge and the Western myth of Serbia is abandoned such a speech and the destruction that surrounds it will not be reported. I hope that such a strategy will emerge so that both Serbs and Albanians will be able to reclaim their homes in Kosovo and that the climate that makes my friend in Belgrade feel ashamed to be a Serb will dispel. To return to the medieval songs of Kosovo:

Go home now to your whitewashed house
with an unbloody hem, unbloody sleeve.[27]

We should hope that all the populations of Kosovo will shortly be able to do this and that this return will be openly and fairly represented in the West.

NOTES

WEBSITES

The following websites, all of which are referred to in short form (e.g. WEB 1) in the notes overleaf, contain much valuable recent information as well as extensive links to other Kosovo-related sites.

WEB 1. http://www.incommunion.org/NATO.htm

WEB 2. http://kosovo.com

WEB 3. http://www.spc.org.yu

WEB 4. http://www.decani.yunet.com

WEB 5. http://stratfor.com/company/index.asp

WEB 6. http://www.Serbian-Church.net/News/archiva.html

WEB 7. http://www.Serbian-Church.net/Genocid/indexe.html

WEB 8. http://www.ecclesia.gr/News/Kosovo/SerbPetitions.html

1   Pennington and Levi 1984: 18.

2   *Ibid*. p. 24.

3   This painting is reproduced as plate 16 in Judah.

4   See Pennington and Levi (1984), pp. xv-xvii. The ethnic balance in Kosovo has actually fluctuated dramatically over the years and although Serb and Albanian historians tell very different stories, it would appear that Kosovo was originally (i.e. in the Middle Ages) largely Serb. The Albanian population grew during the Ottoman period and during the wars of liberation from the Ottoman Empire. Although the Serbian population increased after 1912, it became proportionally less as the twentieth century wore on (at least partly due to higher birth rates in the Albanian community). By the 1980s Serbs were leaving Kosovo which, by that time, had a high degree of autonomy within the Yugoslav Federation and was overwhelmingly Albanian. How the tensions of that period would have worked themselves out cannot be known as Mr Milosevic chose instead to exploit them for his own purposes.

5   See WEB 1, the site of the Orthodox Peace Fellowship for some texts that illustrate Serbian opposition to the war and the Milosevic regime.

6   The classic account of this has become Glenny 1992. See also Glenny 1999: 634–62. Since this article was written, Tim Judah's book, *Kosovo, War and Revenge* (New Haven: Yale University Press, 2000) has appeared.

7   See Tanner 1997: 272–4.

8   See Judah 1997: 151–2; Malcolm 1994: 192; Tanner 1997: 151–2.

9   See Malcolm 1998:12–14.

10 Although it is generally thought that all Albanians are Islamic, this is not the case. There are Orthodox Albanians in the south and Roman Catholic Albanians (who have played an important role in the history of Kosovo) in the north.

11 See Judah 1997: 30–1; Glenny 1999:11; Goodwin 1999: 12; and Malcolm 1998: 58–60. Serb friends have often observed with some sadness that it is a strange thing to be part of a culture that sees defeat as its most glorious moment.

12 For a well-illustrated introduction to this topic see Peic 1994.

13 See Judah 1997: 1–2. The planning is reproduced as Plate 1.

14   See Judah 1997: 133–4.

15   See Gounaris *et al*. 1994; Zahariadas 1996.

16   It should be mentioned that various atrocities committed during the Second Balkan War and World War I put Bulgaria fairly high in the demonology of Serbian history.

17   *New York Times*, 6: 2000 and WEB 3.

18   See Judah 1997: 2; Tanner 1997: April 296–8.

19   See WEB 3 and WEB 4.

20   Having lived for a brief period just beside this stretch of the Danube I can testify to the gloomy atmosphere that still pervades the spot.

21   See WEB 5.

22   See WEB 6 where a daily updated register of such events, and worse, is maintained. One of the difficulties in dealing with recent events in Yugoslavia is ease with which one can write about deaths and displacements measured by the thousand. To mention these six boys might help to keep perspective on the enormity of even one death in such circumstances.

23   The best recent account of the Gypsies of this region is to be found in Fonseca (1995).

24   See Outlook 1999: 14–15; WEB 3; and Mileusnic 1997. The book is available in its entirety via WEB 7. In it the deliberate destruction of Orthodox sites in Bosnia-Herzegovina, Croatia and Slovenia is chronicled. Since this article was written, a section of the BBC's *Correspondent Europe* (broadcast 12 May 2000) dealt briefly with the destruction of Kosovo churches and monasteries. This programme also illustrated the difficulties Western commentators have had in understanding the Orthodox perspective. The reporter, Dennis Murray, was appalled when a priest showed a grieving woman a photograph of her dismembered son who had been killed, allegedly by Albanians, since the end of hostilities. Although this plainly broke her heart, anyone familiar with Orthodox funeral rituals and beliefs about mourning would have seen this apparently insensitive act as a gesture of great compassion.

25   See WEB 8.

26   *Outlook 1999*: 6.

27   Pennington and Levi 1984: 24.

13

THE UN: SQUARING THE CIRCLE

DAVID TRAVERS

THE KOSOVO CRISIS PRODUCED SEARCHING QUESTIONS for the UN both in its political as well as its operational activities, which this chapter attempts to explore. These questions are:

- Why did the Security Council fail to use preventive diplomacy to defuse the crisis?

- Has the primacy of the Security Council in maintaining international peace and security been undermined by unauthorized Nato threats to use force against the Federal Republic of Yugoslavia in order to prevent violations of Council mandatory resolutions, and by the Nato bombing campaign to avert a humanitarian disaster?

- Is there an emerging internationally accepted concept of humanitarian intervention in which support for individual human rights overrides the rights of states?

- Did the UN High Commissioner for Refugees maintain international refugee law in a highly charged political atmosphere?

- Has the organization a sustained interest in bringing to trial indicted war criminals?

- Will the compilation of human rights violations lay the groundwork for preventing abuses occurring in the future?

- Can regional organizations co-operate with the UN in maintaining both international and internal peace and governing part of the territory of a sovereign state?

The crisis also demonstrated the extent to which the UN is dependent upon the political, financial and human support of member states, the length to which members are prepared to go in order to make an agency a scapegoat to cover their own failings and, finally, the way in which the various components of the UN organization adjusted to changing conditions and created new precedents for possible future use.

THE ROLE OF THE SECURITY COUNCIL

First a few preliminary remarks on the role, make-up and operational framework of the Security Council. The Security Council has primary responsibility for maintaining international peace and security. It acts on behalf of the whole international community. States and regional organizations are not allowed to threaten or use force in their international relations except in collective or self-defence against an armed attack. Any other use of force has to be approved by the Security Council. Thus a regional institution (such as Nato) cannot take enforcement action without the authority of the Security Council.

The Council is composed of 15 members: five are permanent – China, France, the Russian Federation, the UK and the US – and ten are non-permanent. The non-permanent members are elected by the General Assembly for two years on a staggered basis, five retiring and being replaced each year. Thus the composition of the Council changes each year. The Council takes substantive decisions by nine votes out of 15, including the affirmative votes of the five permanent members. In practice, affirmative includes absence, not participating in the vote and abstention, but a non-affirmative vote – the veto – prevents the Council from acting. The Council possesses both peaceful settlement and enforcement powers. In the former it has powers of recommendation only; but in the latter it may take decisions that are binding upon member states. If the Council, using Article 39 of Chapter 7 of the Charter, states that there is a threat to the peace, or that a breach of the peace or aggression have occurred, it can order a range of activity including ceasefires, arms embargos, economic sanctions and authorize the use of force. But it can only request, not demand that states, coalitions of states and regional institutions provide armed forces for enforcement.

The Council had passed only one resolution on Kosovo before March 1998. In August 1993 it had requested vainly that Yugoslavia allow the continuation of the CSCE Mission of Long Duration in Kosovo, Sandjak and Vojvodina that had been operating since September 1992. Although the crisis had been long anticipated the Council had been unable to prevent or defuse it. First the problem was complex: it involved the quality of government, the systematic violation of the civil, political and human rights of the Kosovo Albanians and the total rejection of their peaceful pursuit of self-determination by Yugoslavia because of the emotional, religious, historical, strategic and political importance of Kosovo to Serbs and Serbia. But, in addition to these issues, and because of long standing fundamental international principles, i.e. sovereignty, territorial integrity and non-intervention in internal affairs, the Security Council could intervene only if invited by Belgrade, or if it decided that there was a threat to the peace. Such a finding would override any claim to domestic jurisdiction. However, President Milosevic did not want international help, a position Russia, as the Great Power in the Balkans, was likely to support; and other members of the Council were then wary of regarding such unsatisfied demands for self-determination in Kosovo as human rights violations, and police action to curb demonstrations as threats to the peace.

66 **Kosovo did not have a high priority on the international agenda** 99

Moreover, Kosovo did not have a high priority on the international agenda because time and resources were being devoted to securing and maintaining peace in Bosnia for which, at the time, the cooperation and support of President Milosevic was regarded as indispensable. Thus any attempt at preventive diplomacy, for which members of the Council would receive scant reward even if successful, was likely to be thwarted.[1]

When the Security Council did become involved in March 1998, the problem had increased in difficulty. The emergence of the Kosovo Liberation Army had radicalized Kosovo Albanian politics. It demanded independence and was willing to use force, particularly against Serbian and Federal security forces, to achieve this, unlike some of the politicians, such as Ibrahim Rugova, who still desired independence but were willing to accept some form of self-government as an interim measure achieved by peaceful means. Because of this split among the Kosovo Albanians the issue of who should represent them became a major problem in any negotiations called for by the Security Council.

While the international community accepted that a government could use force against terrorists to maintain public order and security, the Yugoslav response had been excessive, resulting firstly in egregious humanitarian abuses particularly in areas where the KLA was active, and yet further displacement of the Kosovo Albanian population and destruction of property. Subsequently the Secretary-General reported to the Security Council concerns that the disproportionate use of force and actions of the security forces were designed to terrorize and subjugate the population as a collective punishment to teach them that the price of supporting the Kosovo Albanian paramilitary units was too high.[2]

The Council, however, faced formidable difficulties in attempting to manage this crisis. The members, particularly the permanent ones, found it difficult to reach a common analysis of, and possible solution to, the dispute. Russia and China strongly endorsed Yugoslavia's view that Kosovo was an internal problem, but Russia, and to a lesser extent China, gradually accepted a role for the Security Council provided that it did not create a precedent for international intervention in a sovereign state. Indeed, neither state, apart from a reluctantly agreed arms embargo, which in practice froze the armaments advantage of Yugoslavia, would allow the Security Council to take any coercive measures within Chapter 7 of the Charter against Belgrade. Thus these measures, that might have been used to persuade Belgrade and to a lesser extent the KLA to comply with Security Council resolutions, and in particular to negotiate the future political status of Kosovo, were denied to the Council. The international community was not prepared to see the human and political rights of the Kosovo Albanian population repressed, nor was it prepared to support separation and independence. Partly as a consequence, the management of the crisis was shared, sometimes competitively, certainly often without coordination, between different institutions and states.[3]

> 66 The international community was not prepared to see the human and political rights of the Kosovo Albanian population repressed, nor was it prepared to support separation and independence 99

The Contact Group comprising France, Germany, Italy, Russia, the UK and the USA, and its delegated envoys, had been meeting since September 1997. There was a general fear that violence in Kosovo had the potential to spread throughout the Balkans and in particular could undermine the Dayton Agreement. The Group became the primary body that undertook diplomatic initiatives. Many of these were endorsed by the Council and some, particularly the Rambouillet and Kleber negotiations, were welcomed and supported by the Council. The Contact Group had been allowed to take the lead by the non-permanent members of the

Council because it was thought that Russia would have influence in Belgrade. However, the EU, the OSCE, Nato, the Group of 7 industrialized states and Russia, and individual states including Russia and the USA also took diplomatic initiatives.

The EU, the Contact Group – apart from Russia – and individual states including EU associates, the USA, Canada and Japan undertook a range of economic sanctions.[4] The OSCE, absorbing the Kosovo Diplomatic Observer Mission, monitored the cease-fire, and Nato undertook contingency planning for air and ground action including operations to enforce a cease-fire agreement or peace settlement in Kosovo. Its activities were varied. It conducted air exercises over Albania and Macedonia, states adjacent to Yugoslavia, to demonstrate its military capabilities. It threatened to use force against Yugoslavia to secure agreements with President Milosevic. It operated air surveillance over Yugoslavia to verify that all parties had ceased hostilities and were maintaining a cease-fire as demanded by Security Council resolution 1199 (1998) and the terms of resolution 1203 (1998). It deployed troops to Macedonia to extract the KVM should that be necessary, and also to Albania. Finally, it threatened and then used force against military targets in Yugoslavia without the permission or approval of the Security Council in order to avert a humanitarian catastrophe.

Yet this is not to suggest that the Security Council did not play important roles before, during and after the bombing campaign. It approved three resolutions before the bombing campaign started (1160 (1998) 31 March 1998, 1199 (1998) of 23 September 1998 and 1203 (1998) of 24 October 1998) which clearly set out the demands that the international community had made to the parties in the dispute. There were a number of important features about these resolutions. First there were major debates on the first and third resolution, which was relatively unusual in a Council that had become increasingly cohesive since 1987. Normally private consultations about a draft resolution initially take place between the permanent, and then all, the members of the Council. The agreed draft is then formally approved in a public meeting of the Security Council that lasts for a few minutes. Whereas there is no public record of the diplomatic negotiations that led to the drafting of a resolution, in a public debate positions are revealed and political compromises exposed. This was the case with these three resolutions. Indeed, even though the public debate focused on the first and third, the second also received public scrutiny: Russia and China spoke before the vote, and the UK and the US spoke after it. China abstained on all three resolutions while Russia abstained on the third. Other institutions and states justified and legitimized their actions against Yugoslavia by claiming they were supporting the precise and clear demands expressed in the Security Council's mandatory resolutions.[5] There were common themes in all the resolutions.

THE CONTENT OF THE COUNCIL'S RESOLUTIONS

The Council stated in all three resolutions that it was acting under Chapter 7 of the Charter. In the first resolution it did not cite any reason for this judgement, but presumably it was implying that this was a situation where the violation of human rights was so serious that it threatened international peace and security, and therefore came under the jurisdiction of the Council. Had this been stated explicitly it would have invited a Russian or Chinese veto. But in the second resolution it affirmed that the deterioration of the situation in Kosovo constituted a threat to peace and security, and in the third that the unresolved situation in Kosovo constituted a continuing threat to peace and security. The Council was even-handed towards the parties. It condemned the excessive use of force by the Serbian police and the Yugoslav armed forces, as well as terrorist acts by the KLA and all external support for such activity in Kosovo, including finance, arms and training. The Kosovo Albanian leadership was required to condemn all terrorist action and all elements in the Kosovo Albanian community were to pursue their goals by peaceful means only. It called upon the authorities in Belgrade and the leadership of the Kosovo Albanian community urgently – without preconditions, with international involvement, and to a clear timetable – to enter into a meaningful dialogue with the aims of agreeing confidence building measures to encourage the return of the displaced and refugees, and to solve the political problems of Kosovo. The Council also stated that the principles for a solution of the Kosovo problem should be based upon the territorial integrity of Yugoslavia and should be in accordance with OSCE standards and that such a solution must also take account of the rights of the Kosovo Albanians and all who lived in Kosovo. It expressed its support for an enhanced status for Kosovo which would include a substantially greater degree of autonomy and meaningful self-administration. It also

> 66 The Council condemned the excessive use of force by the Serbian police and the Yugoslav armed forces, as well as terrorist acts by the KLA and all external support for such activity in Kosovo 99

called upon the parties to cooperate fully with the Prosecutor of the ICTY in the investigation of possible violations within the jurisdiction of the Tribunal.

Another important feature of the Council's demands was for a progressively deeper international involvement in Kosovo and a greater degree of accountability for Belgrade. In the first resolution, in an attempt to reduce the spread of violence, which had the potential to destabilize the whole Balkan region, the Council imposed an arms embargo on Yugoslavia including Kosovo. The Council's conditions for terminating this embargo included:

- a substantial dialogue between the parties seeking settlement, with international participation
- the withdrawal of police units and the cessation of action against the civilian population by the security forces
- access to Kosovo by humanitarian organizations and representatives of the Contact group and other embassies
- the acceptance of a mission by the OSCE and the return of the OSCE long-term mission
- the facilitating of a mission to Kosovo by the UN High Commissioner for Human Rights (UNHCHR).[6]

In the second resolution the Council demanded that all parties, groups and individuals immediately cease hostilities and maintain a cease-fire in Kosovo. An earlier call in a presidential statement of 24 August had been ignored.[7] The Council demanded further that the Serbian and the Kosovo Albanian leadership take immediate steps to improve the humanitarian situation – it was estimated by the UNHCR that over 230,000 people had been displaced, including up to 50,000 that were without shelter and other basic necessities – in order to avert the impending humanitarian catastrophe. The Council also endorsed steps taken to establish effective and continuous international monitoring of the situation in Kosovo, and the establishment of the Kosovo Diplomatic Observer Mission was welcomed.[8] Yugoslavia was required to issue expeditiously appropriate travel documents to, and provide access and complete freedom of movement for, the monitors. It also had to facilitate, in agreement with the UNHCR and the International Committee of the Red Cross, the safe return of refugees and displaced people to their homes and allow free and unimpeded access for humanitarian organizations and supplies to Kosovo.

> 66 Over 230,000 people had been displaced, including up to 50,000 without shelter and other basic necessities 99

In the third resolution the Council endorsed and supported the agreements reached between Yugoslavia and the OSCE, and Yugoslavia and Nato. These agreements had been concluded after Nato had threatened to use force against Yugoslavia because Belgrade was not complying with the demands of the previous resolutions. The OSCE was to provide a 2000-strong mission that initially had verification, reporting, force monitoring and refugee assistance roles. Once a political settlement had been reached by a defined date the mission would also assume electoral supervision, institution-building and police-development tasks. The Nato agreement provided for unarmed air surveillance flights over Kosovo during which the Yugoslav armed forces were not permitted to use the relevant radar systems. The flights would supplement the reporting of the verification mission and assess the extent to which Belgrade was reducing its security forces to the level agreed with Nato. The Council, by demanding in a mandatory resolution that Yugoslavia cooperate fully with the OSCE and Nato agreements, had ensured that the terms of those agreements had now become legal obligations to the Council itself.[9] Moreover, President Milosevic had moved from a position where Kosovo was an internal problem to one where he had to accept, at least publicly, that the international community would play a significant role in resolving its problems. But despite these important achievements, any attempt by the Council to authorize the threat or use of force to ensure that the agreements would be kept had been removed to avoid a Chinese veto. Furthermore, Nato's threat to use force without consulting and receiving the approval of the Security Council was criticized by two permanent and two non-permanent members, perhaps the sharpest criticism coming not from Russia and China but from Brazil and Costa Rica. Their questioning of the legality of the threat of force and the relationship between Nato and the UN was a foretaste of the emergency debate that would be held in March 1999 in the Security Council.

> 66 Nato's threat to use force without consulting the Security Council was criticized, the sharpest criticism coming from Brazil and Costa Rica 99

Finally the Council asked the Secretary-General to report regularly on the implementation of the resolutions. This posed a problem because the UN had no direct political presence on the ground in Kosovo. He therefore relied on information provided by the offices of the UNHCR and the UNHCHR, and the OSCE, the EU, Nato and latterly the Kosovo Diplomatic Observer Mission and the KVM. Once the latter became fully operational Mr Annan restricted his reporting to the arms embargo and humanitarian affairs but the other institutions continued to report to the Council through him.[10]

In addition to the three resolutions, the Security Council expressed further views on Kosovo in two presidential statements of 19 and 29 January 1999. In these the Council strongly condemned the massacre of Kosovo Albanians in Racak and deplored the decision by Belgrade to declare the head of the KVM *persona non grata* and sought his reinstatement. It also condemned the decision by Yugoslavia to refuse access to the Prosecutor of the ICTY and condemned the shooting of KVM personnel. On 29 January the Council expressed its deep concern at the escalating violence in Kosovo and welcomed the summoning by the Contact Group of the Yugoslavia and Kosovo Albanian leaders to talks at Rambouillet in France to negotiate a political settlement.[11]

THE BOMBING CAMPAIGN

During the bombing campaign the Council met to discuss the Nato bombing, the attack on the Chinese Embassy in Belgrade and the humanitarian situation. The first debate provided an opportunity for both Russia and China to mount a legal and practical attack against Nato and to express their displeasure, but it also offered Nato members of the Council an opportunity to explain and defend their doctrine of humanitarian intervention and allowed both sides to assess their degree of support from other Council members. On the issue of the Embassy bombing, China used the Council meetings as a safety valve to vent its anger and secure an international apology. On the humanitarian situation, the debate demonstrated the capacity of a range of states, principally Muslim, to persuade the Council to build unity and to express itself on the humanitarian situation in Kosovo and other parts of Yugoslavia.[12]

On 24 March at the request of Russia the Council met urgently

to consider an extremely dangerous situation caused by the unilateral military action of Nato members against the Federal Republic of Yugoslavia.

Two broad views were expressed in the Council. The first by Russia and China made seven principal points:

1 The bombing was a blatant violation of the UN Charter.

2 Members of Nato were obligated to be guided by the Charter, including Article 103 which emphasized that Charter obligations took precedence over all others.

3 The Council alone could decide what measures should be taken regarding maintaining or restoring international security.

4 Attempts to justify the air strikes as preventing humanitarian catastrophe were not recognized by international law.

5 The use of unilateral force would lead to a situation with devastating humanitarian consequences.

6 A dangerous precedent had been set in the alliance's attempt to enter the twenty-first century in the uniform of an international gendarme.

7 No considerations of any kind could serve to justify aggression: the virus of a unilateral approach could spread and those who embarked on the military venture bore complete responsibilities for the consequences.

The other view, argued by the USA, the UK and France and their Nato allies on the Council, contained the following counter-points.

1 President Milosevic had rejected the Security Council demands that Belgrade end actions against its civilians.

2 He had refused to withdraw security forces responsible for repression.

3 He had refused to cooperate with organizations engaged in humanitarian relief.

4 Belgrade had refused to fulfil its agreements with the OSCE and Nato.

5 He had failed to pursue a negotiated agreement with the Kosovo Albanians, providing a substantial degree of self-government while respecting the territorial integrity of Yugoslavia.

6 Military action had been taken with great regret in order to save lives.

7 The action being taken was legal and justified in international law as an exceptional measure to prevent an overwhelming humanitarian catastrophe.

8 Appropriate force would be directed only towards disrupting the violent attacks being committed by the Serb security forces and weakening their ability to create a humanitarian catastrophe.

On 26 March in the Security Council a draft resolution tabled by Russia, Belarus and India demanding an immediate end to Nato bombing against Yugoslavia was decisively defeated by 12 votes to 3 (Russia, China and Namibia). But the legality of the Nato action was neither condemned nor endorsed by the Security Council. It remained in a legal vacuum. Nato claimed, however, that the vote, given the political and geographical spread of the Council membership, was evidence of broad international support for the military action that it had to take. Others contended that the Security Council had no choice other than to defer to the Nato action. Lawyers still differ on whether the Nato action was another strand in an evolving standard of humanitarian intervention in a developing area of international law. In so far as it was developing, it seemed to suggest that force could be used against a state to protect the lives of its citizens in exceptional circumstances *without the approval of the Security Council* after all other means had failed. If established by the Kosovo precedent, humanitarian intervention would join collective- and self-defence against armed attack as exceptions to the general prohibition on the use of force by states and international institutions against other sovereign states.[13]

THE BOMBING OF THE CHINESE EMBASSY IN BELGRADE

The Security Council met at 3.42 a.m. on 8 May at the request of China, having already held consultations about a presidential press statement on the bombing. The Chinese government stated that at midnight on 7 May 1999 Nato, led by the United States, flagrantly attacked the Embassy of China in Belgrade. It also noted angrily that two people had died, two were missing and many were injured. For China this was a clear violation of its sovereignty and of the basic norms of international relations. It reminded members that even in times of war it was recognized that diplomatic institutes should not be violated and the protection of diplomats should be guaranteed. China demanded that Nato investigate and account for this incident and stop the air strikes immediately. Nato members on the Council, led by the USA, stated that the facts had not yet been confirmed but informed the Council that Nato was investigating the incident. It was asserted that Nato did not target civilians or Embassies, and that if Nato was responsible for a bombing error, it was deeply sorry. Even so, the UK representative could not restrain himself from adding that despite more than one million people being beaten out of their homes, and several thousands having been killed, resulting from President Milosevic's decisions, no midnight Council meetings had taken place about this.

The Council, on 14 May 1999, in a presidential statement that had been carefully negotiated, expressed profound regrets over the bombing and deep sorrow for the loss of lives, injuries and property damage caused by the bombing. It also noted that regrets and apologies were expressed for this tragedy by members of Nato. The Council, bearing in mind the Charter of the UN, reaffirmed that the principle of the inviolability of diplomatic personnel and premises must be respected in all cases in accordance with internationally accepted norms. The Council stressed the need for a complete and thorough investigation of the bombing by Nato. It took note that an investigation had been initiated by Nato and awaited the results. The US government subsequently issued a formal explanation for the bombing mistake. Nato and various organs of the US government formally apologized and accepted full responsibility for the incident. In addition the US government separately apologized and agreed to pay US$28 million in compensation to the Chinese government and US$4.5 million to the families of those killed and injured.[14]

THE HUMANITARIAN SITUATION IN YUGOSLAVIA

The Security Council passed a resolution 1239 (1999) on the 14 May by 13 votes to zero with Russia and China abstaining.[15] The sponsors of the resolution were concerned that the Security Council had not pronounced on the humanitarian tragedy that was unfolding in Kosovo. They wanted the Council to build unity, to regain its primacy, by inviting the UNHCR and other international humanitarian relief organizations to extend relief to all who had been affected by the ongoing crisis and for access to be granted to their personnel. They also emphasized that the humanitarian situation would continue to deteriorate unless there was a political solution based on the principles adopted by the Group of 7 industrialized states and Russia on 6 May 1999. They urged all concerned to work towards this aim.[16]

THE CIVIL AND SECURITY PRESENCE IN KOSOVO

On 10 June 1999 the Security Council, acting under Chapter 7 of the Charter, adopted resolution 1244(1999) by 14 votes with one abstention – China – which established an international civil and security presence in Kosovo under UN auspices. This resolution had evolved through a number of sequential steps. On 6 May the Group of 7 industrialized states and the Russian Federation, drawing upon an earlier proposal of the Secretary-General, agreed the principles for a political solution of the crisis. These principles were then incorporated into a paper presented to, and accepted by, President Milosevic on 3 June by the President of Finland, Mr Ahtisaari, representing the EU, and the Special Representative of the President of the Russian Federation, Mr Chernomyrdin. In Cologne on 7 and 8 June, the foreign ministers of the Group of 7 and Russia then agreed to the terms of a draft Security Council resolution which contained the 3 June agreement. Finally, Nato and the Federal Republic on 9 June signed a military technical agreement which required Yugoslavia to withdraw its military and police forces from Kosovo within 11 days. The start of the withdrawal of the Serbian and Yugoslavia forces on 10 June was followed immediately by the order of the Nato Secretary-General, to suspend all bombing. Russia and China had refused to meet formally to approve the resolution until the bombing had been halted. The Yugoslavia and Serbian force withdrawal was completed on time by 20 June and Mr Solana formally terminated the air campaign.

> 66 The international military presence, which was to be led by Nato, had a wide-ranging mandate 99

The international military presence, which was to be led by Nato, had a wide-ranging mandate:

1   to deter renewed hostilities and to demilitarize the KLA.

2   to establish a secure environment for the safe return of the refugees and the displaced, and the operation of the civil presence

3   to ensure public safety until the civil presence could become responsible for this (including the removal of landmines)

4   to support and coordinate closely with the international civil presence

5   to conduct border duties and to ensure its own protection and freedom of movement and that of the international civil presence and other international organizations.

The civil presence, called the UN Interim Mission in Kosovo (UNMIK), was to be established by the Secretary-General who was requested to appoint a special representative to lead it. It too had a wide-ranging mandate designed to promote substantial autonomy and self-government in Kosovo. Within this overall framework its objectives were as follows:

1   to perform the basic interim administration of the province and to facilitate a political process to determine its future status

2   to support the reconstruction of key infrastructure

3   to provide humanitarian and disaster relief

4   to maintain civil law and order, promote human rights and assure the safe and unimpeded return of all refugees and displaced persons to their homes in Kosovo.

Both the military and civil presence was established for an initial period of 12 months and would continue unless the Security Council decided otherwise.[17]

There are a number of interesting points about this resolution of 10 June. It would have been expected, for example, that the major role in Kosovo would have been played by the OSCE as indicated in the agreement endorsed by the Security Council in resolution 1203(1998) of 24 October, and in Rambouillet. Significantly, however, the UN was chosen for this task instead of the OSCE. Russia and China had insisted on this change despite the resolution clearly establishing a precedent for international intervention inside a state (with the temporary transfer of sovereignty over Kosovo from Yugoslavia to the UN). In addition, Belgrade wanted a UN role to justify ending the war. Nato viewed such a modification as beneficial to its own position: it wanted to return to legality as quickly as possible having become very sensitive to criticism that its bombing campaign lacked Security Council approval.[18]

The civil and military presences were separately led and were directed by different institutions. There was no single person in charge of the whole operation. The UN would not be responsible for paying for the military presence because, although it was Security Council approved, it was not run by the secretariat. On the civil side the UN was conducting a unique experiment. Under the overall authority of the Special Representative, who was to be the civil administrator, the UN was cooperating simultaneously with several international agencies. It was working with the EU in reconstruction and rehabilitation, with the OSCE in institutional building, and with the UNHCR in the return of the refugees and the displaced. Such cooperation on the civil side, however complicated and difficult, still presented fewer problems than the political objectives targeted by the Security Council. These political objectives were going to be more difficult to achieve. The Special Representative had to act on the basis, which the Security Council had constantly affirmed and reaffirmed, that Kosovo remained part of Yugoslavia. However, such affirmations ran counter to those of the Kosovo Albanians who, after being radicalized by the KLA and their recent experiences at the hands of the Serbs, were demanding independence.[19]

Finally, the operation was of indefinite duration.

THE ROLE OF THE SECRETARY-GENERAL

Although it is difficult to assess the full role of the Secretary-General in the Kosovo crisis, because of the volume of confidential diplomacy he engages in, it is nevertheless clear that he played adroitly the role of an international civil servant, protector of the principles of the organization, conscience of the world and stimulator of action by the Security Council. When the Security Council imposed a mandatory arms embargo on Yugoslavia, the Secretary-General was asked, in consultation with appropriate regional organizations, to recommend a comprehensive regime to monitor the implementation of the resolution. The UN, for budgetary reasons, was unable to establish and administer the regime and the Secretary-General therefore turned to the OSCE, Nato, the EU, the Western European Union (WEU) and the Danube Commission. These all had experience in providing unprecedented monitoring assistance to the neighbours of Yugoslavia when UN comprehensive sanctions were imposed against it during the violent collapse of the former Yugoslavia. All were willing to help but none wished to be the leading coordinator. In consequence, the Secretary-General had to recommend that periodic meetings be held between the participating institutions, the UN peace-keeping force in Macedonia and the secretariat in order to exchange information and discuss practical problems arising from the monitoring of violations. Such procedures raise the question of whether the embargo was meant to be symbolic: a warning to Belgrade that this was the beginning of international intervention, if it did not comply with resolution 1160. It also raises the further question of whether these institutions were not willing to apply an embargo which, in reality, would only affect the Kosovo Albanians. This is because the Serbs had been rearmed by Russia and were probably self-sufficient in the type of weapons being used in Kosovo.

Mr Annan was also requested to report on the evolving situation in Kosovo and the extent to which Belgrade was complying with the terms of the resolutions. But as has already been noted, the UN had no political presence in Kosovo to provide the Secretary-General with first-hand information. Therefore Mr Annan was unable to provide an independent assessment. He relied, instead, on information and assessments provided by other sources. But, in October 1998, the Security Council had asked how the secretariat might acquire a first-hand capability to help him to fulfil these functions. In order to answer this question, Mr Annan sent a mission to Yugoslavia, including Kosovo, and on receiving its report he pointed out to the Council that it had now endorsed the establishment of the KVM by the OSCE. The latter already had the responsibility of reporting to the Council, which would now subsume his responsibilities for political reporting and assessments. Thus, there was no need for a separate political presence on the part of the secretariat. Information coming from one source, the KVM, would prevent parallel reporting channels which otherwise might lead to confusion as well as unnecessary expense. Mr Annan continued to report on humanitarian and human rights issues.[20]

At the outset of the bombing campaign Mr Annan made a very balanced statement which appeared to recognize Nato's dilemma and yet upheld the principles of the Charter. He deeply regretted that in spite of all the efforts made by the international community, the Yugoslav authorities had persisted in their rejections of a political settlement, which would have halted the bloodshed in Kosovo and secured an equitable peace for the population there. It was indeed tragic that diplomacy had failed but there were times when the use of force might be legitimate in the pursuit of peace. In helping to maintain international peace and security, Chapter 8 of the United Nations Charter assigned an important role to regional organizations. But as the Secretary-General had pointed out many times, (and not just in relation to Kosovo), under the Charter, the Security Council had primary responsibility for maintaining international peace and security, a fact that was explicitly acknowledged in the North Atlantic Treaty. It followed, therefore, that the Council should be involved in any decision to resort to the use of force.[21]

> 66 It was indeed tragic that diplomacy had failed but there were times when the use of force might be legitimate in the pursuit of peace 99

Mr Annan worked on humanitarian problems while seeking a political solution that would require legitimization by the Security Council and provide an important role for the UN. He expressed his profound outrage at reports of a vicious and systematic campaign of ethnic cleansing by Serbian military and paramilitary forces in Kosovo. He called on the international community to give immediate financial, material and logistical support to the authorities in countries where the refugees were arriving. He appealed to the president of Macedonia to keep the borders of his country open to the refugees. He reviewed the UN humanitarian response and sought ways of improving it, including the appointment of a regional coordinator for UN assistance in the Balkans. He went to Albania and Macedonia to gain a personal sense of the plight of the refugees and the burden on the two asylum countries. He obtained the permission of Yugoslavia to send a humanitarian mission to Kosovo and other parts of Yugoslavia in order to provide an initial assessment of the emergency needs of civilian populations and of the medium-term rehabilitation requirements in the state in light of the approaching winter. He informed Nato but did not seek a bombing pause. Also, with the Under-Secretary-General for Humanitarian Affairs, he briefed the Security Council on the humanitarian problems, in particular, on the findings and recommendations of the assessment team.[22]

In his diplomatic search for a political solution the Secretary-General consulted widely including in New York, Geneva, Moscow and Bonn. On 9 April he called urgently on Belgrade to undertake five commitments and urged Nato to suspend air operations on the acceptance of these conditions. These commitments were echoed by the Nato foreign ministers meeting on 12 April and the Nato Washington Summit of 23–25 April. They were also absorbed into 6 May statement of the Group of 7 and Russia. Mr Annan established a secretariat task force in April that produced a blueprint for the administration and reconstruction of Kosovo that foreshadowed the one adopted by the Security Council in resolution 1244. He appointed two special envoys to the Balkans: former Swedish prime minister Carl Bildt and Foreign Minister Eduard Kukan of Slovakia. They assisted the Secretary-General in his peace quest and prepared for the implementation any proposed agreement. They consulted with senior UN political, peace-keeping and humanitarian officials as well as with representatives of Nato, the EU and the OSCE. Finally, they briefed the Security Council on the status of UN contingency plans for the operation in Kosovo, an operation they described as the most challenging and complex peace implementation operation undertaken in modern times.

THE ROLE OF THE OFFICE OF THE UNHCR

The UNHCR had been working in Kosovo since 1992, assisting refugees who had fled from the violent dismantling of the former Yugoslavia. When the fighting started in March 1998, the office appealed for funds to expand its operations to look after those who had sought refuge in

Montenegro and Macedonia, and to help find, feed, shelter and protect the internally displaced, particularly those living in the open. When security conditions improved, the UNHCR helped those who wished to return and, where necessary, helped to repair their homes. The High Commissioner also visited Kosovo and Belgrade twice in the second part of 1998 and told President Milosevic that no lasting solution would be possible without a fundamental change in the Yugoslavia's attitude to the Kosovo Albanians.[23]

On 23 March 1999, a day before the bombing began, the office had to withdraw its staff from Kosovo where it had provided assistance to 400,000 people displaced or affected by the fighting in the province. Mrs Ogata, the High Commissioner, said that the decision had been a tormenting one. The office could no longer be with the people it worked for at a time of their greatest need. Like almost every government the agency did not forecast, nor have contingency plans for, the calculated deportation of Kovoso Albanians that resulted in one of the largest and most rapid flow of refugees Europe had seen in the twentieth century. The field staff were overwhelmed. In the ensuing crisis, the UNHCR faced fundamental challenges to its role of protecting refugees and acting as lead humanitarian agency. Macedonia was concerned that a large influx of Kosovo Albanian refugees, by altering the ethnic balance, would strain the unity of the multi-ethnic government and cause political destabilization. Moreover, it felt that if it did accept the refugees, there was no guarantee it would obtain the political, economic and financial support of the international community. It therefore decided not to grant unconditional asylum but to use the refugees as bargaining counters, often closing the border, separating families and forcing some refugees back into Kosovo. The government insisted that it would provide temporary protection for only 20,000 refugees and that any more would only be allowed entry on the condition that they would be evacuated to other states.

> 66 The calculated deportation of Kosovo Albanians resulted in one of the largest and most rapid flow of refugees Europe had seen in the twentieth century 99

The UNHCR, however, sought to maintain its universal standards. It argued that Macedonia should uphold the 1951 United Nations Refugee Convention to which it became a party in 1994. It believed that all those fleeing Kosovo had a valid fear of persecution as defined in the 1951 Convention and should be considered as *bona fide* refugees, and that Macedonia must permit unconditional first asylum and not turn refugees back to life-threatening situations. Furthermore, it also insisted that access to asylum should not be dependent on burden-sharing arrangements first being in place.

The US and the UK, however, placed greater emphasis on the political damage inflicted by images of refugees stranded in dreadful conditions, in the open, on the border between Kosovo and Macedonia, the destabilization of Macedonia, and the need for continuing access for Nato troops, which Macedonia threatened to withdraw, than on the maintenance of universal standards of refugee law that the High Commissioner was seeking to maintain. The US therefore, relentlessly encouraged the office to develop an innovation: the Humanitarian Evacuation Programme. Refugees on a voluntary basis were flown from Macedonia to third states that had offered them a temporary home. Almost 92,000 refugees were flown to 29 other states. Critics of the programme were concerned about how much information was made available to the refugees, particularly on the degree of protection they would receive, which varied considerably among the participating countries and because the UNHCR had been unable to maintain its preferred approach of keeping refugees in the region.

Another strategy used by UNHCR, again at the behest of the US, to relieve refugee pressure on Macedonia was to encourage, with the assistance of the two governments, the voluntary transfer of some refugees from Macedonia to Albania. While this move to relieve the pressure was undoubtedly effective, some critics questioned the degree to which some of the transfers were voluntary. A further problem emerged when Nato offered assistance to the UNHCR on 2 April 1999. This posed an acute dilemma. The agency wanted to save lives but, at the time, lacked the means to do so. Nato was available with the necessary resources. Nato members were among the leading donors to the agency. The problem was that the agency was non-political and had responsibilities in other parts of Yugoslavia. Assistance from such a prominent actor in the crisis clearly risked compromising UNHCR's status. Moreover, Nato did not have explicit Security Council approval for its bombing campaign. Despite these obstacles, Mrs Ogata decided to accept the offer, on certain conditions:

- that the protection and assistance to refugees had to remain civilian and strictly humanitarian in character
- that she defined the precise logistical areas in which she sought assistance
- that the miliary involvement in humanitarian activities would continue only as long as extraordinary circumstances prevailed.[24]

In addition to these complexities, a third problem emerged. The UNHCR was prevented from co-ordinating the humanitarian response, which was its mandated responsibility, by its own internal weaknesses, and by important donor governments and refugee host states acting bilaterally. They believed that refugees were too important politically to be left to the Refugee Agency. Yet despite these problems and further difficulties with registration of the refugees and maintaining the civilian character and the security of the refugee camps, the UNHCR did contribute to meeting

the immediate life sustaining needs, with minimal avoidable deaths among many hundreds of thousands of refugees. This surely is the ultimate measure of any such operation.25

THE INTERNATIONAL CRIMINAL TRIBUNAL FOR THE FORMER YUGOSLAVIA

The ICTY was established by Security Council resolution 827 on 25 May 1993. It is located in The Hague in the Netherlands. It is mandated to prosecute persons responsible for serious violations of international humanitarian law committed on the territory of the former Yugoslavia since 1991. Its prosecuting authority covers grave breaches of the 1949 Geneva Conventions; violations of the laws or customs of war; genocide and crimes against humanity. The work of the ICTY generally has been constrained for several reasons. States do not always honour their international obligations imposed upon them by Chapter 7 of the Charter, to cooperate with all aspects of the work of the ICTY, including providing information, assisting with investigations and executing arrest warrants. The Tribunal, lacking enforcement powers is dependent upon the Security Council taking action against errant states. In this respect, the Council did not respond effectively when the President of the ICTY twice cited Yugoslavia for non-compliance concerning the Prosecutor's investigations into possible violations of humanitarian law in Kosovo. In addition, the budget is seldom sufficient and although the General Assembly made special provision for the initial investigations in Kosovo, this had to be supplemented by voluntary contributions from interested states. Finally, for major investigations the Prosecutor is dependent on states providing intelligence information and specialist seconded staff – especially forensic pathology and crime scene teams whose continuing availability is partly dependent upon international interest being sustained.[26]

The Prosecutor, Louise Arbour, creating a precedent by commenting on current investigations, first announced the Tribunal's interest in Kosovo on 10 March 1998. She had received information about Yugoslavia's military campaign in areas where the KLA was active, which had involved the shelling of towns and villages, loss of lives on both sides, widespread destruction of property and expulsions of the civilian population. She stated that the territorial and temporal jurisdiction of the Tribunal covered any serious violations of international humanitarian law taking place in Kosovo and that she was empowered to investigate such crimes.[27] This was presumably an attempt to deter further violence and to counter claims by some states that the temporal jurisdiction had ended with the signing of the Dayton Accord, which brought peace to Bosnia-Herzegovina.

Arbour believed that the nature and the scale of the fighting indicated that an 'armed conflict' within the meaning of international law existed and that the Tribunal's jurisdiction included crimes committed by persons on both sides of the conflict. She reaffirmed that combatants involved in armed conflict were obligated to observe the laws of war and that any violations of such laws could be punished. She also made clear that those in superior responsibility could be held criminally liable for the atrocities committed by their subordinates.[28] The importance of this statement was the implication that the KLA was now recognized as an organized armed movement controlling a significant part of the territory of Kosovo and that its members were subject to the laws of war. If they committed atrocities, it was emphasized that they would be liable to prosecution. Equally, for the opposing side, it meant that Yugoslavia could no longer sustain its claim that it was engaging in an internal police action to combat terrorism. The Security Council repeatedly reaffirmed the Prosecutor's jurisdiction over Kosovo in three resolutions: 1160 of 31 March 1998; 1199 of 23 September 1998 and 1203 of 24 October 1998.[29]

> 66 The KLA was now recognized as an organized armed movement and its members were subject to the laws of war 99

Until October 1998, the Prosecutor was able to investigate and gather evidence in Kosovo without any obstruction from Yugoslav officials. Then Belgrade refused to grant any further visas, most notably refusing entry to the Prosecutor in January 1999 as she sought to enter Kosovo from Macedonia to investigate the Racak massacre, claiming that the ICTY had no jurisdiction to conduct investigations in Kosovo and would not be allowed to do so. Indeed investigations were regarded as a violation of Yugoslavia's sovereignty. But this meant Yugoslavia was disregarding Security Council resolution 1207 of 17 November 1999, which demanded that it facilitate access for the Tribunal. Belgrade also ignored a presidential statement in January 1999, following the Racak massacre, calling for its full cooperation with the Tribunal in carrying out an investigation in Kosovo.

Despite the lack of access, the Prosecutor established an investigation team dedicated to Kosovo and, after the bombing commenced, she moved a large number of investigators into the region. They sought the assistance of various government and non-government organizations to distribute a brief questionnaire to those fleeing Kosovo. The aim was to identify key witnesses who would be interviewed by the investigators about crimes falling within the competence of the ICTY. Governments responded to the Prosecutor's request for intelligence information. Britain, for example, appointed an officer in the foreign office to liaise with the Prosecutor and to ensure that all British intelligence on possible crimes was collated and shared with the Tribunal. The USA, Germany, France and Holland also attempted to provide information as quickly as it became available.[30]

On 27 May, the ICTY announced the indictment of President Milosevic and four senior Yugoslavian officials for crimes against humanity – including, specifically, murder, deportation and persecutions – and for violations of the laws and customs of war committed since the beginning of 1999 in Kosovo.[31] Arrest warrants were issued against all five accused and for the first time the Tribunal requested that all states search for and freeze assets of the accused under their jurisdiction. Such measures were intended to deny the use of the assets for the evasion of justice, and enable them to be used for restitution if the accused were convicted.[32] This was the first time that a Head of State had been indicted during an existing military campaign and was deemed by at least one Western government, Britain, to have important consequences, one of which would be that it added to the psychological pressure upon President Milosevic to seek a diplomatic solution.[33]

> 66 On 27 May, the ICTY announced the indictment of President Milosevic and four senior Yugoslavian officials for crimes against humanity 99

Once the international security presence had been established in Kosovo, the Prosecutor's office, with the assistance of forensic pathology and crime scene teams from 14 states, acted quickly before evidence was lost. Initially, the work concentrated on the seven villages and sites listed in the indictment against President Milosevic and the other leaders. Subsequently, this was expanded to include the KLA crimes committed against Serbian civilians in 1998 and 1999. The Prosecutor reported in November 1999 that she had received reports of 529 grave-sites; approximately one-third of those had been examined and work had been completed at 195 sites. Reportedly, 4,266 bodies had been buried in those sites and 2,108 bodies had been exhumed. She believed that the final exact figure would never be known because of the steps taken to conceal the crimes.[34] In 2000 the Tribunal is seeking to complete exhumation at 300 separate sites of reported graves in Kosovo. Although in the aftermath of the war it would be more difficult to maintain international interest and forensic support for the Tribunal's work in Kosovo, there were two factors that contributed to ensuring the continuing activity into 2000. First, a morgue built and equipped to European standards had been established that could accommodate bodies from four different sites simultaneously thus allowing them to be cleared more quickly. Secondly, compared with 1999 when the Tribunal worked from July to October, the 2000 season would be much longer.[35]

NATO AND WAR CRIMES IN YUGOSLAVIA

On 14 May 1999 the then Prosecutor established a committee of legal and military experts to examine allegations received by the Prosecutor that senior political and military figures from Nato countries had committed serious violations of international humanitarian law during the bombing campaign, and that she prepare indictments pursuant to Articles 18(1) and (4) of the Tribunal Statute. The Prosecutor – now Carla Del Ponte – addressing the Security Council on 2 June 2000 stated that, after examining all the available evidence, she had found no basis for opening an investigation into any of the allegations that Nato personnel and leaders may have committed war crimes during the bombing campaign. She stated that, while Nato had made some mistakes, she was satisfied that there was no deliberate targeting of civilians or unlawful military targets by Nato during the campaign. Then, in an unprecedented move, designed to refute the allegation that the ICTY was an instrument of Nato, the Prosecutor decided to make public the committee's report that she had drawn on to reach her decision.[36]

HUMAN RIGHTS AND THE ROLE OF THE UNHCHR

A clear pattern of serious and systematic violations of the human rights of Kovoso Albanians has been documented by the special rapporteurs of the Human Rights Commission, by the office of the High Commissioner, and by the treaty-based bodies since 1993. The Human Rights Commission, the third committee and the plenary session of the General Assembly have discussed the rapporteurs' reports and specific resolutions about Kosovo and these have been addressed to Belgrade. Repeated requests from the General Assembly for an adequate monitoring mission in Kosovo were partially met in 1996, when Yugoslavia consented to the opening of a UNHCHR office in Belgrade which also covered Kosovo, and fully in 1998 when a sub-office opened in Pristina. The activities of the office can be summarized as follows:

- The office received reports of arbitrary arrest by the police and abductions by armed Kosovo Albanians (believed to be KLA members), and categorized the occupations of people being arbitrarily arrested and illegally detained.

- It reported on the difficulties lawyers and families had in seeing and speaking to the detainees, many of whom were later transferred to prisons in Serbia.

- The office made contact with the Serbian Ministry of the Interior inquiring about cases brought to its attention, and monitored trials of persons charged with crimes against the state, including terrorism.

The Commission on Human Rights at its 1999 session first debated the situation in Kosovo and then requested the High Commissioner to report on conditions and events there, and on the actions she had taken to assist the international community's efforts to deal with the massive outflow of refugees. During the session the High Commissioner provided four weekly briefings; submitted a report on 31 May and a consolidated report on 27 September. After the session ended she visited the area on two occasions. In March 1999 the High Commissioner sent a personal envoy to the area along with the special rapporteur. She also established the Kosovo Emergency Operation, the purposes of which were to:

- establish a human rights presence as close as possible to actual developments in Kosovo and to interview refugees and seek impartial verification of alleged violations of human rights

- seek to identify patterns and trends in human rights violations

- consult and help coordinate among international partners the assembling and analysis of information relating to human rights violations in Kosovo

- assemble information in reports to the High Commissioner, the special rapporteur and other UN human rights mechanisms, including the ICTY

- explore opportunities for technical reconstruction and security of the region.

The staff of the emergency operation, supplemented by human rights monitors provided by the governments of Switzerland and Norway, conducted in-depth interviews in Albania, Macedonia and Montenegro with carefully selected refugees drawn from all the geographic areas of Kosovo. These interviews provided information, recorded in the consolidated report, on the displacement and deportation of ethnic Albanians from Kosovo, killings and executions, violence against women and children, arbitrary arrest and detention, torture and mistreatment, and destruction and confiscation of property. The High Commissioner stated that the report again confirmed that the Serb forces committed shocking crimes during the Nato air campaign and that it was essential that those responsible for such criminal violations be brought to justice.

66 The office of the High Commissioner stated that it had been unable to gather reliable and impartial information on the role played by the KLA 99

The office of the High Commissioner stated that it had been unable to gather reliable and impartial information on the role played by the KLA during the 11-week Nato campaign. However, it was able to report on the impact of the armed conflict particularly Nato bombing on civilians in Serbia and Montenegro.

Once the Security Council had established the security and civilian presence in Kosovo by resolution 1244 (1999) the Kosovo Emergency Operation was terminated, and UNHCR staff stationed in Yugoslavia returned to Kosovo with the advance team of UNMIK.[37]

THE ADMINISTRATION OF KOSOVO: CURRENT EVALUATION

The UN with the assistance of KFOR, has been administering Kosovo for a year in pursuit of stability, peace, democracy and prosperity in the shattered province.

UNMIK has, however, faced considerable difficulties. On initial deployment there was no functioning government – no civil service, no police, no armed forces, no border guards and controls – although members of the KLA and other armed groups were seeking to fill the administrative and security vacuum. Indeed, there was the danger of internecine conflict among the Kosovo Albanians themselves. There was no functioning economy and the housing stock and infrastructure were severely damaged. Moreover, the international community has failed to provide sufficient finance, administrative staff and international police to allow the mission to function fully. Nor have relations with the Kosovo Albanians and minority groups, who all have their own internal differences, been easy. Predictably, perhaps too, cooperation from Belgrade has been partial and Russia and China, not unexpectedly, have been critical of the operation. The mission has never had the full support of all the permanent members, let alone the Security Council as a whole.

Despite the flawed nature of support, the mission has had some important successes. UNMIK and KFOR have been very well coordinated. The UNHCR and its working partners have been so successful in meeting the emergency needs of the returning displaced and refugees that the humanitarian pillar, as a formal component of the UNMIK structure, was dismantled on 30 June 2000. The KLA was disarmed and demilitarized by KFOR and some of its former members either joined the Kosovo Protection Corps, which is intended to provide emergency response and reconstruction services, or entered police training programmes. The Joint Interim Administrative Structure has been established in which Kosovo citizens, including the minorities, share with UNMIK the administration of Kosovo at both the central and local levels. Preparations are under way for the registering of electors for the municipal elections later in 2000 although the Serbs and other minorities are currently boycotting this, and Belgrade refuses to help in the registering of Serbs who have fled Kosovo. These elections will be the first step towards self-government. The economy in Kosovo is slowly improving although unemployment remains at a very high level. However very serious problems remain. The first is that KFOR and the UNMIK police have been unable to provide a secure environment for the minorities within Kosovo. They are still subject to harassment, violence, intimidation and arson. Their freedom of movement and their ability to gain access to social and public services is restricted and there are doubts as to whether the mission can promote reconciliation between the communities. The UNMIK police force has never reached its authorized figure and, indeed, some of the personnel have been of such poor quality and lacking in basic skills (such as driving and use of firearms), that they have had to be returned home. Organized crime flourishes, allegedly with former members of the KLA participating. In addition, the judicial system is only functioning intermittently and a climate of impunity has emerged. Witnesses are unwilling to testify because of threats of intimidation or death, and judges are intimidated or appear to show signs of ethnic bias in their conduct. In an attempt to develop public confidence in the judicial system UNMIK intends to appoint international judges and prosecutors throughout Kosovo and to establish a Kosovo war and ethnic crimes court. It is claimed that the creation of such a court will be a factor in the re-establishment of the rule of law, in consolidating peace through justice and in paving the way to justice.[38]

CONCLUSION

From this analysis of the activities of the UN in the Kosovo crisis we can draw certain conclusions. First, it might seem at first sight that the Security Council, despite its responsibilities to maintain international peace and security, played only a marginal role compared to other international actors. It was unable to defuse the crisis. It was unable to establish a political presence in Kosovo. It was unable to secure the consistent co-operation of the parties. It did not oversee the ceasefire. It did not use economic sanctions. And it did not authorize either the threat or the use of force by Nato.

Yet, if such a view was accepted it would ignore the range of roles played by the Council some of which cannot be undertaken by other institutions. The Council passed three binding resolutions, despite the differences between the permanent members, that had an important influence on the management of the dispute by the international community. First, the Council established that the international community had a legal and legitimate interest in Kosovo and in how the dispute was to be resolved. Second, it upheld the principle that violence should not be used to settle political disputes and that there were legal limits to the amount of force that governments could use to maintain security and internal law and order. It attempted to reduce the means of violence available to the disputants by imposing an arms embargo. It stated the method, and the legal and political principles for peacefully settling the dispute. It welcomed, endorsed and legitimized the agreements reached between states, regional organizations and Yugoslavia which sought to achieve Security Council objectives. It upheld the principle that the disputants had to permit humanitarian access to the victims of the violence. The Council supported the position of the Prosecutor that the ICTY had jurisdiction in Kosovo. Finally, the reports it requested from the Secretary-General provided the information to judge the extent to which the parties were complying with Security Council resolutions.

The second role played by the Council was to provide a forum in which the members debated whether or not Nato's use of force in attempting to prevent massive violations of humanitarian law by Yugoslavia against its Kosovo Albanian citizens was legally justified. One of the legacies of Kosovo is that the members of the Council are exploring how the Council might prevent future humanitarian crimes while respecting state sovereignty and international law and how it might establish criteria to help it decide when the threat or use of force for humanitarian purposes is necessary and justified. And the UK, to stimulate this debate, has submitted to Kofi Annan a framework of six principles to guide international intervention.[39]

The Council played a third role when it encouraged the Secretary-General to consult and present principles for a possible settlement between Nato and Yugoslavia and to appoint envoys including one with experience of administering a Balkan peace settlement.

The Council also played a fourth role when both Nato and Yugoslavia sought its imprimatur for agreements that would end the hostilities. This demonstrated the importance that states attach to the legal authority and the political importance of the legitimizing role of an organ which acts on behalf of the whole international community. No other institution has similar powers and mandate.

The Kosovo crisis also provided opportunities for the Secretary-General and the international secretariat to play important roles. The secretariat was initially reluctant to be drawn into the political aspects of the crisis. Kofi Annan adroitly sidestepped any responsibility for deciding whether Yugoslavia was complying with the Security Council resolutions. This helped to maintain his independence of action. Yet both privately and publicly he protested at the use of force and urged the parties to negotiate and avoid further bloodshed. When Nato resorted to force he made a careful, principled stand acting as guardian of the Charter and conscience of the world. He urged the members of the Council to restore their unity and sought support for his humanitarian and political activities. He ordered the secretariat to prepare contingency plans for the UN to administer Kosovo. And he presented a set of principles for the settlement of the dispute that all parties could use without any loss of face because they originated from an international civil servant.

The Secretariat also played significant roles in the UN operational activities. The UNHCR maintained international refugee law in very difficult circumstances, established principles for accepting assistance from Nato, worked with the USA and refugee host states in establishing new precedents, and, in the light of criticism of her office's performance in coping with the speed and the size of the refugee flow, ordered an independent review. The UNHCR organized an emergency field operation to collect information on human rights abuses. And the Prosecutor of the ICTY created a number of precedents in responding to the crisis including the indictment of a head of state, but she has not been able to secure the indispensable cooperation of Yugoslavia. Without this there is little chance of bringing the indicted to trial. But overall, possibly aside from the office of the High Commissioner for Refugees, the secretariat has been strengthened by their activities. This is important because they represent an international interest in what can be a world of selfish ethnic and national interests.

> 66 In administering Kosovo the UN and its partner organizations have rediscovered that states will provide resources more easily for waging violence than for building the peace 99

And finally, the crisis showed that states could use the Security Council for a variety of cooperative and divisive purposes. It also provided evidence that some states will support or castigate and push aside secretariat-run operations whenever it suits their national interests. Finally, in administering Kosovo the UN and its partner organizations have rediscovered that states will provide resources more easily for waging violence than for building the peace.

NOTES

1   Meckel 2000: paras 4 to 45.

2   United Nations S/1998/912 para 7.

3   FCO Memorandum 1999 Kosovo: History of the Crisis para 17.

4   These included the refusal to supply equipment which could be used for internal repression or terrorism, the denial of visas to officials responsible for the repression, and a freeze on funds held abroad by the regime and a moratorium on government financed export credits.

5   Weller 1999: 187.

6   The committee appointed by the Security Council to monitor the arms embargo reported on 3 March 1999 that it had received 53 replies containing a brief statement that the state concerned had adopted all necessary measures to comply with the embargo. Of the states bordering Yugoslavia, only Croatia had submitted in December 1998 an interim report on an incident that occurred on its territory in contravention of the embargo. All reports and all press reports with one exception that reported on one possible violation by Yugoslavia dealt with the flow of arms and funds to Kosovo Albanians. This was perhaps not surprising because Russia had provided arms to Yugoslavia and perhaps more importantly Belgrade was probably self-sufficient in the range of arms used in Kosovo and thus there was little need to breach the embargo.

7   This is a consensus text read out by the Council President at a formal meeting. It is an expression of the Council's views on an issue of substance but is non-binding on member states. It is an official Council document.

8   President Milosevic had refused to allow the European Monitoring to be enlarged but conceded the establishment of the Diplomatic Mission composed of staff from states having embassies in Belgrade presumably to avoid a Security Council prescribed mission or an OSCE presence, which he had been refusing until Yugoslavia had been allowed to rejoin the organization.

9   Weller: 187.

10   UN Press Releases SC/6496, SC/6577 and SC/ 6588; and UN reports by the Secretary-General:S/1998/361; S/1998/470; S/1998/608; S/1998/712; S/1998/834; S/1998/912; S/1998/1068; S/1998/1147; S/1998/1221; S/1999/99; S/1999/292.

11   UN Press Releases: SC/6628 and SC/6637.

12   The Council also received briefings from the Secretary-General and the secretariat on diplomatic and humanitarian developments and from Mrs Ogata, the United Nations High Commissioner for Refugees, on the plight of the refugees.

13   UN Press Release SC/6657, SC/6659; NATO: Kosovo: one year on; Weller 1999.

14   It was later revealed that three people died in the bombing. (UN Press Release SC/6674/Rev 1, SC6675, Final Report to Prosecutor 2000 paras 81 and 84.)

15   This resolution had been drafted by a range of states principally Muslim.

16   UN Press Release SC/6677.

17   UN Press Release SC/6686.

18   Devenport (1999).

19   It is conceivable that the Kosovo Albanians might argue that the resolution refers back to the Rambouillet Accords, which stated that the Kosovo Albanians would be consulted about the status of the province after three years.

20   S/1998/1068.

21   SG/SM6938.

22   Briefing to the Security Council 2 June 1999.

23   UNHCR is a General Assembly established agency whose mandate is regularly renewed. It has an administrative budget but for each of its field operations helping refugees or the internally displaced it has to appeal for funds. Donors therefore have an important influence on the role of the office and the programmes that can be sustained.

24   Ogata: Security Council briefing 5 May 1999.

25   Response to the Select Committee on International Development Third Report from the United Nations High Commissioner for Refugees para 25. Morris 1999; Ogata, Geneva 6 April, 1999; Talk Back: Special Issue; 'The Kosovo refugee crisis: an independent evaluation of UNHCR's emergency preparedness and response.' And comments by UNHCR.

26   Since its inception the tribunal has indicted publicly 91 accused; six have died and charges were dropped against 18 others; one has been tried and sentenced; 34 are currently in proceedings before the tribunal and 35 remain at large mainly in Yugoslavia, the Serb Republic and Croatia. There are also an undisclosed number of sealed indictments that have been confirmed by Judges of the Tribunal. (International Criminal Tribunal for the Former Yugoslavia; Fact Sheet 27 October, 1999: PIS/FS-54 page 1).

27   Office of the Prosecutor CC/PIO/302-E, The Hague, 10 March 1998.

28   CC/PIU/329-E, The Hague, 7 July 1998.

29   Boelaeert-Suominen 2000; Weller 1999: 239–40.

30   Annual Reports of the International Tribunal for the Former Yugoslavia: A/53/219; 1999 A/54/187.

31   Earlier on 26 March the Prosecutor had addressed a letter to the President and 12 other top Yugoslavian officials warning them of their responsibility to prevent their subordinates committing war crimes and to punish those who did. The Yugoslav Embassy in The Hague, however, refused to accept the letter which was made public two days later.

32   JL/PIU/403-E and JL/PIU/404E: The Hague, 27 May 1999. One of the consequences of these indictments had been to end all cooperation between the ICTY and Yugoslavia. The Prosecutor believed that allegations that the ICTY was biased against the Serbs were hollow when the Office of the Prosecutor was denied access to the evidence and the victims, which would enable the ICTY to bring indictments where the Serbs were the victims. The Office was making extraordinary efforts to try to identify and locate witnesses from Yugoslavia through non-official channels and to encourage those people to leave Yugoslavia to enable interviews to be conducted in neighbouring countries where it would be safe for them to do so (ICTY Weekly Press Conference 7 June 2000).

33   FCO Memorandum: Kosovo: History of the Crisis 1999 para 85.

34   Press Briefing, New York, 10 November 1999.

35   ICTY Weekly Press Conference 10 May 2000.

36   Committee Report on Nato Bombing 2000; ICTY Weekly Press Conference 7 June 2000.

37   E/CN.4/2000/10 27 September, 1999; Report of the United Nations High Commissioner for Human Rights 1999 A/54/36.

38   Report of the Secretary-General: S/2000/538; 6 June 2000; UN Press Release SC/6856 and SC/6873; Pardew 11 April 2000.

39   See the speech by the Foreign Secretary Robin Cook to the American Bar Association on 19 July 2000.

14

CONCLUSION: RETROSPECT AND PROSPECT

STANLEY HENIG

A STARTING POINT FOR REASSESSING the war in Kosovo in the light of the various perspectives offered in this book may be to freeze it as a moment in time. The Western world went to war in the Balkans; it has been victorious; it has suffered no casualties; it may be the last armed conflict in Europe in which the USA is a participant. In the Balkans one nationality gains ground (in a very literal sense) and another loses. There the war is entering its eighth century with the widespread perception that nothing has been (finally) resolved. The West has now committed forces to monitor an arrangement on the ground that is neither signed nor accepted by the two ethnic groups involved. Two concepts of international law vie for our attention – one based on traditional sovereignty of independent states and the doctrine of non-interference; the other based on fundamental human rights. Back on the ground there remains a suspicion that the old rules apply – to the victor the spoils!

It is conceivable that the above offers the basis for at least a semantic consensus between those who have contributed towards this book, but it scarcely conceals the conflicts that occasioned the Kosovo crisis and which remain largely unresolved.

Over the last decade, the international community has sought, with great difficulty, to come to terms with fundamental change occasioned by the ending of the bipolar system. At one level the collapse of Soviet-style communism has left the West as undisputed victor, waving the twin flags of liberal democracy and market capitalism. At another level it has landed the apparent victors with an almost terrifying responsibility for resolving world problems, and it (the West) is proceeding quite literally 'by the seat of its pants'. After a successful war to drive Iraqi forces out of Kuwait, the West backed off from enforcing or even enabling a change of regime in Baghdad. It watched as the internal opposition was crushed, but it has retained a costly military capacity in the Gulf

> 66 Over the last decade, the international community has sought, with great difficulty, to come to terms with fundamental change occasioned by the ending of the bipolar system 99

to avert any further threats to regional peace. The USA intervened to try to end the chaos caused by the civil war in Somalia. The 'bloody nose' it then received may have contributed to the Western decision to do nothing in the face of genocide in Rwanda. The international community – UN, Nato and the EU – 'huffed and puffed' during the early stages of the implosion in Yugoslavia. It seemed that no amount of tough talking could avert a growing pattern of inhumanity – burnt villages, massacres, murders, rape, ethnic cleansing – with the reaction that 'we must not let it happen again'.

The very phrase 'the West' suggests, of course, a uniformity that simply cannot exist where different parties compete for political power, with the result settled through the ballot box and where, in the name of a free press, proprietors, editors, reporters and commentators have at their disposal the vast power of modern technology to promote their own discourse and agenda. If governments are indeed more or less blundering into a series of international hot-spots, there is even less consistency and certainly less uniformity in what might be termed anti-establishment views. Thus governments are castigated on the grounds that 'something ought to be done' (televisual responses to Bosnia/Rwanda); military involvement is deemed inappropriate at the end of the twentieth century (anti-Nato pressure groups reacting to war in the Gulf/Kosovo); and economic sanctions are condemned as an inexact weapon that hurts victims rather than perpetrators ('soft' liberal opinion on Iraq/Yugoslavia). For over half a century western Europe has relied on the USA to pick up the major responsibility and most of the tab for extra-territorial activity. The chapter on the USA in this book poses, but does not answer, the key question – was the internal opposition to Nato's war in Kosovo driven simply by Republican hatred of President Clinton and moral outrage –

genuine or phoney – about a stain on a woman's dress, or does it harbinger an agonizing reappraisal of post-Cold War priorities and a move back towards isolationism?

There is a sense in which the former Yugoslavia was itself virtually a concept held afloat by the Cold War. The country lay clearly within the Soviet sphere but without alignment. Precisely because this independent Communist federal republic stood astride so many European fault lines – linguistic, religious, cultural – there is a sense in which it was interdependent with the world order that emerged from the ruins of World War II. Yugoslavia both depended on, and sustained, that world order. With the metamorphosis occasioned by the collapse of the Soviet Empire, Yugoslavia simply imploded. It is worth reflecting on the hypothetical ramifications of such an implosion at the height of the Cold War. Would it be an exaggeration to suggest that this might have brought the entire edifice of international order crashing down with unpredictable implications? It is easy enough to recognize that Tito 'saved' Yugoslavia from being forced into the regular mould of the Cold War: he also safeguarded Europe's most obvious fault lines from both the great powers and the danger of conflict.

> 66 With the metamorphosis occasioned by the collapse of the Soviet Empire, Yugoslavia simply imploded 99

Looking back on the history of the Balkans it is not difficult to feel some empathy with those nineteenth-century statesmen who worried about the implications of the collapse of the Ottoman Empire even if ultimately and in reality they could do little about it. Several hundred years of Ottoman rule had led to a jumbling of national and ethnic groups and a very inexact identification with any specific territory. The serendipity of the final collapse of the Empire with the allied decision after World War I also to break up the Austro-Hungarian Empire promoted a new and highly unstable state system in the Balkans. Against a background where each national group claimed the right to territory based, sometimes quite fictionally, on the greatest extent of its power several hundred years previously, it was virtually impossible to construct any set of stable inter-state relations that might bind the sub-region together. The victors in the series of wars that had engulfed the Balkans from 1912 to 1918 not unnaturally appeared to fare best on the ground, while the losers had to bide their time. In quick succession, Turkey – the apparent main loser – gained some revenge on Greece, – until then seemingly a major victor; most states abandoned even the trimmings of liberal democracy for cruder, more extreme and often bloody politics; and Yugoslavia – the one ostensible multi-ethnic state – began to fall prey to national rivalries. The Balkans region was sucked into the vortex of World War II by extraneous forces but the conflict within the sub-region had its own coloration. The new post-war settlement or truce, necessarily reflecting the situation on the ground, simply froze frontiers which in many cases had no legitimation – historic or ethnic. The end of the Cold War could be heralded as occasioning the re-integration of the Balkans into the rest of Europe and with this the actual or potential re-emergence of many of the old disputes – predominantly national and ethnic but overlaid with religious, cultural and linguistic implications. The most cursory reading of the chapters in this book dealing with the motivations and responses of Russia and Yugoslavia, on the one hand, and the leading western European states on the other, illustrates graphically the differing mindsets of Western (Christian) and Eastern (Orthodox) perspectives.

This is particularly apparent when we consider how the media in various countries interpreted the conflict and war. History and competing national claims ruled out any possibility of a clean break between Serbs and Croats. The fact that the Yugoslav army was largely inherited by the Serbs meant there was a vast disparity in power between the two sides. It can be argued that neither side accepted all the 'rules of war', but the Serbs were both much stronger and far more ruthless. These characteristics came particularly to the fore during the civil war in Bosnia where Serbs, Croats and Muslims had conflicting claims. *Prima facie* the Serbs were responsible for most of the excesses and they all too often seemed to be carried out either by official forces or with their connivance. By the time the Bosnian war was over Serbia retained little support in the West; historic memories of old alliances during World War II had largely disappeared; and, of perhaps still greater significance, the international community and the Western powers felt humiliated – before their own domestic public opinion and on the world stage. Even if governments had been content to forget, Western media remained ready to remind the public of past Serbian excesses. Acts of war became 'crimes against humanity', 'massacres', 'ethnic cleansing' and even – utterly inappropriately – 'genocide'. Serbs were held to be largely responsible and Yugoslavia as an established state was on its way to pariah status. The different national chapters show that perspectives in Berlin, London, Paris, Rome and Washington were far from being identical – but there was clear

> 66 Even if governments had been content to forget, Western media remained ready to remind the public of past Serbian excesses 99

agreement that what had already happened in the former Yugoslavia was simply unacceptable in the new Europe. The Serbs simply had to be stopped. Kosovo – their own backyard in a sense that was not true for Croatia or Bosnia – was the inevitable occasion for the West to stand firm.

It is equally clear from those national chapters that there was little if any enthusiasm for a ground war. Offering ground troops to monitor a peace was different, but would only be possible if somehow the Serbs and Albanians could be persuaded to reach agreement on at least a procedure for a way forward. Cynics may argue that if they could do that, there would perhaps be less need for monitors. During the course of the aerial bombardment, there was no real change in the reluctance of the main Western allies to commit ground forces for active military involvement. There are suggestions earlier in this book that the British and French governments might have gone along with ground forces had there been strong support elsewhere, but there was no enthusiasm at all in Germany and Italy, and clear opposition in the USA, the country that would have had to contribute the greater part of any force that fought its way into Kosovo.

As well as looking at different reactions among the major Western players, this book has also considered the work of three relevant arms of the international community – the UN, Nato and the EU. The structure of the UN meant that it could offer its good offices as a route to agreement between the parties to the conflict and it could help coordinate humanitarian and other forms of international aid. Divisions between (major) member states ensured that it could not under any likely circumstances become a participant in the struggle between the Albanians of Kosovo and Serb dominated Yugoslavia. These were not the factors restraining the EU from action, although following historic precedent there was the usual support for Serbia in Greece. As the prime regional organization, the EU had a commitment and a motive for intervention. One of the cements that binds the Union is a commitment to human rights. It was accepted policy that most of south-eastern Europe would ultimately come within the EU and should perhaps already be bound by some of its norms. Furthermore, the break-up of Yugoslavia was having major economic, political and social implications for the entire continent. The problem was that the EU still possessed only a limited capacity in classic foreign affairs and virtually none in defence and security matters. Its traditional machinery for external policy – the 'old wine' graphically described in the EU chapter – of financial assistance could not of itself resolve deep-seated historic national rivalries.

> ❝ The break-up of Yugoslavia was having major economic, political and social implications for the entire continent ❞

Nato was thus, almost by a process of elimination, the chosen instrument once the Western powers had reached a consensus that they should on this occasion intervene. The Nato action was justified by reference to the UN and the need to prevent further 'crimes against humanity'. Insofar as international law is a static concept and can only be formally changed by some kind of agreement enshrined into a widely recognized charter, convention etc. the Nato action might appear to have been illegal. However, it is possible to argue with equal validity that international law has to be dynamic and responsive to circumstance and that it needs to find a way to legitimize the protection of peoples as well as states. Logically Nato cannot be judge and jury in its own case, but there is little moral value in suggesting that potential victims of war and oppression should wait for assistance while the international community sorts out the long-standing and possibly irresolvable issue of people *vis-à-vis* states. Different contributors to this book have adopted different stances on this core issue and they reflect a variety of outside opinion. There is no need to doubt the sincerity either of those who argued from the position of traditional international law or of those who felt a moral responsibility to intervene and prevent a series of humanitarian disasters. The problem is that their respective positions are not easily reconcilable.

This book is not about the course of the actual war in Kosovo. From the allied point of view it was a war by remote control. It is unclear whether the allies initially expected the bombing campaign to be of shorter duration or whether the final 'surrender' of Milosevic, aided by pressure from Russia, again took them by surprise. What is clear is that the allies stuck together without any major public disagreements, and the sustained bombing campaign ultimately achieved the goal of removing Yugoslav forces from Kosovo without any land invasion. As with any war there was a quota of mistakes and other incidents – the Chinese Embassy, the convoy of refugees and the deaths of civilians. This is inevitable in war, but the process of instant reporting helped by Yugoslavia continuing to allow access for the media magnified each such incident. In retrospect there was nothing remarkable about the conflict in terms of unexpected and unnecessary casualties. War is indeed brutish: even in an age of high technology there can be no guarantee of always hitting the right target. A more potent criticism might be that the bombing precipitated more expulsions of Albanians from their homes, while the allied victory subsequently led to exclusions of Serbs. Western governments disclaimed responsibility, but this too is what happens in war especially where civil strife is also involved.

The previous paragraph encompasses matters reported, photographed and filmed at the time. Once the international media circus moved on, Kosovo largely faded from view, its infrequent reappearances occasioned by specific events – gruesome discoveries of victims; further clashes between Albanians and Serbs; arrests of Westerners by Yugoslav authorities. The remainder of this concluding chapter will, therefore, focus on some longer-term implications. The analysis will consider consequences of the crisis and the war in the region and beyond – for the participants and for international relations, organizations and law.

The first set of implications focuses on Yugoslavia and its former constituent parts. Even before the war in Kosovo, independent status for Slovenia, Croatia, Macedonia and Bosnia had effectively dismembered what was Yugoslavia or the Union of Southern Slavs. In the likely event that Kosovo will not again be reintegrated with Serbia, Yugoslavia has – regardless of the future relationship of Serbia and Montenegro – to all intents and purposes ceased to be a multi-ethnic state. Indeed its very name is now a misnomer. Recent history suggests that any future confederation or even looser association between the successor states will be difficult to forge. Aspirations for Serbian hegemony over the region that once was Yugoslavia have effectively been thwarted. In the event that Kosovo too is 'lost' Serbia will for the first time since the Balkan wars at the beginning of the last century be an aggrieved nation, dissatisfied with the boundaries of its state and with the international system which sustains them. Given Serbia's geographic centrality this is hardly conducive to a more stable Balkans. The Milosevic regime defied any crude classification: it was autocratic and secretive but it was certainly *not* fascist. The replacement of Milosevic by Kostunica was occasioned by an election – not normally the route by which dictators are removed! Withdrawal of support for Milosevic by the police, security services and armed forces was an echo of events in the former Czechoslovakia a decade previously. His downfall was brought about by the perceived failure of his policies for asserting Serbian national interests and the heavy economic price paid. Political leaders – democratic or autocratic – rarely flourish after lost wars. There is no evidence of any Serb support for Nato's intervention in Kosovo, but ultimately its success and the huge economic price paid by Serbs undermined the Milosevic regime. Any perception that the removal of Milosevic was purely an internal event, unmotivated by the external

> ❝The Milosevic regime defied any crude classification: it was autocratic and secretive, but it was certainly *not* fascist❞

world, ignores an important reality. Milosevic 'took on' that external world: he lost and paid the price.

Nonetheless the legacy for Kostunica and succeeding Serb governments is complex. Even the most cursory reading of Chapter 12 demonstrates the centrality of Kosovo to the Serb psyche. Independent status for Slovenia, Croatia, Bosnia and Macedonia may be accepted in time, but for the vast majority of Serbs, Kosovo will for long be an integral part of their own homeland. If an immediate priority for the new regime is to end its pariah status, the prospects for Serb/Yugoslav evolution towards a political system more in tune with those prevalent in the EU will not be helped by indefinite continuation of a huge national sense of grievance. The apparently massive costs of reconstruction pose a further problem. The best prospects for economic and political regeneration may rest with 'old wine' of the EU, but external investors/donors would be well advised to avoid any crude linkage with Serb acceptance of the current status quo in the Balkans.

Nato and the EU are the guarantors of Kosovo: the internal problems of economic, political and social reconstruction are already turning out to be far greater than expected. There is seemingly no prospect of Albanians and Serbs living in any kind of harmony. An independent Kosovo would hardly be viable. It is doubtful that Serb hostility could ever be bought off by any kind of partition (which would make the rump even less viable). Nato would have to take major responsibility for the creation, defence and security of any sort of independent Kosovo. Such a division of Yugoslavia would be an unwanted consequence of a war theoretically undertaken on 'behalf of the UN'. If there were no partition the Albanian majority would almost certainly seek to evict the remaining Serb minority – hardly an action to merit Nato protection. Perhaps logically, and also improbably, the only long-term solution might be to split the province between Albania and Serbia with both joining the EU. It is hard to see this happening very quickly: in the interim Kosovo would remain occupied by Nato forces and a financial drain on the EU and the USA.

It was suggested earlier in this chapter that for some forty years in the context of the Cold War, Yugoslavia was interdependent with the bipolar international system. Relics of this interdependence remained on show throughout the crisis, and were particularly demonstrated through the differing phases of Russian involvement. Pro- and pan-Serb emotions, coupled with a determination not to be sidelined from an area of historic interest conditioned a series of Russian responses. The Russian government sought to ensure that its legitimate interests were recognized without running any significant risk of being dragged into the conflict. It can be argued that both goals were achieved. Russian involvement in bringing about the settlement which ended the war, and subsequently in facilitating the final stages of what was ultimately a peaceful transference of political power from Milosevic to Kostunica, will turn out to have helped to stabilize the slightly shaky post bi-polar international system.

Three international organizations were involved in the Kosovo crisis. The UN has a proven, if limited, capacity to broker agreements and maintain peace: it is very rarely an organization capable of going to war. In this sense, the crisis over Kosovo has not brought about any significant change. This is not the case for Nato or the EU. The chapter on Nato explores links with its own member states and the notion of war on 'behalf' of the UN. What is particularly interesting is that this can be considered the first full-scale 'hot' war for an organization that, above all, epitomizes the Cold War; it was also 'out of area', suggesting an on-the-ground extension of Nato interests. Perhaps most significant is that Nato members held together despite differing perceptions about the Balkans and the presence in governments of a variety of political groups, including pacifists and ex-communists. Equally noteworthy was the active participation of France in the military activities. Finally, it needs to be recognized that whether or not intervention led in the short-term to an intensification of ethnic cleansing in Kosovo and a lack of regard for complications of future status, Nato can claim a success. The majority Albanian population were enabled to return to their homes; what was in effect Serbian military occupation of Kosovo was brought to an end; and events were set in train which ultimately precipitated the downfall of the Milosevic regime.

For the EU, Kosovo was a meeting with its own destiny. The break-up of Yugsolavia is pre-eminently a European problem and its repercussions impact directly on the EU. On the negative side, the EU simply lacked the instrumentalities required to deal with the situation and was forced, as ever, to rely on the USA. The pressure within the Union to develop a security and defence capacity has increased, particularly influenced by uncertainty over future willingness on the part of the USA to be involved in similar campaigns in the future. The first consequence seems likely to be the creation of a European Rapid Reaction Force that

> **66 The pressure within the Union to develop a security and defence capacity has increased. 99**

will operate within the continent in association with Nato. There is, however, another equally positive side as far as the Union is concerned. It was argued earlier in this concluding chapter that Milosevic's downfall was the ultimate result of his military defeat. Insofar as Nato and EU governments accept this as normative, there will be an inevitable revisionist argument that similar processes of cause and effect have not always been apparent in other regions subjected to Western military action. Iraq is the obvious example: its military defeat was much more conclusive and extensive than those of Serbia/Yugoslavia or, in the 1980s, of Argentina over the Falklands. The economic price paid by the people of Iraq for their country's pariah status has been far greater than that met by the Serbs. Yet unlike Milosevic or Gualtieri, Sadam Hussein has survived. It is possible to offer all kinds of specific reasons for this, but ultimately political culture is critical. Yugoslavia is part of Europe, affected by the same norms and attitudes as the rest of the continent.

> **In actuality Milosevic, for all that he may be charged by the international community with war crimes, was not a despot**

Many of the successor states are knocking on the door of the European Union seeking membership. In that sense the Union is a powerful centripetal force, affecting the behaviour of all in the region. Europe is not free from unpleasant political parties and sometimes they may gain some political power, but fascist or communist despots are part of its past, not its present or likely future. In actuality Milosevic, for all that he may be charged by the international community with war crimes, was not a despot. To have hung on to power in the face of electoral defeat and a popular rising, he would have had to become such a despot, ready to use armed force against his own people. There are parts of the world, above all Europe, where this is no longer conceivable.

It may be appropriate to end by considering the implications for international law. I mentioned earlier two alternative approaches – one posited on international law as static and based on agreed texts; the other more dynamic. There is a need to widen the discussion. The classic view is that the main (perhaps even the sole) concern of international law is the behaviour of sovereign states and its primary purpose is to regulate relations between those states. This reflects a very traditional view that they are the sole legitimate players in international politics. In recent times regional organizations – the EU is the most obvious – have clearly become major players in their own right. In addition the big multinational corporations wield much international power even if their legitimacy is contested. *Prima facie* the classic approach to international law would place on states the onus of regulating the behaviour of these other potential players. The problem with this approach is that individual states may well cede considerable national sovereignty to regional and other international organizations, partly motivated by the need to seek modes of control over the multinational corporations.

International law is not *prima facie* concerned with individuals, but it does recognize human rights. If a state takes action prejudicial to the rights of foreign nationals, this is clearly a matter for international law. The difficulty is the automatic assumption that any state is the sole arbiter and protector of the rights of its own nationals resident within its boundaries. Historically, this has helped to reinforce the rule of non-interference in domestic matters. On one reading, humanitarian concerns offered a moral, but not necessarily a legal, basis for allied intervention in Yugoslavia. However, if international law takes precedence over national laws, the argument can be developed. It may be reasonable to claim that under international law human rights for co-nationals are a responsibility of states and that Yugoslavia was palpably failing to fulfil that responsibility. This would offer a legal justification for the allied action.

The absence of consistency in the Western world's responses to international crises and abuse of human rights have inevitably fuelled various critiques of the war over Kosovo. Some have simply based their arguments on alternative views of international law, while others fall back on different possible responses. There have also been assertions about hidden agendas – although these have not been demonstrated with any compelling evidence. What we can see at the beginning of a new millennium is a growing commitment to the notion of accountability – of nations and individuals. Allied insistence on ending the suppression of Kosovo Albanians, international judicial rulings about General Pinochet, and various war crimes trials fall into the same category. These remain largely uncharted waters for the international community and inconsistency is inevitable. However, all these events lay down tiny markers over the future behaviour of both states and their leaders. In the long run, this may be the most important legacy of the last war of the twentieth century.

REFERENCES AND FURTHER READING

CHAPTER 2 KOSOVO: A FUSE FOR THE LIGHTING

Ali, T. (1999) 'Springtime for NATO', *New Left Review*, 234, March–April, 62–72.

Amnesty International (1999) Annual Report on Yugoslavia cited at www.amnesty.org.

Bandow, D. (2000) 'NATO's hypocritical humanitarianism' in Galen Carpenter, T. (ed.) *NATO's Empty Victory: A Postmortem on the Balkan War.* (Washington DC: CATO Institute), 31–51.

Bugajski, J. (1999) 'Problems of Balkan Reconstruction', Center for Strategic and International Studies paper cited at www.csis.org/hill/ts990804bugajski.html.

Chomsky, N. (1999) *The New Military Humanism: Lessons from Kosovo.* London: Pluto Press.

Fields, J. (1999) 'Historical perspective: Yugoslavia: a legacy of ethnic hatred', 19 February cited at www.associatedpress.html.

Galen Carpenter, T. (2000) (ed.) *NATO's Empty Victory: A Postmortem on the Balkan War.* Washington DC: CATO Institute.

Georgieff, A. and Blocker, J. (1999) 'How to handle Post-Kosovo Serbia?' *Central Europe Online*, 21 March cited at www.centraleurope.com/features.

Gowan, P. (1999), 'The NATO powers and the Balkan Tragedy', *New Left Review*, 234, March–April, 83–105.

Group 17 report (1999) 'Economic consequences of NATO bombing: Estimates of damage and finances required for Economic reconstruction of Yugoslavia', June cited at seerecon.org/outside sources.

Human Rights Watch (1999) 'Abuses against Serbs and Roma in the New Kosovo', 11 (10D) August.

Human Rights Watch (2000) 'Civilian deaths in the NATO air campaign', 12 (1D), February.

ICG (2000) 'What happened to the KLA?', ICG Balkans report, 88, 3 March.

Jatras, J.J. (2000) 'NATO's myths and bogus justifications for intervention' in Galen Carpenter, T. (ed.) *NATO's Empty Victory: A Postmortem on the Balkan War.* Washington DC: CATO Institute, 21–31.

Johnston, D. (1999) 'Notes on the Kosovo Problem and the International Community' cited at www.kosovo.serbhost.org/diana_johnston.html. Accessed 23 April 2000.

Judah, T. (1997) *The Serbs: History, Myth and the Destruction of Yugoslavia*. New Haven and London: Yale University Press).

Judah, T. (1999) 'Kosovo's Road to War', *Survival*, 41 (2), Summer, 5–18.

Judah, T. (2000), *Kosovo: War and Revenge*. New Haven and London: Yale University Press.

Kosovar Albanians: The Other Side (1999) 22 August cited at www.emperors-clothes.com/interviews/alban.htm.

Lampe, J. R. (2000) *Yugoslavia as History: Twice there was a country*. 2nd edn. Cambridge: Cambridge University Press.

LaPorte, E. (1999) 'The Criminal race: The Demonization, Dehumanization and Criminalization of the Serbian people' cited at www.suc.org/politics/kosovo/papers/propagandapro.html.

Layne, C. (2000a) 'Miscalculations and blunders lead to war' in Galen Carpenter, T. (ed.) *NATO's Empty Victory: A Postmortem on the Balkan War*. Washington DC: CATO Institute, 1–21.

Layne, C. (2000b) 'Collateral damage in Yugoslavia' in Galen Carpenter, T. (ed.) *NATO's Empty Victory: A Postmortem on the Balkan War*. Washington DC: CATO Institute, 51–8.

Lee, M. (1983) 'Kosovo between Yugoslavia and Albania', *New Left Review*, 140, July–August, 62–91.

Lutovac, Z. (1997) 'All Kosovo Options', *Vreme* (Belgrade), 10 May cited at www.cdsp.neu.edu.

Malcolm, N. (1998) *Kosovo: A Short History*. London and Basingstoke: Macmillan.

Mazower, M. (1997) 'Ethnicity and War in the Balkans', *National Humanities Research Center paper* cited at www.nhc.rtp.nc.us:8080/publications/hongkong/mazower.htm.

Mertus, J. (1996) 'A wall of silence divides Serbian and Albanian opinion on Kosovo', *Transition*, 22 March.

Moore, P. (1999) 'Questions and Answers on Kosova', *Radio Free Europe/Radio Liberty Balkan Report*, 3 (13), 7 April.

Posa, C. (1998) 'Engineering Hatred: The Roots of Contemporary Serbian nationalism', *Balkanistika*, 11, 69–77.

Rama, S.A. (2000) 'The Serb–Albanian war and the international community's miscalculations', *International Journal of Albanian Studies* cited at www.albanian.com/IJAS/vol2/is1/art1.html. Accessed 23 April.

Ramet, S. (1997) *Whose Democracy? Nationalism, religion and the doctrine of collective rights in post-1989 Eastern Europe.* Lanham and Oxford: Rowman and Littlefield.

Ramet, S. (1999) *Balkan Babel.* 3rd edn. New York: Westview Press.

Roberts, A. (1999) 'NATO's "Humanitarian War" over Kosovo', *Survival,* 41 (3), Autumn, 102–33.

Rothschild, J. (1983) *East Central Europe between the Two World Wars.* Seattle: University of Washington Press.

Sigler III, J.C. (1999) 'A look at Albanian nationalism and the KLA' cited at www.suc.org/politics/kosovo/papers/sigler.html.

Snegaroff, C. (2000) 'Multi-ethnic Kosovo still a distant dream one year after war', *Central Europe Online,* 21 March cited at www.centraleurope.com/features.

South Balkans report (1999) 'Violence in Kosovo: Who's killing whom?', 2 November cited at www.intl-crisis-group.org.

Tomova, M. (1997) *Imagining the Balkans.* New York: Oxford University Press.

UNHCR (1996) *Background paper on Refugees and Asylum seekers from Kosovo,* June.

UNHCR (1999) report on asylum applications from citizens in the former Yugoslavia, 20 July cited at www.unhcr.ch/statist/990/euro/text.htm.

US State Department report (1999) *Ethnic cleansing in Kosovo: An accounting.* Washington DC: December.

Vickers, M. (1998) *Between Serb and Albanian: A History of Kosovo.* New York: Columbia University Press.

World Bank (1999a) 'Towards stability and prosperity; A program for reconstruction and recovery in Kosovo', report dated 3 November.

World Bank (1999b) 'Kosovo: Building peace through sustained growth; The Economic and Social policy agenda', report dated 3 November.

CHAPTER 3 BRITAIN: TO WAR FOR A JUST CAUSE

Crampton, R.J. (1994) *Eastern Europe in the Twentieth Century.* London: Routledge.

Glenny, M. (1999) *Balkans 1804–1999: Nationalism, War and the Great Powers,* London, Granta.

Ignatieff, M. (2000) *Virtual War: Kosovo and Beyond.* London: Chatto and Windus.

Judah, T. (2000) *Kosovo: War and Revenge.* Yale University Press.

Kaplan, R.D. (1994) *Balkan Ghosts.* London: Vintage.

Magas, B. (1993) *The Destruction of Yugoslavia: Tracking the Break-up 1980–92.* London: Verso.

Malcolm, N. (1998), *Kosovo: A Short History.* London: Macmillan.

CHAPTER 4 ITALY: THE RELUCTANT ALLY

Catone, A. (1999) 'Glossario di guerra. Il discorso ideologico di giustificazione', *Giano*, 32: 36–55.

D'Alema, M. (1999) *Kosovo*. Milano: Mondadori.

Desiderio, A. (1999) 'Che cosa rischia l'Italia', *limes*, supplemento al n. 1, 1: 87–92.

Editorial (1999) 'Lo Stato d'Europa', *limes*, 2: 7–14.

Fubini, F. (1999) 'Il paradosso italiano: siamo importanti ma contiamo poco', *limes*, (4) 17–26.

Haski, P. (1999) 'Kosovo: dans les coulisses du "club des cinq", *Libération*, 1er juillet.

L'Abate, A. (1999) *Kossovo: una guerra annunciata*. Molfetta: edizioni la meridiana.

Morozzo della Rocca, R. (1998) 'Italia e Usa: due modi di affrontare la crisi del Kosovo', *limes*, (1) 243–9.

Morozzo della Rocca, R. (1999) *Kosovo*. Milano: Guerini.

Panebianco, A. (1999) 'Democrazie in guerra', *il Mulino*, (2) 211–20.

Paolini, M. (1998) 'Una strategia per i Balcani adriatici', *limes*, 1: 227–34.

Paolini, M. *Per una pace giusta* (1999) Roma: Idee in cammino.

Rusconi, G.E. (1999) 'Obiettivi e risultati della guerra del Kosovo', *il Mulino*, 3: 407–14.

Salvoldi, G. and V. and Gjergji, L. (1999) *Kosovo non violenza per la riconciliazione*. Bologna: EMI.

Scotto, G. and Arielli, E. (1999) *La guerra del Kosovo*, Roma: Editori Riuniti.

Serpicus (1998) 'Perché aiutiamo la Serbia', *limes*, (1) 235–41.

Tonello, F. (1999) 'Quando parlano le bombe', *Problemi dell'informazione*, 3: 293–304.

CHAPTER 5 GERMANY: THE FEDERAL REPUBLIC, LOYAL TO NATO

Elsasser, Jurgen (ed.) (1999) *Nie wieder Krieg ohne uns. Das Kosovo und die neue Deutsche Geopolitik*. Hamburg: Konkret.

Illyria (1999) The Bronx, 27 January–3 February.

Klaus Kinkel (1999) interview in *Der Spiegel* (12/1998), as cited in Ralph Hartmann *'Die ehrlichen Makler': Die deutsche Aussenpolitik und der Bürgerkrieg in Jugoslawien*. Berlin: Dietz Verlag.

Lipsius, Stephen (1999a) 'Kosovo: Politische Führung zerstritten', in *Südost Europa*, 48 (7/8) July–August, 359–60.

Lipsius, Stephen (1999b) 'Neue Minister und Ressorts in Kosovo', in *Südost Europa*, 48 (9/10) September–October.

Petranovic, Branko (1992) *Srbija u drugom svetskom ratu 1939–1945*. Belgrade: Vojnoizdavacki i novinski centar.

Ramet, Sabrina P. (1999b) 'Kosovo: A Liberal Approach', in *Society*, 36 (6) September–October.

Ramet, Sabrina P. (1999a) *Balkan Babel: The Disintegration of Yugoslavia from the Death of Tito to the War for Kosovo*. 3rd edn. Boulder, Colo.: Westview Press.

Reuter, Jens (1998) 'Internationale Gemeinschaft und der Kreig in Kosovo', in *Südost Europa*, 47 (7/8) July–August.

Schlarp, Karl-Heinz (1986) *Wirtschaft und Besatzung in Serbien 1941–1944*. Stuttgart: Franz Steiner Verlag.

Steinberg, Jonathan (1990) *All or Nothing: The Axis and the Holocaust, 1941–1943*. London and New York: Routledge.

Stenger, Michael (1999) 'Tödliche Fehlenschatzung. Kein Asyl: Warum Flüchtlinge aus dem Kosovo bis zuletzt abgeschogen wurden' in Thomas Schmid (ed.) *Krieg im Kosovo*. Reinbeck bei Hamburg: Rowolht Taschenbuch Verlag.

Troebst, Stefan (1998) *Conflict in Kosovo: Failure or Prevention? An Analytical Documentation, 1992–1998*. ECMI Working Paper No. 1 Flensburg: European Centre in Minority Issues.

Troebst, Stefan (1999) 'Chronologie einer gescheiterten Prävention. Vom Konflikt zum Krieg im Kosovo, 1989–1999', in *Osteuropa*, 49 (8) August.

Zumach, Andreas (1999) '"80 Prozent unserer vorstellungen werden durchgepeitscht". Die letzte Chance von Rambouillet und die Geheimdiplomatie um den "Annex B"', in Schmid (ed.), *Krieg im Kosovo*. Reinbeck bei Hamburg: Rowohlt Taschenbuch Verlag, 63.

Lexis-Nexis Academic Universe

codoh.com/newsdesk/99326.html

www.bundeskanzler.de/03/13/

www.cdu.de/presse/archiv/pr047-99htm

www.kirchenzeitung.de:81/kizartik

www.pds-online.de/1/zukunft/9904/wittich.htm

www.spd.de/politik/kosovo/scharpinghtm

www.spd.de/politik/kosovo/parteig120499.htm

www.spiegel.de/politik/deutschland/nf//0,1518,16770.html

www.welt.de/daten/1999/06/18/0618del118198.htx

www.welt.de/extra/brennpunkte/kosovo/artikel317.htm

www.yahoo.co.uk/headlines/1999524/news/9275441000-3-1.html

www.yahoo.de/schlagzeilen

w3zdf.msnbc.de/news/32906.asp

CHAPTER 6 FRANCE: QUESTIONS OF IDENTITY

Lamizet, B. (1998) *La médiation politique*, Paris: L'Harmattan.

CHAPTER 7 THE EU: OLD WINE FROM NEW BOTTLES

Adam, Bernard (1999) 'Après la guerre au Kosovo – Quelles leçons pour la sécurité européenne', la guerre du Kosovo, éclairages et commentaires. Les livres du GRIP.

Andreani, Gilles (1999) 'Europe's uncertain identity' CER Essay, February.

Baer, Alain (1999) 'Les enseignements stratégiques de l'opération de l'OTAN au Kosovo', *Défense nationale*, 12.

Bavarez, Nicolas (1999) 'Guerre propre paix sale', *Commentaire* 87, Autumn.

Biermann, Rafael (1999) 'The Stability Pact for South Eastern Europe – potential, problems and perspectives', discussion paper ZEI, Bonn.

Birnbaum, Norman (1999) 'Europe, NATO and the transatlantic future', Peace and Security 1999-06 31 (1).

Bruckner, Pascal (1999) 'L'Amérique diabolisée', *Politique Internationale*, 84, été.

Buyse, A. (1999) 'Kosovo en Europa's veiligheid', De Kosovaarse kwestie en haar impact op de europese veiligheid, Defense Studiecentrum, Brussels symposium 8 December 1999.

Cabada, Ladislav & Ehl, Martin (1999) 'The Kosovo Crisis and the Prospects for the Balkans', *Perspectives*, 13.

Chenu, Paul (1999) 'Kosovo: ambiguités et perspectives d'un plan de paix', *Esprit*, Octobre.

David, Dominique (1999) 'Kosovo: de vraies et de fausses leçons stratégiques', *Défense nationale*, 12.

De Schoutheete, Philippe (1997) Une Europe pour tous, Paris: éditions Odile Jacob, September.

Delors, Jacques (1991) 'European Integration and Security', *Survival*, XXXIII (2) March/April.

Duchène, François (1973) 'The European Community and the Uncertainties of Interdependence' in Kohnstamm, M. and Hager, W. 'A Nation Writ Large? Foreign Policy Problems before the European Community', Institut de la Communauté Européenne pour les Etudes universitaires.

Duke, Simon (1999) 'From Amsterdam to Kosovo: lessons for the future of CFSP', EIPASCOPE 99/02.

Farrell, Deirdre (1998) 'The European Union as a Civilian Power in its Relations with Central and Eastern Europe', College of Europe.

Forget, Michel (1999) 'A propos du Kosovo', *Défense nationale*, 12.

Friis, Lykke and Murphy, Anna (1999) 'Negotiation in a Time of Crisis', revised version of the paper presented at the Colloquium 'The EU as a Negotiated Order', Burleigh Court, Loughborough University, 22–23 October.

Garde, Paul (1999) 'Kosovo: missile intelligent et chausse-pied rouillé', *Politique Internationale*; 84, été.

Gautier, Louis (1999) 'L'Europe de la défence au portant', *Politique Etrangère* 2/99.

Gere, François (1999) 'Le jeu sans la règle', *Défense nationale*, 12.

Glucksmann, André (1999) 'Le Kosovo: une nouvelle forme de conflit dans l'après-guerre froide', *Défense nationale*, 12.

Gnesotto, Nicole (1998) 'La Puissance et l'Europe', Presses de Sciences Po.

Gnesotto, Nicole (1999) 'L'OTAN et L'Europe', *Politique Étrangère*, été.

Grant, Charles (1999) 'European defence post Kosovo?' CER working papers, June.

Hassner, Pierre (1999) 'Le barbare et le bourgeois', *Politique Internationale*, 84 été.

Heisbourg, François (1999) 'L'Europe de la défense dans l'Alliance Atlantique', *Politique Étrangère*, 2.

Hendrickson, David C. (1999) 'Albania and NATO. Regional security and selective intervention' Security dialogue, 30 (1) mars.

Hoffmann, Stanley (2000) 'Towards a Common European Foreign and Security Policy?', *Journal of Common Market Studies*, 38 (2) June.

Lord, Christopher (1999) 'Now America takes over', *Perspectives*, 13/99.

Mollard de la Bruyere, Yves (1999) 'La politique européenne face aux balkans', De Kosovaarse kwestie en haar impact op de europese veiligheid, Defense Studiecentrum, Brussels symposium, 8 December 1999.

Ortega, Martin (1999) 'Una capacidad europea para la gestión de crisis', *Politica Exterior*, 70, Julio/Augosto.

Peterson, John and Sjursen, Helene (ed) (1998) *A Common Foreign Policy for Europe?* Routledge, European Public Policy Series (215 pages).

Pick, Otto (1999) 'NATO, European defence and the lessons of Kosovo' *Perspectives*, 13/99.

Pierre, Andrew J. (1999) 'De-Balkanising the Balkans: Security and Stability in South-eastern Europe', United States Institute of Peace Special Report, 20 September, http://www.nyu.edu/globalbeat/balkan/USIP092099.html.

Rupnik, Jacques (1998) 'L'Europe dans le miroir des Balkans', Transeuropéennes, 12–13.

Sloan, Stanley R. (2000) 'The United States and the European Defence', Chaillot Papers 39, Institute For Security Studies, WEU, Paris, April.

Smith, Karen Elizabeth (1997) 'Paradoxes of European Foreign Policy. The Instruments of European Union Foreign Policy', EUI Working Paper RSC 97/68, 18.

Tatu, Michel (1999), 'Kosovo: une chance pour l'Europe', *Politique Internationale*, 85.

Teunissen, Paul J. (1999) 'Strengthening the Defence Dimension of the EU: An Evaluation of Concepts, Recent Initiatives and Developments', European Foreign Affairs Review, 4.

Vimont, Pierre (1999) 'Les enjeux de la crise au Kosovo pour l'Europe', Revue du Marché Commun et de l'Union Européenne, 429, juin.

Vukadinovic, Nebojsa (2000) 'Les enjeux de la stabilisation et de la reconstruction des Balkans', *Politique Étrangère*, 1.

Weller, Marc (1999) *The crisis in Kosovo 1989–1999, from the dissolution of Yugoslovia to Rambouillet and the Outbreak of Hostilities*, Cambridge, International Document and Analysis, 1 (501 pages).

Woodward, Susan (1999) 'Should we think before we leap?', Security Dialogue, 30.

Zięba, Ryszard (1999) 'The Need for a New Approach in Research on European Security', *Perspectives*, 13.

OFFICIAL DOCUMENTS

Franco-British Summit – Joint Declaration on European Defence, 4 December 1998, Saint-Malo.

Presidency Conclusions
(htttp://www.europa.eu.int/en/Info/eurocouncil/index.htm)

Vienna 11 and 12 December 1998

Cologne 4 and 4 June 1999

Helsinki 10 and 11 December 2000

Lisbon 23 and 24 March 2000

Santa Maria da Feira 19 and 20 June 2000.

CHAPTER 8 THE MEDIA: INFORMATION AND DEFORMATION

Amnesty International (1998) *Kosovo, the Evidence,* London; Ennifield Print and Design.

Benn, Tony (1999) *Outlaw War: New Labour and the Kosovo Crisis.* Video from Platform Films.

Halimi, S. and Vidal, D. 'Media and Disinformation' in *Le Monde Diplomatique,* March 2000, (English edition), Guardian Publications.

Hobsbawm, Eric, (1994) *Age of Extremes,* London: Michael Joseph.

OSCE (1999) *As Seen as Told.*

Weymouth, T. and Lamizet, B. (1996) *Markets and Myths.* Harlow: Longman.

CHAPTER 9 THE USA: TO WAR IN EUROPE AGAIN

The American Heritage Dictionary of the English Language (1970), Boston and Mew York: American Heritage Publishing Co. & Houghton Mifflin Co.

Horowitz, Irving Louis (1999) 'The Vietnamisation of Yugoslavia', in *Society,* 36 (5) July–August.

Illyria (1999) The Bronx, 19–21 May.

Madsen, Wayne, (1999) 'Mercenaries in Kosovo: The U.S. connection to the KLA', in *The Progressive,* 63 (8) August, 29.

Rub, Matthias (1999) '"Phoenix aus der Asche". Die UCK: von der Terrororganisation zur Bodentruppe der Nato?' in Schmid, Thomas (ed.) *Krieg im Kosovo.* Reinbeck bei Hamburg: Rowohlt Taschenbuch Verlag.

Sadkovich, James J. (1998) *The US Media and Yugoslavia, 1991–1995.* Westport. Conn.: Praeger.

Zumach, Andreas (1999) '"80 Prozent unserer Vorstellungen werden durchgepeitscht". Die letzte Chance von Rambouillet und die Geheimdiplomatie um den "Annex B"', in Schmid (ed.) *Krieg im Kosovo,* Reinbeck bei Hamburg: Rowohlt Taschenbuch Verlag. 65.

Lexis-Nexis Academic Universe

Lexis-Nexis Congressional Universe

thomas.loc.gov/cgi-bin/query

www.eu-praesidentschaft.de/03/0302/0075/index.html

www.house.gov/curtweldon/pr

www.house.gov/paul/press/press99

www.ireland.com/newspaper/opinion

www.Salonmag.com/news/feature/1999/05/06/war/index.html

www.spintechmag.com/002/gb0200.htm

www.startribune.com

www.suntimes.com

www.suntimes.com/output/special/cong28.html

CHAPTER 10 AIR STRIKE: NATO ASTRIDE KOSOVO

Ali, T. (1999) 'Springtime for NATO', *New Left Review*, 234, May, 62–72.

BBC (1999) 'NATO's War: the untold story', *Newsnight*, London: BBC.

Channel Four (1999) *War in Europe*, London: Channel Four.

Eliot, T.S. (1970) *Murder in the Cathedral*, London: Faber and Faber.

European Union (1999) *The Development of a Common European Security and Defence Policy – The Integration Project of the Next Decade*. Speech by J. Solana, 17 December, accessed via http://ue.eu.int/pesc/article.asp?lang=en&id=4900007.

Foreign and Commonwealth Office, British–Italian Summit: 19–20 July 1999 – *Joint Declaration Launching European Defence Capabilities Initiative*, http:www.fco.gov.uk/news/newsteext.asp?2664.

Gowan, P. (1999) 'The NATO Powers and the Balkan Tragedy', *New Left Review*, 234, May, 83–105.

Marshall, A. (1999) 'Alliance that held together in a crisis', *Independent*, 4 June, 4.

NATO (1999a) press release, 24 April 1999, *The Alliance's Strategic Concept*, approved by the Heads of state and government, participating in the meeting of the North Atlantic Council in Washington DC on 23 and 24 April 1999, accessed via http://www.nato.int/.

NATO(1999b) *Speech of Lord Robertson, NATO Secretary General to the French Institute For International Relations*,18 May 1999, accessed via http://www.nato.int/.

NATO (1999c) *Press conference on the Kosovo Strike Assessment*, by General Wesley K. Clark and Brigadier General John Corley, NATO speech, press conference SACEUR, NATO HQ, 27 April 1999.

NATO (1999d) *Secretary General Javier Solana's Remarks to the Press on His Last Day*, 18 May 1999, accessed via http://www.nato.int/.

Steele, J. (1999) 'Clinton's soft words belie hard facts', *Guardian*, 19 November, 16.

CHAPTER 11 RUSSIA: WALKING THE TIGHTROPE

Antonenko, O. (1999–2000) 'Russia, NATO and European security after Kosovo', *Survival* 41 (4), Winter, 124–44.

Balkan Report (1999) 'Moscow's third way' and 'Russians go home', 3 (23), 15 June.

BBC News (1999) 'Russia warns against third world war', 9 April.

Black, J.L. (2000), *Russia Faces NATO Expansion: Bearing gifts or bearing arms?* Lanham, Maryland: Rowman & Littlefield.

Bowker, M. (1998) 'The wars in Yugoslavia: Russia and the international community', *Europe–Asia Studies* 50 (7), 1245–61.

Buszynski, L. (1996) *Russian foreign policy after the Cold War.* Westport, Connecticut/London: Praeger.

Christian Science Monitor (1999) 'Russia's dilemma', 30 March.

Cichock, M. A. (1990) 'The Soviet Union and Yugoslavia in the 1980s: A relationship in flux', *Political Science Quarterly* 105 (1), 53–74.

CNN (1999) 'Russian Premier cancels US visit over Kosovo crisis', 23 March.

Cornell, S.E. (1999) 'International reactions to massive human rights violations: The case of Chechnya', *Europe–Asia Studies* 51 (1), 85–100.

Csongos, F. T. (1999) 'Alliance updates post-Cold War mission', RFE/RL report, 26 April.

Dannreuther, R. (1999–2000), 'Escaping the Enlargement trap in NATO-Russian relations', *Survival* 41 (4), Winter, 145–64.

Davydov, Y. (1999) 'Problema Kosovo v Rossiiskom vnutripoliticheskom kontekste' in *Kosovo: Mezhdunarodnye aspekty krizisa*, Moscow Carnegie Centre, 247–79.

Frost, M. (1999) 'Kosovo peace force divides West and Russia', RFE/RL report, 7 May.

Global intelligence update (1998) 'Kosovo crisis sets template for new Russian politics' at www.stratfor.com, 15 October.

Goldgeier, J. and McFaul, M. (1998) 'Flawed pragmatism', *Moscow Times*, 10 October.

Guskova, Y. (1999) 'Dinamika kosovskogo krizisa i politika Rossii' in *Kosovo: Mezhdunarodnye aspekty krizisa*, Moscow Carnegie Centre, 32–78.

Hedges, C. (1999) 'Kosovo's new masters?', *Foreign Affairs*, May/June, 24–42.

Hoffman, D. (1999) 'Yeltsin renews threat over Kosovo', *Washington Post,* 14 May, A26.

Hoffman, D. (2000) 'New Russian security plan criticises West', *Washington Post*, 15 January, A01.

Hughes, C. (1999) 'Russian envoy reports progress as NATO jets pound Yugoslavia', *Associated Press report,* 29 May.

Irish Times (1999) 'Russia's voice on Yugoslavia', 5 April.

Izvestiya (1999a) 9 April.

Izvestiya (1999b) 23 April.

Izvestiya (1999c) 7 May.

Izvestiya (1999d) 9 June.

Johnston, D. (1999) 'Russia reacts to war in Yugoslavia', Centre for Defense Information, *Weekly Defense Monitor*, 3 (14), 8 April, 2–4.

Karpov, M. (1998) 'NATO confrontation is senseless for Russia', *Moscow News*, 31 December–4 January, 4.

Lagunina, I. (1999) 'NATO experts hope for resumption of contact with Russia', RFE/RL report, 30 April.

Levada, Y. (2000) '1999: An explosive year', *Moscow News*, 29 December 1999–4 January 2000, 4.

Levitin, O. (2000) 'Inside Moscow's Kosovo Muddle', *Survival*, 42 (1), Spring, 130–40.

Lukyanov, F. (1999) 'Serbs want a Slavic Union', *Moscow News*, 14–20 April, 1.

Malashenko, A. (1999) 'Moscow between Yugoslavia and Chechnya: The Kosovo factor in Russia's policy on the Caucasus', Moscow Carnegie Center Briefing papers, 7, July.

Matloff, J. 'Engaging Russia in the search for a settlement in Kosovo' in Christian Science Monitor, 13 April, 1999.

McLaren, B. (1999) 'Covering Kosovo: Russia's reaction to Kosovo', *International Press Institute report*, 3.

Monitoring Obshchestvennoe Mnenie (1999) 5 (43) September–October.

Moskovskii, Komsomolets (1999) 30 April, 2.

Partridge, B. (1999) 'Russia moving closer to NATO on Kosovo', RFE/RL report, 30 April.

Pikayev, A. (1999) 'Russian–US cooperation and the Kosovo crisis', Moscow Carnegie Center briefing paper, 5, May, 1–5.

Pounsett, R. (1999) 'Russia and the Kosovo Crisis', *Russia Today*, 6 April.

RFE/RL report (1999) 'Chernomyrdin says Kosovo solution closer', 4 May.

Rousso, A. (1999) Peace in Yugoslavia: Who gains?', Moscow Carnegie Center briefing papers, 6, June, 1–6.

Roy, S. (1999) 'Hysteria or disgust?', *Moscow News*, 7–13 April, 3.

Rubinsky, Y. (1999) 'Politika zapadnoevropeiskikh derzhav v otnoshenii kosovskogo konflikta' in *Kosovo: Mezhdunarodnye aspekty krizisa,* Moscow Carnegie Center, 212–79.

Russia Today (1999) 11 May.

Sevodnya (1999) 28 October.

Starr, K.L. (1999) 'Consequences of Kosovo – Views from Russia, NIS and the Baltic States', US Information Agency, Issue Focus at www.usia.gov/admin/005/wwwh97j8.html.

Stein, S. (1999) 'Crisis in Kosovo: overview of Eastern and Central European media', US Information Agency, Foreign Media Reaction Daily Digest, 9 April at www.usia.gov/admin/005/wwwh9a08.html.

Stratfor Special Report (1999a) 'Russian political and military posturing', 1 April.

Stratfor Commentary Archive (1999b), 'Chernomrydin puts pressure on Milosevic', 30 April.

Stratfor Special Report, (1999c) 'It's the Russians stupid', 14 June.

Stratfor Commentary, (1999d) 'Russia in Cologne,' 19 June.

USIS (1999) 'US opposes any political partition of Kosovo', US State Dept. report, 7 May.

Vershbow (2000) 'Amb. Vershbow on European Security Post-Kosovo', NATO Security Issues Digest No. 57, 23 March, at www.Grmbl.com/S20000323b.html.

Vinokurov, G. (1995) 'Media coverage of the Chechen conflict' at www.medialaw.ru.

Voronkov, L. (1998) 'Russian foreign policy formation and its Balkan cross-road', *Montenegro Journal of Foreign Policy,* 1–2 at www.diplomacy.cg.yu/12982.htm.

Vremya (1999) 23 March.

VTsIOM (1999) poll of 5 June. The results can be viewed at the public opinion foundation website: www.fom.ru.

Weller, M. (1999) 'The Rambouillet conference on Kosovo', *International Affairs,* 75 (2), 211–51.

Williams, D. (2000a) 'Russia strengthens Yugoslav ties', *Washington Post,* 17 May, A18.

Williams, C. (2000b) 'The New Russia: From Cold War strength to post-communist weakness and beyond' in P. Anderson., G. Wiessala and C. Williams (eds.) (forthcoming) *New Europe in Transition,* London: Pinter.

Williams, C., Chuprov, D. and Staroverov, V. (eds.) (1996) *Russian Society in Transition* Aldershot: Dartmouth.

Williams, C. and Sfikas, T. D. (eds.) (1999) *Ethnicity and Nationalism in Russia, the C.I.S. and the Baltic States,* Aldershot: Ashgate.

CHAPTER 12 KOSOVO: THE DESECRATED ICON

Fonseca I. (1995) *Bury Me Standing. The Gypsies and their Journey.* London: Chatto & Windus.

Glenny, M. (1992) *The Fall of Yugoslavia*, London: Penguin.

Glenny, M. (1999) *The Balkans 1804–1999*, London: Granta.

Goodwin, J. (1999) *Lords of the Horizons. A History of the Ottoman Empire*, London: Vintage.

Gounaris, B. and Michailidis I. (1994) 'Slav Speakers and Macedonian Slavs in Modern Greek Macedonia: Selected Bibliography' in *Modern Greek Society: A Social Science Newsletter*, XXII, 1–93.

Judah, T. (1997) *The Serbs. History, Myth and the Destruction of Yugoslavia*, New Haven: Yale University Press.

Judah, T. (2000) *Kosovo, War and Revenge.* New Haven: Yale University Press.

Malcolm, N. (1994) *Bosnia. A Short History*, London: Macmillan.

Malcolm, N. (1998) *Kosovo. A Short History*, London: Macmillan.

Mileusnic, S. (1997) *Spiritual Genocide 1991 – 1995 (7).* Belgrade: Museum of the Serbian Orthodox Church.

Outlook (1999) *Orthodox Outlook*, XII (6).

Peic, S. (1994) *Medieval Serbian Culture*, London: Alpine Fine Arts Collection (UK) Ltd.

Pennington, A. and Levi, P. (1984) *Marko the Prince, Serbo-Croat Heroic Songs*, London: Duckworth.

Tanner, M. (1997) *Croatia. A Nation Forged in War.* New Haven: Yale University Press.

Zahariadas, N. (1996) 'Greek Policy toward the Former Yugoslav Republic of Macedonia, 1991–1995' in *Journal of Modern Greek Studies*, 14 (Special issue on Macedonia), 303–27.

CHAPTER 13 THE UN: SQUARING THE CIRCLE

Primary Sources:

Meckel, M. (2000) General Rapporteur. Committee Reports: Kosovo *Aftermath and its implications for Conflict Prevention and Crisis Management.* 28 April. Nato Parliamentary Assembly.

Robertson, Lord (2000) 'Kosovo One Year On: Achievement and Challenge'. 13 April.

Weller, M. (1999) The Crisis in Kosovo, 1989–99: International Documents and Analysis, Vol.1, Cambridge: Documents and Analysis Publishing Ltd.

United Nations

Security Council press releases:

SC/6496 31 March 1998: Security council imposes arms embargo on Federal Republic of Yugoslavia, pending action to resolve Kosovo Crisis.

SC/6577 23 September 1998: Security Council demands all parties end hostilities and maintain a ceasefire in Kosovo.

SC/6588 24 October 1998: Security Council demands Federal Republic of Yugoslavia comply fully with NATO and OSCE Verification Missions in Kosovo.

SC/6628 19 January 1999: Security Council strongly condemns massacre of Kosovo Albanians in Southern Kosovo.

SC/6637 29 January 1999: Security Council expresses deep concern at escalating violence in Kosovo.

SC/6657 24 March 1999: NATO action against Serbian military targets prompts divergent views as Security Council holds urgent meeting on situation in Kosovo.

SC/6659 26 March 1999: Security Council rejects demand for cessation of use of force against Federal Republic of Yugoslavia.

SC/6674/Rev 18 May 1999: China, at Security Council meeting, registers strongest possible protest over attack against its embassy in Belgrade.

SC/6675 14 May 1999: Security Council expresses profound regrets over bombing of Chinese Embassy, deep sorrow for loss of lives, injuries, property damage caused.

SC/6677 14 May 1999: Security Council calls for access for UN and humanitarian personnel operating in Kosovo and other parts of the Federal Republic of Yugoslavia.

SC/6686 10 June 1999: Security Council welcomes Yugoslavia's acceptance of peace principles, authorises civil, security presence in Kosovo.

SC/6687 10 June 1999: Secretary-General, in Council Meeting on Kosovo, says UN is determined to lead civilian implementation of peace effectively and efficiently.

SC/6856 11 May 2000: divergent views expressed as Security Council hears Kosovo Mission Report.

SC/6873 9 June 2000: Security Council hears briefing by Head of UN Interim Administration Mission in Kosovo.

Secretary-General's reports:

S/1998/361 30 April 1998: Report of the Secretary-General prepared pursuant to Security Council Resolution 1160 (1998)

S/1998/470 4 June 1998: Report of the Secretary-General prepared pursuant to Security Council Resolution 1160 (1998)

S/1998/608 2 July 1998: Report of the Secretary-General prepared pursuant to Security Council Resolution 1160 (1998)

S/1998/712 5 August 1998: Report of the Secretary-General prepared pursuant to Security Council Resolution 1160 (1998)

S/1998/834 4 September 1998: Report of the Secretary-General prepared pursuant to Security Council Resolution 1160 (1998)

S/1998/912 3 October 1998: Report of the Secretary-General prepared pursuant to resolutions 1160 (1998) and 1199 (1998) of the Security Council

S/1998/1068 12 November 1998: Report of the Secretary-General prepared pursuant to Resolutions 1160 (1998), 1199 (1998) and 1203 (1998) of the Security Council

S/1998/1147 4 December 1998: Report of the Secretary-General prepared pursuant to Resolutions 1160 (1998), 1199 (1998) and 1203 (1998) of the Security Council

S/1998/1221 24 December 1998: Report of the Secretary-General prepared pursuant to Resolutions 1160 (1998), 1199 (1998) and 1203 (1998) of the Security Council

S/1999/99 30 January 1999: Report of the Secretary-General prepared pursuant to Resolutions 1160 (1998), 1199 (1998) and 1203 (1998) of the Security Council

S/1999/293 17 March 1999: Report of the Secretary-General prepared pursuant to Resolutions 1160 (1998), 1199 (1998) and 1203 (1998) of the Security Council

General Assembly offical records:

General Assembly: Official Records 53rd Session: A/53/219: Annual Report of the International Tribunal for the Former Yugoslavia 1998.

General Assembly: Official Records 54th Session: A/54/187: Annual Report of the International Tribunal for the former Yugoslavia 1999.

General Assembly: Official Records 54th Session: supplement No 36 (A/54/36) Report of the United Nations High Commissioner for Human Rights, 23 September, 1999.

Economic and Social Council:

Commission on Human Rights: 56th Session: E/Cn.4/2000/10: Report of the High Commissioner for Human Rights on the situation of human rights in Kosovo, Federal Republic of Yugoslavia.

International Criminal Tribunal for the former Yugoslavia

Final Report to the Prosecutor by the Committee established to review the Nato bombing campaign against the Federal Republic of Yugoslavia
ICTY Weekly Press Conferences

INDEX